KT-592-355

Eden, Suez and the Mass Media: Propaganda and Persuasion During the Suez crisis

TONY SHAW

I.B. TAURIS

LONDON · NEW YORK

New paperback edition published in 2009 by I.B. Tauris & Co Ltd
6 Salem Road, London W2 4BU
175 Fifth Avenue, New York NY 10010
www.ibtauris.com

Distributed in the United States and Canada Exclusively by St Martin's Press
175 Fifth Avenue, New York NY 10010

First published in hardback in 1996 by I.B. Tauris & Co Ltd

Copyright © Tony Shaw 1996, 2009

The right of Tony Shaw to be identified as author of this work has been asserted by
the author in accordance with the Copyright, Designs and Patents Act 1988.

All rights reserved. Except for brief quotations in a review, this book, or any part
thereof, may not be reproduced, stored in or introduced into a retrieval system, or
transmitted, in any form or by any means, electronic, mechanical, photocopying,
recording or otherwise, without the prior written permission of the publisher.

ISBN: 978 1 84885 091 0

A full CIP record for this book is available from the British Library

A full CIP record for this book is available from the Library of Congress

Library of Congress catalog card number: available

Set in Monotype Ehrhardt by Ewan Smith, London

Printed and bound in India

Contents

Acknowledgements

Thanks must go, first of all, to my doctoral supervisor, Dr Roger Owen, for his support of this research. My examiners, Anthony Smith and Peter Calvocoressi, gave me useful advice on how to convert the thesis into a book. I am also indebted to Dr Richard Cockett, Dr Ross McKibbin, Keith Kyle and Professor Asa Briggs for their constructive criticism. Needless to say, none of the above bears any responsibility for the final text; all of the opinions and conclusions are entirely my own.

The research could not have been undertaken without the assistance of the staffs of the Public Record Office at Kew in London; the Bodleian Library in Oxford; the BBC's Written Archives in Caversham; Independent Television News; Colindale Newspaper Library; the *Manchester Guardian* and *The Times* archives; the House of Lords Records Office; Birmingham University Library; Churchill College and Trinity College, Cambridge; and King's College, London. I am also grateful to numerous journalists, politicians and Foreign Office officials for their time and recollections.

Over the past six years, I have received financial assistance from the British Academy, the University of Oxford and the Scouloudi Foundation in association with the Institute of Historical Research. I am grateful to the *Guardian*, the *Daily Mail* and Solo Syndication Limited for the permission to use copyright material. Frank Cass and Oxford University Press have also allowed me to cite extracts from my related articles in *Contemporary Record* and *Twentieth Century British History*. The map on p. xii is reproduced from Wm. Roger Louis and Roger Owen (eds), *Suez 1956: The Crisis and Its Consequences* (1991, p. xviii), by permission of Oxford University Press.

Finally, I would like to thank my family and friends for their tolerance and support during this project. Dr John Bell deserves particular mention for his companionship and constant encouragement. Michael Thornhill cast a sharp eye over the final drafts. Shirley Heckles read the proofs, helped me to channel my ideas positively and enabled me to maintain a healthy distance from the material. It is to her that this book is dedicated.

Tony Shaw

Preface to the Paperback Edition

This book provides a fully-documented case study of media-government relations in Britain during the 1956 Suez crisis. The Suez crisis is now half a century old and has therefore been consigned by many people to the dark and distant past. But we would do well to recall that for Britain 'Suez' was, along with the 1938 Munich crisis, the most divisive and controversial episode of the twentieth century. Centred on a narrow man-made canal linking the Mediterranean with the Red Sea, it was a crisis that caused fighting on London's streets, that split families and friendships (some permanently), and that destroyed a prime minister. It was a crisis that tested a government's propaganda skills to the full and pushed the mass media's independence to breaking point. Suez would come to symbolise the end of the British Empire and has haunted British governments for two generations.

I had two main intentions when I first wrote this book in the mid-1990s. The first was to both freshen and broaden the terms of the debate among 'Suezologists' by examining the role played by propaganda during the crisis. It struck me back then how so few Suez scholars had up to that point bothered to look seriously at the public dimensions of policy-making and diplomacy during the crisis. As a result, scholars had in my opinion over-looked one of the chief reasons for Anthony Eden's notorious decision to collude with the French and Israelis in October 1956 – a need to fulfil the expectations his propaganda campaign demonising the Egyptian leader, Gamal Abdel Nasser, had raised among Conservative Party ranks, elements of the press, and large swathes of the general public. It was this, as much as anything else, that led to Britain's disastrous 'police action' in Egypt in early November, the Cabinet's humiliation at the hands of the United States later that month, and Eden's resignation in January 1957.

When the book appeared several scholars took umbrage at my assertion of neglect, at my argument that an important piece of the Suez jigsaw had been left out. However, I still stand by it. Indeed, I think that neglect is even more glaring today. In the past decade, a number of historians have enriched our understanding of the battle for hearts and minds that was waged during the Suez crisis. Richard Aldrich and Stephen Dorril have given us a partial insight into MI6's secret propaganda activities designed to unseat Nasser. James Vaughan has placed Suez within the wider context of Anglo-American propaganda policies in the Arab Middle East from the end of the Second World War to the introduction of the Eisenhower Doctrine in 1957. And Laura James has drawn on new Arabic material to shed light on Nasser's propaganda's techniques and output during the crisis.[i]

Nevertheless, I find it disappointing that, more than fifty years after the crisis, the vast majority of books on Suez continue to treat the crisis as an episode in which politicians, military chiefs and ambassadors – in Britain and overseas – by and large took decisions in a hermetically-sealed, publicity-free environment. Whenever journalists and broadcasters feature in these historical accounts it is usually merely to add a hint of colour. The 'public', meanwhile, still tends to be treated as a homogenous mass. Consequently, readers get no sense of the lengths to which Eden and other politicians in Britain and overseas tailored their policies for public consumption and how this affected the outcome of the crisis. We also hear precious little about the important lessons Suez taught future governments – like Margaret Thatcher's during the 1982 Falklands conflict – about the value and methods of successful propaganda in wartime.[ii]

This brings me to the second intention of my book: to write a case study of media-government relations in Britain that might be used as a template for scholars and students interested in analysing those relations at other times of war or (perceived) national emergency, in the past or the future. When this book first appeared in 1996, both the Suez crisis and the general issue of media-government relations in Britain were subjects of great interest. This can partly be put down to the recent release of declassified documents relating to Suez principally in Britain, France, Israel and the United States. Such documents, the life-blood of academic historians, appeared to set the seal on the full, unexpurgated history of the Suez crisis. For my part, unprecedented access to official propaganda materials, BBC files and Fleet Street records, plus interviews with previously tight-lipped journalists and politicians who had been major players during Suez, allowed for a near microscopic study of media-government relations during the crisis. I felt this depth of analysis based on such a wide range of primary sources was essential in order to elevate my findings beyond the sociological, often discourse-based studies of contemporary media-government relations in Britain which argued that political news was inherently biased in favour of powerful forces.

For ordinary people, however, the reason why Suez had resurfaced after so many years was the 1991 Gulf War. As in 1956, in 1991 Britain found itself fighting a war in the Middle East, this time centred on Iraq's invasion of its oil rich neighbour, Kuwait. Britain was far less divided in 1991 than in 1956, but for many commentators the parallels with Suez were nonetheless striking, especially in propaganda terms. Like in 1956, in the run up to the Gulf War, the British government, supported by many newspapers, labelled its enemy, Iraq's Saddam Hussein, a 'second Hitler' who had ambitions to dominate the Middle East. As during Suez, Downing Street cultivated its friends in the press and the Foreign Office briefed journalists unattributably about the enemy's links with terrorists. For his part, Saddam, acting a lot more openly and in Western eyes more crudely, like Nasser thirty-five years earlier wrapped himself in the garb of anti-colonialist Pan-Arabism. If Nasser had argued that the Suez Canal was Egyptian property, Saddam claimed that Kuwait should rightly be regarded as Iraq's lost, nineteenth province.

Unlike Nasser in 1956, Saddam was roundly defeated in 1991. His warnings of a 'Mother of all Battles' came to nothing as the US-led Operation Desert Storm rid Kuwait of Iraqi forces within a mere six weeks. In 1956, the British government had adroitly sanitised media coverage of the Suez combat phase. In 1991, the US and British governments went several steps further, diverting the public's attention from the deaths of an estimated 50,000 Iraqis via 'live' satellite TV images of 'smart bombs' pinpointing legitimate targets. In the conflict's aftermath some commentators were deeply troubled by this manipulation of words and images, but the general public in Britain appeared to believe they had been given a grandstand view of the most visually transparent war of all time.[iii]

If these events helped regenerate interest in the propaganda dimensions of Suez in the 1990s, more recent conflicts have underlined the continued relevance of my study. Since 1996, Britain has conducted military operations in several places, including Kosovo, Iraq and Afghanistan. In the wake of September 11, 2001, the British government has also played a key role in the US-led War on Terror. In each of these conflicts, the British government has utilised a range of media management techniques, some seen during the Suez crisis and others invented for today's 24/7 news culture.

The Iraq War, which started in 2003, bears an uncanny resemblance to Suez. Britain was bitterly divided over Prime Minister Tony Blair's right to use force against Saddam Hussein's regime. Like in 1956, demonstrators took to the streets, this time in even greater numbers. Like Eden in 1956, Blair dubiously claimed he was acting on the authority of the United Nations. There were even echoes of secret collusion, this time surrounding the misuse (or 'sexing-up') of intelligence by Washington and London to prove that Saddam Hussein possessed weapons of mass destruction. And, once again, the war brought into sharp focus the relationship between the state and journalists in Britain during conflict.

The Iraq War showed Tony Blair to be far more adept at media management than Anthony Eden. He also had a much closer and more effective relationship with his Director of Communications, Alastair Campbell, than Eden had with his Press Secretary, William Clark. It was Campbell who, like Eden in 1956, conducted a campaign accusing the BBC of anti-government bias. This would eventually lead to the 2004 Hutton Report, which heavily criticised the Corporation and prompted the resignation of its Chairman and Director-General. Ironically, academic analysis would later show, rather like mine of Suez, that the BBC had in fact been the most pro-war of the main British news broadcasters. Further scholarship would show that on the whole the Blair government had actually enjoyed a good 'media war'. This could partly be accounted for by the fact that the Iraq War produced a number of technological and logistical shifts in the reporting of conflict, like the Pentagon's decision to 'embed' journalists into military units on signed contracts that limited what they were allowed to report. It was only when Saddam Hussein's weapons of mass destruction failed to materialise and the war in Iraq turned into a long and bloody occupation that the British media as a whole really started to criticise Downing Street.[iv]

In the light of the Iraq War and the War on Terror, much has been published recently on the subjects of propaganda and media-government relations during conflict. However, I believe that what I wrote about Suez in 1996 has stood the test of time, and, consequently, I have resisted making any changes to this paperback edition.

Thanks again to Shirley, and to Isaac, who wasn't here first time around.

Notes

i. Richard Aldrich, *The Hidden Hand: Britain, America and Cold War Secret Intelligence* (John Murray, 2001); Stephen Dorril, *MI6: Fifty Years of Special Operations* (Fourth Estate, 2000); James R. Vaughan, *The Failure of American and British Propaganda in the Arab Middle East, 1945-1957* (Palgrave Macmillan, 2005); Laura James, *Nasser at War: Arab Images of the Enemy* (Palgrave Macmillan, 2006).

ii. Recently published books on Suez include James W. Fiscus, *The Suez Crisis: War and Conflict in the Middle East* (Rosen, 2004); Wm. Roger Louis, *Ends of British Imperialism: The Scramble for Empire, Suez and Decolonization* (I.B.Tauris, 2006); Martin Woollacott, *After Suez: Adrift in the American Century* (I.B.Tauris, 2006); Jonathan Pearson, *Sir Anthony Eden and the Suez Crisis: Reluctant Gamble* (Palgrave Macmillan, 2002); Simon C. Smith, *Reassessing Suez: New Perspectives on the Crisis and its Aftermath* (Ashgate, 2008); Michael T. Thornhill, *Road to Suez: The Battle of the Canal Zone* (Sutton, 2006); Barry Turner, *Suez 1956: The Inside Story of the First Oil War* (Hodder and Stoughton, 2006); Derek Varble, *The Suez Crisis 1956: Essential Histories* (Osprey, 2003); Bertjan Verbeek, *Decision-Making in Great Britain during the Suez Crisis: Small Groups and a Persistent Leader* (Ashgate, 2003).

iii. Philip M. Taylor, *War and the Media: Propaganda and Persuasion in the Gulf War* (Manchester University Press, 1998).

iv. Justin Lewis, et al, *Shoot First and Ask Questions Later: Media Coverage of the 2003 Iraq War* (Peter Lang, 2005).

Preface

The Suez crisis of 1956 has fascinated British and international historians, political commentators and foreign affairs analysts for almost four decades. It is not difficult to see why: the Anglo-French use of force against Egypt in October–November 1956 caused arguably the single most dramatic public split over a foreign policy issue in twentieth-century British history, leading to the downfall of a prime minister; the affair cruelly exposed the frailties of a once great imperial power, whose dominant role in the Middle East was replaced by the Americans; it further complicated the Arab–Israeli dispute, already one of the world's most intractable and dangerous conflicts; it provided a test case for the authority of the United Nations; and it involved the controversial issues of personal political intrigue and diplomatic collusion. All of this took place against the backdrop of the Cold War and the threat of a localized conflict escalating into a nuclear holocaust.

There is a common agreement amongst scholars of history and communications alike that the British mass media played a vital part in the national and international debate surrounding the Eden government's policies during the Suez crisis. Indeed, conventional wisdom suggests that the principal opinion-formers – the press and the BBC – not only reflected but perhaps even caused the historic cleavage amongst the British people, thereby significantly weakening Eden's case against the Egyptian leader, Gamal Abdel Nasser. Yet little attempt has been made to examine the relationship between the mass media and the government during Suez, or, for that matter, the larger question of what role public opinion played in ministers' calculations.

Most of the reputable works on Suez tend to look at the crisis from either the diplomatic or the high political point of view. David Carlton and Robert Rhodes James are the well-established scholars of Anthony Eden's part in the affair, whilst Keith Kyle, W. Scott Lucas and Steven Z. Freiberger have recently written detailed accounts relating the Suez episode to Britain's deteriorating post-war influence in the Middle East.[1] Most of the above at least touch on Eden's notorious attempt to control the BBC. Kyle and Lucas, together with Fullick and Powell's

Suez: The Double War (1979), also offer an insight into the government's psychological warfare campaign directed at the Egyptians. A comprehensive examination of the government's propaganda strategy has not been attempted, however. Moreover, all these accounts generally accept the British newspapers' various policies at face value.

Since the Vietnam, Falklands and 1991 Gulf Wars highlighted the issue of crisis media management, academic interest has grown in whether, and if so, how, the Eden government sought to control the news during the Suez crisis. Comparative works by Valerie Adams, Derrik Mercer et al. and the former editor of *Picture Post*, Tom Hopkinson, have proved particularly useful in this regard.[2] The problem with most of these studies, however, is that they tend to look at the government's handling of information purely from the military point of view and focus their attention only on the 'war' phase of Suez in October–November 1956. Moreover, their almost unanimous verdict is that Eden's public relations policy – if he had one at all – was a complete disaster. The present study seeks to revise this interpretation.

A number of key figures directly involved in one way or another with the government's propaganda campaign during Suez have released their own accounts of the crisis over the past forty years. The daily diaries of Eden's press secretary, William Clark, provide an indispensable insider's view of how Number 10 sought to manipulate the domestic mass media. Even Clark was unaware of much of the Foreign Office's and Ministry of Defence's activities, however, particularly in the later stages of the crisis, when he was made the scapegoat for ministers' own errors and banished from the inner circle of propaganda practitioners. Bernard Fergusson, director of psychological warfare during Suez, throws some light on the generally amateurish efforts made to undermine Egyptian morale in his autobiography, *The Watery Maze* (1961). Similarly, Douglas Dodds-Parker's *Political Eunuch* (1986) gives an indication of the importance which he, as parliamentary under-secretary of state at the Foreign Office, attached to the presentation of policy in the summer of 1956 – though without disclosing the true extent of his own role in the propaganda campaign and the variety of methods the government used. The impression gained from the numerous memoirs of more senior ministers and officials tends to be a misleading one of indifference to public opinion.[3]

Of the accounts written by those on the receiving end of the government's actions, perhaps the most useful are Harman Grisewood's *One Thing at a Time* (1968) and James Margach's *The Abuse of Power* (1976). As the BBC's director of spoken word in 1956, Grisewood was in a position not only to suffer government pressure personally but also to witness the subsequent divisions within the Corporation over the

interpretation of such hallowed concepts as independence and impartiality. For all its candour, however, Grisewood's overly-influential
account provides no assessment of the BBC's actual programme output
during Suez. Margach's book, coming from an experienced member of
the Westminster lobby in 1956, with wide connections in politics and
journalism, is in many ways the perfect accompaniment to William
Clark's diaries. His criticism of Eden's supposed naivety in handling
the press is contradicted, however, by the degree of support the prime
minister won from *The Times* during the crisis, referred to in Iverach
McDonald's *A Man of The Times* (1976) and *The History of The Times:
Volume V* (1984).

For a ready insight into the government's efforts to carry leading
US opinion during Suez we can draw on the work of the then *New
York Times* London correspondent, Kennett Love.[4] Yet although Love
was familiar with the preferential treatment given American journalists
during the crisis, including the Foreign Office News Department's
confidential 'sabre-rattling' briefings, he was unable to judge how the
Foreign Office managed to dictate the US media's coverage of the
eventual military assault on Egypt. Nor was he in any position to
assess the work of British Information Services, the Foreign Office's
chief organ of propaganda in the United States itself.

This book, then, attempts to provide the first detailed assessment
of the British government's involvement in propaganda during the
Suez crisis, from July through to December 1956. It does this via an
analysis of largely unpublished British and American government
documents, private and party papers, interviews and media sources.
Through an examination of the methods employed and the content of
the material produced, the book presents a revisionist interpretation of
the Eden government's attitude towards public opinion and the importance of policy presentation. By highlighting the integral part propaganda played in the government's policy and diplomacy throughout
the crisis, the book also adds to the historical debate concerning the
cabinet's decision to opt for collusion with the French and the Israelis
in October 1956 rather than a negotiated settlement. Only by taking
into account the government's whole propaganda exercise is it also
possible to understand fully the relatively limited effects of the crisis
on the Conservatives' political fortunes.

The book sets out to explain, first of all, why effective propaganda
was essential to support Anthony Eden's hidden agenda during Suez –
the removal of Gamal Abdel Nasser from power. Parts One and Two
then concentrate on how the government sought to persuade the British
public of the justification for the use of force against Egypt. From the
outset of the crisis, Eden worked on the assumption that the more

aggressive the British public appeared, the greater the prospects of the Egyptian regime either tamely acquiescing or angrily retaliating. The government's assiduous efforts to control the main domestic opinion-formers – Fleet Street and the BBC – are therefore examined in detail.

It is argued that, despite being a relative amateur in the matter of handling the mass media, and having a flawed policy, Eden had a considerable degree of success. By exploiting the intimate relationship that exists between the government, press and broadcasting in Britain, the prime minister managed to fashion news and current affairs reporting during Suez to a remarkable extent. This is therefore a study of the system of government manipulation of the media – a system that exists in the 1990s – as well as of Eden and Suez. Questions to be answered include whether the BBC really did – as conventional wisdom would have us believe – maintain its impartiality under extreme government pressure; and how much the British public got to know about a war that was fought in its name.

The third, and final, Part turns its attention to the issue of international opinion. In this respect the book is by no means comprehensive. Throughout the text periodic references are made to the government's efforts to persuade Commonwealth, and especially Arab, opinion of the justness of its cause. However, partly because of the material already published in the latter area,[5] but mainly because of the overriding importance attached by ministers to the United States during Suez, the focus is on American opinion. As the crisis ultimately proved so conclusively, Eden could not expect the US administration to allow him a free hand in Egypt in the summer of 1956. In fact, the State Department and Foreign Office had, since 1945, acted at times more like rivals than allies in the Middle East. Consequently, throughout Suez the Foreign Office sought to do all it could to enlist the support of the Eisenhower administration for a policy of force. A major facet of this campaign was the necessarily subtle yet systematic cultivation of American leadership opinion. It is argued that whilst this attempt to influence American opinion-formers was an overall failure, the work of the Foreign Office's propaganda officials in the US played a significant part in helping to patch up the 'special relationship' in the immediate aftermath of the Suez crisis.

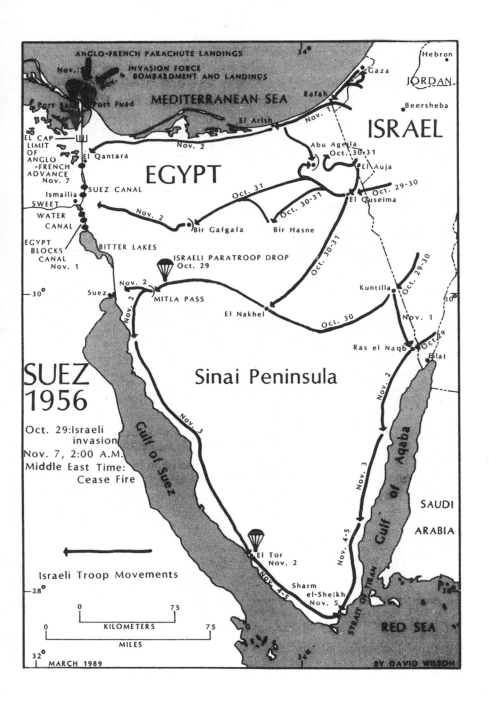

ANGLO-FRENCH PARACHUTE LANDINGS
Nov. 5
INVASION FORCE
BOMBARDMENT AND LANDINGS

MEDITERRANEAN SEA

Port Said Port Fuad

El Arish
Nov.

Gaza
Rafah
Hebron
JORDAN
Beersheba

EL CAP
LIMIT
OF
ANGLO
-FRENCH
ADVANCE
Nov. 7

El Qantara
Nov. 2

EGYPT

Abu Ageila
Oct. 30-31
El Auja

ISRAEL

SUEZ CANAL

Ismailia
SWEET
WATER
CANAL

Nov. 2

Oct. 31

El Quseima
Oct. 29-30
Oct. 30-31

Bir Gafgafa
Bir Hasne

EGYPT
BLOCKS
CANAL
Nov. 1

BITTER LAKES

ISRAELI PARATROOP DROP
Oct. 29

Oct. 30-31

Oct. 29-30

—30°

Suez
Nov. 2

Nov. 2

MITLA PASS

El Nakhel

Kuntilla
Oct. 29-30

Nov. 1

Oct. 30

Ras el Naqb
Oct. 29
Eilat

SUEZ
1956

Sinai Peninsula

Gulf of Suez

Nov. 3

Gulf of Aqaba

Nov. 3

SAUDI
ARABIA

Oct. 29:Israeli
invasion
Nov. 7, 2:00 A.M.
Middle East Time:
Cease Fire

Nov. 4-5

El Tor
Nov. 2

Nov. 4-5

Israeli Troop Movements

—28°

Sharm
el-Sheikh
Nov. 5

STRAIT OF TIRAN

RED SEA

0   75
KILOMETERS

0   75
MILES

—32°
MARCH 1989

BY DAVID WILSON

I

Introduction:
the propaganda strategy

> In what was to be my worst moment of the crisis, I had to go to the Prime Minister and tell her that it looked as if the whole thing had started off with a major disaster. She was unmistakably very shaken and needed a lot of reassurance. It did not take too much imagination to see the thought going through her mind: 'Is this going to be another Suez?' [Admiral Sir Terence Lewin, chief of the Defence Staff, informing Mrs Thatcher of the loss of two Wessex helicopters at the start of the operation to retake South Georgia, 21 April 1982][1]

During the 1982 Falklands crisis British ministers, civil servants and the military were haunted by memories of 'Suez' and, in particular, by what they perceived as Anthony Eden's abject failure to keep the British public united and international opinion sympathetic the last time the country went to war. Aside from his notorious attempt to control the BBC during the crisis (itself widely interpreted as a graphic lesson in how not to manipulate the media), the received impression of Eden was one of a prime minister fatally ignorant of the power and importance of public relations. As a direct consequence of his myopia and naivety – so the argument goes – Eden (and Britain) had lost the Suez 'war' not on the field of battle but on the information front, where it had barely competed. This was a mistake British policy-makers were determined not to repeat during the Falklands crisis. Unlike the Egyptians, the Argentinians would not be allowed to have it 'all their own way' in the realm of public persuasion, as the commander-in-chief of the Anglo-French forces during Suez had put it.[2] Margaret Thatcher, for one, was adamant that, this time, Britain would not 'lose the propaganda war'.[3]

It is one of the contentions of this study that from the very beginning of the Suez crisis in July 1956 the British government appreciated the importance of 'presenting' its policy to a far greater extent than the public then realized and historians since have given it credit. There was no clear-cut 'propaganda policy' during Suez in the sense of some sort of hastily revitalized ministry of information or a coherent set of guidelines detailing what should (and should not) be told to the media. Nevertheless, propaganda was regularly discussed at the highest levels, most notably at meetings of the government's *de facto* war cabinet, the Egypt Committee. What emerges from a variety of sources is the picture of an improvised yet concerted effort on the part of different branches of the government and military – for most of the crisis working individually, though sometimes collectively – to persuade domestic and international opinion of the justification of the use of force against Egypt. At the heart of this propaganda campaign was the government's manipulation of the British media.[4] It will be shown that so intent was Eden on getting the British press and broad-casters to act according to his interpretation of 'the national interest', and thereby give their full support to his policy, that at times it appeared as if the prime minister was waging war on sections of his own people rather than on the Egyptian president, Gamal Abdel Nasser. But before I move on to discuss in detail why the government was so quick to see the need for a propaganda campaign during Suez, and what form that propaganda took, it would be as well to explain briefly my use of this most emotive of words.

Throughout Suez, British ministers were constantly at pains to condemn Nasser publicly for his use of 'propaganda' to further his cause, especially during the war phase in November 1956 with his fabrication of 'atrocity stories' concerning the number of Egyptian civilians killed by the Anglo-French forces.[5] The clear implication was: his was a totalitarian regime dependent for its survival upon its ability to tell lies, whereas democratic governments, like the British, were, even at times of crisis, beholden to their people and therefore forced to stick to the facts. However, contrary to popular misconception (then and now), to define propaganda as lies or at best half-truths is far too simplistic and highly misleading. It should instead be viewed in a much broader perspective. The social psychologist Kimball Young sees propaganda as:

> the more or less deliberately planned and systematic use of symbols, chiefly through suggestion and related psychological techniques, with a view to altering and controlling opinions, ideas and values, and ultimately to changing overt actions along predetermined lines. Propaganda may be open or its purpose avowed, or it may conceal its intention. It always has a setting within a social-cultural framework, without which neither its psychological nor its cultural features can be understood.[6]

According to this definition, propaganda should therefore be seen essentially as a process of persuasion, involving amongst other methods the deliberate selection and omission of accurate information as well as falsehoods. Thus, a great deal of the 'information' which the British government disseminated during Suez – the amount of cargo which annually passed through the Suez Canal, for example, or the difficulty the United Nations had in making economic sanctions effective – was certainly true. Yet this was still propaganda because of the intent behind its dissemination. The government chose to spread these facts because they strengthened its message. The notion that democratic governments are inherently incapable of conducting propaganda is, of course, fallacious. The key difference is that their techniques of persuasion have to be more sophisticated than those used in closed societies, with news guidance and suppression more subtle. The need for subtlety is accentuated if, as was the case during the Suez crisis, the government has hidden motives and envisages conducting a policy of limited war, possibly in the face of strident domestic opposition.

It is significant that the opening shots of the Suez crisis themselves took place in the full glare of publicity, centred around what was then the world's largest civil engineering project, the Aswan high dam. Since assuming the office of prime minister of Egypt in April 1954 (he was appointed president in June 1956), deposing the more pluralist-minded General Neguib after a four-month power struggle, Colonel Nasser had sought to consolidate his position and provide his regime with the necessary popular appeal. Eighteen months later, negotiations opened between Egypt, the United States, Britain and the World Bank over a loan to finance the construction of a high dam at Aswan near the Sudanese border. This was designed to transform Egypt's economy and society by adding over 850,000 hectares to the area of cultivable land, rendering the Nile navigable as far south as Sudan and generating the electricity necessary for industrialization. At first, talks between the parties went well, reflecting Western support for the nascent Egyptian administration. During the first half of 1956, however, with Nasser seen to be increasingly courting the Russians and Red China, they stalled. Finally, on 19 June 1956, the Americans, swiftly followed by the British, announced their decision to withdraw their offer of a loan, thereby scuppering the whole project. The unbearable pressure a loan of $400 million would impose on the Egyptian economy was cited publicly as the reason.[7]

To what extent this withdrawal could be attributed simply to the Anglo-American fear of losing their money, or whether it was driven more by the desire to punish Nasser for flirting with communists, is something of a moot issue.[8] The key point is that Nasser suspected revocation might occur and consequently was at the time more concerned with how Egypt's plea for financial assistance had been turned down than with why. The manner in which the State Department's press statement emphasized the fragility of the Egyptian economy and its consequent inability to sustain heavy repayments was seen as deliberately insulting and designed to humiliate Egypt. Then, by implying via the private briefing of journalists that the Egyptian ambassador to the US had, on Nasser's orders, threatened to accept a 'very generous' offer from the Russians if Western help was not forthcoming, the impression given was that the US and Britain had delivered a justifiable slap in the face to a third world upstart.[9]

Nasser's reaction was to retaliate in kind. For all the West's fears and allegations throughout this period, the Egyptian president was not about to become a satellite of Moscow. Having only just escaped the political dominance of Britain, principally via the Anglo-Egyptian Treaty of October 1954, he felt little inclination to submit to that of Russia, lured by offers of aid apparently without strings attached.[10] Still determined to build the dam and fulfil Egyptians' expectations, however, Nasser therefore turned his thoughts to the only other credible source of finance he and his advisers knew: the revenues from the Suez Canal. However, even if, against all the odds, the canal's Anglo-French operator, the Suez Canal Company, adhered to Egypt's demands for a greater share of its profits, the sums gained would only go part of the way towards paying for the dam. Moreover, what Nasser wanted, aside from ready cash, was a spectacular, substantial riposte to those who regarded him as a political and diplomatic lightweight. Only this would prove Egypt's new-found independence and confirm Nasser's own emerging reputation amongst the younger generation as the leader of an Arab renaissance.[11]

How this riposte was to be presented was for Nasser, however, almost as important as the act itself. It is essential to realize that the Egyptian president was deeply conscious of the power of propaganda and was one of its most skilful exponents in the Middle East in the 1950s. In part this derived from the coincidence of a revolution in the media of communications which occurred in the Middle East post-1945 and the emergence of revolutionary Arab nationalism in the region. The symbiotic relationship between these two phenomena led to a veritable propaganda boom which had a direct effect on Middle East politics and society.[12] Nasser himself was one of the first to harness the influence of radio, launching the Voice of the Arabs station in 1953 (with the help of the CIA) 'as a means of building the myth of Arab nationalism, to designate the foreign enemies to it, and to establish criteria by which the people would identify "imperialist enemies in our midst"'.[13] Two years later, having achieved complete power, he had instituted a comprehensive propaganda programme directed to the Arab world and against the British in particular, with the Voice of the Arabs at its heart.[14] According to Nasser, radio was by this point the nation's 'general university'.[15] The fact that throughout his rule Nasser's closest adviser was the journalist Mohamed Heikal is indicative of the importance he attached to the role of propaganda and the mass media.[16]

It is therefore in the light of both of the above factors – the need to hit back at the West, and in a fashion which attracted maximum publicity and sympathy – that we should view Nasser's famous announcement of the nationalization of the Suez Canal Company in Alexandria on 26 July 1956. That Nasser's proclamation, coupled with a simultaneous takeover of the company's offices, delivered an effective blow to the West is beyond doubt.[17] Equally important, however, was its style and context. The Egyptian leader calculated that the success of his coup depended on two things: whether, after twenty-four hours, two convoys, northbound and southbound, had passed freely through the canal; and, secondly, whether Egypt's friends in Asia and Africa offered their support.[18] His speech on the night of the 26th, chosen to coincide significantly with the anniversary of King Farouk's abdication, and naturally broadcast live, was therefore crafted for a home and overseas audience. Breaking with tradition, Nasser spoke directly to the people in the Arabic of the streets. He painted a graphic picture of the historic victimization of Egypt at the hands of the imperialists and of the latter's continued favouritism towards Israel. Referring directly to the Aswan dam débâcle, he then castigated the US and the World Bank in turn, calling upon those listening to 'defend our nationalism and our Arabism'. The overall effect of this *tour de force* was that by the time the Egyptian leader actually got around to announcing the takeover of the Suez Canal Company the atmosphere was such that many of those listening felt they themselves were active participants in the whole drama.[19] It was powerful rhetoric such as this that helped to set the tone and agenda for the unfolding crisis.

News of Nasser's coup reached 10 Downing Street late in the evening of Thursday, 26 July 1956, during a dinner hosted by Eden in honour of King Faisal of Iraq and his veteran prime minister, Nuri Said. The immediate reaction amongst those assembled, who included the leader of the Opposition, Hugh Gaitskell, was a mixture of shock and anger. 'You have only one course of action open and that is to hit, hit hard and hit now. Otherwise it will be too late' was Nuri's alleged advice to Eden.[20] To say that Nasser had astonished Number 10 and the Foreign Office would, however, be misleading. As the breakdown of the negotiations over the Aswan dam scheme suggested, relations between Britain and Egypt had been deteriorating for some time.

Nasser's assumption of full control over Egyptian affairs in April 1954 had initially been greeted with optimism in London. He had long been considered the real driving force behind the 1952 revolution and consequently was seen as potentially offering a strong but steadying influence in an increasingly volatile region still of great value to Britain, given its Cold War and imperial interests. Despite his obvious emotional dislike of the British, the Foreign Office also believed that Nasser was the best chance to settle Anglo-Egyptian differences, centred on the 1936 Treaty, symbol of British occupation and domination.[21] The subsequent Anglo-Egyptian Treaty of October 1954, by which the British agreed to evacuate all troops from the Canal Zone within twenty months in return for the right to re-enter in the event of an attack on the Arab states or Turkey, appeared to confirm this. Eden, foreign secretary and the principal architect of the settlement, looked forward cautiously to a new and constructive era of Anglo-Egyptian friendship founded on the basis of equality.[22]

With Egypt now apparently quiescent, the British renewed their efforts to form a regional security organization along the lines of NATO. This initiative had twin aims: to ensure the primacy of Western influence in the Middle East, and to strengthen Britain's leading role in the region in particular, increasingly under threat from the US.[23] At the same time, the Foreign Office and State Department worked energetically (though ultimately forlornly) behind the scenes for a permanent solution to the Palestine problem, the ALPHA project. This envisaged an Israeli abandonment of large tracts of territory in return for secure and guaranteed frontiers, the sort of settlement thought to appeal to the Arabs.[24] However, given even General Neguib's antipathy to joining an earlier British-sponsored defensive system, the Middle East Defence Organization (MEDO),[25] it was always highly unlikely that Nasser would be associated with any pact dominated by outside powers. His whole political philosophy rested, after all, on anti-imperialism and independence for the Arabs.[26] Nevertheless, by then establishing Iraq, Egypt's bitter rival for the leadership of Arab world, as the nucleus of the alliance, Nasser's very hostility was assured. Thenceforth, the Baghdad Pact (formed in February 1955 and eventually comprising Turkey, Iraq, Britain, Iran and Pakistan) became one of the chief targets of Egyptian propaganda. Xenophobic and pan-Arabist broadcasts wreaked havoc with the Foreign Office's efforts to enlist other Arab states to the pact and with Britain's reputation in the Middle East in general.[27] Attempts by the Foreign Office to counter these attacks via its own broadcast outlets, namely the BBC's Arabic Service and Sharq al-Adna, a covert station in Cyprus, had little effect other than to sour Anglo-Egyptian relations further.[28]

Angered by Nasser's interfering tactics, Eden retaliated by depriving him of British arms, on which Egypt was still dependent. This embargo could not have come at a worse time for Nasser: in March 1955 Egypt experienced an exceptionally damaging Israeli attack in the Gaza area. The threat to Egypt from Israel, now apparently heavily armed by the French, was particularly acute throughout the summer of 1955.[29] Consequently, having been shunned by Washington, in September 1955 the Egyptian premier struck a deal with Moscow whereby Czechoslovakia would supply Egypt with a wide range of weapons, including 80 MiG 15s, 45 Ilyushin bombers and 115 heavy tanks equal to the best in the Russian army. News of this arrangement caused near-panic in Western capitals, where it was interpreted as a dangerous shift in Egyptian policy and in the regional balance of power.[30] Eden, now prime minister, sought an immediate estimate from the British ambassador in Cairo, Sir Humphrey Trevelyan, 'as to Nasser's present position, the extent of his support, and the chances of any rival'. Though the reply was discouraging – 'there are no reliable signs of the regime losing its grip of the situation or of its opponents gaining ground' – the frustration felt by those in London who were now beginning to see the Egyptian leader as a conspirator who, either by design or by accident, might open up the Middle East to communism was abundantly clear.[31] As it happens, the consternation caused by the Czech arms deal and the West's fear of losing such an important state as Egypt to the Soviets led directly to the opening of talks between Britain, the US and Egypt on the financing of the Aswan high dam in November 1955. Britain's policy towards Egypt was, for the time being, to be one of 'moderation' combined with inducements, designed to illustrate London's interest in the welfare of the Egyptian people rather than to help Nasser personally.[32] The role which long-term projects like the Aswan dam could play in this scheme was outlined by Eden to the cabinet on 20 October:

> The allocation of the Egyptian High Dam project to the Egyptian consortium, if it could be secured, would be of immense importance in restoring the prestige of the West, and particularly of the older European powers in the Arab world generally. In our dealings with Egypt it could be a trump card.[33]

Eden's policy of appeasement, and Anglo-Egyptian relations generally, were dealt a significant blow in March 1956, however, when King Hussein of Jordan abruptly dismissed General Sir John Glubb from his command of Jordan's Arab Legion. This was an army largely officered and financed by Britain and had thus been a potent source of British influence for decades. It is now known that the king's decision to eject Glubb was taken primarily for domestic political reasons.[34] In the wake of the humiliating failure of Field Marshal Sir Gerald Templer's mission to cajole the Jordanians into joining the Baghdad Pact, however, itself blamed on Radio Cairo,[35] the British cabinet was in no doubt as to who was behind the move. Nor was the British press, which had long regarded Glubb as a legend in the mould of T. E. Lawrence.[36] Unfortunately for Eden, there was little positive the government could do, bar send the young king thinly veiled threats designed to change his mind. An overwrought prime minister then had to undergo a testing Commons debate, during which, he later admitted, he made one of the worst speeches in his career.[37] By the end of this episode, with questions being asked about his suitability as Churchill's successor, Eden appears to have concluded that Nasser was an arch-enemy of Mussolini proportions whose 'object was to be a Caesar from the Gulf to the Atlantic, and to kick us out of it all'. 'It is either him or us, don't forget that', he warned his closest Middle East adviser, Evelyn Shuckburgh.[38]

In contrast with the nervousness and indecision manifest during the Glubb affair, Eden's reaction to the news of the nationalization of the Suez Canal Company was altogether more self-assured. On the same night, 26 July, the prime minister held an immediate post-prandial meeting with three of Britain's chiefs of staff, the French ambassador and the American chargé d'affaires, at which he made clear his intention not to allow Nasser 'to get away with it'.[39] Having talked privately of 'destroying' him in March,[40] Eden (and many others) now saw the Egyptian leader as an insurmountable obstacle to the progress of British policy in the Arab world. As such, he had to be removed. Moreover, by expropriating the Suez Canal Company, the Egyptian had not only launched a personal assault upon Britain and France, the company's major shareholders, but he had also threatened the smooth operation of arguably the single most important international waterway. Nasser's act therefore provided Eden and like-minded ministers with the possible pretext for effecting his overthrow. This order of priorities was clearly and unambiguously stated during a meeting of the Egypt Committee on 30 July: 'While our ultimate purpose was to place the Canal under international control, our immediate purpose was to bring about the downfall of the Egyptian Government.'[41]

It was made clear to Eden in the early hours of 27 July, however, that Britain was militarily ill-prepared to carry out his wishes. Any expedition against Egypt would be a complicated affair and would take several weeks to mount. In fact, though Nasser himself was not fully aware of it,[42] he could hardly have chosen a more opportune time to test the readiness and morale of the British armed forces. Fulfilling the 1954 Anglo-Egyptian agreement slightly ahead of time, the last British troops had left the Suez Canal Zone in June 1956. A major defence review was in progress, threatening the future role of the navy in particular; from both the army and the RAF came complaints of major problems with equipment and training. Indeed, so seriously did the chiefs of staff view affairs that they threatened the prime minister with resignation if immediate operations were pursued.[43] Consequently, Eden's hopes that British forces in the area could have ridden in on the first waves of international indignation at Nasser's action, regained control of the canal, toppling the Egyptian dictator in the process, and thereby presented the world with a *fait accompli*, were immediately dashed. Instead, ministers had to recognize that it was going to be a long crisis and one in which public opinion would necessarily be an important, perhaps critical, factor.

Later in the morning of 27 July, the cabinet discussed, in the light of this embarrassing military unpreparedness, and with an eye clearly already on the 'presentability' of its case, what was 'the basis on which Britain could sustain, and justify to international opinion, a refusal to accept Nasser's decision to nationalise the Suez Canal Company'. It was at this point that Eden suffered his third shock in less than twenty-four hours. Ministers had to recognize immediately (much to their distress) that 'Britain would be on weak ground in basing its resistance on the narrow argument that Nasser had acted illegally'. The first point to note was that the Suez Canal Company did not actually own the canal but merely had a concession to operate it – until 1968, in fact, when everything was to revert to the Egyptian state. Moreover, as the Suez Canal Company was registered as an Egyptian company under Egyptian law and Nasser had indicated that he intended to compensate the shareholders at ruling market prices, the cabinet admitted that 'from the strictly legal point of view, his action amounts to no more than a decision to buy out the shareholders'. The only way in which Nasser would find himself on the wrong side of the law was if he broke the terms of the 1888 Convention. This bound the parties to keep the canal open to all ships in times of war and peace, and never to blockade it.[44]

This revelation posed a real dilemma for Eden. Nasser's coup was interpreted by many, including the prime minister himself, as a public affront not only to Britain but also to him personally. Following his mishandling of the Glubb affair in March, Eden had been under considerable pressure to strengthen his image from sections of the Conservative Party and leading Tory opinion. This went well beyond the Suez Group die-hards, led by Captain Charles Waterhouse, MP, who represented the staunch imperial position and had been a thorn in Eden's side ever since his promotion of the February 1953 Sudan Agreement. No direct challenge to his leadership was in the offing but any further humiliations could threaten to damage his status irreparably.[45] As far as many in the party were concerned, therefore, Eden's long-awaited showdown with his Middle Eastern *bête noire* had now arrived; both of them could not survive this crisis. And yet, if Nasser had not even technically broken the law, how could the British government brand him as an international criminal whose act merited the strongest of retaliatory measures, even armed force outside the United Nations? The answer to this problem lay in the marginalizing of the legality issue (though, for public consumption, a case would certainly be filed against Nasser) and the presentation of the government's case, as the cabinet euphemistically put it, 'on wider international grounds'.[46]

What this meant in practice was a twin-track policy of rapid military preparations supported by a propaganda campaign vilifying Nasser and whipping up public opinion in favour of the use of force. However, the key to this policy was for the government to dissemble. Were the public to discover Eden's real purpose, whole sections of opinion that trusted him as 'a man of peace' would be alienated. The trick, therefore, was to have the public opinion-formers do the government's bidding whilst the latter stuck to the line that its only objective was to 'restore' international control of the Suez Canal. This called for media manipulation of the highest calibre, not to mention Machiavellian nature.

One advantage that Margaret Thatcher had when formulating her propaganda strategy during the Falklands crisis was the relative lack of interest which most of the international community had in what happened in the South Atlantic. The government could therefore afford the luxury of concentrating its information efforts almost entirely on winning the hearts and minds of the British people. The 1956 Suez crisis was, however, of a fundamentally different nature. The canal itself, the focus of the dispute, was vital to Western Europe. In 1955, 14,666 ships had passed through it, one third of them British, three quarters of them belonging to NATO countries. Annually 70 million tons of oil came through the canal, of which 60 million tons were for Western Europe (accounting for two thirds of that region's total oil supplies). Hence, anything which jeopardized its efficient operation had potentially worldwide implications.[47]

Added to this, not only was the Middle East, which provided the setting for the crisis, seen by so many countries as the vital provider of cheap oil, but it also rivalled Europe as the centre of the Cold War. In July 1956, Britain still had the single most powerful military presence in the area (including bases in Jordan, Libya and Cyprus),[48] but she could no longer consider the Middle East as her own personal sphere of influence. The world might accept another AJAX, the covert operation run jointly by the CIA and British intelligence in Iran in 1953 which toppled Musaddiq and restored the shah to power.[49] Indeed, MI6 busied itself throughout the Suez crisis with plans to replace Nasser with an 'alternative' government, without the knowledge of the Foreign Office or the approval of all the cabinet.[50] But, for a war to be fought on Egyptian soil it was essential that Eden should carry with him not just British but international opinion as well. This the chiefs of staff added weight to on 31 July 1956:

> It was ... necessary to obtain the support of as many other countries as possible: no logistic or administrative difficulty should be allowed to stand in the way. Every effort should be made to encourage Nasser to put himself further in the wrong. At the same time public opinion in this country and in the world should be prepared to support any action we might eventually take.[51]

Some countries or peoples were of course worth more effort than others, depending on the diplomatic, political or economic weight they wielded. A high priority was given to the old Dominions, owing to their seniority in the Commonwealth; to India, owing to her membership of both the Commonwealth and the newly formed group of Non-Aligned Nations (which included Egypt); and, with a view to isolating Nasser from his own brethren, to the Arab world itself.[52] Of the utmost importance, however, and which is therefore examined at length, was American opinion. This was due not only to the considerable discord which had prevailed between Britain and the United States in the Middle East post-1945, but also to the highly influential role that public opinion was thought to play in the foreign policy-making process in the US. Furthermore, it was the United States that the cabinet believed held the key to the Soviet Union's behaviour, particularly if Britain and France decided to use military force. As it was, the longer the crisis went on and the more opposed to intervention the US administration became, the greater the emphasis put by Eden on appealing over the heads of President Eisenhower and Secretary of State Dulles to the American people themselves. Consequently, the Foreign Office school of thought which argued that the route to US foreign policy was through American public opinion came increasingly to the fore.

Throughout all this, Eden also had to bear in mind that Nasser himself attached considerable importance to the public projection of his policies. As explained earlier, the Foreign Office had already learned to its cost the degree of control Radio Cairo exerted over the Arabs.

Eden and his foreign secretary after December 1955, Selwyn Lloyd, had themselves personally intervened on several occasions in 1955 and early 1956 to try to persuade Nasser to conclude a moratorium on the airwaves, mindful of the damage these attacks were inflicting on Britain's image in the Middle East.[53] In the mid-1950s, the Foreign Office kept a keen eye on the burgeoning size and sophistication of the Egyptian propaganda 'machine', and its growing influence both at home and abroad.[54] The upshot was that by the summer of 1956 London had developed a grudging but deep respect for Nasser's ability to combine his propaganda with an overall appreciation of local, regional and international sentiment. Given this, it seems safe to assume that when Suez erupted ministers calculated that unless they competed effectively on the information front they ran the risk of losing their case by default.

Throughout the late summer and autumn of 1956, then, the British government launched an intensive propaganda campaign aimed at capturing the moral high ground in advance of any conflict against Egypt. 'Colonel Nasser', as he would always be referred to by official spokesmen, was presented as a fanatic nationalist, and the autocratic nature of his regime was emphasized. He was a second Hitler whose 'plunder' put the world 'at his mercy' and who therefore could not be 'appeased'. The Suez Canal Company employees, forbidden to leave their employment, were, it was claimed, being treated as virtual hostages. As for the canal itself, 'seized by force', this was nothing less than Britain's 'artery' whose continued smooth operation amounted to 'a matter of life and death'. For Arab consumption, great play was made of Nasser's avowed intention to dominate the Middle East, clearly outlined in his own version of *Mein Kampf*, *The Philosophy of the Revolution*. His unwillingness to consult fellow Arab leaders prior to the nationalization coup was evidence of his lack of respect and regard, especially for those countries whose healthy development relied upon their oil trade. With the American public particularly in mind, Nasser was portrayed as a Soviet 'stooge' whose dangerous antics could threaten US interests in the Middle East and ultimately lead to war in this most unstable, but strategically and economically vital, region. Finally, in addition to all this, Britain and France had to depict themselves as the policemen of the Middle East, as the only powers physically capable of enforcing 'international law' in that region.[55]

PART ONE

The British Press

2

Eden and the press: the state of play in July 1956

It is a long time, I think, since any Government has been so active in seeking to influence the press by every possible means ... as this Government has done during the Suez crisis.[1]

Compared with the lengths to which Anthony Eden is known to have gone in trying to control the BBC during the Suez crisis, the perceived wisdom is that the British press got off virtually scot-free. Attention has been brought over the years to the efforts of William Clark, Eden's press secretary, to, as one writer puts it, 'stoke up the sense of tension in the press' in the earliest days of the crisis,[2] but any antics of this kind have generally been dismissed by historians as harmless tinkering. The fact is that the press's performance during Suez is commonly thought to be a model of how it should operate in a liberal democracy, with 'independent' newspapers 'freely' articulating the divergent views of public opinion. Indeed, the press's success in fulfilling its duty as the 'watchdog of government' is often held up as one of the few redeeming features of the whole Suez debacle.[3] It automatically follows from this that if the government did try to manage the press during Suez then, firstly, it can only have done so in a half-hearted manner, otherwise the papers, given this view, would have exposed it themselves; and, secondly, if there was anything amounting to a campaign by the government it obviously failed anyway. Certainly, there can have been few other occasions in British history when so many newspapers have collectively and explicitly called for a prime minister's resignation, as happened at the height of the Suez crisis.

It is the contention of this study that the Eden government made a far more determined effort to manage the press during Suez than historians of the crisis have hitherto argued. Moreover, its exertions were, at times, highly successful. The fact is the British press was a, if not the, vital medium by which the government communicated with the public during Suez. There are two main reasons for this. Firstly, in the mid-1950s newspaper reading in Britain was at its zenith. In 1956 itself the total readership of the main daily morning newspapers was 49 million out of a population of 51 million (needless to say some people read more than one paper).[4] Thus, whilst the press could no longer claim to be the dominant medium of communication that it had been in the days of Northcliffe (competition from the cinema, radio and television had put paid to that), it was still clearly a formidable opinion-former, and one that any government ignored at its peril. Indeed, given the rapid increase in television sales in Britain from the late 1950s onwards and the subsequent establishment of TV as the undisputed means of communication between the public and the opinion-formers, Suez perhaps ranks as the last great international crisis in which the press could play a direct and profound role as a source of information – and persuasion.

Secondly, as already stated, Eden's policy objective – of toppling Nasser from power – dictated that he had somehow to conduct a war of nerves against the Egyptian regime and whip up public opinion in favour of aggression, but without himself revealing his true intentions. This called for other elements, outside the government, but within the realms of 'power', to do his bidding for him. The British press, with its reputation for independence, coupled with a long-established susceptibility to executive manipulation, particularly at times of 'national crisis', appeared the perfect instrument for this policy of 'war by stealth'.

In order to get the press to do this it will be shown that Eden employed a combination of three tried and tested manipulative techniques: personal contacts between ministers and key press figures, consistent exploitation of the lobby system of non-attributable political briefing, and the dubious use of wartime censorship powers. His aim throughout was to use the newspapers to create and maintain a climate of opinion at home in favour of war, whilst simultaneously obscuring his hatred of Nasser, and the true scale and nature of the military preparations for that war. By encouraging the press to advocate the need for force on the grounds of the dangers posed to Britain and the Middle East by Nasser, and yet at the same time giving the impression that it was itself surprisingly moderate, the government hoped it could justify a progressively aggressive policy by claiming that it was merely yielding to public opinion as manifested in a 'free' and 'independent' press. This, in turn, would increase the pressure on the Egyptian president, who was known to be a voracious reader of the British and American press.[5]

How effectively this strategy operated was dependent to a great extent on the state of play between Eden and the press prior to Suez;

no government would expect to enlist Fleet Street's support for such an ambitious, to some highly questionable, scheme simply from scratch. It is therefore important to assess what might be called the government's press base in July 1956, that is, its popularity rating in the main newspapers, the extent of its Fleet Street contacts, and the efficiency of its news dissemination system. Since the focus of Whitehall's machinery of information was then, and still is, Downing Street, we shall concentrate primarily on Eden's attributes as a practitioner of press manipulation.

Anthony Eden has gone down in history, paradoxically, as a superb image-builder but an inept media-manager. His authorized biographer calls him 'a complete innocent' in the matter of handling the press; James Margach, commentator on twentieth-century prime ministerial-press relations and the *Sunday Times* lobby correspondent during Suez, goes so far as to call him a 'natural loser' in the traditional battle for supremacy between Fleet Street and Number 10. In fact, of the twelve prime ministers – from Lloyd George to Callaghan – evaluated by Margach in terms of their press management skills, none comes off worse than Eden.[6]

Such a strong indictment is centred on Eden's failure throughout his career to develop a firm press base for himself. Unusually for a Conservative prime minister, Eden had few close contacts, let alone friends, in Fleet Street. The only real exceptions to this were a coterie of experienced diplomatic correspondents and his close relationship with Lord Kemsley, chairman of Kemsley Newspapers and editor-in-chief of the *Sunday Times* (about which more will be said later). Two main reasons are regularly given to explain this relative isolation. First, that Eden lacked the necessary manipulative streak or political killer instinct with which all the best media-managers have been blessed. Even after his resignation as foreign secretary in protest against Chamberlain's policy of appeasement in February 1938, for example, Eden remained conspicuously aloof from the press.[7] His ignorance of when and how to use the press in this instance stood in stark contrast to Chamberlain's masterly manipulation of journalists and proprietors during his tenure at Number 10.[8] The second reason is Eden's over-concentration throughout his career on foreign affairs. Had he regularly switched departments like most politicians, Eden would conceivably have made contacts with a wider range of correspondents, all eager to develop intimate and mutually beneficial links. By closeting himself in the Foreign Office for thirty years, however, Eden had isolated himself from the majority of the most influential (and useful) grass-roots journalists, especially those who were members of the Westminster lobby.

When Eden finally succeeded Churchill in April 1955, therefore, Britain had a prime minister peculiarly naive and ill-educated in the realm of press management. Robert Rhodes James writes that on entering Number 10 Eden was genuinely astonished, shocked even, to learn that under Churchill's guidance a small group of ministers had regularly met to decide which confidential documents should be leaked to the press.[9] This is most instructive. For Eden to be unaware of such machinations not only casts doubt on the lines of communication within the Churchill government, it also begs the question as to whether he had learned anything about the subtleties of cultivating the press from his three decades in politics. The fact that Eden was outside this select team of briefers suggests that he was neither regarded as a skilled publicist by his colleagues nor had many press contacts of use to the government.

Eden appeared to have sensed this weakness in September 1955, however, when he appointed William Clark, diplomatic correspondent of the *Observer*, as his press secretary. Clark had excellent media connections, a wide knowledge of domestic and international affairs and was a current-affairs broadcaster. He also had experience in public relations, having worked for British Information Services in the United States during the war. For a prime minister so bereft of media contacts as Eden, it was surely only logical that he should attempt to buy himself some such contacts by proxy, that is via a well-connected press adviser. Moreover, the press itself welcomed the appointment for precisely the reasons that Conservative Central Office distrusted it: Clark was a non-Tory and a widely respected, progressive journalist who would hopefully urge upon Eden the need for a greater measure of open government. Clark himself certainly saw things this way. His diary entry for the night of his appointment waxes lyrical about how much in agreement Eden and himself were on the benefits of an 'informed democracy'. Furthermore, Clark appeared fully confident that Eden would grant him the necessary freedom to handle the press as he thought best. 'I have found the Prime Minister extremely obliging and absolutely prepared to let me try and play this as a non-party, impartial job', he wrote in a letter to A. P. Wadsworth, editor of the *Manchester Guardian*. 'I think, in fact, that it is a credit to have picked on someone who is not a regular, safe party man.'[10]

Nevertheless, Clark's optimism faded very quickly when he came to realize, as many others did in the Eden government, that the new prime minister was a compulsive interferer, especially in press affairs. The first evidence of a serious dispute between Eden and Clark over how to cope with critical press comment surfaced within a month:

> Prime Minister worried about *Daily Mail* on Middle East again. I advised
> him against seeing the Editor to reprimand him but PM determined to
> do so and I arranged it at House of Commons this afternoon.[11]

Its apparent success failed to enamour Clark of what he considered a
heavy-handed technique of press management. Not only was this, in
Clark's eyes, a naive and crude method of manipulating the press, and
one that could not be very durable, it would, in the long run, probably
prove to be dangerously counter-productive. Clark's diary entry for
the weekend of 6–9 April 1956 emphasized this very point:

> Several times when papers have attacked him [Eden] he has sent for the
> editor or the proprietor, over my strong protests. The result has been to
> let them know that he was moved by their words.[12]

In Clark's opinion, an altogether more effective and sophisticated way
of securing the government a positive press was via the unattributable
briefing of his own elite class of specialist reporters, the lobby. Since
the lobby was to be one of the government's main channels of communication with the press and public during Suez it is worth outlining
briefly how it works.

As a group of select political journalists whose privilege it is to have
free and unfettered access to any MP or minister that wishes to speak
confidentially to the press, but whose rules oblige its members to keep
secret the actual sources of their information, the lobby is unique to
British politics. The original idea behind its creation (in 1884) was to
facilitate news-gathering and make for more open government. In fact,
so open to government manipulation has the lobby proved to be over
the years, especially since the establishment in the 1920s of an office at
10 Downing Street designed to improve the prime minister's press
relations, that it has gradually fallen deeper and deeper into disrepute.
This culminated in the 1980s in the withdrawal from the lobby 'system'
of two highly respected national newspapers, the *Independent* and the
Guardian, on the grounds that it had been reduced to nothing less
than a tool of the government of the day.[13]

Back in the 1950s little of the modern-day controversy surrounding
the lobby existed; however, this is not to say criticism was not as
applicable. On his very first day on duty in Number 10, William Clark
was immediately and genuinely shocked by the ease with which he
could influence his erstwhile colleagues: 'It is amazing to see how
much of one's lightest guidance over the phone appears in the papers
next day from the political correspondents.'[14] Coming from someone
with as wide an experience of the media as had Clark, this comment
was extremely significant. It suggested that even the most hardened

journalists, never mind the general public, were unaware of the executive's power of manipulation. What especially struck Clark about
the lobby was its over-emphasis on self-discipline and outright subservience to the providers of information (such as himself): 'it is a
tight loyal professional body of people with a devouring interest in
rather dull "scoops" e.g. all fear that one day the announcement of
Cabinet changes will find them napping.'[15] Clearly, if a government
had the wish, and was versed in the requisite skills, the lobby represented a most useful instrument with which to set the tone and agenda
for political reporting in Britain. As a pseudo news cartel system it
enabled a government to release information or inspire stories without
being held publicly responsible for them. As we shall see, given the
secret nature of the government's policy during Suez it was precisely
this sort of clandestine news dissemination system that Eden needed.

Despite the malleable nature of the lobby and the inspired appointment of William Clark, Eden's government received a remarkably bad
press from a very early stage. 'Of all Prime Ministers' honeymoons
[with Fleet Street],' writes James Margach, 'his was the briefest.'[16]
This could be attributed to a number of factors: unnaturally high
expectations due to Eden's image as Churchill's crown prince, his
obvious lack of self-confidence in domestic affairs, plus his apparent
loss of touch in foreign policy. The Soviet–Egyptian arms deal of
September 1955 was particularly damaging, discrediting the Anglo-
Egyptian Treaty which Eden had negotiated with Nasser a year earlier
and suggesting that the Middle East was about to go communist.[17]
What should not be underestimated when attempting to explain this
drop in popularity, however, is Eden's very mismanagement of the
press.

The root cause of this was the prime minister's over-sensitivity to
all media criticism, no matter how trivial. At times this bordered on
paranoia. When the *Daily Telegraph* demanded a cabinet reshuffle in
October 1955, for example, Eden compared the paper with the Nazis
and, again contrary to William Clark's advice, instinctively retaliated.[18]
Smelling blood, in January 1956 Fleet Street assailed the prime minister
with an almost unprecedented barrage of hostility. Allegations of
fumbling and indecisiveness rained down on him from newspapers
across the political spectrum; Clark was in despair.[19] Eden himself
appears to have been hurt most by an article written by the *Daily
Telegraph*'s deputy editor, Donald McLachlan, demanding the 'smack
of firm government'. This ridiculed Eden's habit, when emphasizing a
point during a speech, of holding up both hands like a boxer and then
bringing the right fist down into the left palm – but without the
expected resounding smack.[20] There seems little doubt that most of

the papers involved in this campaign aimed to put a shot across Eden's bows rather than bring him down. There is certainly no evidence whatsoever of any Fleet Street conspiracy.[21] What this showed, however, was that Eden had quickly lost the confidence of a large section of the press, including many newspapers on which a Conservative leader could normally rely.

Had Eden kept his head down and ridden out this storm, his standing in the press might have slowly risen. However, when the Sunday press then spread the rumour of his imminent resignation, he panicked and issued an official statement to the effect that such talk 'was false and without any foundation whatsoever'.[22] In his memoirs, R. A. Butler, then Lord Privy Seal and the minister who most regularly met the lobby, wrote how 'unwise' this denial was.[23] It only served to confirm to the press the prime minister's weakness. To James Margach, then the *Sunday Times* lobby correspondent, it was this fundamental error more than the 'Eden Must Go' campaign itself that 'proved in advance [of Suez] that in the conflict for power between Downing Street and Fleet Street Anthony Eden was the natural loser – the easiest and quickest victim on record'.[24]

This analysis of the state of play between the government and the press before Suez shows the latter in the clear ascendancy. In the year since his arrival in Number 10, Eden had given a series of classic lessons in how not to handle the press. This was due to his failure to establish anything remotely close to a system of media-management. The prime minister had proved to be too easily distracted, too obsessed with detail. The result was a political and publicity policy which lacked any sense of design or planning. The one man who perhaps could have masterminded a clear publicity strategy, and whose job it was to keep the prime minister in close touch with media and public opinion, William Clark, found himself after the January 1956 debacle seeing less and less of Eden. 'I feel more and more cut off from his views', wrote Clark in late March. 'Is that my fault? Does he not trust me?'[25] By the summer, their relationship appeared to be at breaking point:

> I [am] partly feeling very low as a result of a general persecution complex arising out of a whispering campaign designed to make me appear disloyal to the PM. The difficulty is that I no longer do see enough of the PM to feel that I enjoy his full confidence. Perhaps I don't since the steady attack on him by the *Observer* certainly must be a disappointment to him ... Sunday he rang up to say he was pleased about the Saturday press on his Norwich speech. Then he began to carp. 'I hear Massingham [the *Observer*'s political correspondent] is never out of your room – he's my enemy so it's not much good seeing him, is it?'[26]

The signs are that by this stage Clark's place was being gradually usurped by the prime minister's parliamentary private secretary, Robert Allan.[27]

In early July, the cabinet ordered a complete investigation into the existing arrangements for coordinating the presentation of the government's publicity. An early draft written by Frederick Bishop, Eden's private secretary, pinpointed several serious problems:

> The present set-up is of a number of departmental public relations outfits, some (like the Treasury Information Service and the Foreign Office News Department) considerably bigger and more important than the others, and operating more or less independently. Such co-ordination of their activities, or forward planning to integrate them, as takes place, comes about through the central position of the Office of the Prime Minister's Public Relations Adviser. This is at best a somewhat haphazard process, without regular arrangements for co-ordination or forward planning. This is necessarily so, since there is no one sufficiently free from the daily business of talking to the Press, etc., to be able to look around and think ahead over the whole field of Government activities.
>
> The Ministerial responsibility for co-ordinating the presentation of Government policy to the public is with the Lord Privy Seal (who is also responsible on behalf of the Prime Minister for the policy direction of the Conservative Central Office). The Central Office have their own publicity (or propaganda) organisation, the direction of which is effected mainly through the Liaison Committee of which the Lord Privy Seal is Chairman.
>
> There are thus two 'publicity machines', without connection save that they are both under the Ministerial control of the Lord Privy Seal.
>
> There is in addition the Central Office of Information – an entirely separate Department which is in effect no more than a publicity agency; it undertakes publicity operations, in the main long-term or educational ones, at the instance of Government Departments, but it does not initiate current policy nor does it do any forward planning to co-ordinate the publicity activities of the Government.

To meet these shortcomings, Bishop suggested dispensing with the Number 10 press secretary altogether, replacing him with a powerful backroom 'brooder and planner' based in the Lord Privy Seal's Office.[28] Radical proposals, even if agreed upon, could not be implemented immediately, however. A week later, on 16 July, following yet another dressing down from Eden, Clark and Bishop were still at a loss and 'saw no easy way to improve the mechanics and the direction of the Public Relations policy.'[29] Evidence of such low morale reflected the disarray in which the government's practitioners of propaganda found themselves on the eve of a crisis which would test their ability to the full. When Suez did erupt, only ten days later, the government, not surprisingly, appears to have concluded that this was precisely the wrong time to undertake a fundamental shake-up of its propaganda machinery and the review was put on hold.

3

Nationalization

Historians have on the whole been perfectly justified in emphasizing the overwhelming hostility of the vast majority of the British press to Nasser in the immediate aftermath of his nationalization of the Suez Canal Company on 26 July 1956. Rarely had Fleet Street reacted to a foreign event with such interest and, in the case of many newspapers, such unbridled aggression. 'The British government will be fully justified in taking retaliatory action,' declared the Liberal *News Chronicle*. 'No more Adolf Hitlers!' shouted the Labour party's ally, the *Daily Herald*. 'There is no room for appeasement.'[1] Coming little more than a month after the last British troops had withdrawn from the Canal Zone under the terms of the 1954 Anglo-Egyptian Treaty, Nasser's act was interpreted by several papers as in distinctly bad faith. One, the pro-Conservative *Daily Mail*, suggested reoccupying the Zone immediately.[2] To attribute all this to the government's skilful manipulation would be patently absurd; the coup caught the government completely by surprise.

Where these historians have gone astray, however, is to overlook the criticism which many papers levelled at the government as well during the first heady days of the crisis. This was particularly true of the Tory press, on whom Eden counted to take the lead in campaigning for war. In so doing, these historians have not only tended to exaggerate the degree of unity that existed in Britain in response to Nasser's action, especially on the thorny issue of a resort to military force, but they have also underestimated the pressure on Eden to control the press from the very outset.[3]

The press's real, as opposed to assumed, reaction to the news of nationalization was apparent the very morning after.[4] Given that the coup was, at least in the prime minister's eyes, virtually equivalent to a declaration of war, Eden must have been immensely cheered by the *Daily Telegraph*'s and *Daily Mail*'s immediate comparison of Nasser with Hitler, together with the *Daily Express*'s warlike editorial, 'A Time

23

To Resist'.[5] What cannot have escaped Eden's attention, however, was the manner in which all three of these normally loyal Conservative papers interlaced their calls for action with criticism of the government, and of the prime minister in particular. As far as they were concerned, Eden and the Foreign Office had to a great extent brought this latest blow to their and the nation's prestige upon themselves for having been so naive as to trust Nasser in the first place. The *Daily Express* led the charge:

> President Nasser's proposal to grab the Suez Canal should surprise nobody. It is an act of brigandage which follows naturally from what has gone on before: the scuttle from the Suez base; the American decision, supported by Britain, to give no money for the Aswan Dam; and the very nature of Nasser's government which owes its existence to hatred of the Western Powers ... Is Britain going to tolerate this new arrogance? With each act of surrender to Nasser the task of resistance has become harder.[6]

Considering Eden already knew by this stage that any effective military 'resistance' would take some weeks to mount, these cutting remarks, bordering on threats, did not bode at all well. They could certainly not be ignored in the hope that they would fade away. The chances were that the longer the government did not act as these papers demanded, the more virulent would be the attacks. A paper like the *Daily Telegraph*, with its strong links with the Conservative party rank-and-file, could cause an immense amount of damage in such a situation. When, therefore, on top of all this, an increasingly beleaguered Eden was forced to realize the weakness of the government's legal case against Nasser at that morning's cabinet meeting,[7] we can reasonably presume that this only confirmed what was already going through his mind: that the government needed to set the press's agenda, and swiftly.

So it was, only a matter of hours later, in the afternoon of 27 July, that the government made its first recognizable contact with the press when Eden himself held the first of what would develop into a series of detailed, secret talks throughout the Suez crisis with Iverach McDonald, foreign and deputy editor of *The Times*. As McDonald, via *The Times*, would come to form the keystone in Eden's policy to recruit the press during Suez, their close relationship deserves scrutiny.

In many ways it was inevitable that McDonald should be Eden's first point of contact with the press. As already explained, Eden was, as prime ministers go, remarkable for the sheer dearth of contacts he possessed in Fleet Street, particularly at the grass-roots level. However, if there was one group of journalists which Eden had assiduously courted over the years and on which he consequently felt he could call in his hour of need, it was Fleet Street's diplomatic correspondents. According to James Margach, so successfully had Eden fostered relations with this close-knit band of journalists throughout his career that amongst them 'were an inner circle of special confidants, identified as an arm of the Foreign Office, who adored him with total loyalty.'[8]

Iverach McDonald, though no longer a diplomatic correspondent (he had risen to be *The Times*'s foreign editor in 1952), was at the heart of this inner circle; he was also the closest thing to a friend that Eden had in Fleet Street. Their 'special relationship', as the *Times* man referred to it in his memoirs,[9] dated from the 1930s. McDonald had then found himself in the deeply uncomfortable position of being an anti-appeaser working for an autocratic, pro-appeasement editor, Geoffrey Dawson. This included an agonizing and humiliating stint as *The Times*'s correspondent in Prague during the months that led to the Munich settlement.[10] Eden had of course resigned from high office in February 1938 in protest against Chamberlain's wooing of Italy and his snubbing of President Roosevelt, an act which won him great respect and admiration amongst anti-appeasers like McDonald. Back in the Foreign Office during the war, Eden then kept the *Times* man fully informed of relations with the Soviet Union. By the time of Suez, therefore, McDonald had been reporting for more than twenty years on what he and many others saw as Eden's Midas touch in foreign affairs.[11] Thus, if there was one man in Fleet Street who trusted Eden's judgement, and whom Eden could equally trust to accept, and persuade others to accept, that judgement, it was McDonald. For this reason Eden not surprisingly saw McDonald as his most useful ally in enlisting the support not only of the all-important diplomatic correspondents but of the press in general during Suez. Indeed, so important was McDonald to Eden that it can be said that throughout the crisis he was privy to more cabinet thinking and secrets than most members of the government. In return for such privileges, the *Times* man was to see his friendship with the prime minister exploited to the full.

That Eden should find time in the afternoon of 27 July to see Iverach McDonald, in between that morning's long cabinet meeting and the despatch of his crucial first cable to President Eisenhower, is a mark of the importance the prime minister attached to the press at the very outset of Suez. As to the significance of what Eden actually told McDonald, it is essential to realize that up to this point in the crisis the only public statement any member of the government had yet made was that by Eden only a few hours earlier in the Commons. This had been of a completely bland nature, giving no clue whatsoever as to the depth of the prime minister's anger with Nasser:

LIVERPOOL JOHN MOORES UNIVERSITY
LEARNING SERVICES

The unilateral decision of the Egyptian Government to expropriate the Suez Canal Company, without notice and in breach of the Concession Agreements, affects the rights and interests of many nations. Her Majesty's Government are consulting other Governments immediately concerned, with regard to the serious situation thus created. The consultations will cover both the effect of this arbitrary action upon the operation of the Suez Canal and also the wider questions which it raises.[12]

The nature of Eden's conversation with the man from *The Times* was, on the other hand, anything but bland. This was a deliberate ploy on Eden's part. He clearly sought to have his real views on Nasser and the canal question aired through the press – unattributably, of course – whilst maintaining a peaceful, conciliatory image in public.

Despite McDonald's long-standing admiration for him, Eden could not afford to come straight out and tell him of his intention to use the dispute over the Suez Canal Company as an opportunity for toppling Nasser. This might scare McDonald off. At the same time, if *The Times* was to strike the right tone and help create that much-needed war mentality, McDonald, who would be writing the paper's foreign leaders, presumably had to be convinced of the sheer gravity of Nasser's action and of the government's right to use force if and when it chose. In short, Eden needed to frighten McDonald, but carefully. This he succeeded in doing via a subtle mixture of calmness and aggression, washed down with liberal doses of highly classified, confidential information. Thus, McDonald was told that the government had every intention of negotiating with Nasser but the Egyptian 'dictator' had to be made to realize the error of his ways; on this the cabinet and the chiefs of staff had already agreed. Though it would go out of its way to work with its natural allies, the government, as McDonald's contemporaneous account of the interview attests, 'was determined that we should act, alone if necessary'. As for the United Nations, for which Eden knew McDonald had the greatest respect, there was 'the interminable problem of the Soviet veto', not to mention, as the prime minister significantly confessed, the fact that 'it could hardly be argued [at the UN] that Egypt's action was a threat to peace and security'. So serious was Nasser's act that 'if necessary, force would be used'. Ultimately, though the priority was to achieve an up-to-date agreement on the running of the canal, the present Egyptian regime could not be trusted with the control of it and might therefore have to be deposed.[13]

In divulging this information to McDonald, Eden was taking a grave risk. Excepting the details of how soon Britain would be prepared militarily to use force, McDonald might as well have been given a copy of that morning's cabinet minutes. Nevertheless, the prime minister's gamble paid off. *The Times*'s immediate reaction to Nasser's act – that is, before McDonald had seen Eden – had by no means been conciliatory.[14] But, after McDonald had been briefed the paper adopted an extremely hardline anti-Nasser, pro-force stance. A whole series of editorials, written either by McDonald himself or by *The Times*'s editor, William Haley,[15] bore a noticeable similarity to what Eden had told McDonald during this first meeting, not only in their tone but right down to the phrases used.[16] The most graphic example of this was *The Times*'s editorial on 1 August, entitled 'A Hinge of History'. This warned of the threat to the West's interests throughout the Middle East should Nasser be allowed to get away with it and the danger of getting involved in 'legal quibbles' concerning Egypt's right to national- ize the Suez Canal Company – precisely the form of words in fact used by Eden in his supposedly confidential first telegram to Eisen- hower of 27 July.[17] Little wonder that Eden later quoted extensively from this editorial in his memoirs as evidence of, as he put it, 'a general conviction throughout the country that Nasser must not be allowed to get away with his theft and that we should be fully justified in taking forcible steps to prevent him'.[18]

Writing some thirty years later, Iverach McDonald referred to the 'unusually strong' nature of his paper's editorials during this early period of Suez but claimed that they were designed to keep up the pressure on Nasser to come to the negotiating table, not to encourage force.[19] This is extremely disingenuous. As an examination of McDonald's own contemporaneous notes of his first meeting with Eden shows, he knew exactly how aggressive the prime minister was. He himself had urged Eden that if Britain was going to use force, 'the sooner we went in the better'.[20] This in itself is hardly the mark of a disinterested, objective journalist (as McDonald likes to portray him- self). Moreover, many in Printing House Square soon themselves began to question the origins and wisdom of the paper's uncharacteristically 'hawkish' stance. However, there was little they could do. Eden's private briefings of McDonald and other sympathetic members of the *Times* staff, including the autocratic Haley, a man who hitherto had prided himself on maintaining a healthy distance from politicians lest his independence should be compromised, had the effect of paralysing the paper's regular system of editorial conferences. This is one thing to which McDonald does admit:

> These frank talks with Eden were highly informative but had one un- foreseen and unfortunate consequence within Printing House Square. Haley and McDonald were given so much secret information that they found it difficult to have the usual round-table easy talks with the leader writers as a group. Without planning it, they got into the way of

discussing policy between themselves or with only Green and Woods, deputy foreign editor, brought in on occasions. Knowledgeable men such as Teddy Hodgkin and Richard Harris, most uneasy in any case at some of the paper's tougher leaders in the first few weeks, felt excluded from its Suez policy, although the usual discussions on all other subjects went on. With hindsight it is clear that the Suez talks within the office should have been broadened.[21]

By claiming that both Eden and *The Times* advocated from the start a policy of force as only the last resort, McDonald tried to hide the fact that his paper became the government's chief vehicle for testing the possibility of war on the public during Suez. Eden courted *The Times* more avidly than any other paper, continually offering it preferential treatment, for several reasons. Despite the damage inflicted upon its independent reputation by Geoffrey Dawson's notorious collusion with Chamberlain in the late 1930s, two decades later *The Times* still enjoyed the highest status of all British newspapers. Its editors' traditional access to the policy-makers continued to underpin the paper's pre-eminence. To be able to quote *The Times*'s unequivocal support (which the government could, and did, do throughout almost the whole of Suez)[22] was therefore quite a coup for Eden. Whilst he could not expect the backing of *The Times* miraculously to convert his opponents, it could act as an invaluable reinforcer of that section of British press and public opinion which believed the government to be right on this most vital of issues for the nation. Moreover, because *The Times* traditionally stood at the centre of the political spectrum, which was where the press war over Suez was always going to be won or lost, its importance to the government grew still further. Not to be discounted, either, was the even greater significance attached to *The Times* abroad, where it was still regarded as something of a government mouthpiece. If the paper was steadfast on Suez then this would increase the pressure on Nasser; if, on the other hand, it showed signs of uncertainty, then the government itself would appear to be dithering and the pressure consequently diminish.

Eden's first meeting with McDonald, then, bore all the hallmarks of a successful briefing session. Both parties had got what they wanted: the journalist his inside information and sense of even greater influence, the politician his 'line' publicized confidentially. This mutually beneficial arrangement set the pattern for the government's meetings with favoured correspondents during Suez, with Eden hoping to use them as an instrument for publicizing policies on which the inner cabinet had privately decided, but to which it had not publicly committed itself, and for which it could therefore escape responsibility if the newspaper stories it inspired evoked an unfavourable response.

Eden had another visitor to Number 10 on the afternoon of 27 July – Arthur Christiansen, editor of the *Daily Express* and a director of Beaverbrook Newspapers. Given its self-styled reputation as 'The Imperialist Crusader', one might be forgiven for thinking that Eden could have counted on the *Express*'s unflinching support during Suez without having to lift a finger. After all, in meddling with the Suez Canal had not Nasser threatened Britain's very imperial lifeline? The fact is, however, that the Tory–Imperialist papers had, each in their own way, to be cultivated just as much as the Labour–Liberal press, if not more. In Lords Beaverbrook, Rothermere and Kemsley, plus Michael Berry, proprietors of the *Daily Express*, *Daily Mail*, *Sunday Times* and *Daily Telegraph* respectively, the government could readily call on a phalanx of autocratic press barons, all with a shared interest in maintaining Britain's world status and her empire. But, if this highly influential press was to be used to its utmost during Suez, essential given the nature of Eden's policy, it would first have to be convinced of the government's determination to hit back at Nasser. This in itself would be no mean achievement for a prime minister whose first year in office had been, as far as the Tory press was concerned, at best an huge anticlimax, at worst a betrayal of the party's ideals. As already mentioned, on the very first morning of the crisis the Big Three – the *Telegraph*, *Mail* and *Express* – had gone out of their way to confirm their suspicions of Eden's dubious attachment to Empire. Having accomplished this, the government would then have to guide the Tory press, that is tell it what to say and when. Eden knew even at this very early stage that any military operation against Egypt would take at least six weeks to prepare.[23] Whilst encouraging aggression in the press, therefore, the government had simultaneously to discourage demands for the immediate use of force. Only with the Tory press playing, in this way, the same patient tune could the government build up and maintain the required war psychology amongst the British people over a long period.

Having suffered years of imperial rundown whilst continually warning both Labour and Tory governments that their 'surrenders' would come back to haunt them, the *Daily Express* had more reason than any other paper to turn nasty with Eden when news came through of Nasser's nationalization of the Suez Canal Company. 'A Day of Sorrow – A Day of Shame' was how it had greeted his completion of the 1954 Anglo-Egyptian agreement, for example.[24] If Eden had had any doubts about the *Express*'s loyalty to his cause, however, they were soon to be dispelled by his interview with Christiansen. Despite having been editor of the Express since 1933, Christiansen was still a relatively humble journalist: he recounts his meeting with Eden that afternoon as being 'only my second private audience with a Prime Minister'. Eden, doubtless realizing this, played on the *Express* man's inexperience and modest pretensions to the full, as Christiansen's memoirs reveal:

> I spent the afternoon of my 52nd birthday in the Cabinet Room alone with Mr. Eden while he explained the situation to me ... Eden sat in the Prime Minister's large arm-chair ... I took the chair on the Prime Minister's right ... I formed the view that Britain was going to fight. He seemed calm and resolute ... and I went away impressed with his firmness of purpose.[25]

Plying Christiansen with secret, unattributable information was one thing; getting the unqualified support of Lord Beaverbrook's full array of press holdings was another. Eden knew that Christiansen was not an independent, policy-forming editor. Like all the editors of Lord Beaverbrook's newspapers, he was very much his master's voice, especially when it came to imperial issues (like Suez). To make doubly sure of getting the line he wanted in the *Daily Express*, *Sunday Express* and *Evening Standard*, therefore, Eden, as Christiansen recalls, 'indicated that he had been in previous communication with Lord Beaverbrook, but that as he was in the South of France he would like me to get the facts of the situation to him'. Dutifully, Christiansen did as he was asked, writing to 'the Beaver' that night. The letter makes it abundantly clear that Eden had fed the *Express* man as strong a line as he had to McDonald earlier. As with *The Times*, Eden hoped to have the *Express* readers whipped up in favour of the use of force, without himself coming out into the open. A key difference between the two meetings, however, was the emphasis which Eden put on when the government could be expected to use force. Whereas McDonald was told that military action could be effected in a matter of days (presumably to instil in the traditionally sedate *Times* the necessary sense of urgency), Christiansen was informed that 'the operation [against Nasser] was so big that it would take time to mount'.[26] By letting the *Express* in on this secret, Eden clearly sought to pre-empt any politically damaging pressure that the paper would otherwise have mounted on the government. As we shall see, the prime minister's approach evidently had its desired effect.

What direct action, if any, Lord Beaverbrook himself took on receiving this urgent plea for help from Eden is not known. Christiansen makes no mention of any reply; nor is there any reference to it in either Beaverbrook's or Eden's private papers. This would seem to bear out the widely held theory that the old press magnate's role during Suez was marginal to the point of being non-existent.[27]

Whilst it may be true that Beaverbrook was unable to play any direct part in the proceedings when Suez reached its climax in November, owing to the speed of events and his being in the Bahamas, it is difficult to believe that on receiving the news of Nasser's coup, quickly followed by a personal SOS from the prime minister, the man who owned papers 'purely for the purpose of making political propaganda' simply did nothing. Beaverbrook was certainly closer to Eden than many historians, including his biographer, A. J. P. Taylor, would have us think.[28] Only a few months before Suez he had given Christiansen explicit orders to 'support Eden in all our newspapers'.[29] As this shows, and his biographer verifies, even at the grand old age of seventy-seven 'the Beaver' was also still very much a hands-on press proprietor when he wanted to be.[30] Moreover, there is strong evidence to suggest that Beaverbrook broke his routine of spending the summer in France and returned to England in September solely in order to play a more influential part in Suez.[31]

Whatever Beaverbrook himself may have done at various stages of the crisis, it is clear that journalists on his papers wrote with the courage of their master's strong imperialist convictions throughout. In so doing, the government could not have asked for a more vigorous and loyal bunch of Fleet Street activists. This is reflected in a letter that Eden wrote to Beaverbrook immediately after his resignation in January 1957:

> Dear Max, As I leave for New Zealand I would like to send you this message to try to thank you for the consistent support you have given me, especially in these last difficult months. We did not achieve all we hoped for in the Middle East, mainly because of US opposition. But they are beginning to learn.[32]

Whether it was Beaverbrook or Christiansen who was determining policy at the early stage of Suez, Eden got exactly what he wanted from the *Express*. Of the newspapers pressuring the government to intervene forcibly immediately, the *Express* was, contrary to all expectations, not the most outspoken. This dubious distinction was instead shared by the *Daily Telegraph* and *Daily Mail*. The *Express* was without doubt extremely hostile to Nasser and clearly chafing at the bit. However, and this is the key point, unlike the *Telegraph* and *Mail*, the *Express* had not, by the end of July, begun to criticize the government for its inaction. Instead, the *Express* was doing its level best to increase public support for the use of force but without demanding that the government took such action immediately. Hence, whilst the *Mail* declared on 28 July 'We wait for action ... much more drastic action than has yet been taken' and the *Telegraph* on 31 July accused Eden of having been 'too gentle' in his first substantial Commons speech on the crisis, the *Express* continued to call for 'resistance' but evinced patience and confidence in how the government was handling the crisis.[33]

On Monday, 30 July, the inner cabinet, the Egypt Committee,[34] agreed on the priority of ousting Nasser and heard the foreign secretary, Selwyn Lloyd, reveal his plan for bringing the crisis to as quick a climax as possible. The conference of maritime nations for which the Americans had been pressing from the outset would be called, but merely to present Nasser with an ultimatum. 'In the event of an unsatisfactory reply, action would follow.'[35] The government's ability to carry this out, however, given Britain's own military unpreparedness, depended to a great extent on its French ally. The socialist administration in Paris, led by Guy Mollet, had been outraged by the events of 26 July and immediately lent its full support to the British cabinet's hardline stance. Nasser's patronage of the FLN rebels in Algeria, where over 300,000 French troops were stationed in 1956, had long since earned him a reputation as the Mussolini of the Arab world in French eyes. Moreover, Mollet himself felt that the Egyptian leader was in many ways a Western creation that the French and British therefore had the responsibility to crush.[36] Nevertheless, hopes that the Egypt Committee had of the French spearheading an early attack to recapture control of the Suez Canal were dispelled at the same 30 July meeting. Eden had to inform the committee that the French contingent of the military force which was being hastily prepared, and with whom he had pledged the government to work, would itself not be ready for action until late August at the earliest.[37]

This must have confirmed what had clearly already been going through the prime minister's mind (judging from the behaviour of the Beaverbrook press): that public opinion would not only have to be stirred but also controlled. The biggest danger to the government at this point was for public opinion to get too far ahead of the military–diplomatic schedule. If the public demand for the use of force against Nasser reached fever pitch too soon, that is, before the military preparations were complete, Eden would once again find himself in the dangerous position of being labelled a ditherer. Public frustration might then all too easily turn into doubts concerning Britain's right to use force. The end result could be a policy which lacked a sufficiently strong public mandate. Eden would then ultimately be faced with either going ahead with his attempt to topple Nasser and hoping that in the heat of such action public opinion would tag along, or giving up his secret objective, following the dictates of those like the US administration who were already perceived as more conciliatory[38] and, in the process, running the risk of facing a coup himself from within his own party. William Clark, whom Eden appears to have reluctantly welcomed back into the fold when Suez broke owing to the value of his media contacts, was perhaps more aware than anybody of the pressure the prime minister was under at this stage, and, consequently, of the importance of getting him a good press: 'Certainly this is the most critical moment in my tour of duty. It is certainly the gravest for Eden, for if he does not act strongly and effectively he will be out.'[39]

No doubt prompted by fears of this worst-case scenario, during its meeting on 30 July the Egypt Committee held the first of what would emerge as a series of regular discussions during Suez recorded under the rather paradoxical title 'Security of the Press'. On this occasion, Peter Thorneycroft, president of the Board of Trade, expressed concern about 'inflammatory articles in the press, e.g. on the prospects of the use of force', and enquired whether it would be possible to 'remind editors of the UK papers of the importance of reasonable discretion in the present circumstances'. According to the minutes, Eden then said that he would consider the possibility of some such action but felt that the 'awkward repercussions' following such an approach had to be borne in mind.[40] Whatever qualms the prime minister may initially have had about asking for such 'editorial discretion', they did not last long. The next day he asked William Clark to arrange for him to see the editors of the *Daily Express* and *Daily Mail*, adding 'at the last moment' the *News Chronicle*.[41] As already mentioned, the *Express* had up to this point caused the government surprisingly little trouble but Eden obviously felt a further 'reassuring' session with Christiansen would do no harm. The next day the *Express*'s editorial, 'Eden means Business', struck the right tone so much that it might as well have been penned by the prime minister himself:

> [Military] preparations have begun which cannot come to fruition quick-
> ly. In a situation like this, sureness and efficiency are important. A vast
> operation is not to be improvised in haste. But the government is clearly
> going to do what, in fact, it must do – secure the jugular vein of the
> British Empire from Nasser's threat.[42]

The *Daily Mail*, on the other hand, together with its sister paper, the *Daily Sketch*, had been among the government's most persistent critics in the last days of July, constantly demanding that Eden use force and increasing the pressure on him with tendentious headlines like 'Service Chiefs Urge Eden to Send in Troops' (28 July).[43] Clearly some papers could play Eden at his own game. If the prime minister was to maintain a solid Tory front during this crisis he could not allow the Rothermere press, which comprised Britain's second largest chain of newspapers, to continually undermine his authority. What exactly Eden said to the *Mail*'s editor, Arthur Wareham, on 31 July, we cannot be sure, as no records were kept of their meeting. Whatever it was it certainly paid off, for the *Mail* overnight shifted its ground significantly. The paper maintained its warmongering stance – Eden was livid when the day after his briefing the *Mail* splashed '20,000 Reservists Called Up' across its front page[44] – but switched attention from the government's pusillanimity to joining Eden in cracking Nasser's nerve. The *Mail* continued to equate negotiation with appeasement but for the first time evinced a greater confidence in the government's policy, even praising Eden personally for having shown Britain's teeth.[45] How long the patience of 'hawkish' papers like the *Express* and *Mail* would hold was not known, but at least Eden knew that he had bought himself a much needed breathing space.

Of the big three Tory press dynasties who needed to be reassured about the government's firmness of purpose this left the Berrys. Gomer Berry, better known as Lord Kemsley, was chairman of Britain's largest group of newspapers, of which the most prominent and politically influential was the *Sunday Times*. According to the afore-mentioned James Margach, the *Sunday Times* Lobby correspondent during Suez, Eden was in regular contact with Kemsley throughout the crisis, especially when war came. Indeed, evidence suggests the two were so close that Eden sought to use Kemsley as some sort of 'fixer' amongst the Tory press during Suez. Margach writes that his proprietor repeatedly received telephone calls from the prime minister protesting not about the attitude of the Kemsley papers (which were steadfastly loyal from the beginning to the end of the crisis) but about the national dailies. For his part, Margach recalls how he himself was always kept up to date with 'the detailed and secret versions' of Eden's policies, either by William Clark or by Eden's parliamentary private secretary, Robert Allan. Analysis of Margach's reports during Suez more than testify to this (though it should be stated that only *The Times* was told the full truth about the Anglo-French-Israeli collusion in late October).[46]

Whether Lord Kemsley ensured that his papers were faithful to the government's cause simply out of loyalty to the Tory party (his contacts at Central Office were numerous), or whether it was because he had a vested interest in the success of Eden as prime minister (Kemsley had played a vital role in persuading his old friend Churchill to stand down in 1955) is open to question.[47] The fact is his personal friendship provided Eden with a considerable amount of political and press leverage during Suez, especially when the military operation launched against Egypt in November threatened to tear the *Sunday Times* asunder. Moreover, with the only other 'quality' Sunday paper, the *Observer*, at that time demanding the prime minister's resignation, the *Sunday Times*'s support was invaluable.[48]

The other side of the Berry family was not nearly so pliant. Michael Berry, Kemsley's nephew, only controlled the *Daily Telegraph*, but this paper was arguably the most important to Eden, since it traditionally provided the principal cues for Conservative activists. If the prime minister was to hold the Tory press and party together over Suez he needed to control the *Telegraph*. However, Eden could be forgiven for thinking, long before Suez, that the *Telegraph* had nothing less than a personal vendetta against him. William Clark's diary of his tenure as Eden's press secretary (September 1955–November 1956) contains more references to the *Telegraph*'s criticism of his master than all the other papers put together. To be fair, Eden was, as already mentioned, unduly sensitive to press criticism. But, in the *Telegraph*'s case the prime minister's anger and frustration at the treatment consistently meted out to him was perhaps justified. Certainly, since his arrival at Number 10 no other paper – either on the right or the left – had come anywhere near to matching the *Telegraph*'s constant obsession with Sir Anthony's personal faults. It was the *Telegraph*, of course, which had helped lead the 'Eden Must Go' press campaign of January 1956, giving the prime minister such a mauling he had still not fully re-covered by the time of Suez.[49]

By an ominous coincidence, the government's frustration with the paper's hostility had reached its climax on the eve of the Suez crisis. On 24 July, William Clark noted in his diary that the press had been universally good on Eden's latest foreign policy speech – except, that is, for the *Telegraph*, which had been 'vicious, even on its newspage'. Clark felt that it was in fact Lady Pamela Berry, the proprietor's wife, who was the *éminence grise* behind these personal attacks, stemming apparently from the Edens' avoidance of her social functions:

> This finally made me write a … note to the PM about Lady Pam, and the general tenor of the paper – in particular her attempts to sow dissension between the senior members of the Cabinet. It created quite a sensation and led the PM to call a meeting of a few senior colleagues to discuss the relations of the party and the paper.[50]

Given this state of affairs, the *Telegraph* was true to form when its initial hostility to Nasser after his shock move quickly began to take second place to criticism of what it saw as ministerial procrastination. The emergency Anglo-US-French talks which took place in London in late July–early August 'reminded many members [of the Commons] of the government's well-known weakness for regarding the calling of a meeting as a substitute for policy'.[51] The government needed to react sharply if it was to nip such accusations in the bud.

Thus, on the same day that Eden was briefing the *Express*, *Mail* and *News Chronicle* (the latter is yet to be dealt with), two of the Tory party's most senior figures and members of the Egypt Committee, R. A. Butler and Lord Salisbury, called to see Michael Berry. Whilst Butler flattered Berry by emphasizing the 'considerable influence' of his paper and sought to mollify him by accepting that there was 'nothing personal' in the *Telegraph*'s continual attacks on the government, Salisbury accused the paper of contemptuousness and aggressively picked holes in that morning's critical leader. As was the custom by now, all of this was accompanied by liberal doses of secret, unattributable information concerning the government's 'absolute determination to take every possible action, even including "war"'. If the *Telegraph* would only realize, Salisbury argued, that the 'government could talk tougher in private than they yet could in public' then the paper might appreciate the delicate position that Eden was in. The fact of the matter was the government was going to make a stand – Eden had already gone beyond the assumption that the canal would revert to Egypt in 1968 by announcing that it must never be under the control of a single power (something the government was publicly trying to obfuscate) – but 'Military action could not be mounted in under a fortnight.'[52]

Despite Berry's continuing doubts about the government's fortitude,[53] Butler's and Salisbury's combination of flattery and intimidation seems to have worked. Suggestions of government appeasement in the *Telegraph* promptly abated; the paper instead subsequently concentrated on giving the lie to allegations that the government's stance was evidence of imperialism being alive and kicking in the Tory party.[54] Thus, as with the *Mail* and *Express*, Eden could not entirely drop his guard from the *Telegraph*, but the troublesome paper had, at least for the time being, been persuaded to look at Suez more from his point of view.

By the end of the first week of the crisis, therefore, the government had managed, via the simple expedient of contacting acquaintances in high places, to gain control of the Conservative press. Because of its military weakness the government may well have had to ask these newspapers to soften their demands for the immediate use of force. However, this had in no way diminished their hostility to Nasser; on the contrary, one could argue that it had increased it. By secretly confiding in its natural Fleet Street allies and assuring them of its intention not to let Nasser 'get away with it', the government soon found that criticism of its policy halted. Instead, the Conservative press concentrated all its efforts on abusing the United Nations and outlining in the most emotive terms the threat which Nasser posed to Britain and the Middle East. The implication was clear: force was inevitable sooner or later, unless something snapped in Cairo beforehand. This willingness of more than half of the national press, with a combined daily readership totalling twenty-five million,[55] to place itself at Eden's disposal would not have been so questionable had the government itself been openly advocating force. As it was, government spokesmen (on the record) were going out of their way to deny any allegations that the first military moves announced on 2 August – the deployment of certain units to the Mediterranean and the call-up of a limited number of reservists – were anything other than 'precautionary',[56] let alone that Eden had ulterior designs on Nasser. The role which a significant proportion of the national and provincial press played, therefore, in enabling the government to run an entirely unattributable and extremely tendentious news campaign throughout Suez should not be underestimated. It must take a great deal of the credit for helping to create the necessary war mentality on the home front.

Having the active support of the Conservative press, together with *The Times*, was doubtless of great value to Eden. However, embarked as he was on a policy which ultimately meant taking the country to war, Eden could not simply sit back and ignore the rest of the press in the hope that it would patriotically acquiesce when the fighting started. As it was, by the end of July – only a mere five days after Nasser's move had shocked the nation, and hence much earlier than historians have hitherto noted – a significant number of papers had already come out against force unless Nasser used it first. These were the *Daily Herald*, *News Chronicle*, *Manchester Guardian* and *Observer*.[57] If the government was to create and maintain any semblance of national unity it would have to make in-roads into this section of the press and prevent this fast-emerging anti-war group from becoming the focus of opposition to its policy. Achieving the 'right' press was as much about curbing the critical papers as it was about recruiting natural Fleet Street supporters.

It was for this reason that Eden had asked William Clark on 31 July to set up an urgent meeting with the editor of the *News Chronicle*. This was a shrewd move by Eden. Of those major papers not yet briefed by the government the *News Chronicle* appeared the most open to persuasion. Unlike the *Daily Mirror* and *Daily Herald*, fellow 'popular' dailies, the *Chronicle* was not tied in any fashion to the Labour party; nor was it as elite-based as the *Observer* and *Manchester Guardian*. Moreover, although the *Chronicle* had a distinguished Liberal pedigree, it was apparent even to the uninitiated that it was suffering in the mid-1950s from what one writer has called 'a political identity crisis'.[58] In essence, with the continuing post-war demise of the Liberal party – to which it had at one time been formally affiliated – the paper lacked political focus; it knew not whether to appeal to the right or to the left. To Eden, therefore, the *Chronicle* must have looked a potential ally, and, in terms of capturing that all-important political middle ground, a valuable one at that. According to its former editor, Robin Cruickshank, the *Chronicle* might well have been in the political and economic doldrums in this period of its history (the paper would go out of business in 1960), but it still remained a 'paper of considerable importance' with an ability to tap 'the liberal and middle-of-the-road sentiments in this country'.[59]

Unfortunately, exactly how Eden tried to recruit the *Chronicle*'s editor, Michael Curtis, on 31 July remains a mystery as, again, no record of their meeting exists (though Clark does testify that it, as well as those meetings with the *Express* and *Mail*, took place).[60] Nevertheless, it is abundantly clear from analysis of subsequent *Chronicle* editorials that whatever it was that Eden said failed to elicit the required response; the meeting might in all probability have proved counter-productive.

The *Chronicle* had, like all papers, been taken aback by Nasser's action on 26 July but the most it had called for, two days later, was 'severe diplomatic pressure'.[61] By 30 July it was already urging that the dispute be taken to the United Nations.[62] Given Eden's opposition to any such line of action, the motive behind his meeting with Curtis the next day can only have been to reverse the *Chronicle*'s stance on Suez. Yet, if Eden hoped that Curtis would prove amenable, and be open to persuasion by a 'progressive Tory', he was to be sorely disappointed. Curtis might only have been editor of the *Chronicle* for two years and, at thirty-five, a relatively inexperienced journalist, but, as a protégé of Walter Layton, the *Chronicle*'s former chairman and guiding light for over two decades, he was a dedicated internationalist. In the event, only two days after his interview with the prime minister, Curtis reaffirmed, in the strongest terms yet, his paper's commitment to solving the Suez dispute via the United Nations. Moreover, *Chronicle* editorials began, for the first time, to criticize government policy explicitly.[63]

Eden's failure to persuade the *News Chronicle* to act, as he saw it, in 'the national interest' was not in itself a disaster for the government. Greater cause for concern was what the failure illustrated. It revealed in sharp focus what would prove to be the government's Achilles heel *vis-à-vis* the press during Suez – the inner cabinet's dearth of grass-root contacts in Fleet Street, especially in the Labour–Liberal press. As he climbs up the parliamentary ladder, moving from one department to another, a politician will invariably make contact with a wide range of correspondents spanning the political spectrum, all eager, as has been pointed out, to develop intimate and mutually beneficial links. These contacts then come in extremely useful if and when that politician finds himself in positions of real power; indeed, one might consider them as an indispensable weapon in the ministerial armoury. Unfortunately for the Eden government during Suez, this ability to call on a wide range of journalistic acquaintances was unusually restricted. Several key ministers, most notably Harold Macmillan, chancellor of the exchequer and leading Suez 'hawk', and the foreign secretary, Selwyn Lloyd, were conspicuously short of Fleet Street friends despite their considerable political experience. Thanks to such a stultified first year in Number 10, Eden himself, already isolated because of his failure to ride on the ministerial merry-go-round, had arguably fewer confidants than when at the Foreign Office.[64]

Had the prime minister simply accepted this weakness and given his more than able press secretary *carte blanche* to manipulate journalists in the manner he thought best, the government might well have gone some way towards overcoming this problem. As an ex-*Observer* correspondent, William Clark was much admired by that very section of the press that Eden was finding most troublesome. However, the relationship between Eden and Clark was fundamentally flawed well before Suez erupted. The longer the crisis went on the more Eden proved himself to be as compulsive an interferer in the matter of handling the press as he had been before it. The result was a progressively sidelined press secretary and an increasingly muddled press policy.

4

'Rattling the sabre'

On 2 August, the outcome of the talks between the British, French and American governments on what collective action should be taken in response to Nasser's act was announced: the twenty-four nations principally concerned with the use of the Suez Canal would meet at a conference in London on 16 August. Its avowed purpose was to place the canal under international control. Eden had mixed feelings about this. On the one hand, the delay – of two weeks before the conference even started, and then probably another to enable the large number of participants to thrash out the issues – allowed for the military preparations to approach completion. On the other, there was the obvious danger that over the whole three-week period the crisis would go off the boil and sufficient public support for force would disappear.[1]

In the immediate wake of nationalization Eden had enjoyed a considerable degree of cross-party support for his stance. At Number 10 on the night of 26 July, Hugh Gaitskell, the Labour party leader, had seemingly given the government a blank cheque for military action.[2] However, by the end of the first week of the crisis there were already ominous signs that the initial parliamentary consensus on Suez was on shaky ground. In his speech to the House of Commons on 2 August, Gaitskell sharply denounced Nasser, but also reminded MPs of the UN Charter, 'and how, for many years in British policy, we have steadfastly avoided any international action which would be in breach of international law, or, indeed, contrary to the opinion of the world'. Britain, he said, must not run the risk of being denounced in the Security Council as the aggressor or of being in a minority in the General Assembly.[3]

It was imperative, therefore, that the government, having conceded the notion of a conference, did not, in Eden's own words, 'lose momentum'.[4] This second phase of the crisis was going to make or break his policy *vis-à-vis* the public. The conference, and the run-up to it, therefore had to be used as a device for bringing the crisis to a climax. Suez had to be kept at the forefront of the public's mind in the fortnight before the conference met. The nation had to be continually reminded of the importance of the Suez Canal to Britain's very economic survival and the dangers of appeasing dictators, thereby maintaining pressure on Nasser in the hope that he, or something within the Egyptian military, would crack, either at the conference or before. However, this powerful message could not be disseminated via the conventional route, the front and back benches of the House of Commons. The second of August had been the last day before the parliamentary recess. If the government was to persuade the British people it would have to do so primarily through the mass media.

Eden has been accused by one historian of adopting an ambivalent attitude towards publicity during this period, doing his best to build up a war psychology via unattributable briefings but at the same time weakening this by his nervousness of press reports about actual war preparations.[5] This strikes at the very heart of the government's propaganda dilemma throughout the crisis. Eden was indeed very keen to build up a war psychology but feared that if too much publicity was given by the press to the government's 'precautionary measures' then Nasser might panic and complain to the Security Council that Britain's actions were a threat to peace.[6] This was the last thing Eden wanted. Any reference of the Suez issue to the United Nations would more than likely scupper any hopes the government had of toppling Nasser.[7] What this delicate situation required was a subtle combination of propaganda and censorship. Only this would produce what Selwyn Lloyd referred to (in conversation with Chauvel, the French ambassador, about guidance to the press) as 'the best possible atmosphere for the London Conference'.[8]

Given his pivotal role as the prime minister's press secretary, and therefore the government's chief spokesman, William Clark had naturally been doing his utmost to fashion the press to his master's liking from the moment he heard the news of Nasser's act. The first few days of the crisis had been, according to his diary, 'very hectic', with Sunday, 29 July, being 'the first rest I've had'. Clark, for one, had no doubts either about the gravity of the crisis or about the importance of his position within it. The prime minister, for his part, seemed to recognize the crucial role his press secretary could play (at least at this stage of the crisis) by allowing him to attend meetings of the Egypt Committee, where all of the most important decisions were taken throughout Suez. This had enabled Clark to impress on selected journalists the utter seriousness with which the war cabinet itself viewed the Egyptian ruler's latest act.[9]

However, it was during this crucial second phase of the crisis –

after the press's immediate disgust at Nasser's act had begun to wane, and when Eden had woken up to the sparsity of his press contacts – that Clark's more subtle manipulative services were more heavily called upon. The increasingly harassed but ever loyal press secretary was instructed by Eden to conduct a full-scale yet discreet campaign aimed at convincing the public and Nasser that military force was both legitimate and necessary. Whilst the nation ought not to regard the forthcoming conference as simply a means of imposing a Versailles-style 'diktat' on the Egyptian regime, argued Clark, nor should it be seen as evidence of the government's weakening resolve. This Clark sought to achieve primarily via his twice-daily unattributable lobby briefings. In the meantime, ministers themselves would continue publicly to preach moderation and evince their hopes for a peaceful solution to the dispute.[10]

The clearest evidence of Clark's exploitation of the lobby came the very day after the announcement of the London Conference. On the morning of 3 August virtually every newspaper carried a story, written by either its political or its diplomatic correspondent, to the effect that unless Colonel Nasser accepted the conclusions of the forthcoming conference, which would itself work to a rigid timetable, the government would have no alternative but to impose a solution to the dispute by force. The *Daily Mail* best summed up the press's interpretation of the Three Power Communiqué, issued the previous evening, with its headline 'Come and Talk – or Else'.[11] In contrast to this, in his speech to the House of Commons only the day before, Eden had been the epitome of moderation and caution; so much so that Denis Healey, hitherto one of the government's shrewdest Suez critics, complimented the prime minister on distancing himself from the 'tremendous shouting and screaming in the press about the insult to our national prestige'.[12] Eden was in fact playing a double game. What he was not willing to tell the House he had his press secretary disseminate via the lobby. In this way the government (or, perhaps more accurately, the inner cabinet) could conduct its war of nerves against Nasser safe in the knowledge that none of its warmongering remarks to the press was traceable. If asked for the source of such stories ministers would simply either plead ignorance or blame them on 'extremists' within the party.[13]

This episode is only the most obvious, recognizable example of Clark's cultivation of the lobby during this phase of Suez. In fact, his diary for the whole of this period is peppered with references to how he discharged his responsibility for, as he later put it, 'rattling my sabre in the direction of the Press'.[14] At times this could take the form of a discreet chat with a group of editors from the provincial press whose papers Eden felt needed 'hardening';[15] at others it could manifest itself in unbridled scare tactics and impassioned appeals to the press *en masse* to act in 'the national interest'. For instance, on the eve of the London Conference the cabinet heard, much to its distress, that the TUC was about to issue a strong resolution calling upon the government to act within the UN. This sparked off a lengthy discussion of domestic opinion. Ministers were forced to admit that, for all their endeavours, British public opinion 'had not fully realised the serious implications of the recent action by Colonel Nasser'. It was essential therefore 'to impress on the public that, if Colonel Nasser were allowed to get away with his recent illegal action, the UK's position in the Middle East would be undermined, with serious consequences for trade and employment'.[16] The next day Clark was again on his mettle, using all his powers of persuasion to convince the Lobby 'that there really was a serious emergency for us, that the [Suez] issue was literally one of "life and death" [one of the government's favourite propaganda phrases throughout the crisis]'.[17] Whilst the effect of this particular briefing was not suddenly to convert any paper, it certainly gave a much-needed shot in the arm to those papers like the *Daily Mail* which were in danger of wilting under incessant allegations of out-of-date blimpishness. Judging from an analysis of editorials on the eve of the London Conference, Clark also seems to have successfully raised the temperature of the crisis at a key point.[18]

In his campaign to build up a national war psychology and frighten Nasser into cracking, Clark was more than ably supported by White-hall's other chief practitioner of media manipulation, the Foreign Office News Department. It was of course important for domestic and international consumption that the government and Foreign Office should appear united on how to deal with the crisis in hand. If the Foreign Office gave any hint of a doubt concerning the illegality of Nasser's act or the government's right to use force, the public would immediately form the impression that policy was in the hands of a belligerent clique. To this end, Eden could take comfort in the fact that, unlike most other section chiefs of the Foreign Office, the head of the News Department routinely received his orders directly from either the permanent under-secretary or the foreign secretary himself.[19] During Suez both of these positions were filled by staunch advocates of aggression, especially the former; Sir Ivone Kirkpatrick, who acted as a personal adviser and draftsman for the prime minister in 1956, was a mandarin deeply scarred by the inter-war years and in total agreement with the Edenites that Nasser represented as great a threat to Britain and the free world as had the dictators of the 1930s.[20] Added to this, the News Department, like the Number 10 Press Office, had its own coterie of specialist reporters, the diplomatic correspondents, that could be used to do the department's bidding if handled skilfully. That many of these journalists had, as mentioned earlier, grown over the years to revere Eden's handling of foreign affairs made them potentially all the more malleable.

Throughout August, Sir George Young,[21] head of the News Department, worked assiduously behind the scenes to impress on the diplomatic correspondents just how incensed the traditionally sedate, pro-Arab Foreign Office was with Nasser. Young himself, like many others in the Foreign Office, actually believed that any resort to military action would do Britain's reputation immense damage, especially in the Middle East. Nevertheless, he stuck faithfully to the line dictated to him by Kirkpatrick and Lloyd until, at some indeterminable point later in the crisis, he was transferred to a different department. Whether this move was due to Young's opposition to the Egypt Committee's policy is unclear, but the effect was to render the News Department headless for a number of weeks. Until Sir Peter Hope was appointed as Young's successor in October, therefore, the department's workload was the responsibility of the relatively inexperienced deputy head, Anthony Moore.[22]

For their part, the diplomatic correspondents painted a picture of a foreign service united in its approach to a dangerous dictator and fully behind the government's policy. By meeting with the diplomatic correspondents *en masse* daily at noon, then holding private sessions later with selected journalists, Young and Moore had the perfect opportunity to spell out to a receptive audience the finer details of Foreign Office thinking and the reasoning behind the government's tough stance. In this way many of the awkward questions which ministers refused to address in public were given a more than fair hearing. Why, for example, Nasser's move had been a clear breach of international law and yet referral of his crime to the United Nations was inapplicable; why the Anglo-American decision not to finance the Aswan dam scheme had been an entirely economic one whilst Nasser's nationalization of the Suez Canal Company was wholly political; why the US administration appeared to be giving out different signals as to how it wished to solve the dispute; and, above all else, why Britain and France had the right to impose internationalization of the canal alone, and by force. By outlining such views the diplomatic correspondents were not, it must be said, necessarily lending their support to Eden. Journalists did not suddenly suspend all their critical faculties and blindly accept the prime minister's interpretation of events. Nevertheless, they did allow the government to dictate the crisis agenda and some even became willing pawns in Eden's game of nerves against Nasser.

One journalist who noticed the News Department's deft manipulation of its 'lobby' during this phase of the crisis was Richard Scott, diplomatic correspondent of the *Manchester Guardian*. Scott was furious when, at the Tory party conference in mid-October, by which time things had significantly calmed down, Eden accused the press of having played tricks with government statements in the early part of the crisis, of having made the 'fantastic' claim, for example, that he was deliberately steering clear of the United Nations and hence away from a peaceful solution to the Suez dispute. Scott was adamant that the boot was on the other foot. As he saw it, the government, supported by the Foreign Office, had been double-dealing:

> it must be recalled by any correspondent who sought guidance from the Foreign office or Downing Street during that [early] period that the spokesmen went out of their way to emphasise that the crisis which Colonel Nasser had provoked was one which the British and French Governments were determined to settle quickly and if necessary by force. Any suggestion at that time of an approach to the UN was, to say the very least, most strongly discouraged ... I cannot believe that I am alone in having received the strongest impression that an imposed rather than a negotiated settlement was what the government wanted in those early days – imposed not necessarily but if required, by military means. The line then adopted by the Foreign Office and 10 Downing Street was that it was essential for the whole Arab world to be shown it would not be allowed to get away with anti-Western actions such as the nationalisation of the Suez Canal Company – that such actions would be resisted by whatever means might be necessary.[23]

However, not all journalists were as wary, nor indeed as critical, of the Foreign Office's methods as Scott was. Some actively collaborated with ministers and officials in seeking to influence the press. One such journalist was Donald McLachlan, deputy editor of the *Daily Telegraph* and, ironically, author of the infamous 'smack of firm government' editorial which had troubled Eden so much in January 1956. Foreign Office records show that McLachlan acted as a self-appointed government 'mole' in Fleet Street during Suez. His main conduit was Douglas Dodds-Parker, parliamentary under-secretary at the Foreign Office and a former member of the Sudan lobby. Since June 1956 Dodds-Parker had been intimately involved with countering Egyptian propaganda in the Middle East, a role which expanded during the Suez crisis to incorporate the government's domestic propaganda strategy.[24] From early August 1956 onwards, Dodds-Parker and McLachlan would regularly discuss how the government could get the best out of the press. On 17 August, for instance, McLachlan gave the minister a valuable insider's view of Fleet Street's current thinking on Suez and a few tips on the best way to present the outcome of the London Conference to the general public.[25]

McLachlan could also be found advising Walter Monckton, minister of defence, on how to operate the government's censorship programme more effectively. On 13 August, for example, Monckton consulted a number of journalists about the handling of news before and during the forthcoming London Conference. At this point he and several other ministers were in two minds about whether to initiate daily conferences to guide the press on a regular, constructive basis. According to the minutes of this meeting, 'the representative of the *Daily Telegraph*', which evidence suggests was McLachlan, advised against any such conferences as they 'would involve leakages of important information'. The same journalist then suggested that an officer experienced in censorship work be sent to Tripoli, Malta and Cyprus in order to see how far uniformity of news treatment could be attained. Finally, he suggested that the minister of defence should get in touch with the US authorities to see whether they would be prepared to help in any way.[26] Clearly Suez had the effect on some journalists of making them abandon altogether their customary role as the watchdogs of government.

Whether or not journalists realized what sort of game the government was playing with the press during Suez, only a tiny minority came out and said so in public, presumably for fear of breaking that all-important confidence. As a result Eden was able to run an extremely tendentious propaganda campaign aimed at giving him the option of going to war completely unbeknown to the average newspaper reader, in whose name, of course, any war would be fought. The bankruptcy of the whole Lobby system of non-attributable briefing can best be illustrated by a message which Dodds-Parker, who had himself just been briefed by Donald McLachlan, passed on to his superiors on the second day of the London Conference:

> Journalists commented that it was impossible to pinpoint any remarks of the Prime Minister or Secretary of State as advocating the use of force; at the same time there was undoubted guidance coming out from the Foreign Office that force might well be used if a satisfactory solution was not reached through or after the conference.

'This', the energetic parliamentary under-secretary stated, 'seems to show that our psychological warfare is working.'[27]

To complement the work of these professional media manipulators, Eden and several other ministers continued their more direct method of personally briefing editors and journalists in the run-up to the London Conference. Sometimes this was done on a one-to-one basis, on other occasions in groups, always depending on what was felt would be most effective. Walter Monckton was particularly busy in this regard. As minister of defence and a member of Eden's inner cabinet he was much sought after by the press for inside information on the government's military and political strategy. Given that he also had the reputation of being one of the government's most 'dovish' characters it suited Eden to have Monckton assiduously playing up the dangers of Nasserism; coming from him it would be more credible. On 13 August, Monckton informed Eden that he had seen the editors of the *Daily Mail, Daily Herald, News Chronicle* and *Daily Mirror*, as well as the deputy editors of the *Daily Express* and *Daily Sketch*, together that afternoon to draw 'their attention to the indications of a stiffening in the US attitude and their determination with us to get the result upon which we were resolved'.[28] Quite what the American administration had said or done to merit such an assertion is unclear. All the evidence suggests that Eisenhower and Dulles were, if anything, distancing themselves further from the Anglo-French position the nearer the conference drew.[29] At some point during the same day Monckton also met the London editors or correspondents of the main provincial papers separately, in order, as he put it, 'to try and sustain them in their firm attitude ... by the argument (which needs constant repetition) that this is a life and death matter for us'.[30]

Actively encouraging the press to maintain as much pressure as possible on Nasser and to stir up public opinion in favour of war was one thing. It was quite another, however, to have that same press publicize in detail the huge military preparations that were accompanying the government's avowedly peaceful policy of 'restoring international control of the Suez Canal', let alone speculate on their ultimate purpose. At all times, but especially in the run-up to the London Conference when so many people (in Britain and abroad) would have their opinions formed on Suez, it was imperative for the British government not to appear the aggressor. Any such charges – rumours even – would only strengthen Nasser's position. As Selwyn Lloyd told Gladwyn Jebb, ambassador in Paris, on 8 August, 'Nothing could put us in a worse position in the eyes of international opinion than to accompany our preparations for the conference with ostentatious military moves.'[31] A way had to be found, therefore, of getting the press to play down the Anglo-French troop movements, though not one that would itself arouse controversy and thereby lead to allegations of political censorship. This would only serve to reveal the government's hidden agenda.

It is clear from ministers' diaries and records of the Egypt Committee that many in the government desperately wanted to impose a strict censorship on the media's coverage of the military build-up in the Mediterranean in the early phase of the crisis. Harold Macmillan, chancellor of the exchequer and the leading 'hawk' in cabinet, saw no alternative: 'We have no censorship powers ... and there is no way of stopping the most detailed accounts of shipping, troop movements and the rest. Personally I doubt that we shall get through all this without taking back the old war powers.' William Clark recalls how Eden himself 'blew his top' on the evening of 2 August when he heard the BBC News disclose what to him was politically embarrassing military information. On 6 August, Winston Churchill offered the prime minister his advice: 'The military operation seems very serious. We have a long delay when our intentions are known. The newspapers and foreign correspondents are free to publish what they choose. A censorship should be imposed.'[32]

However, hopes of somehow reactivating the old wartime censorship apparatus were simply unrealistic in the circumstances of the summer of 1956. Walter Monckton quickly produced a report for the Egypt Committee saying just that. For a start the machinery was no longer available. More importantly it was politically impossible. Although, from Eden's own point of view, Nasser had been waging for months what amounted to a war against Britain in the Middle East and North Africa, even he had to admit that war had not yet been officially declared. Perhaps when hostilities broke out this form of censorship would be justified; until then it would prove politically suicidal.[33]

After consultation with his press secretary and the Egypt Committee Eden chose instead a more subtle technique of controlling the press: one that the government could deny was censorship at all. This was the time-honoured arrangement whereby a government 'asked' – in the nature of formal letters of request or warning known as D-Notices – newspaper and broadcasting editors to refrain from publicizing certain items of news relating to defence or security matters. What made this 'D-Notice system' so appealing to the Eden government during Suez was, first of all, its confidentiality. Protocol stated that any newspaper editor who complied with a request to doctor his copy was forbidden to inform his readers that what they were looking at was subject to censorship (the same went for broadcasting editors and their viewers or listeners). Secondly, because there was no official compulsion behind any D-Notice the whole system could be described as purely voluntary. Whether this was entirely valid, given that any editor knew full well that publishing classified information carried the risk of prosecution under the Official Secrets Act, is highly debatable.

Thirdly, the fact that any one D-Notice could not be issued to editors unless its form and content had first been approved of by the long-standing Services, Press and Broadcasting Committee, half of whose members were representatives of the media, gave the system an air of political impartiality and independence from government. However, to believe that this committee had as its priority the protection of media freedom would be very wide of the mark, especially in times of 'national crisis'. Finally, precisely because this system purported to provide a flexible middle ground between a rigid application of the Official Secrets Act and a written code, in any given set of circumstances there was always scope for a government to exploit that grey area between security and political matters.[34]

Getting the press to comply with this system of self-censorship during Suez was going to be tricky. By the time the government had announced the movement of forces in early August a significant number of newspapers had already signalled their opposition to any premeditated military action against Egypt. In these circumstances, were the Egypt Committee simply to foist upon the press a number of D-Notices whilst bluntly claiming that they were in the national interest, the likelihood was that Fleet Street would be in uproar. What was needed was for the government to create a climate conducive to collective press constraint.

On Friday, 3 August, the day after the announcement of the London Conference, and only hours after he had discussed with his cabinet colleagues the thorny problem of military publicity ('with no sense of reality', according to William Clark),[35] Eden held his first full-scale Downing Street press conference since the crisis had erupted. By all accounts this meeting was extraordinary. Rarely can such a large number of national and provincial newspaper editors have been invited to Number 10 at any one time. So many turned up to hear what the prime minister had to say that the cabinet room was full to the brim.[36] Doubtless this was a deliberate ploy on Eden's part. The greater the number of top-ranking editors in attendance, the more an atmosphere of national crisis and unity could be engendered. This mood was perfectly captured by Arthur Christiansen, who 'sat in an armchair buried behind the PM and reflected ... that the Big Brass present might not frighten the Egyptians but they put the fear of God into me'. In order to increase the pressure on the editors and urge upon them the need for military security, accompanying Eden was the minister of defence and censorship coordinator himself, Walter Monckton.

In the event, the meeting itself did not go exactly according to Eden's plan. Christiansen, for one, dismissed the whole affair as an awful muddle, recalling later how when Monckton offered to set up a committee to which military messages would be submitted he himself expostulated, 'Hey, that's censorship in peacetime.'[37] Nevertheless, by cleverly calling the editors' bluff in appearing to offer them all manner of military secrets, something which horrified the on-looking William

Clark, Eden in fact got the end result he was looking for. No responsible, patriotic editor wished to be put in the position of having to decide for himself which piece of military information could be safely published and which might put a British soldier's life at risk. Consequently, the editors (Christiansen included) did indeed agree to censorship in peacetime.[38]

The next day the government, via the Services, Press and Broadcasting Committee, issued its first D-Notice, followed by another on 15 August (significantly on the eve of the London Conference). The press complied with both. At first sight these notices seem completely innocuous. However, on closer inspection, and when matched with how the newspapers actually reported the summer's military build-up, they reveal shrewd distortion of the D-Notice system. For example, by calling upon the press to 'abstain from speculating in detail on the form which possible operations may take should it become necessary to safeguard the free use of the Suez Canal', the first notice in effect banned newspapers from commenting on the purpose of the military preparations.[39] Such cleverly worded requests could just about be validated on security grounds, but this was not the government's priority. Several memoranda which Monckton produced for the Egypt Committee prove this.[40] On 10 August, for example, Monckton stressed how important it was that he saw the press to 'play down the fact that it would shortly be necessary to take up ships for tactical loading with M/T [motorized transport]'. This was not because the publishing of such information would compromise security, and thereby threaten soldiers' lives, but because 'it would be the first unmistakable indication that the Government was preparing to carry out an offensive operation'.[41]

On meeting the press three days later the minister of defence told the assembled editors that 'he had no wish to teach them how to present the news', and then proceeded to do just that. Any editor who insisted on publicizing in the days ahead the fact that British forces in the Mediterranean area were being greatly strengthened, Monckton argued, would be personally responsible for jeopardizing the conference and the chances of a peaceful solution to the canal crisis. In other words, it was the editors, not the politicians, who would be to blame if British soldiers lost their lives.

The D-Notice which was issued following this meeting, emphasizing 'the importance of not giving any indication of the strength of units which are being moved to the Mediterranean in connection with the present situation', pays testimony to the success of the minister of defence's emotional blackmail.[42] Monckton's path was smoothed by the consent given to these D-Notices by the secretary of the Services,

Press and Broadcasting Committee, Admiral George Thomson, whom he met regularly. Editors tended to trust Thomson's judgement. This was due to journalists' general lack of time and the fact that Thomson had successfully won the confidence of the newspapers during World War Two when acting as chief press censor.[43]

Analysis of newspapers from this period, and throughout the crisis as a whole, reveals how successfully the government exploited the D-Notice system and the British press's over-willingness to censor itself. Reports of the initial Anglo-French military moves were published – photographs of the departure of the training carrier H.M.S. *Theseus* on 5 August, for example, made the front pages of most of the 'popular' papers – but once the forces left their own shores news of their progress was mostly of a vague, low-key nature. Even papers opposed to the government's overall policy tended to steer clear of any specific criticism of the scale of the military moves and what they hinted at. A notable exception to this conspicuous silence was many papers' reaction at the end of August to the announcement of the decision to station French forces in Cyprus. However, even in this instance, criticism focused on the political ramifications of the manoeuvre rather than on its being evidence of a further escalation in an already massive military build-up.[44]

The upshot of this is that by consistently under-playing what amounted to the biggest military operation since World War Two, the press validated the government's 'precautionary measures' and prevented the public from obtaining a real picture of the nature of the military preparations and their purpose. Of all the papers which played Eden's game, only the *Manchester Guardian* made any public reference to the dilemma in which censorship had put patriotic editors who were in no position to judge how far individual D-Notices were justified on security grounds, but who recognized that their cumulative effect was to keep essential information regarding government policy from the public. At the beginning of September the paper called upon the press to break this voluntary censorship because it was playing into the government's hands:

> as we are now seeing, to play down the military and strategic preparations is to reduce the sense of urgency, to obscure the forces that are being built up. Because of the silence of the newspapers people just do not know the facts of the new balance of forces that is being built up. This ignorance helps the Government. It enables it to be, if it pleases, hypocritical, two-faced; it can look wholly peace-loving while actually it prepares for attack.

The *Manchester Guardian*'s plea fell on deaf ears. As the paper said itself, 'patriotic newspapers will always choose the side of "security"'.[45]

Had the world been informed of the true scale and nature of the military build-up in the Mediterranean in the first weeks of August via the British and French press (which were in the best position to find out these things), the chances are that far fewer nations would have accepted their invitations to the London Conference than the twenty-two who did. The Egypt Committee was acutely aware of the need to damp down press speculation about the possible operations against Egypt at this delicate stage lest countries were 'led to believe that the conference was merely a facade to cover military operations which had already been planned'.[46] On the other hand, whilst playing down the military side of things made sense diplomatically, it deprived the government of potentially one of the most powerful devices for creating the necessary war psychology. Thus, the government was prevented from highlighting the strength and prowess of the task force being sent to the 'dangerous war zone', from evoking memories of the heroic battles in which many of the same battalions or brigades had fought during World War Two; as a consequence, it missed the opportunity of playing the jingoistic card to the full. Unlike coverage of the build-up to the two other major post-war conflicts in which Britain has been involved (the Falklands and Gulf wars), there were no reports from journalists travelling or stationed with the British forces to emphasize the troops' belief in their mission. As a result the government was reduced to fighting for the hearts and minds of the British public with one hand tied behind its back.

For all the government's efforts at manipulation, it was apparent long before the London Conference opened that what Eden had feared had indeed happened: time had proved a debilitating factor and the press had gone off the boil. As early as 7 August, barely two weeks into the crisis, William Clark and George Young were lamenting 'that the first fine careless rapture in the press has almost entirely died away, and the weasels are at work asking whether we should be so bold'.[47] No major newspaper had actually made a *volte-face* on Suez, which meant that the government could still rely on a full half of the national daily and Sunday press (and an even greater proportion of the provincials) to support war. But, what press opposition there had been at the end of July to the use of force had, by the time of the conference, hardened into a solid, recognizable pro-UN, anti-war block, spear-headed by the *Daily Herald*, *News Chronicle*, *Manchester Guardian* and *Observer*.

The two latter papers, both owned by trusts designed to guarantee their editorial independence,[48] were particularly influential in undermining the confidence of moderate, liberal opinion in Eden's policy.

The *Manchester Guardian* had led the way with a constant stream of editorials urging 'negotiations first' and arguing that there was no justification for violent action while the canal remained open.[49] These were partly inspired by ominous warnings about Eden's jumpiness sent by the paper's Washington correspondent, Max Freedman, perhaps based on US State Department leaks.[50] The *Guardian* also directly refuted the prime minister's claim that there was a true parallel between Hitler in 1938 and Nasser in 1956.[51] The *Observer*, although it had itself initially called Egypt's nationalization tactics 'Hitlerian',[52] was nevertheless, under the strong leadership of David Astor, consistently and coherently against any 'childish retaliation', firstly because it would be morally and legally wrong – Nasser's act alone was no *casus belli*; secondly because it would ruin Anglo-Arab relations and Britain's whole reputation in the third world; finally, and perhaps most tellingly, because it would require a reoccupation of Egypt, something which Britain was simply no longer strong enough to carry out.[53] Both papers instead proposed practicable alternatives based on the genuine nationalization of the canal under UN jurisdiction, combined with the building of supertankers for the Cape route and a pipeline from Eilat on the Gulf of Akaba to Haifa on the Mediterranean.[54]

Moreover, those papers which at the start of the crisis had sat on the fence as regards a military initiative had since come down firmly against it. The most notable example was the *Daily Mirror*, the nation's biggest-selling daily newspaper. The *Mirror*'s policy during Suez was essentially a product of two minds: Cecil King and Hugh Cudlipp, chairman and editorial director respectively of *Daily Mirror* and *Sunday Pictorial* Newspapers. When the crisis first broke and it seemed that British troops might be sent in immediately, King and Cudlipp were at loggerheads over what stance their papers should adopt. Mindful of the working-class hatred of Nasser, King supported force; Cudlipp was against it on the grounds that the sanctioning of gunboat diplomacy contradicted their newspapers' progressive image.[55] As a result, the *Mirror*'s editorial column for the first fortnight of the crisis was a masterpiece of ambivalence and evasion. It was not until the week before the London Conference was due to open that the paper really found its feet and began to feel comfortable. The two consecutive front-page editorials on 14 August ('No War over Egypt') and 15 August ('Eden's double talk') mark the point at which the *Mirror* stopped equivocating and placed itself firmly in the anti-force party.[56]

Prompted by Eden, William Clark had tried his best to halt this 'softening-up process', only to find, on talking to many journalists, that their doubts about the wisdom of military action 'went far deeper than appeared on the surface'.[57] Not to miss a trick, the dedicated press secretary also worked in the opposite direction, contacting old friends in the liberal press in the hope of convincing them that Eden was not as warlike as they made him out to be. On 14 August, for example, Clark told his old friend Alastair Hetherington, foreign and defence editor of the *Manchester Guardian*, that so far as he knew the government had never intended to start military action unless Nasser triggered it off. That same day Hetherington also called on Walter Monckton, at Eden's specific request. Monckton likewise was, to say the least, economical with the truth, promising Hetherington that although Britain's forces were being brought to a state of readiness in the Mediterranean there had been no decision as yet to launch an operation. This was also part of the MoD's efforts to get the press to play down the government's preparations for war on the eve of the conference. In the *Guardian*'s case it failed.[58]

To Clark this shift in press opinion led him to the conclusion that war was now out as a realistic policy – 'the country couldn't be held together on it'.[59] Although one would not have guessed it from the continued belligerency of *The Times*, Iverach McDonald was, significantly, in private saying much the same thing. On 10 August, he wrote a detailed memorandum to William Haley which ended on a sombre note:

> The more I think about it, the more I believe that the time for landing a force was immediately after Nasser's proclamation. Now the opposition to the use of force is growing more explicit, especially in this country ... Looking facts and forces in the face, it is now going to be extremely difficult for us to use force unless Nasser blocks the Canal (which he will take care not to do so for some time).[60]

All this appeared to cast serious doubt on Douglas Dodds-Parker's boasts a week later that his 'psychological warfare was working'.

5

Losing the initiative

Despite all the signs that the government had shot its bolt – even the cabinet was forced to admit, two days before the London Conference opened, that there would be insufficient public support for the use of force against Egypt 'unless some new incident occurred'[1] – Eden was not about to admit failure. After all, he more than anyone else had helped create a situation in which his very survival as prime minister depended on the overthrow of Nasser, or at least his humiliation. To back down now and agree to reach a compromise with the Egyptian regime would be political suicide. 'I remain firmly convinced', Colonial Secretary Alan Lennox-Boyd told Eden on 24 August, 'that if Nasser wins, or even appears to win, we might as well as a Government (and indeed as a Country) go out of business.'[2] There was, therefore, apparently no alternative but to continue to appeal to domestic and international opinion, and step up the pressure on Nasser.

In this sense the London Conference, which met between 16 and 23 August at Lancaster House, was an undoubted success for the government. It tied the US administration publicly closer to the Anglo-French position and produced a strong resolution, subscribed to by two thirds of the nations present, calling upon Egypt to accept that the Suez Canal should be run by an international board and that it would be illegal for it to be closed by any user for political purposes. This last point was thought particularly useful by Eden as it raised the tantalizing question of how Nasser could possibly manage to lift his embargo on the Israeli use of the canal without losing all face with his fellow Arabs. A five-power group was chosen to take these proposals to Cairo in early September, headed by the Australian premier, Sir Robert Menzies, an enthusiastic supporter of the Anglo-French case.[3]

However, if this resolution was to be translated into something tangible and bring the prime minister closer to achieving his real objective, the manner and atmosphere in which it was to be conveyed to Nasser were crucial. Secretary of State Dulles had ruled out Eden's idea of presenting Nasser with a formal ultimatum, but the prime minister was in no mood for prolonged negotiations which Egypt would merely use to strengthen its control over the canal. As Selwyn Lloyd told Loy Henderson, the American Middle East expert to whom Dulles had deputized the task of serving on Menzies' delegation, 'If your committee ... is to be of any use we must have an answer without delay and the answer must be clearcut'.[4] According to Eden's plan, Nasser now had two options: either to accept the Eighteen Power proposals, relinquishing his role as Arab champion in the process, or to reject the scheme and risk having the UN Security Council – 'consultation' with which ministers by now realized was essential – then swiftly call for international control of the canal. This would provide the diplomatic pretext for an Anglo-French invasion. 'We must secure the defeat of Nasser, by one method or another,' Eden informed the Egypt Committee on 24 August. Four days later, the committee set D-day for Operation MUSKETEER at 26 September.[5]

It was here that the government still saw a vital role for the press. During the London Conference Dulles had left Eden in no doubt that, in his opinion, the Egyptians were well ahead of the British in the propaganda stakes; for a start, the prime minister could not even count on the support of his own people in the event of war.[6] Whether Eden interpreted this as criticism of his policy or of his public relations is debatable. Either way, given the importance of the Americans to his plan at this stage, it was imperative that he should exert greater control over domestic opinion to show firmer backing for military action. Ministers also calculated that the likelihood of Egypt succumbing would itself be enhanced if Fleet Street impressed on Nasser that unless he agreed to accept the Eighteen Power proposals the British and French governments would launch their attack regardless of domestic and international opinion. Looking at it from the other angle, such an aggressive press would simultaneously increase the pressure on the Menzies mission not to over-accommodate its hosts. Meanwhile, the cabinet would stave off mounting opposition demands for an early recall of Parliament to discuss the Suez situation, thus leaving the press, together with the BBC, as the only true national forum for debate on the issue and the most up-to-date barometer of British public opinion.[7]

It was *The Times* that led the way for the government in stoking up the heat of the crisis at this critical juncture when on 27 August it published its most bullish and controversial editorial yet. Written personally by William Haley, who feared that the whole dispute was being comfortably shelved, 'Escapers' Club' was, even by *The Times*'s Suez standards, an astonishingly scathing assault on those in Britain who questioned Eden's policy and in particular his right to use the military option. Such 'dissidents' were not only unrepresentative – 'public opinion ... is remarkably firm' – but also profoundly dangerous, being part of 'a certain masochistic strain in our present national conscience' which believed that 'any troublemaker anywhere is bound automatically to have right on his side'. The editorial called for an end to this British 'disease' of self-guilt, blindness and paralysis. As to the question of how this particular dispute should be settled, the London Conference had changed nothing:

> Of course, it [public opinion] wants to avoid the use of force. So does everyone and we hope no one does so more than the British Government. But that is a far cry from saying that because there seems little we can do about it the best thing is to find excuses for, and forget, the whole business. Nations live by the vigorous defence of their interests ... Doubtless it is good to have a flourishing tourist trade, to win Test matches, and to be regaled by photos of Miss Diana Dors being pushed into a swimming pool. But nations do not live by circuses alone. The people, in their silent way, know this better than the critics. They still want Britain great.[8]

It must be said that there is no concrete evidence to prove that 'Escapers' Club' was prompted directly by Eden or any other member of the government, as had certainly been the case with a number of *The Times*'s editorials earlier in the crisis. At the same time, however, one might argue that the government no longer really needed to make such specific requests; so imbued with Eden's interpretation of the national interest were Haley and McDonald that, by this stage, they could automatically intuit the prime minister's wishes. Certainly it is indicative of the close, almost incestuous, relationship that by now existed between certain elements of *The Times* and the government that Haley immediately received a note from William Clark congratulating him on his editorial, which had 'caused the widest approving comment among the Cabinet'.[9] *The Times*'s editor, for his part, was clearly more than glad to have been of assistance: 'One of the heartening things is the way in which when *The Times* has a leader of this kind it seems to ring a bell. We have already had a number of encouraging messages.'[10] The two of them arranged to meet the next day, 28 August, doubtless so that the approving cabinet could express its gratitude in the customary mutually beneficial manner – by giving its most useful Fleet Street ally the fullest insight into its present thinking on Suez. This was followed by a personal *tête-à-tête* between Haley and Eden on the 29th, after which, significantly, the former produced a detailed guidance memorandum for Printing House Square to be used in his absence (Haley was committed to a US tour). 'It is essential', the memo concluded, 'that the public constantly have kept before them exactly what they have at stake.'[11]

'Escapers' Club' was one of those rare newspaper editorials whose contentiousness drew an immediate reaction from the rest of the press. Over the next few days Fleet Street was a hotbed of debate over who were the Suez realists and which papers could legitimately claim to be speaking on behalf of the silent majority in Britain. Respectful disagreement turned to contemptuous animosity. To papers like the *Manchester Guardian*, *The Times*'s eloquence amounted to nothing less than an attack on the very right to speak out against government at times of crisis.[12] In private the *Guardian*'s long-serving editor, A. P. Wadsworth, was simply at a loss to know what had caused his old friend and ex-colleague, Haley, to adopt such a reactionary line.[13] Though *The Times* could not claim to have significantly altered any newspapers' views, the overall effect of this press war was to bring the Suez issue back to the top of Fleet Street's and the public's agenda. This was exactly what Eden needed.

Whilst *The Times* focused attention on the enemy within, the Foreign Office increased the pressure on Nasser again via the diplomatic correspondents. Beginning on the same day that Haley's editorial hit the doormats and continuing on into September as the Cairo talks got under way, a veritable deluge of propaganda highlighting the government's readiness to use force was disseminated through the press. Typical of this was a front-page article written by Norman Ewer, the *Daily Herald*'s veteran diplomatic correspondent, on 29 August:

> In Government and Tory Party circles in London the talk is again of the Menzies mission becoming not a prelude to negotiations but a prelude to war against Egypt ... [If Nasser failed to agree to Menzies' proposals] Britain and France would 'act' without further delay. And action means an all-out military operation. Even if the US, even if the other allies, even if members of the Commonwealth, disapprove, Britain and France would 'go it alone'.[14]

The temperature was increased still further on 30 August, when virtually all newspapers carried as their headline story the news of the decision to station French troops in Cyprus.[15] Given that up to this point the government had gone out of its way to actually hide the true details of its military preparations in the Mediterranean, the fact that this move took place when it did (on the very eve of the Menzies committee's departure for Cairo), and in such a blaze of publicity (a special press conference was held to announce the decision), suggests that the motive behind it was more psychological than logistical. Even

William Clark had to admit to himself that 'the official excuse' that the French needed a site to protect their nationals in the area 'is a bit thin'.[16]

Clark also worked in unison with *The Times* during this period to prepare the ground for the government's brief referral of the dispute to the United Nations should Menzies draw a blank. This required a certain amount of ingenuity since Eden and the paper had hitherto dismissed the organization as unwieldy and incapable of producing swift results.[17] On 31 August, William Haley told Clark that he was greatly worried by a *News Chronicle* story from Washington to the effect that the US might bring the Suez issue to the Security Council to save Britain and France from being charged before it. Haley had been told by Eden two days before of the government's intentions as regards the UN, that is using it not as a talking-shop but as an instrument solely to prove Nasser's guilt and justify force. Clark agreed with Haley that it would be most unfortunate if the impression were to grow that Britain was likely to be taken before the Security Council by the Americans, and he suggested that something should be done to counteract this possibility. This had two results. Firstly, the Foreign Office wrote to its Washington embassy to ask the State Department to deny the report as quickly and completely as possible. 'If not killed it may do much harm.' This the State Department did. Secondly, the next day, 1 September, saw *The Times* advocating for the first time an approach to the UN, albeit of a strictly limited nature:

> The objection to the matter being simply referred to the UN and left there has all along been, and remains, that the UN is likely to be dilatory and certain to be ineffective as a means of freeing the Canal. But whatever international control is eventually brought about by negotiation or otherwise should certainly be under the aegis of the UN and the sooner the UN is officially informed of what has happened the better.[18]

So that there should still be no doubt in people's minds which side of the dispute was in the wrong, Eden appears to have scoured the press for material with which to sully Nasser's name still further. On one occasion prior to the London Conference, he had sent the Foreign Office two items from *The Times* for use, as the letter puts it, 'both in building up HMG's case and in propaganda'. The latter was thought particularly useful as it gave the lie to one of Nasser's most emotive, anti-imperialist propaganda themes, that as many as 120,000 Egyptians had died in digging the Suez Canal.[19] On 28 August, an article appeared in the *Evening Standard* 'exposing' the existence of Egyptian concentration camps, many run by ex-Nazis. Spotting a propaganda opportunity, Eden asked the Foreign Office to look into the allegations.

Its verdict was that 'the circumstantial evidence for the existence of internment camps is very strong'. 'Good for a speech', Eden put in the margin.[20]

The prime minister's campaign was also given a boost from a more conventional source at this juncture, albeit somewhat irresolutely. On 1 September, Lord Beaverbrook informed Eden that he had that day met Winston Churchill, who 'is in full support of your programme and talks about making a speech in Parliament'. Eden was already fully aware of Churchill's hostility to Nasser but, probably out of pride, had not yet called for the former premier to make his views known publicly. 'This is very good news about Winston,' Eden replied on 7 September. 'I should not have liked to ask and it is brave that he should now volunteer. If in the event a speech would prove physically too much for him a published statement would have almost the same effect.'[21] Why, in the end, Churchill waited until early November before proclaiming his support for Eden's Suez policy is unclear. Whatever the reason, as Beaverbrook's note shows, it did not prevent the old warrior from adding his considerable weight to the case for force against Egypt in a more subtle fashion. His entertaining of another press proprietor, Gomer Kemsley, at the Churchills' retreat in the south of France in mid-September is a further illustration of this.[22]

Finally, when the Cairo talks themselves were at a crucial stage, stories were circulated about the swift, overwhelming 24-hour coup that could be executed against Egypt once the button was pressed. This followed yet another cabinet request for Clark to 'harden' the press, on 5 September.[23] It was also at some point during this period that Cecil King, chairman of *Daily Mirror* Newspapers and a man known to be not entirely at ease with his papers' strong opposition to the government during Suez, was briefed personally by the chancellor of the exchequer, Harold Macmillan, who left him in no doubt that a military operation was indeed being planned, and 'that the moment the troops landed Nasser would fall and be replaced by a leader more friendly to Britain'. Though King was adamant that he opposed Macmillan's scheme when recounting this episode years later (calling it 'insane'),[24] evidence suggests that this briefing helped to cause the *Daily Mirror*'s initial ambivalence when the military assault was eventually launched in late October 1956.

Despite all the support – witting and unwitting – which the government managed to gather from the press during this period, Nasser, instead of cracking under the pressure of inspired leaks, simply dug his heels in further. The Menzies committee spent a whole week in Cairo but left on 9 September with nothing to show for its efforts bar a vague Egyptian counter-proposal for a new convention fixing tolls for the canal. This was immediately dismissed by the Foreign Office as a device 'designed to waste as much time as possible in preliminaries' and consequently not even worthy of comment.[25] Nasser had calculated from the outset that the longer the crisis went on the less chance Eden would have of using force against him. So long as the canal operated as smoothly under its new Egyptian tutelage as it had done when in the hands of the old company, Nasser believed that he was relatively safe from attack. Faced with a plan which amounted to a 'restoration of collective colonialism' he was therefore neither going to acquiesce tamely nor retaliate angrily. He would instead stall, make his own appeals to international opinion and hope that as time passed his opponents would grow fractious with one another rather than with him. Moreover, since the British and French could no longer claim that the dispute was essentially a private matter between them and the Egyptians, and at least eighteen nations now had a legitimate stake in it, the likelihood of the crisis being settled militarily had, he estimated, receded still further.[26]

Having effectively rejected the London Conference proposals, Nasser had apparently fallen into the Egypt Committee's trap. The road now seemed clear for perfunctory discussions at the UN confirming Egypt's aggressive intransigence followed by military action. Such logic failed to take into account the US administration's continued search for a peaceful settlement, however. Anticipating Nasser's response to Menzies, Dulles had withdrawn over the Labor Day weekend (1–3 September) to his vacation home in Canada to reflect on how to block Eden's appeal to the Security Council and wrest the initiative from the British. His answer was the CASU (Co-operative Association of Suez Canal Users), or 'SCUA' as it became known, which envisaged the signatories of the 1888 Convention coming together to organize convoys and take tolls from the vessels in them, thus depriving Nasser of his canal revenue. Eden initially dismissed this as merely a 'promising suggestion', but gradually warmed to the scheme the more he realized its potentially devastating impact on the Egyptian economy and consequently on Nasser's nerve. As it was Dulles' own idea, it also seemed to offer the best prospect yet of co-opting the Americans in a process ending in the forceful compulsion of Egypt. For Eisenhower and Dulles, on the other hand, the scheme was a means of derailing the Anglo-French drive to war or, at the least, of gaining a breathing space.[27]

By itself, SCUA would probably not have been appealing enough to divert Eden from the UN. However, the emergence of Dulles' scheme coincided with a British overhaul of Operation MUSKETEER. On 7 September, Eden received a detailed note from its commander-in-chief,

General Charles Keightley, recommending a completely new plan that
would be more flexible in terms of timing and, most importantly, would
lead to far fewer casualties. Keightley pointed explicitly to the current
adverse climate of public opinion:

> It is … of the greatest importance that this invasion is launched with
> our moral case unassailable and the start of the war clearly and definitely
> Nasser's responsibility and no one else's … The problem is whether it
> appears likely that this moral case can be achieved within the next few
> weeks and, if not, therefore, whether some other plan which can be
> launched at a much later date is not required.

Rather than an orthodox, direct assault on Alexandria and Cairo, this
new plan, MUSKETEER REVISE, envisaged toppling Nasser via bombing
and psychological warfare followed by an allied landing at Port Said to
secure the Canal Zone. Because it was less prone to the vagaries of the
Mediterranean weather it could be operational until the end of October,
three weeks later than the original plan.[28]

Eden took issue with virtually every aspect of Keightley's note,
except, significantly, for the importance of Britain's 'moral case'. Nevertheless, owing to his failure to establish a diplomatic pretext for an
invasion in the near future, the prime minister relented.[29] Knowing
that REVISE would be at least another month in preparation, this sealed
his acceptance of SCUA. He was also keenly aware that a significant
element of his own cabinet, led by Walter Monckton, by now showed
signs of being unsustainably divided on the unilateral use of force.[30]
Three days later, therefore, on 10 September, the Egypt Committee
agreed to postpone the approach to the UN in order to explore Dulles'
proposals.[31] Eden would later call this last decision nothing less than
the greatest mistake of his whole career, but in retrospect it would
appear that he had little alternative.[32]

If the Egypt Committee had any doubts after the Menzies mission
about having lost the political, diplomatic and publicity initiative they
were to be progressively dispelled over the next month as the crisis
became increasingly bogged down. The result of Nasser's measured
obstinacy was a series of failed attempts to force him to negotiate, all
of which watered down Eden's initial proposals and defused the dispute
to the point at which most people no longer considered it a 'crisis' at
all. Any possibility of SCUA putting Nasser on the spot, for instance,
was effectively destroyed before it even got off the ground. Furious at
Eden for having presented his plan in Parliament on 12 September as
a virtual ultimatum, Dulles held a press conference the next day and
duly stated that 'the United States would never shoot its way through
the Suez Canal, even if Egypt should halt the traffic'.[33] During the

second London Conference a few days later he then refused any commitment to force American shipowners to pay duties to SCUA instead of Egypt.[34]

With the Americans pursuing their own agenda and dampening down any prospect of force, the British and French governments could do little but drift with the rising tide of public apathy. Opinion polls showed that what sporadic public support there had been for force near the start of the crisis had diminished by September. In the third week of August, according to a Gallup poll, when asked, 'If Egypt will not accept the decision of the [London] conference, should we take military action against her, or confine ourselves to economic and political actions?', 33 per cent opted for the former, 47 per cent the latter, with 20 per cent undecided. When asked, a fortnight later, 'If Egypt deliberately interfered with the free passage of shipping in the Suez canal, should we take military action right away or refer the matter to the UN and only act with the UN's approval?', only 27 per cent chose the former, whereas 64 per cent opted for the latter, leaving 9 per cent undecided.[35] By the time the Eden government eventually referred the Suez issue to the UN Security Council in early October,[36] therefore, it was in entirely different circumstances than those en visaged earlier, diplomatically and politically. The move attracted considerable public backing, not because it was seen as a precursor to war, but as the means to a sensible, peaceful end to the dispute.

The government's inability to control events was inevitably reflected in the press. Throughout this phase a significant proportion of the national daily newspapers continued to be consistently more aggressive than the majority of British people (judging by opinion polls). This included *The Times*, *Daily Telegraph*, *Daily Express*, *Daily Mail*, *Daily Sketch* and *Financial Times*, representing over 26 million daily readers.[37] However, Eden could do little to prevent the opposition press further 'softening', as he called it. The prime minister's task was made doubly difficult in this respect by the Labour party's cultivation of its own press contacts. Thus, both the *Daily Herald*, the party's semi-official newspaper, and the *Daily Mirror*, with its own strong connections with Transport House,[38] provided firm support for a negotiated settlement brokered by the United Nations. The *Mirror*'s leading columnist and pro-Zionist Labour MP, Richard Crossman, was especially vociferous, labelling Eden's belligerent policy 'demented'.[39] Towards the end of August, as government leaks made war appear imminent, Hugh Gaitskell himself went onto the propaganda offensive by giving two detailed interviews, one to *Reynolds News*, a Sunday paper owned by the Co-operative Press, the other to the *Manchester Guardian*.[40] Subsequent letters to *The Times* and *The Economist*, plus another interview in the *Daily Mirror*, helped to clarify further Labour's position and ensure that the party's message got as wide a hearing as possible. The missive which appeared in *The Times* on 14 September accused Eden of deliberate ambiguity on the question of force during the Commons emergency debate on Suez the day before, thus publicly underlining the gulf which had by now opened up between the two main political parties.[41]

Perhaps one of the most worrying features for Eden of the opposition press during Suez was its sense of solidarity. Twice in early September, for example, the *Daily Mirror* took the unusual step of quoting editorial extracts from the *Observer*, *Manchester Guardian* and *News Chronicle* to support its anti-war campaign.[42] A similar exchange of comment occurred when Suez reached its climax in November. There is no evidence of any explicit agreement between the editors to work as a team. It seems more likely that a few of these papers, the *Mirror* in particular, for all their apparent strength of purpose, harboured fears of being branded appeasers or anti-British by their readers. The ghost of Neville Chamberlain haunted Fleet Street as much as Westminster and Whitehall in 1956. No journalist or politician wished to find himself on the losing side if war came, thereafter stigmatized as a latter-day Guilty Man. The close association with the like-minded offered such pressmen a form of protection, a sense of safety in numbers.[43] The outward effect, however, was to emphasize the extent of distrust there was of the government. As the *Daily Mirror*'s headline above a long and varied list of Eden's critics put it, 'Are they *all* liars and scaremongers?'[44] Meanwhile, the resolve of certain papers was strengthened by the cabinet's inability to keep secret the growing split in its ranks. In early October Walter Monckton told the *Mirror*'s editor-in-chief, Hugh Cudlipp, of his opposition to the use of force without UN approval and his anguish over whether to resign. He was replaced by Antony Head on 18 October.[45]

To make matters worse for Eden, many pro-force newspapers began to show ominous signs of having lost some of their zest for the fight. In this case, the prime minister was to some extent reaping what he had sown. Proprietors and journalists were bound to feel let down, having been persuaded to trust the government's intuition, only to see one anti-climax follow another and ministers fail to support their private promises and public rhetoric with the requisite action. Many newspapers had staked their reputation on the humiliation of Nasser. Furthermore, even the most resourceful papers found it increasingly difficult to present the dispute in the necessary simple terms, as one of tyranny versus democracy, when the government made an already complicated issue even more intractable by supporting such schemes as the Users' Association. Those papers that could understand SCUA had immense problems in conveying such 'a hazy concept' to their readers. Lack of comprehension bred ignorance and apathy.[46]

Finally, in the first weeks of October the popular press was full of rumours of disaffection among the reservists sent to the Mediterranean and of the low morale of troops growing bored waiting for action. Walter Monckton and Antony Head, then secretary of state for war, arranged a meeting with several editors to quell this media speculation, arguing that such reports were against the national interest. This did have some effect – for example on the *Daily Mirror*, whose editor-in-chief later claimed that in playing down the discontent the paper 'could not have been more helpful to the Government or War Office had it been edited by General Shortt [Director of Public Relations at the War Office]'.[47] But the damage to public opinion was already done. How could a newspaper legitimately claim that Britain was ready for war when the very troops sent to defend her interests showed signs of what in an earlier age would have been construed as mutiny?

Given this embarrassing state of affairs for the cabinet, it comes as no surprise to find Eden at the end of September acknowledging the need for an overhaul of the government's propaganda machinery and strategy. On 26 September, the Lord Privy Seal, R. A. Butler, was appointed as the government's chief publicity coordinator, a role which had been tentatively envisaged for him in early July but shelved when Suez erupted. Butler's job was to make the necessary approaches to members of the cabinet, whilst the Conservative party chairman, Oliver Poole, liaised with ministers and junior ministers, the object being to ensure 'that adequate publicity was given, through Ministerial speeches, to the main features of Government policy at the present juncture'. Butler was also delegated to effect closer consultation with the Foreign Office regarding propaganda in the Middle East, and to put pressure on the BBC to improve greatly its Overseas Service.[48]

On 1 October, Ian Bancroft, Butler's private secretary, informed Selwyn Lloyd's office of a significant shift in the direction of propaganda, one which William Clark had been urging upon Eden for weeks: 'The PM wishes to ensure that the Government case on Suez – and in particular the "long haul" concept – should be put over well by both Government and Party spokesmen at the Party Conference and afterwards.' In tandem with this, Butler supervised the preparation of a detailed confidential guidance note for the use of ministers not directly concerned with Suez, for government officials, and for those Party officials who needed to deal with the press at the Llandudno conservative conference, to be held mid-month. The aim was to eliminate an increasing tendency towards repetition and contradiction. The paper produced, after rigorous consultation with William Clark and the Foreign Office's Information, News, Middle East and African Departments, emphasized both the justice of the government's cause and its determination to try every peaceful means of solving the dispute.[49] This was a far cry from the aggressive material the government had been peddling at the start of the crisis.

The extent to which this shift in presentation was also matched by a fundamental change in policy is the subject of considerable historical debate. The Egypt Committee's motive behind taking the Suez issue to the UN was to expose the fragility of Egypt's case via direct negotiations. Eden himself was determined to play for high stakes, as his instructions to Selwyn Lloyd in New York on 7 October reveal: 'It is ... very important that, while appearing reasonable, we should not be inveigled away in negotiation from the fundamentals to which we have held all along and that we should not be parted from the French.'[50] During the talks between Lloyd, Pineau, the French foreign minister, and Fawzi, his Egyptian counterpart, from 9 to 12 October, however, the prime minister seemed to warm to the prospects of a compromise settlement. Evidence for this ranges from Eden's concern at Pineau's initial intransigence at the UN, to the Egyptians' acceptance of the essence of the West's position, articulated in Lloyd's so-called 'Six Principles';[51] and from the sustained pressure by Washington against force, through to the growing restrictions on the military timetable.[52]

That Eden, strongly supported by Lloyd, was having second thoughts in mid-October about going to war over the nationalization of the Suez Canal there is little doubt. Nevertheless, the Egypt Committee was by no means reconciled to the abandonment of its short-term objective – the deposing of Nasser – for the simple reason that it could not afford to. Even if the 'Six Principles' were successfully implemented, this would clearly not amount to the total climbdown for so long demanded of Cairo by London. If anything, it would be the Eden government that would be humiliated by exposing itself to charges of appeasement. Moreover, the opponents of the government's policy, on both the right and the left, would have a field day when the Mediterranean task force returned home, complete with restive reservists. Overall, therefore, it seems likely that British policy was wracked by indecision in the immediate wake of the UN negotiations, with Eden, in the words of one historian, 'hoping, with increasing desperation, for something to turn up'.[53]

6

Collusion and war

All this was to change radically following the visit to Chequers by General Maurice Challe, a deputy chief of staff of the French air force, and Albert Gazier, France's minister of labour deputizing for Foreign Minister Pineau, on Sunday, 14 October. Aware of Eden's pent-up frustration, yet fearful that a compromise settlement was in the offing, the French envoys offered to break the diplomatic logjam and provide the prime minister with his much-needed pretext for invasion via collaboration with Tel Aviv.

Challe's plan hinged on a pre-emptive Israeli strike against Egypt across the Sinai desert. This would enable Britain and France to claim that the safety of the Suez Canal was at risk and justify the despatching of their forces to the Canal Zone to separate the combatants. Eden was immediately enthusiastic. It would – at the very least – puncture Nasser's prestige, mean the reservists would not have to be stood down, and prevent a full-scale Israeli invasion of Jordan, with whom Britain had a defence treaty. Such an assault appeared imminent following a major Israeli raid into Jordanian territory at Qalqilya on 10 October, the culmination of months of cross-border fighting. If this were to occur ministers feared that they would indeed find themselves at war in the Middle East, but against Israel, not Egypt. Eden was determined not to let Cairo off the hook in this way. His anger at the prospect was revealed in an alleged conversation with Anthony Nutting, minister of state at the Foreign Office, on 13 October: 'I will not allow you to plunge this country into war merely to satisfy the anti-Jewish spleen of you people in the Foreign Office.'[1]

Consequently, a little over a week later, on 24 October, the secret plan was officially agreed upon and a treaty signed (against Eden's wishes) at a meeting of British, French and Israeli ministers and officials at Sèvres outside Paris. The gist of this, though not the precise details, was then given to, and agreed by, the cabinet the next day.[2] Opinions still differ about many aspects of this tripartite 'collusion':

for instance, over its implications for cabinet government, the extent to which fraud was committed, and the precise roles of the three participants.[3] What concern us here, however, are the two interrelated questions of what role (if any) the Eden government assigned the press during the conspiracy, and what part the press actually played when the diplomatic and military subterfuge was put into operation.

It could of course be argued that from the very outset of the Suez crisis the British government had been involved in a conspiracy and yet had plainly shown few qualms about divulging this to a whole host of 'trustworthy' newspapermen. However, the sort of intrigue in which ministers embroiled themselves during the latter half of October 1956 was of an altogether more dubious nature. It was one thing to trick one's enemy into providing a necessary *casus belli*; it was quite another to manufacture that *casus belli* oneself and then brazenly ride in as peacemaker. When, therefore, the offer came from the French to break the Suez deadlock, there was little scope for press manipulation – at least not before the Israeli attack (scheduled for 29 October). The key to the success of the operation – militarily, politically and in terms of public relations – was secrecy and surprise. For the government to contact its friends in Fleet street *en masse* in order to seek their prior approval and prepare the ground would have been far too risky. Briefings alerting the press to the recent increase in Egyptian *fedayeen* raids on Israeli territory, for example, thereby encouraging people to expect and sympathize with retaliation, would immediately become transparent once the Anglo-French ultimatums were announced. Any rumours in the press that the government even had foreknowledge of, let alone had taken a hand in fostering, an imminent Israeli invasion of Egypt would not only wreck the whole project but would also threaten Eden's political survival.

The most therefore that ministers could hope for from the press was that it would continue to give the impression, as it had done whilst negotiations at the United Nations progressed during early October, that the British government was more pacific and conciliatory than ever. Anything the papers could do to show that the government was far from desperate to resolve the dispute quickly, the easier it would be to refute the inevitable allegations of skulduggery. This ministers encouraged by sending out signals via the press that the Security Council proceedings had been a great success. On 18 October, during the meeting at which Eden first introduced the cabinet to the possibility of cooperating with the Israelis, it was agreed that public statements before and after the reassembly of Parliament on 23 October should emphasize the degree of support which Britain had obtained in the Security Council for its stand on Suez. Two days later, at the half-yearly meeting of the North West Area Conservative Council in Liverpool, with representatives of the BBC and press invited, Selwyn Lloyd delivered a high-profile speech (written by Eden) highlighting this very point. R. A. Butler, wearing his publicity coordinator's hat, urged ministers to make 'full use' of the foreign secretary's address.[4]

It is a measure of how much the prime minister by this stage regarded *The Times* as his own personal tool rather than an independent-minded newspaper that, on or around the date he condescended to inform his cabinet colleagues of parts of the Challe plan, he personally told Iverach McDonald of the whole plot.[5] Rarely can a journalist have been handed such a bombshell of a scoop. Given the potential for disaster should rumours of this collusion leak out, it is nothing less than extraordinary how much trust was placed in the *Times* man.

By contrast, Eden went to the lengths of sending William Clark on an enforced fortnight's holiday on 15 October, the day after the seminal Chequers meeting, for fear of his confiding in an erstwhile colleague. Having mistakenly doubted Clark's loyalty for months, Eden arguably felt that his press secretary lacked the stomach for what lay ahead. When Clark returned to London he was ordered to keep out of the prime minister's private office. From that point, though curiously he was allowed into some top-level meetings, Clark was effectively in limbo, his job made impossible by Eden's affording him only partial confidence.[6]

However, Eden had seriously misjudged McDonald, who, together with Haley, was utterly appalled at the prospect of what the prime minister was planning. Lunching with McDonald on 1 November, William Clark, who by then was himself aware of what had been going on behind his back, found the *Times* man 'in despair':

> He thought the whole project had been grotesquely mishandled, and above all it was collusive and dishonest. Clearly he had been choked to the marrow by the revelation of duplicity which the Prime Minister had made to him in believing that *The Times* was an unshakeable government supporter. Iverach had only told Haley – no one else – but he had also urged Haley to go and see the PM and warn him off.[7]

Nevertheless, it would be wrong to conclude from McDonald's reaction that Eden's miscalculation cost him the support of his most valuable Fleet Street asset when he most needed it. When, two weeks after the prime minister's confession, the tripartite plan was put into operation, *The Times* undoubtedly failed to back the government in the manner Eden hoped and perhaps expected. Clearly there were lengths to which Haley would not go in supporting Eden's quest to destroy Nasser. On the other hand, to claim, as Harold Macmillan and others did afterwards, that *The Times* actually changed sides once hostilities started, and that this could be attributed to a strong feeling within Printing House Square of having been used by Eden all along, is pushing it too far.[8] The fairest conclusion one can reach about *The Times*'s attitude towards the government during the crucial military phase was that it sat firmly, if awkwardly, on the fence. Considering the paper's earlier steadfast allegiance to Eden's cause, this shift undoubtedly did the prime minister some damage. However, to assert that *The Times*, in a fit of pique, launched an assault on Eden armed with the secrets which he had given it is manifestly erroneous. Indeed, far from assuaging its guilt at having prior knowledge of collusion, as Richard Lamb asserts, by reproducing in its pages every story appearing in the American press that hinted at a conspiracy,[9] it will be shown that *The Times* went out of its way to discredit such stories and generally scotch the whole theory.

On the evening of 29 October, exactly according to plan and taking the whole world, including Fleet Street (minus Haley and McDonald), by surprise,[10] the Israelis launched their assault on Egypt through the Sinai and, by dropping parachutists in the vicinity of the Mitla Pass, posed an apparent threat to the Suez Canal. At 4.30 GMT the next afternoon Eden told a packed House of Commons of the ultimatums (though he was careful not to use that word) which had just been handed to the Egyptian and Israeli ambassadors in London. These 'communications' called upon Egypt and Israel to withdraw their forces to a distance of ten miles on either side of the canal and consent to an Anglo-French force temporarily occupying the Suez Canal. The Egyptian and Israeli governments were asked to reply within twelve hours. If both or either of them did not comply, 'British and French forces will intervene in whatever strength it may be necessary to serve compliance.'[11]

In managing to keep secret its recent dealings with the French and the Israelis and deliver such a shock to the press, the Eden government had undoubtedly scored an important tactical propaganda success. Ministers were inadvertently helped in this regard by Fleet Street's growing interest in the events of late October 1956 in Hungary, where student-led demonstrations against the political system threatened to destabilize the Soviet bloc. As a front-page news story, Suez in comparison had apparently blown itself out.[12] However, there is little or no evidence to suggest that the government had put any thought into how it was going to build on this success and present its plan to the public in general and Fleet Street in particular. In the fortnight which ministers had to prepare their case, no clear strategy on how to deal with an inevitably inquisitive press was devised.

Excuses can be made for this, most notably an understandable fear that the more the talk of propaganda the greater the chance of a leak. The enforced absence of William Clark also suggested that the government's propaganda machinery was by this stage disjointed. And yet, perusing cabinet and Egypt Committee minutes from this period, one cannot escape the impression that, when it came to how the press and public would react to its policy and the threat of war, the government on the whole felt that any pre-planning was unnecessary. Eden's line of thinking appeared to be that so long as the hidden objective – the collapse of Nasser's regime – was achieved quickly and with the minimum of casualties on both sides, then ultimately British, American and even Arab public opinion would accept it. Only if the military operation dragged on, with Nasser still holding the reins of power, would serious difficulties arise and the question of a concerted propaganda campaign then need to be addressed.[13]

Not that Eden was going to leave everything to chance and the press entirely to its own devices now that the crisis was at last reaching its climax. If the prime minister thought he had learned one thing from his dealings with the press over the last few months, it was the fourth estate's abiding fear of betraying (or being seen to betray) the nation's soldiers. It was this that had enabled the government to provide a smokescreen for its Mediterranean military build-up throughout the summer. It comes as no surprise, therefore, to find Robert Allan, Eden's parliamentary private secretary and by now Clark's *de facto* replacement as his chief press adviser, briefing journalists only hours after the prime minister's ultimatum statement in the Commons on 30 October, to the effect that 'the paratroops were going in the following dawn'.[14]

Given that the plan for MUSKETEER REVISE clearly stated that the Anglo-French troops would not in fact be landing on Egyptian soil for at least another five or six days, there are only two rational explanations for this glaring inaccuracy. Either it was part of the government's psychological warfare campaign against Nasser, a fundamental feature of REVISE; or it was designed to get the press to support the troops, and thereby the government, in the false belief that a full-scale invasion was imminent in which the lives of 'our lads' would be immediately at stake. The newspapers would of course soon realize how bogus this information was but would by then presumably have committed themselves and thus be wide open to charges of inconsistency if they changed their tune. Whatever the motive – it was probably a combination of both – this was a blatant attempt to manipulate the press at a most crucial point, when every titbit of news could make a difference to a newspaper's stance.

The next morning, Wednesday, 31 October, virtually all newspapers carried a story to the effect that British troops, even ground forces, would be moving into Egypt that very day. Indeed, some papers even reported that contingents had already done so.[15] How much of an influence this particular piece of disinformation had in determining the press's attitude towards government policy at this early stage is debatable. The fact is, however, that two of the papers hitherto most critical of Eden during Suez and which had previously warned their readers of the prime minister's potential for trickery – the *News Chronicle* and *Daily Mirror* – were conspicuously non-committal and afflicted by indecision.[16]

It is difficult to believe that the fear of appearing to support 'the enemy' as British soldiers went into action did not play at least some part in these papers' decision to equivocate. Michael Curtis, the *Chronicle*'s editor, had for weeks been under intense pressure from the paper's proprietors, Laurence and Egbert Cadbury, to tone down his criticism of Eden's Suez policy. As well as being Conservative party supporters, the Cadburys were acutely aware of the *Chronicle*'s marginal financial position. In 1955, the *Chronicle* had bought and assimilated Kemsley's Manchester-based *Daily Despatch*, many of whose readers were natural Tory sympathizers, and it was these who were reportedly leaving the paper in droves in the summer of 1956. The outbreak of hostilities also caused a 'savage split' in the *Chronicle*'s office.[17] As for the *Mirror*, its powerful chairman had wavered at the outset of Suez when it looked as if British troops might go into action, and he now must have had in mind what Macmillan had told him in September about the likelihood of a short, sharp victory.[18]

With the *Chronicle* and *Mirror* out of the picture this left the *Manchester Guardian* and *Daily Herald*[19] as the only real press opponents of Eden's policy on what was, in effect, day one of the real crisis. (*The Times*, though clearly no longer the staunch ally of Eden as it had been, was wracked with self-doubt,[20] whilst the *Observer*, an expected critic, could not comment until Sunday, 4 November.) The *Financial Times, Telegraph, Express, Sketch* and *Mail*, perhaps bolstered themselves by the news that the nation was on the verge of war, showed little hesitation in supporting Eden's ultimatums. Thus, on the Fleet Street front, things seemed to be going extremely well for the government.[21] The relatively little criticism of the government in the press tended to focus on the expediency of its policy and how poorly it would be received abroad; as such it was hardly the stuff to sway the undecided or make the patriotic think again. Allegations that Eden's ultimatum could be linked directly to his dispute with Nasser over the Suez Canal were made, but implicitly rather than explicitly. As for collusion, the *Manchester Guardian* raised the question only to dismiss it outright.[22]

Unfortunately for Eden this was nothing but the calm before the storm. The deeper opposition politicians and inquisitive journalists delved, the more holes appeared in the government's policy. Ministers and officials, not having been briefed by the public relations men on how the government's policy should be presented and what exactly the prime minister's motives were in issuing his ultimatums to the Israelis and Egyptians, were largely left to make up their own minds. This led to confusion and contradiction. For example, at the same time that Eden was delivering the news of his ultimatums to Parliament on 30 October, a Foreign Office spokesman was innocently telling journalists that the government's policy was to invoke the 1950 Tripartite Declaration. This required Britain, France and the United States to come to the aid of either party to the Arab–Israeli dispute if subjected to invasion by the other, namely, in this case, Nasser's Egypt. [23]

The inevitable result was suspicion and speculation in the press. No journal put this more trenchantly than the *New Statesman* a month later on 8 December:

> Consider what has happened in the last month. To justify their acts of aggression, ministers have deluged parliament with conflicting excuses and explanations. We intervened 'to separate the combatants and to protect shipping' (Sir Anthony), to secure international control of the Canal (Mr Head), to 'put teeth into the UN' (Sir Anthony again), to uncover a 'red plot' (Mr Thorneycroft). Since then, Mr Lloyd has contradicted Mr Thorneycroft (by admitting that the information which Mr Thorneycroft said our action had 'discovered' was known to us before we undertook it), and Mr Heathcoat Amory has contradicted Sir David Eccles, by agreeing with him on the 'principles' which guided British intervention. He has also contradicted Mr Head by stating emphatically that Britain did not intervene to secure control of the Canal. Finally, to complicate matters still further, on Wednesday Mr Lloyd laboured through the whole catalogue. [24]

Just how chaotic the government's propaganda policy was, especially in late October–early November, is illustrated by what transpired at a meeting of ministers on the morning of 1 November. With Eden about to defend his policy in the Commons that afternoon, including by then the use of bombers against Egyptian targets, William Clark made the suggestion that he should say that he had acted on behalf of the United Nations. Though this idea was, according to Clark's own record, rejected – the minister of defence, Antony Head, for one, feared that it would jeopardize the government's prime objective of getting rid of Nasser – Eden in fact went on to make great play of it in his speech later. Clark was 'amazed' when he heard this and 'tried at once all I could to get the press to notice this as a significant passage'.[25] For the government not to have thought through the possible implications of its policy and prepared certain propaganda lines beforehand is quite remarkable. To hit on a convenient justification almost by accident was not the way to conduct a successful propaganda exercise. This was borne out by the furore in the Commons later in the day, which forced the Speaker to suspend the sitting for half an hour, caused by the fact that neither the minister of defence nor the foreign secretary could say for certain whether Britain was now at war.[26]

The government's inability to tell the same story twice was inevitably reflected in the press. Those papers committed to supporting Eden's cause found themselves having to perform linguistic somersaults. As a direct result of his belated adoption of this working-for-the-UN line, for example, the *Daily Mail*, whose editorial on 1 November had confidently stated 'Britain at War', was forced to change it the next day to 'A Police Action' and offer its readers an apology. The *Daily Express*'s leader of 7 November contrasted sharply with its front-page article of 31 October. Having initially described the notion of holding Israel and Egypt apart as 'foolish', preferring to think of the intervention as a straightforward occupation, the *Express* had to fall back on that very notion in order to justify the operation once the premature ceasefire was declared.[27] Not all of Fleet Street was as generous as the *Mail* and *Express*. As the government shifted its ground, so did that element of the press which had initially given Eden the benefit of the doubt. By day three of the crisis both the *News Chronicle* and the *Daily Mirror* were accusing Eden of using the Israeli invasion of Egypt as an excuse to dislodge Nasser and of threatening 'the whole continuity and achievement of British post-war foreign policy'. With editorial confidence restored, the normally sedate *News Chronicle* called on the Conservatives to save the government from its leader and the nation from its humiliation.[28]

Perhaps the most powerful, certainly the most consistent, criticism came from the *Daily Herald*, *Manchester Guardian* and *Observer*. Both the *Herald* and the *Guardian* were credited with denouncing Eden's 30 October ultimatums more swiftly than the opposition in the Commons. Indeed, Gaitskell's condemnation of the government's action as 'an act of folly whose tragic consequences we shall regret for years' on 31 October mirrored their editorials of that morning.[29] The *Guardian*'s vehemence, guided by Alastair Hetherington, now editor, was all the more penetrating because of the paper's traditional sympathy with Israel.[30] All three newspapers were direct to the point of being provocative and used language designed to express the shock and indignation their journalists and readers felt. All three were in the vanguard calling for the removal of Eden 'by constitutional means', an indication simultaneously both of the deep anger the government's policy had aroused and the lengths to which a self-styled respectable and democratic press would go in opposing such a policy.[31] The impact which the *Observer*'s ferocious assault on Eden made on the national consciousness in November 1956 has warranted it being called the paper's 'finest hour' and the most celebrated attack on a government since 1945.[32] At the very least, the paper's cogent allegations of 'crookedness' and its dismantling of the government's words and actions helped to cast grave doubts in many moderates' minds on Eden's claim to have acted impartially in the Middle East.[33]

Thus, having played his trump card, only to see it backfire when the immediate invasion failed to materialize, Eden found himself in a difficult position *vis-à-vis* the press. As had been the case ever since the first weeks of the crisis, the prime minister could at this point still count on the support of at least half of the nation's most influential newspapers. In spite of the Security Council's various resolutions roundly censuring the Anglo-French action,[34] the *Daily Telegraph* emphasized strongly the common ground between the opposing parties on how the security and stability of the Middle East could be secured in the long run: a UN given real power. Beaverbrook's *Daily Express* continued to give Eden's policy an imperial blessing, whilst the *Financial Times* played its part by defying the pundits and declaring confidence in the British economy's ability to withstand a Middle East campaign (so long as it was short).[35]

But the fact was that, despite the successful routing of the Egyptian air force in the first days of November, Nasser was still in power and the use of British troops would consequently be necessary. This full-scale military assault, however, could not itself be effected until 5 November owing to transportation delays. As things were, polls showed that domestic public opinion was already polarizing at a remarkable rate, presumably intensified by the war in the press. When asked by Gallup on 1–2 November, 'Do you think we were right or wrong to take military action in Egypt?' 37 per cent opted for the former, 44 per cent for the latter, leaving 19 per cent undecided. Between 30 October and 3 November, the *Daily Express* posed the heavily weighted question: 'As a result of Israel's invasion of Egypt, Sir Anthony Eden has sent British forces to occupy the Suez Canal Zone to protect British interests and to guarantee freedom of transit through the Canal by British ships and ships of all nations. Do you support or oppose this action?' The results were 48.5 per cent in support, 39 per cent in opposition, with 12.5 per cent undecided.[36] The question was, therefore, whether Eden could afford to allow this deep division within British society to grow wider during the awkward phoney-war phase.

Not surprisingly, given his track record and complacent belief that no strategy would be required to deal with the media once the RAF had intervened to extinguish the fires of war in the Middle East, Eden's answer to this press hostility was to panic and resort to the bully tactics which had for so long demoralized William Clark. James Margach recalls how during this period editors were summoned, in groups of six or eight, to Downing Street to be lectured personally by the prime minister on their duty to rally round the armed forces in action. 'I can't keep coming round to Number 10 to be harangued by the P.M. on what I should be thinking and saying in the national interest', the News Chronicle's Michael Curtis told Margach.[37] When this failed to have the desired effect Eden turned to the telephone instead. Lords Rothermere and Kemsley (Margach's own chief) were his most regular dawn contacts, though these were not, in truth, the proprietors whom Eden most needed to convince.[38] Of an even more desperate and disreputable nature was the request made to William Clark to inform the press discreetly that Anthony Nutting, whose resignation as minister of state at the Foreign Office on 2 November had caused Eden considerable embarrassment, had not acted on principle but 'was terribly under the influence of his American mistress and anyway was not quite himself nowadays'. This Clark refused to do, arguing that it 'was the sort of thing the Party did, certainly not me'.[39]

However, Eden did not draw a complete blank in his efforts to strengthen his case in the press. During this period he received a number of personal telegrams from prominent newspaper or periodical proprietors, each expressing their 'extreme admiration' for his conduct of affairs in the Middle East. On 2 November, Roy Thomson, the Canadian millionaire who in the mid-1950s had just embarked on his addictive purchasing of British newspapers and always disclaimed the slightest interest in editorial policy, told Eden that in the present circumstances he could 'depend on the complete support of The Scotsman'. This was Scotland's most respectable newspaper, with a circulation of 54,000.[40] On 6 November, Edward Hulton, proprietor of the Hulton Press, publisher of Picture Post, offered the prime minister his services. A week later Hulton then asked if he could make contact with someone in Eden's 'PR organisation [to] be of maximum usefulness in the present emergency'.[41] Perhaps the most important, certainly the most effusive, of these messages came from the aforementioned Lord Kemsley. His telegram, which simply said 'Wonderful, wonderful, wonderful', was less an offer of support than a note of unbridled congratulation.[42] Given what we now know of the deep split in the *Sunday Times* office over Eden's ultimatums, this made Kemsley's loyalty to the prime minister's cause all the more significant. It was he who personally ensured that the *Sunday Times* gave its full and un-equivocal backing to the government during this military phase, thus providing an essential riposte to the vehemently anti-war line of the other 'quality' Sunday paper, the *Observer*.[43]

Despite the abuse which he and his paper had suffered at the hands of Eden, there is also evidence that the editor of *The Times*, William Haley, had not completely abandoned the prime minister in his hour of need. On the afternoon of 5 November, following the rowdiest of Commons Suez debates, during which Labour's Tony Benn and Aneurin Bevan had confronted Selwyn Lloyd with evidence of the government's psychological warfare campaign in Egypt,[44] Eden spoke to both Haley and Donald McLachlan at the House and assured them categorically that, contrary to rumours, there were no divisions what-soever in the cabinet.[45] This was in fact a long way from the truth. Only the evening before, the cabinet had seriously split over whether to proceed with the Anglo-French landings and defy the UN's call for a ceasefire. Eden had even threatened to resign if his dissenting colleagues, namely R. A. Butler, Salisbury (leader of the House of Lords), Kilmuir (Lord Chancellor), Heathcoat Amory (minister of agriculture), Buchan-Hepburn (minister of works) and Monckton (now paymaster-general), failed to back his course.[46] Nevertheless, on 6 November, *The Times* duly trotted out the prime minister's line:

> The defection of Mr Nutting from the Government is not taken seriously by his colleagues, and it seems unlikely that any other junior Ministers will follow his example. In the Cabinet there has been complete unanim-ity on the policy of intervention to limit the spread of hostilities in the Middle East.[47]

It is also important to appreciate how at this point the increasingly dramatic events in Eastern Europe, and the media's treatment of them, assisted the government's presentation of the Anglo-French landings on 5–6 November in particular, and its policy in general. On 3 Novem-ber, a day the British and French spent wriggling at the UN insisting that they must be part of any emergency force despatched to Egypt, the crisis which had been brewing for weeks in Hungary exploded. The Soviet Union ordered its forces to bombard Budapest with the aim of crushing the democratic uprising.[48] Initially this worked against Eden, with the Labour party and that section of the press opposed to the government's Middle Eastern policy quick to accuse the prime minister of either having given the Russians the excuse to act following his own disregard for international law, or having split the Western alliance and thereby left the Hungarian dissidents in the lurch.[49] However, the more the British people were made aware of the extent and nature of the Soviets' crackdown, which appeared long in the planning, the less was heard of such allegations. The result was that the Hungarian factor rebounded in Eden's favour. On Sunday and Monday, 4 and 5 November, for instance, during what was a limbo in the Middle East war, the press reported the Russians' repression in Hungary in graphic detail, relegating the latest Suez events to the inside pages.[50]

This acted as a most welcome distraction for the Eden government at a time when many ministers and members of the public questioned whether the planned operation to wrest control of the Suez Canal militarily should go ahead. The relative freedom with which the media covered the Russians' widely reported 'barbarism' also contrasted with its censored version of events in Egypt following the Allied landings. Government spokesmen exaggerated the differences between the Anglo-French action and the Russians' 'flagrant aggression', emphasizing the latter's complete unwillingness to hand over to the UN especially.[51] Headlines referring to the 'Free World's Shock and Horror' (*Daily Telegraph*) and the Hungarians' 'Inspired Resistance to Soviet Brutality' (*Manchester Guardian*) continued to share top billing with Suez events throughout November 1956.[52]

Truth is always the first casualty of war, and Suez was no exception. However, what has hitherto been overlooked by historians is the lengths to which the Eden government went to control the media's coverage of the military operation in Egypt, and the extent to which this might have assisted the government in strengthening the moral justification of its whole policy. With the press and public opinion very much in the balance throughout the first two weeks of November 1956, how successfully the 'police operation' was perceived as having been carried out was one of the most important factors in determining whether many British people accepted Eden's case for intervention. Put simply: the fewer the deaths (on both sides), the more credible the claim that the government had been right to act as peacemaker.

The Suez campaign, as distinct from the crisis, lasted little more than a week. Hostilities began with Israel's invasion of the Sinai peninsula on 29 October. Anglo-French naval and air attacks on Egypt were launched on 31 October. Anglo-French paratroops dropped on Port Said on 5 November, and their seaborne forces went ashore on 6 November. On the same day, at midnight, the British and French governments accepted a UN demand for a ceasefire. Compared with the two other major post-war conflicts in which Britain has been involved, the Falklands and Gulf wars, this was therefore – in strict military terms – little more than a skirmish. However, there was still plenty of scope for news management.

The Eden government succeeded in controlling the press's coverage of Operation MUSKETEER REVISE by four main methods: firstly, and primarily, by restricting correspondents' access to the war front; secondly, by replacing what the journalists could not see for themselves with news via 'authoritative military sources'; thirdly, by restricting what editors were actually allowed to publish; and fourthly, by setting up a powerful, multi-departmental committee based in London which sought to tie these different functions together and offered positive guidance to the press.

The Ministry of Defence had, in conjunction with the press, been trying to arrange for a group of thirty correspondents to be accredited to cover any military operation that might arise ever since the Suez crisis had erupted in late July 1956. However, the Foreign Office had remained adamant throughout August, September and October that no approach should be made to the Press Association on the subject of accreditation until that operation actually began.[53] Whether this was for reasons of security or politics is unclear. Foreign Office personnel were on the whole certainly not as confident as the Services that the operation would be so clean-cut. With so much secrecy and indecisiveness surrounding the military planning in the summer of 1956, the reaction amongst many in the Foreign Office to the prospect of war was one of fear and trepidation. Nasser's nationalization coup had proved immensely popular in Egypt, and it was believed that the Egyptian military and people were therefore unlikely immediately to crumble once any fighting started. Indeed, if the Egyptians showed the same dogged resistance to British troops as the Ismailia police had during the so-called 'Black Saturday' troubles of January 1952, the result might be a bloodbath. To have journalists present in these circumstances would be a distinct liability.[54]

The result of this nervousness is that when REVISE was launched the press was virtually left out in the cold. The government had had three full months in which to listen to the press's requests and afford newspapers genuine, if restricted, access to the biggest military operation the country had been involved in since World War Two. And yet, except for one journalist, Peter Woods of the *Daily Mirror*, who by sheer enterprise managed to drop with the parachute assault force on 5 November (breaking both ankles in the process),[55] no first-hand press coverage was possible for either the bombings, the parachute or the seaborne attacks. As a consequence, most of what really happened in Port Said, including the prolonged street fighting and the killing and wounding of hundreds of Egyptian civilians (detailed later), was missed by the press. Even the two journalists hand-picked by the Army Public Relations Unit to accompany the assault ships, Donald Edgar of the *Daily Express* and the *New York Times* defence correspondent, Hanson Baldwin, were not allowed ashore with the 6 November landings. As Edgar wrote later, his vantage point was on a ship anchored three miles off Port Said, 'distant enough to reduce the scene to the size of a coloured picture postcard and the warships to toys on the Round Pond in Kensington Gardens.'[56] The ship carrying the rest of the journalists from their base in Cyprus did not reach Port Said until after the ceasefire had been declared. According to one reporter, perhaps echoing the MoD's excuse, the vessel's bottom had not been cleaned, rendering it too slow to keep pace with the forces.[57]

To compensate for this failure to place the correspondents where they could do their own job, the MoD provided a service which did their job for them. Defence correspondents are best satisfied when they are granted access to authoritative military sources, and the MoD public relations officers at Suez were regarded as a poor substitute in this respect. Most were lowly subalterns with no previous experience or training in public relations.[58] Thus, one particularly successful information policy innovation at Suez was the daily press conferences taken either by the land force commander himself, Lt General Sir Hugh Stockwell, or by his chief of staff and specialist officers when appropriate. This provision was popular with even the most sceptical and experienced correspondents, who valued the opportunity to talk to, or question directly, those they regarded as useful and legitimate sources of information.[59] Inevitably, however, these briefings at Allied Force HQ in Cyprus tended to be wholly subjective and heavily biased in favour of the Anglo-French forces. But, without any means of verification until correspondents did arrive on the scene, and under the pressure of having to provide their editors with at least some copy, journalists had no alternative but to report what was given them. We therefore find the reports of the bombings, for instance, based almost entirely on the AFHQ communiqués, complete with their emphasis on pinpoint accuracy and the 'scrupulous care taken by the allied air forces in selecting targets so as to spare the Egyptian population'.[60] Similarly, when the seaborne assaults on Port Said and Port Fuad took place, reports, again based on military communiqués, told of 'unharassed landings' and of the whole operation resembling 'an exercise'. Any deaths that were reported were invariably attributed either to Nasser's intervention from Cairo to revoke the Port Said military commander's surrender or to the Egyptian soldiers' cowardice in having donned civilian dress.[61]

Once correspondents did start seeing for themselves what had happened at Port Said in their enforced absence, until censorship was lifted on 7 November all their reports were vetted by a Joint Press Censorship Unit in Cyprus. One journalist, James Cameron, gave a vivid account of the reporting restrictions that were imposed on those filing copy on events in Egypt back from Cyprus during this period:

> I believe I am allowed to speak for those of us who were denied the right to express such things as doubt, or bitterness, or shame, because of an ironclad censorship whose provisions included both military and political [word(s) missing], and whose major weapon was that it banned even the definition of its own existence.

Cameron went on to say that in Cyprus it was forbidden to make a statement 'likely to cause despondency' or to 'bring us into disrepute'. Correspondents were even forbidden to use the word 'war' in relation to events in Egypt.[62]

Reports that managed to survive this network of censorship and make their way back to Britain, usually at least two or three days late because of the poor communications set-up in Cyprus,[63] then faced another obstacle. On 1 November, the government issued its third D-Notice of the crisis. As with the previous two, the vast majority of the information which editors were requested not to publish was justifiable on the grounds of security. Yet again, however, the D-Notice included the banning of material which, under the peculiar circumstances of Suez, and the government's inability to command a clear consensus, was of a politically sensitive nature. Any news concerning casualties or casualty figures, for example, had to be 'referred to the appropriate Government Department', where considerable time was taken over its verification.[64]

Whether it was owing to a fear of contravening these D-Notice guidelines, or because journalists had been prevented from witnessing the fighting in the first place, the fact is that the first, isolated report challenging the official allied figure of one hundred Egyptians killed and wounded was not published until 9 November. On that date, Michael Butler in the *Manchester Guardian* estimated there were approximately a thousand Egyptian casualties, a figure which turned out far more accurate.[65] Given that hostilities only ceased on 6 November this period of three days does not appear to be that significant. On the other hand, had the British public known at the time the full consequences of its government's intervention (as was perfectly possible, give or take half a day), that is, when the crisis was at its height and many people were still undecided about the rights and wrongs of the issue, things might have turned out differently. Certainly the rather curious increase in public support for Eden's policy at this time, as evidenced by the opinion polls of 5–6 and 10–11 November, might not have materialized.[66] The fact that Britain was not even officially at war with Egypt throughout this whole episode made the government's use of the D-Notice system all the more questionable.

Finally, acting as overseer of these various strands of news control during and after MUSKETEER REVISE was the Ministry of Defence Public Relations Committee. Set up by Eden on 1 November and chaired by Walter Monckton, this committee comprised the public relations officers of all three services, together with representatives from the MoD and the Foreign, Colonial and Commonwealth Relations Offices. William Clark was also in attendance until his eventual resignation as the prime minister's press secretary on 6 November.[67] The committee had a wide remit, including the supervision of the news operation in Cyprus and the coordination of publicity arrangements with the French, but its most valuable role was as overall guide to the press on the home front, 'both on the factual detail of operational action and on the political interpretation of the campaign'. Throughout the first fortnight of November Monckton's committee met daily to discuss what titbits of information it should provide the media with. These were then disseminated via the various departmental press lobbies, usually in the form of easily digestible, newsworthy themes. With so little hard news coming back from the theatre of operations, especially in the first week, these themes inevitably formed the basis of most journalists' stories. As the crisis progressed beyond the military phase, the committee to some extent then compensated for the earlier confusion surrounding the publicized motives for intervention by providing a focal point for the government's propaganda policy as a whole.[68]

How this system operated can best be appreciated by a sampling of the committee's minutes. At its fifth meeting on 4 November, for example, it discussed how news of the imminent troop landings at Port Said should be handled. It was reported that Secretary-General Hammarskjöld had apparently told the United Nations General Assembly that the allies were about to bomb centres of population in Egypt. Furthermore, despite reports that Egyptian units were moving west away from the canal towards Cairo, the committee heard that it might still be necessary to fight for Port Said and Suez, with consequent heavy civilian casualties, prejudicing the allied case before the UN. Douglas Dodds-Parker, representing the Foreign Office, therefore stressed the need for the committee's briefings 'to play down the sensational and colourful reports after the landings'. By pre-empting potential problems in this manner the committee helped to save the government from the far worse press its intervention in reality deserved.[69]

On 7 November, the day after the ceasefire, the committee concluded that it should disseminate three main propaganda themes via the media. These were: firstly, that Nasser alone was responsible for the blockage of the Suez Canal which had occurred during the hostilities; secondly, that the allied decision to stop fighting the previous night was not in any way connected with the Soviet threats of retaliation transmitted on 6 November,[70] but was simply because the Israelis and Egyptians had themselves both agreed to an unconditional ceasefire; thirdly, that the Egyptian claims of heavy casualties inflicted by, and on, the allied forces were outright lies. By 9 November, the committee's attention had turned towards exploiting the allies' apparent discovery of large quantities of Soviet military equipment in Egypt, conclusive proof, it was argued, of Nasser's status as a Russian stooge.[71] There is ample evidence of the press taking up these themes, on both sides of the Suez divide.[72]

In his report written shortly after the Suez campaign, Lt General Stockwell complained bitterly of the lack of foresight shown in the creation and handling of the public relations service connected with the operation. He attributed the difficulties encountered at Port Said principally to the poor quality and lack of experience of officers selected for the Army PR Unit; the lack of suitable experience of some of the correspondents; the overloading of the PR Unit beyond the limit at which it was established; and the poor standard and efficiency of communications equipment. Whichever way the report is read, one is left with the overriding impression that in terms of military-media relations Suez was a disaster, and should never be repeated.[73]

For all this, MUSKETEER REVISE got a remarkably good press. There is no doubt that the Anglo-French forces did indeed go out of their way to keep Egyptian casualties to a minimum – it was, after all, a prerequisite of a credible police operation. However, from newspaper accounts of the operation the overall impression is that the military intervention resembled a bloodless training exercise. Without any firsthand accounts of the actual landings, papers were simply unable to present a genuine flavour of the fighting. The result was a sanitized non-war. Reports did eventually filter out questioning how successful REVISE had been and casting serious doubt on the official allied figures of Egyptian casualties, ultimately leading to an independent enquiry.[74] But these reports were in the main too late to have any real impact on the course of the crisis. There is no way of telling whether press and public opinion would have been different had the truth about the operation been known earlier. The real debate centred on the government's right to intervene in Egypt in the first place, and on this most newspapers and people had already made their minds up before the troops went in. Nevertheless, it should not be forgotten how serious the gulf was in British society at the height of Suez. Had it been common knowledge that as many as 1,500 Egyptian soldiers and civilians had been killed and wounded in the name of peacekeeping (fifteen times the figure released by the government),[75] public opinion might well have turned against rather than in favour of Eden's policy. To separate the military from the political factors incumbent on public opinion is difficult at the best of times; during such crises as Suez when the government's use of armed force lacks a clear national consensus it is virtually impossible.

By the second week of the crisis, therefore, the government had recovered from a shaky start and had undoubtedly controlled the war news very well; but it was by no means in the clear yet. Indeed, with the announcement of a premature ceasefire on 6 November, forced upon Eden primarily by the United States' use of economic sanctions,[76] in many ways the real test for the government had only just begun. Eden had staked everything, including his premiership, on a rapid military campaign that would leave the Anglo-French task force in control of the whole length of the Suez Canal. His government would then be seen to have fully achieved its declared objectives – of separating the combatants and protecting the vital waterway. Moreover, it would also be in a strong position both to undertake the job of unblocking the canal, the closure of which threatened the British economy and was therefore a sign of the government's failure, and to dictate its own terms of withdrawal. So heavy was the pressure of international opinion, however, particularly from Washington, that by the time Eden had been forced into calling a halt to MUSKETEER REVISE, the task force had seized only one third of the canal. Consequently, if Eden was to survive, he would somehow have to present this to the British people as a success and keep secret (or at least obscure) the extent of his, and Britain's, humiliation. The prime minister could not do this without at least some help from the press.[77]

First to the rescue came Iverach McDonald. On 6 November, after the cabinet had made what was, for it, the unenviable yet unavoidable decision to call a ceasefire that day, but before Parliament had been informed of this, McDonald was let into the secret by Harold Macmillan at the House of Commons. In the obvious hope that *The Times* would consequently shed as positive a light as possible on the government's 'defeat', the once 'hawkish' but now fast trimming chancellor levelled with McDonald. 'It was risky from the beginning – perhaps too risky.' Nevertheless, 'Eden had won approval for his endorsement of a UN police force in the area. And, after all, we had forced the UN to act. Without our move, the Israeli–Egyptian war would have spread through the Arab lands.'[78] To McDonald's ears, given what he knew of the government's tacit aims, not to mention collusion, this was of course complete nonsense. Despite this (or perhaps, more interestingly, because of it)[79] McDonald and *The Times* did what was asked of them. From 7 November onwards the paper produced a series of editorials calling for an end to the crisis and for Britain to return to normality. Its whole tenor was one of the need for patient reflection rather than a search for scapegoats. The government might have been 'misguided', but the priority was now for the country to 'pull together', draw strength from the torture it had experienced and congratulate itself on the healthiness of its democratic structures. In short, the British people should forgive and forget.[80]

Having Fleet Street's still most respectable voice urging reconciliation rather than recrimination during this volatile period can only have helped the government. However, of much greater importance than the line taken by *The Times* in the aftermath of the ceasefire was that adopted by the Conservative press. Were the *Telegraph*, *Mail*, *Sketch*, *Express* and *Sunday Times* all to have turned against the government, or, as was more likely, Eden alone, during this critical phase, the pressure from the public, Parliament and party for a change at Number 10 would probably have been irresistible.[81] The temptation for these papers to throw Sir Anthony to the lions, thereby assuaging their guilt and protecting the image of the party, was very real. After all, in the eyes of a number of these papers Eden had been a liability even before Suez erupted. Now he had not only failed miserably to topple Nasser but had also capitulated to the Americans. Lord Beaverbrook was probably voicing the opinion of his fellow press proprietors when he wrote to Brendan Bracken, the former minister of information and now part-owner of the *Financial Times*, on 13 November: 'I think that Eden was doing wonderfully well until he gave the order to ceasefire. At that moment he committed his country and himself to damnation.' A few weeks later, when the prime minister was in Jamaica sick and contemplating his political future, Beaverbrook declined to make the journey from his home in the Bahamas to meet him.[82]

Fortunately for Eden, what Michael Berry and Lords Kemsley, Rothermere and Beaverbrook might have said in private did not in this instance make its way into their papers. In the case of the latter two at least it appears that on this occasion they in fact deferred: Beaverbrook to his son,[83] Rothermere to the *Daily Mail*'s editor, A. G. Wareham. Rothermere felt that Eden's policy had been 'a catastrophe for the Tory Party'. However, Wareham, who had become a close contact of the prime minister's during Suez, and was for once sufficiently strong-willed to oppose his proprietor, felt that Eden deserved his paper's total support, and his opinion held sway.[84] Consequently, despite knowing that his policy was by this time shot full of holes, the Conservative press remained loyal to the prime minister. Patently relieved that Britain had not become embroiled in a drawn-out and unpopular conflict against Egyptian terrorism, the Tory papers rejoiced, claiming victory for themselves and vindication for the government. As far as they were concerned all of Eden's objectives had been achieved – the war between Israel and Egypt had been stopped, a larger conflict in the Middle East prevented, and new vigour put into the United Nations.[85]

If these papers ran out of ideas with which to defend the government's policy they could always turn for inspiration to the Ministry of Defence Public Relations Committee. During the second and third weeks of November, Monckton's committee worked feverishly behind the scenes producing stories designed to grab the headlines and legitimize Operation MUSKETEER REVISE. On 9 November, for example, the committee pushed the line that the wanton destruction of port facilities in Port Said, the blocking of the Suez Canal and the blowing up of the oil pipelines elsewhere in the Middle East were all part of a premeditated plan to deny oil to Western Europe. A week later, on 16 November, the committee was informed that Eden was concerned about reports gaining currency in the press that the allied forces would have reached the town of Suez, on the southern tip of the canal, within twenty-four hours but for the ceasefire (which was in fact not far from the truth).[86] It was therefore decided to counter these reports by an off-the-record statement to the effect that the commander-in-chief's own assessment was that it would have required another full week to capture the whole of the canal. The clear implication behind this briefing was that, contrary to rumours, the government had not betrayed the troops and in the process snatched defeat from the jaws of victory.[87] Both these stories found their way successfully onto the pages of the national press. Whilst not necessarily convincing readers, they at least helped to muddy the waters and instil in opponents of the government's intervention an element of doubt.

The one publicity theme pushed more heavily than any other by the MoD Public Relations Committee throughout this period, fully supported by the cabinet, was the allied discovery of Soviet arms in Egypt. On 9 November, the committee urged 'the maximum use of stories of Russian penetration in the Middle East', such as a report of a large party of Russians which had been caught trying to cross the frontier into the Sudan, and another of Russian officers captured by the Israelis in Sinai (neither of which was true). Three days later the committee's Foreign Office representative argued that great play should be made in the press of the on-the-spot reports from Egypt which showed that British intelligence estimates over the last two to three months for the flow of Russian arms into the Middle East were not only confirmed but exceeded.[88] The Foreign Office News Department also helped out by leaking to the press details of the various secret arms dumps which had been found by the Israelis in the Sinai. This had to be done carefully, however, lest officials strengthened further the charge of collusion.[89]

That a large quantity of Soviet military equipment was found in Egypt by the invading Anglo-French and Israeli forces is beyond doubt.[90] However, it had been common knowledge for months that Nasser was trading cotton for arms with the Soviet bloc; his deal struck with the Czechs in September 1955 for Russian fighters, bombers and tanks, along with Soviet military experts to train the Egyptian army, had been highly publicized. Moreover, there is no evidence to suggest that the British cabinet itself was at all surprised by this latest 'discovery'. For the government now to disseminate stories, therefore, claiming that its intervention had been designed not only to 'separate the combatants' but also to arrest the proliferation of Soviet arms (and ultimately communism) in the Middle East, having made no mention of this motive when the operation was first launched, was disingenuous to say the least. Nevertheless, the Tory papers lapped up these latest 'revelations' of a Russian plot to dominate the West's oil and exploited them for all they were worth in order to justify the government's use of force against Nasser. For days on end, articles with such titles as 'Eden Sees Through It', 'Nasser's Big Brother' and 'New Plots For Old' dominated the editorial pages of the majority of the national press.[91] Even readers of those papers opposed to the government's whole Egyptian venture could not fail to be influenced in some way by the sudden spate of 'official' reports which appeared in the news pages outlining the extent of Russia's influence in Egypt. So pleased was the Foreign Office with the results of this campaign at home that it sent details of the arms discoveries to its missions abroad for wider dissemination. 'The London press is devoting much attention to Soviet supplies of arms to the Middle East. For your information this is the result of information supplied by us', stated one guidance telegram.[92]

The one true revelation that would of course have completely demolished the government's case for intervention was its collusion with the Israelis. Looking back at the newspapers of November 1956, one is immediately struck by how much the press already knew of the tripartite conspiracy. A large part of the reason for this was French indiscretion. From the start of the crisis in July, the Mollet government's hardline policy had, in stark contrast to Eden's, enjoyed the virtually unanimous support of parliamentary and press opinion. French journalists and politicians vied with one another to compare Nasser to Hitler, and the 1956 situation with that of the late 1930s.[93] During the summer of 1956, the Foreign Office had managed in the main to impress on the Quai d'Orsay the importance of a moderate image based on limited, legitimate objectives.[94] What cooperation there had been on the propaganda front before the war, however, appears to have counted for little once the fighting started in late October. Constrained by Commonwealth ties, the 'special relationship' with the US, as well as domestic opinion and the UN, Eden went to war publicly in order to restore peace in the Middle East. Mollet, on the other hand, sought to topple Nasser and to help the Israelis and was under little pressure to disguise the fact. Despite repeated pleas from London, therefore, the French did little to hide the assistance they gave to Operation KADESH, the Israeli attack on Egypt. On 1 November, Ralph Murray, Keightley's political adviser, who was involved in directing the psychological warfare operations from Cyprus, cabled Ivone Kirkpatrick: 'As seen from here there is little if anything covert about French close and active support of Israel.' Amongst French misdemeanours, he cited the operation of French aircraft from Israeli airfields with allied force markings and the shelling of Rafah by the French cruiser *Georges Leygues* in direct support of the Israelis.[95] 'Actions of this sort, which cannot possibly remain secret, are extremely embarrassing', Eden complained to Mollet. 'Nothing could do more harm to our role as peacemakers than to be identified in this way with one of the two parties.'[96] A week later, on 8 November, Ambassador Gladwyn Jebb was instructed to ask the French premier whether it was wise that two French squadrons remained with the Israeli air force.[97]

The French government's comparative freedom from the restraints of domestic and international opinion threatened to play havoc with Eden's already flawed case for military intervention. However, the only newspapers willing to take up the issue of collusion seriously were those on the political left. These were papers which had already earned themselves a reputation of being dogmatically anti-Eden anyway. Consequently, their allegations were inevitably interpreted by many people as being guided by malice and self-interest rather than by any genuine search for the truth. The blanket of censorship was again also a significant factor. Israel had itself imposed a strict embargo on the reporting of military activities emanating from its shores throughout the first fortnight of November 1956. This prevented James Morris,

the *Manchester Guardian*'s source in Tel Aviv, for example, fro
reporting as early as 8 November that French fighter pilots had flow
in operational sorties with the Israeli air force against the Egyptians
(this appeared in the paper on 20 November). This delay before editors
and readers received such revealing information was, again, perhaps
crucial. Had newspapers been in the position, armed with such evidence, to raise the question of foreknowledge and collaboration at a
very early stage rather than a fortnight after the end of the war amidst
a growing mood of reconciliation, the government would certainly not
have found it as easy to brush such rumours under the carpet as it did
so effectively in late November.[98] The attempts by editors to sow
discord amongst government ranks by arguing that the charge of
collusion would ultimately be proven, and that the cabinet's policy
ought therefore to be repudiated, might also have been more successful
in these changed circumstances. The *Observer*'s David Astor even tried
this privately by canvassing (forlornly) what he saw as the youthful,
dissenting element within the Tory party, epitomized by the ambitious
minister of labour, Iain MacLeod.[99]

At least one newspaper, the *News Chronicle*, appears to have
considered collusion simply too hot to handle lest any allegations of
such an unsavoury nature it might make proved groundless and its
reputation suffered as a result. The paper did assert on 15 November
that the country 'had been seriously misled, from the start, on facts it
was entitled to know', but this was as far as it was prepared to go. The
whole theme of collusion was conspicuously absent from the *Chronicle*'s
news pages and editorials alike. A clue as to why comes from a letter
sent to Michael Curtis by Laurence Cadbury, senior proprietor, during
the immediate post-crisis period. In this, Cadbury warned his editor
against publishing a series of 'very explosive' Suez articles which
amounted to 'a damaging indictment on the Government' because this
was not the sort of thing that many purchasers of the *Chronicle* now
wanted to see:

> Many of our readers are no doubt still by no means indignant at the
> Government's Suez action. I doubt if very anti-Government articles are
> wise from the mundane but important circulation point of view. If we
> were a committed Labour Party paper, which we are not, it would be a
> different matter ... In my personal experience I have yet to find anyone
> who wants to see any washing of dirty linen at the present moment.[100]

This followed a jittery letter from Egbert Cadbury to Sir Walter
Layton, former editorial and business chief of the *News Chronicle*, on
16 November commenting on Curtis's inexperience and the need for
someone to keep an eye on him. Cadbury noted how senior personnel

in the *Chronicle*'s Manchester premises were 'very upset about our attitude over Suez and the hysterical way we had treated it. It has been most disheartening to see the *Daily Despatch* readers they have been at such pains to keep being literally thrown away.'[101]

A number of papers on the right did grant some coverage to the collusion issue, though only either flatly to dismiss the allegations or argue that if there was any collaboration it involved the French and Israelis alone.[102] Other than this, the subject was steered clear of altogether. As for the one paper that was in a position to completely expose the government, *The Times* did reproduce stories from American papers hinting at some degree of collusion, but then effectively poured cold water on these by making a pointed, yet specious, reference to the actual timing of the Anglo-French intervention in Egypt. Surely, it argued, if there been a conspiracy, the actual invasion of Port Said would have followed the bombings almost immediately rather than being delayed for six days, thereby allowing time for opposition to grow and the Egyptians to ready their defences.[103] In order to maintain this line William Haley was forced to suppress his own and Iverach McDonald's knowledge, as well as the strong evidence of collusion sent him by Alexander Rendel, the paper's diplomatic correspondent.[104]

As a consequence of this institutional silence on the part of more than half of the national press, all the government had to do was rigidly stick to its own story and wait for the minority charges to peter out. This was the low-key strategy agreed by the cabinet on 20 November, as the minutes reveal:

> Attention was drawn to the continuing speculation in certain sections of the press about the extent of the foreknowledge which the UK and French Governments had had of Israel's intention to attack Egypt. While there would be no question of acceding to requests for an independent enquiry on this point, the government might well be pressed to make some further statement on it. It was the general view of the Cabinet that the best course would be to repeat the assurances which had been given by the Foreign Secretary in the debate in the House of Commons on 31 October.

This was a reference to Selwyn Lloyd's earlier outright denial of collusion as British bombers went into action over Egypt.[105] By the end of November the worst of the storm had blown over. Thus it was that the Eden government managed, with more than a little help from its Fleet Street allies, to get away with one of the worst-kept secrets in modern British history.

With the failure to make the allegations of collusion stick, any meaningful or decisive role that the press might have had in the twilight of Suez had disappeared. All that was left was for the crisis to play itself out peacefully. By the time, therefore, that the government was forced to surrender to the United Nations for the second time in less than a month and withdraw its forces unconditionally from Egypt – announced by Selwyn Lloyd in the Commons on 3 December – the terms of the debate in Fleet Street had moved on. No paper explicitly saw this decision for what it was: proof of the moral bankruptcy of the government's whole Suez policy. Instead the opposition press widely regarded it as an opportunity, not to question the government's right to continue holding office, but to call a domestic political truce. Editorials entitled 'A Chance To Advance' and 'The Recovery of Britain' epitomized the mood of a press that only a fortnight earlier had been demanding a new government.[106] Paradoxically, the only papers now condemning the government were those on the right, though these hardly intended to bring about the Conservatives' downfall. Perhaps this is a measure of how successfully the press had been anaesthetized and the government had performed its damage-limitation exercise.

This success was at the same time not enough to save Eden himself. Because he had personalized the dispute with Nasser so heavily, the prime minister was the obvious choice for a scapegoat to many disgruntled Conservatives. His flight to the West Indies in late November on the grounds of illness then encouraged further charges of weakness, even cowardice.[107] It also allowed potential successors to strengthen their hands, particularly, in Macmillan's case, with the Americans, who themselves saw Eden as an obstacle to the restoration of cordial relations.[108] On returning from his Jamaican sojourn in mid-December, therefore, Eden had effectively already lost power. Several embarrassing experiences subsequently in the Commons served to confirm his lack of support. It was these, together with his continued ill-health, that persuaded him to resign, a decision that was announced on 9 January 1957.[109] Not surprisingly, few newspapers greeted this news with either shock or regret; their role in causing Eden's downfall was, however, marginal.[110]

7

The press: conclusion

Suez is often cited, if not directly then certainly by implication, as an illustration of the power and responsibility of the British press.[1] Despite the enormous moral and political pressure for it to toe the government line whilst the country was at war, the press had stuck bravely to the role assigned it by Macaulay in his definition of the fourth estate[2] and had faithfully reflected public opinion. Sir Anthony Eden had sought to deceive the British people on a scale rarely seen, but the press – so the argument goes – had fulfilled its duty as the 'watchdog of government', articulated the public's fundamental misgivings and revealed the truth. As a result, a government's policy lay in tatters and a prime minister was forced to resign. Suez was therefore not just a triumph for British democracy; it marked a watershed in relations between the executive and fourth estate. Thereafter, no government would give such scant regard to the nation's press (and its concomitant, public opinion) during times of crisis.

This study has shown how naive an interpretation of events that is. The first point to note is that at no stage during the entire five months of the crisis did the British press ever faithfully reflect what the British people were thinking. From July through to December 1956 the press was consistently more aggressive and pro-war than was public opinion. This was particularly the case during the first crucial days of the government's intervention in Egypt. At that stage, polls show that only a minority of those people asked actually agreed with Eden's use of force, whereas a clear majority of Britain's newspapers was in full support of it. Even when the war was at its peak and many people inevitably equated support for the government with loyalty to the troops, the percentage of people in favour of the government's policy was significantly lower than the proportion of national and provincial papers singing Eden's praises. All this makes a mockery of assertions that the press was on the whole more hostile to the government during Suez than was public opinion.[3] In fact, the very opposite was true.

That this curious discrepancy was due, at least in some measure, to government manipulation there is no doubt. Simply to say that those papers favouring military action throughout the crisis were natural Conservative party supporters (of which there was a majority in Fleet Street) and that therefore they would have backed Eden anyway is to miss the point. For a start, it is not so much a case of whether these papers supported Eden, but how. When Eden heard the news of Nasser's coup he quickly realized that it would not be possible to use force for quite some time, and that therefore to build up a war psychology too early would prove counter-productive. Consequently, the Tory papers' patience with, and confidence in, Eden's apparently prudent policy during August was of great benefit to the government. Indeed, had the original MUSKETEER plan (scheduled for early September) not been cancelled owing to complications of a mainly diplomatic nature, this measured approach might well have paid rich dividends. Paradoxically, were it not for ministers having confided in these papers, telling either their editors or their proprietors of the prime minister's determination not just to reverse Nasser's act but to oust him, at least some of these papers might not have been so consistently aggressive and personally hostile to the Egyptian president. They might in fact have lost their enthusiasm for the fight much earlier, leaving Eden high and dry.

Thirdly, to argue that these papers simply backed the government is highly misleading. If all these papers did was to agree openly with any given ministerial statement on Suez then this would have been entirely valid and further clarified their position *vis-à-vis* the government. But they did much more than this. Having been secretly informed of the hidden meaning behind such statements, the Beaverbrook, Rothermere and Kemsley press (together with the *Telegraph* and *The Times*) proceeded to do the government's bidding for it, thus enabling the government to seem moderate and presenting the papers themselves as independent sources of judgement. Fourthly, and finally, it is a well-known fact that many people in Britain (as elsewhere) have no idea that most of their national papers, including the one they buy, tend to favour one or other of the major political parties. Thus, the majority of papers supporting the government during Suez might well be classed as 'Conservative', but a great many of their readers would not necessarily have known that. Even if they did, they would certainly not have been aware of how intimate, almost seamless, was the relationship between their paper and certain ministers during the crisis. Given how large a proportion of the national daily readership these newspapers represented, their potential impact in terms of increasing sympathy for Eden's cause should not be underestimated.

Even if we leave aside the question of how much control the government exerted on the Tory press during Suez, and whether this alone accounts for the newspaper–poll discrepancy, there is still plenty of evidence to show how successfully ministers used the press to their advantage. By briefing the appropriate lobbies, for example, the government managed to conduct a war of nerves against a foreign leader on a scale rarely seen and across the whole press spectrum, without itself having to come out into the open. The sense of tension created by extensive leaking at key stages of the crisis was almost tangible. Nasser did not succumb to this pressure, but a lesser man in different circumstances might well have done. At the same time, by subjecting the press to the self-constraints of the 'voluntary' D-Notice system the government helped keep military information of a highly sensitive political nature from the public. Thirdly, by the exploitation of so-called Fleet Street friends, Eden succeeded in enlisting the support of certain newspapers whose allegiance he otherwise could not have expected and the value of which was therefore doubled. The assiduous courting of Iverach McDonald and *The Times* stands out in this respect. Finally, by a deft combination of conventional censorship and new-style guidance, during MUSKETEER REVISE itself the government succeeded in limiting reporters to doing little more than public relations for the Anglo-French forces, thus sanitizing the press's coverage of the war and contributing to the validity of Eden's whole policy. As one American newspaper editor put it during World War Two: 'The final political decision rests with the people. And so that they may make their minds the people must be given the facts, even in wartime, or perhaps especially in wartime.'[4]

That Eden, however, failed abjectly throughout the crisis to control a number of other newspapers in the manner he would have wished there is equally no doubt. The damage which papers like the *Manchester Guardian*, *Observer*, *Daily Mirror* and *Daily Herald* inflicted on the government's claim of acting in the national and free world's interest was considerable. Many of those people inevitably confused by the government's motives for intervention latched onto the hostility generated by this section of the press, finding in their editorials a clear and strong articulation of their serious misgivings. Politicians opposed to the government's disdain for the United Nations and to the eventual use of military force against that body's specific wishes readily used these papers to support their own criticisms. Foreign governments set against a military solution to the crisis exploited the absence of British national unity, graphically illustrated by the deep cleavage in the press. This created particular difficulties for Eden in discussions with John Foster Dulles (who, as Part Three will show, continually questioned the prime minister on the thorny issue of British public opinion), and is attested to by the prime minister's own desperate efforts to stop the BBC's Overseas Service carrying its customary reviews of the British press, parts of which were naturally less than complimentary to the government.[5]

Whether all this press criticism played any direct part in the failure of the government's policy is nevertheless extremely debatable. There is not one piece of evidence to show that the Egypt Committee had to make any major decision affecting the course of the crisis based, even in some small part, on what the press had said or might say. Even the decision to call a premature and humiliating halt to MUSKETEER REVISE, often cited as the prime example of a government having buckled under the unprecedented hostility of press and public opinion, can now be attributed, almost for certain, to factors of a completely external nature. As to Eden's resignation in January 1957, any theories that this was caused in any way by the newspapers' continual harassment of a man they considered a virtual criminal are pure fantasy. This was a straightforward palace coup, with a little meddling by the US administration thrown in. As we have seen, the press on the whole eased up on its search for the truth behind the collusion rumours and its criticism of the government, including Eden, very soon after the end of hostilities. The Conservative party might have come to regard Eden as a liability, but this had very little to do with the press branding him a liar. If anything, so intent on reconciliation were the majority of British papers, one could in fact say that the press helped pave the way for Eden's continuation as prime minister.

Suez is therefore as much an illustration of the innate weakness of the British press, its structure and *modus operandi*, as it is a celebration of its in-built strength. By using the well-established system of un-attributable news dissemination heavily loaded in favour of the pro-vider; by capitalizing on the unhealthy intimacy between the press and government in Britain; and by exploiting the British press's over-willingness to censor itself, supported by an arsenal of powerful legal weapons, Anthony Eden's attempts to fashion the press to his liking proved to be remarkably successful for someone who throughout the crisis failed to develop any real public relations strategy and who was in many ways a complete amateur in the realm of press manipulation. Indeed, had Eden not been so peculiarly innocent and his chief ministers so lacking in journalistic contacts one cannot escape the impression that the newspapers would have proved even more malleable. This is hardly the mark of a free and independent press, of which Suez is supposed to make us so proud.

PART TWO

The BBC

8

Collision course

In contrast with its manipulation of the press, the government's attempt to control, some say even take over, the BBC during Suez has long been a matter of controversy, not least because the BBC itself has consistently set so much store by it. Indeed, if Suez is said to rank as a success story for the British press, to the BBC the episode represents nothing less than 'a triumph'[1] and proof of the corporation's independence. In 1972, as part of the celebrations to mark the BBC's fiftieth birthday, the then director-general, Charles Curran, went out of his way to evoke memories of the crisis:

> In 1956 the BBC had to face pressures stronger than any which had threatened its editorial independence in the thirty years since the General Strike ... The pressure on the External Services, broadcasting to the world, including the area of conflict, was particularly severe ... Against formidable arguments about the national interest, the duty to provide an impartial service was held by the BBC to be paramount, and the pressures were successfully resisted.[2]

With a mass of evidence to support Curran's assertion, both from the BBC and from historians,[3] Suez has become a central reference point for those inside and outside the BBC with faith in the institution's attachment to truth and objectivity.

Part Two of this book sets out to reassess the relationship between the government and the BBC during the Suez crisis by placing it within the wider context of Eden's propaganda policy. In doing so, it looks at the issue as much from the government's side as from the side of the BBC, and is supported by an unprecedented analysis of the corporation's news and current affairs output. Its contention is that, like the press, the BBC had a number of weaknesses in its system of operation and organizational structure which the Eden government could, and did, turn to its advantage. Consequently, the BBC's cherished reputation for having successfully withstood the challenge from Whitehall and proved its value as 'a great national asset'[4] is in many ways invalid. Again, as with the press, ministers were able to use a combination of direct and indirect manipulative techniques, designed to turn the BBC into a straight organ of propaganda. These ranged from close and informal contacts with the corporation's senior personnel, through to the planting of a Foreign Office liaison officer at Bush House; and from the imposition of pro-government speakers, through to parliamentary manoeuvres designed to clip the BBC's wings. Eden's aim throughout was to impose on the BBC his belief that the nation's interest was synonymous with that of the government.

Owing to the priority ministers attached to winning the hearts and minds of British public opinion during Suez, attention will focus on the government's efforts to manipulate the BBC's Domestic, as opposed to Overseas, Services. To separate the BBC's two roles entirely, however, would be both artificial and misleading. For one thing, whilst the Domestic Services were financed out of licence-fee income and the Overseas Services by grants-in-aid, even the government itself was not always clear about the handling of these different budgetary modes. Any threat of cuts in financial support consequently had potential implications for both services.[5] Periodic reference will therefore be made to the considerable pressures exerted on the Overseas Services, especially when these rebounded directly onto the home front. Finally, because television played such an important role in informing the public during Suez – indeed, the crisis arguably ranks as the medium's first big test in Britain[6] – account must also be taken of the government's attempts to control Independent Television (ITV), which had started broadcasting in September 1955.

Before looking at events during Suez, however, it is first necessary to examine the nature of the relationship between the government and the BBC prior to July 1956. This serves to highlight two factors which were to be of paramount importance during the Suez crisis itself: firstly, the substantial scope that Whitehall already had for controlling political broadcasting (much of which remains today); and secondly, despite this, ministers' intense distrust of the broadcasting authorities. In fact, so convinced of the BBC's radicalism was Eden, evidence suggests that the two were on collision course even before Nasser's nationalization coup transformed the political scene and heightened each of their roles.

The 1950s witnessed significant developments in British broadcasting, particularly in the coverage of current affairs and political issues. These were for the most part linked to the growth of television, a service closed down by the BBC during World War Two but by 1956 available to 95 per cent of the UK population.[7] Nineteen fifty-one, for example, saw the first ever television party election broadcast, made by Lord Samuel for the Liberals; three years later, television cameras were allowed into the party conference halls for the first time, starting with the Conservatives in Blackpool. To complement this wider coverage of politics, broadcasters slowly began to inject greater depth and analysis into their programmes. *Panorama*, relaunched by the BBC's Television Talks Department in September 1955, signalled an attempt by the corporation to cover news and current affairs in a more robust, less deferential fashion than had hitherto been the case. *Tonight*, which started two years later, continued this process.[8] Independent Television News (ITN), which went on the air also in September 1955, adopted an even more questioning approach towards politics and politicians. As the decade progressed its 'newscasters', men who would help write the news themselves and thus became authoritative figures in their own right, set new investigative standards by probing politicians as never before.[9]

Notwithstanding these changes, broadcasting remained wedded to the state, with the politicians, and the government especially, holding the strongest hand. To provide for its independence the BBC had been established under Royal Charter, but that same charter gave the government formal powers of veto and the authority to revoke the corporation's licence. The fact that the government also appointed the BBC's Board of Governors and, as already mentioned, controlled the annual licence fee, created opportunities for further interference. The BBC and the Independent Television Authority (ITA), like the press, were subject to the Official Secrets Act and the D-Notice system.

Added to this, both authorities actively restricted themselves by obeying the so-called Fourteen Day Rule, invented by the BBC itself in 1944 to escape pressure from politicians seeking to use the airwaves to comment on current legislation. The 'fortnight gag', as it became known, forbade the discussion on radio and television of issues while they were being debated in Parliament, and for two weeks before parliamentary debates.[10] This propensity to channel politics through the parties was reaffirmed after the war when, following lengthy negotiations, in 1947 the BBC, government and opposition drew up an '*Aide-Mémoire* on Political Broadcasting'. This document, which would come under intense scrutiny during the Suez crisis, both formalized the Fourteen Day Rule and established the ground rules concerning the resumption of controversial political broadcasts. Politicians were given access to radio primarily via ministerial and party political broadcasts. Whereas the latter allowed for controversy, the former were obliged to be purely factual and to be used for national appeals, say for fuel economy. In the unlikely event that the opposition considered a ministerial broadcast to have infringed the rules, provision was made for it to take the matter up with the chief whips. If this resulted in dead-lock, it was then left to the BBC Board of Governors to 'exercise its judgement'. Over and above these limited broadcasts on major policy, the BBC was free to invite MPs to take part in controversial broadcasts of a round-table character, so long as different sides were represented.[11] 'It is clear from this story', writes Asa Briggs,

> that it was the BBC and not the political parties which sterilised political broadcasting at the end of the war, doubtless fearing that if it were to seek to become a more active influence there would be so many pitfalls ahead that the independence of the BBC, secured with difficulty during the war, would be in danger.[12]

The end result was that by the mid-1950s coverage of current affairs and political issues was considerable but 'not very systematic and very little of it was topical'.[13]

When Suez erupted, Eden had only been in Number 10 a little over a year. Yet within that relatively short space of time, his ad-ministration had succeeded in shifting the balance of power between the government and the broadcasting authorities even further in the former's favour. In February 1955, the panellists on radio's *In the News* used the ban on their discussion of the hydrogen bomb because of an upcoming parliamentary debate as an opportunity to launch an open assault on the Fourteen Day Rule. This sparked off a joint BBC and press campaign to remove what many called an undemocratic 'lunatic restriction', culminating with the BBC informing the govern-ment on 14 July that it would no longer consider the rule as binding.[14] The corporation's roar soon turned into a whimper, however. On 27 July, the new postmaster-general, Charles Hill, supported significantly behind the scenes by Sir Alexander Cadogan, the chairman of the BBC's Board of Governors,[15] converted what hitherto had been a typically English gentlemen's agreement into actual law. The corpora-tion's campaign summarily collapsed amidst allegations of timidity.[16] The government's ability to suppress coverage of potentially sensitive issues was therefore strengthened.

This was followed in the spring of 1956 by an agreement between the political parties and broadcasting authorities opening the way for ministerial broadcasts on television. As was the case with such broad-casts on radio, it was stated that the opposition could seek a right of reply if it considered the subject matter in the least bit controversial. Whether such a request was granted, however, depended on the in-terpretation of the rules laid down in the 1947 *aide-mémoire* and the definition of 'controversy'. This had proved to be problematic on numerous occasions over the years,[17] and accounted for the strong resistance which Hugh Gaitskell, the newly installed leader of the Labour party, offered in early 1956 to the idea of extending ministerial broadcasting facilities. Gaitskell argued that the impact of television was so great that the effect of ministerial broadcasts could never be entirely without party advantage and that a 'build up' for the minister would ensue. Moreover, even if the opposition was consistently granted a right of reply this could still hardly be described as a fair system. The fact that the Opposition could only reply and therefore not initiate discussion of any given issue via either broadcasting medium meant that the procedure was inherently weighted in favour of government and entitled it alone to set the political agenda.[18] Gaitskell eventually succumbed to the pressure from both senior ministers and the BBC in April, on condition that the procedure for television ministerial broadcasts be reviewed in 1957. At the same time, he pushed strongly for the revision of the *aide-mémoire*.[19]

Behind the new prime minister's actions lay an enthusiasm for the medium of television which mirrored his predecessor's penchant for radio. Eden had been one of the first politicians to recognize the potential power of the medium as well as to have the confidence to put himself at the mercy of the cameras. (In contrast, Churchill never gave a television interview and dismissed TV as a 'peepshow'.)[20] In 1951, the then shadow foreign secretary had been the star of the Conservatives' first and only television election broadcast.[21] Four years later, during the general election of May 1955, Eden attached great importance to television as a medium. He also set the pattern for future election campaigns by speaking directly to the voters in a live, fifteen-minute television solo, later described as a '*tour de force*' by the psephologist David Butler.[22] In a confidential letter sent to Number 10 on the eve of election day, Mark Chapman-Walker, the chief publicity officer at Tory Central Office, waxed lyrical in his admiration for Eden's 'courage in encouraging us to use the new medium with risk and pioneering spirit'. He ended, 'Many thanks from all of us concerned for your imaginative leadership.'[23]

Having personally played such a key role in the first, mouldbreaking television election in Britain, and emerged triumphant with an increased majority, Eden was determined to exploit to its utmost what he saw as 'his' medium by turning TV into a fully fledged tool of government. This thought process was confirmed two months later when, at the Geneva summit of July 1955, Eden compared himself unfavourably with Eisenhower and the French prime minister, Edgar Faure, both of whom made regular nationwide broadcasts on their respective television networks. According to William Clark, afterwards

'Eden discussed with me about setting up the same kind of thing in Britain. He wanted to use television as a new instrument, a new weapon for national unity and purpose.'[24] With approximately 35 per cent of the adult population in Britain already with TV sets, and commercial television about to be launched in September, this was perhaps only natural.[25] Moreover, it is also likely that Eden initially regarded television as the potential antidote for what he perceived as an acutely critical press.

However, mixed in with Eden's fondness for television was a deep suspicion amongst the major members of his government, including the prime minister himself, of the nation's broadcasting authorities. If their reinforcement of the restrictive Fourteen Day Rule was not by itself sufficient evidence of this, then subsequent actions and effusions surely were. In December 1955, Eden instructed Tory Central Office to give an account of what steps were being taken to keep a check on radio and television current affairs programmes. He expressed particular concern with ITA broadcasts and wanted them carefully monitored for evidence of what he detected as anti-government bias. At the same time, in order to counter the Labour party's increasingly skilful use of television for propaganda purposes, Eden actively encouraged the studio training of Tory MPs. Courses were held at Central Office to familiarize MPs and other notable party members with the type of broadcasting techniques that the BBC and programme companies now required.[26]

A few months later, in May 1956, Douglas Dodds-Parker, parliamentary under-secretary at the Foreign Office, chose the showing of a television film on the visit to Britain of the Soviet leaders as the occasion on which to vent his spleen on the BBC:

> I consider this a disgraceful occurrence in an organisation as big as the BBC. It *cannot* be just the result of Harman Grisewood [Chief Assistant to the Director-General, whom Dodds-Parker trusted] being away for a few days. Many people, far beyond the confines of the Tory Party, believe that there are sinister, extreme left influences in the BBC, who since the war have slanted news, etc. against HMG's long term interests. Ever since I returned to the FO at Christmas 1955, there have been several inaccurate items of news about the Middle East which I refuse to accept as merely chance occurrences. It is high time that one or two patriots were put into these key positions.[27]

Such dark threats were in fact aimed more at the BBC's External, rather than Domestic, Services at this point. Indeed, it might be fair to say that, as far as the External Services were concerned, by the summer of 1956 the BBC had lost the confidence of the government almost completely. Over the years ministers had grown increasingly impatient with what was seen as the BBC's refusal to reorganize its foreign broadcasting operations to take into account changing national priorities. (The BBC, for its part, consistently blamed the government for irrational economies.)[28] Relations then turned sour in 1955–56 owing primarily to events in the Middle East, where it was felt by ministers that the BBC's long-established Arabic Service was doing little to counter the powerful impact of Cairo Radio. The corporation's strict adherence to impartiality was described by one official as 'a fetish'; Eden himself pushed forcefully for the siting of broadcasting stations in Iraq and Aden to compete with Nasser's 'Voice of the Arabs'.[29] Consequently, in the spring of 1956, Foreign Office information officials drew up radical proposals to reshape the BBC's External Services and to make its output in the Middle East in particular more vigorous.[30] In early July the cabinet set up a committee chaired by Dodds-Parker to consider the whole issue of overseas broadcasting.[31] That same week, the foreign secretary, Selwyn Lloyd, had 'a frank discussion' on overseas broadcasting with Sir Ian Jacob, the BBC's director-general. Lloyd criticized the BBC for being 'too respectable' and urged the corporation to be 'more aggressive' in certain instances.[32]

Meanwhile, in June 1956, only a month before the Suez crisis broke, Frederick Bishop, head of the Number 10 Private Office, informed Charles Hill that Eden was 'concerned to notice that the BBC have added yet another socialist commentator (Aidan Crawley) to their staff. They seem to be leaning rather too much in that direction in recent appointments.' The postmaster-general concurred, offering his own theory on such appointments, and with it a useful insight into the government's distinctly jaundiced attitude towards the BBC, particularly in the newly dawning television era:

In the twenty odd years that I have known the Corporation [Hill had been the BBC's avuncular Radio Doctor during World War Two] there has always been a tendency for it to lean to the Left. There is something about big bureaucracies that acts as a magnet to the pinkish planner ... This sort of thing mattered less when the BBC was more cautious about controversy, when it was limited to sound and when the main vehicle was the ten or fifteen minute talk. Today, with the advent of TV, with the greater captivity of the viewer, with the growing appetite for 'snappier' controversy and, most important of all, with the arrival of the commentator as distinct from the talker, the bias to the Left is of much greater moment. Add to this that the main BBC commentators now are Francis Williams, Aidan Crawley, Christopher Mayhew and Woodrow Wyatt, and the gloomy story is up to date.[33]

A week later, having acted on the prime minister's 'concerns', Hill again wrote to Eden, this time relaying the essence of a discussion he had had with Alexander Cadogan and Ian Jacob on the increasingly problematic subject of the corporation's political impartiality (or lack of it). Hill and Jacob had clearly clashed on the question of the government's right to scrutinize the BBC's objectivity:

> I detect, through the insistence of Jacob rather than Cadogan, a deter-mination to keep Parliament off the Corporation's 'sacred ground'. The BBC Governors are wise and sensible men, he argues, and the main-tenance of impartiality is their responsibility and not that of Ministers. If allegations are made, let the Governors and them alone deal with the matter. Parliament, after all, is rather a nuisance and the Governors know better. [34]

So seriously was the government treating the matter of broadcasting impartiality by the summer of 1956 that on 5 July the issue was raised in cabinet, in conjunction with a debate on the government's overall machinery of presentation.[35] If this alone was not enough to highlight the ominously poor relations between the government and broadcasters on the eve of Suez, a week later we see William Clark having con-siderable difficulty in convincing the prime minister that the BBC and ITA were not part of a 'conspiracy' to oust him.[36]

It could of course be argued that all of this was not unique, or even new. After all, since 1922 every government, of whatever political persuasion, has at some point during its period of office accused the broadcasting authorities of bias. Furthermore, it must be said that since the advent in September 1955 of Independent Television News, with its robust style of political coverage, broadcasters did appear to ministers to be developing more dangerously aggressive traits (if only because hitherto they had proved positively supine). However, the fact that the government's complaints against the broadcasters seemed to be reaching a climax in the summer of 1956 did not bode at all well for BBC–ministerial relations during Suez. Despite having had con-siderable success in rewriting the rules governing political broadcasting very much to his own advantage, Eden himself was clearly displaying the sort of near paranoia that was already the hallmark of his relations with the press. Talk of 'pinkish planners', media 'conspiracies' and the government's right to define impartiality gave more than a hint as to the sort of tactics ministers might employ against any errant broad-casters during a period of national crisis.

Moreover, given that the broadcasting authorities themselves had been made increasingly aware of the power of their positions, it was by no means guaranteed that these ministerial machinations would not work. During his very first meeting with the BBC's Director-General following his appointment as Eden's press secretary in September 1955, it had immediately dawned on William Clark the extent to which the corporation was reliant on government goodwill and consequently how limited its avowed independence was. On that occasion Jacob inundated Clark with requests, including guidance on how to handle the current press speculation surrounding the engagement of Princess Margaret, and, perhaps more significantly, that the newly established Independent Television Authority not be given parity with the BBC. This latter point reflected the BBC's fear that the recent birth of commercial television would lead to the corporation rapidly losing its position as the main instrument of broadcasting.[37] These requests do not, by themselves, rank as proof of the BBC's subservience to government. Nevertheless, they do illustrate the potential leverage which ministers had even without recourse to the extraordinary powers at their disposal during a crisis. More ominously, perhaps, they also showed how the BBC instinctively looked to the government for advice on matters deemed to be of national interest. In this regard the corporation bore an unhealthy resemblance to the Westminster press lobbies.

9

'Are they enemies or just socialists?'

Given the importance which Eden clearly attached to the use of broad-casting for political purposes, combined with the deep distrust he felt for the broadcasting authorities, one is immediately struck by the length of time it took him to go on the air after Nasser had nationalized the Suez Canal Company. Here was a situation tailor-made for the prime minister's famous charm and diplomatic assuredness. On the one hand, the government needed to conduct an anti-Nasser propaganda campaign; on the other, the British people cried out for guidance. What could be better than to meet both of these requirements by Eden himself making a direct, controlled, yet impassioned appeal to the nation? This was exactly what Churchill had done to such great effect during World War Two; only now his successor had the additional advantage of television.

Quite why it took Eden until the end of the second week of the Suez crisis to appear on television, having only recently fought so tenaciously for this right, is unclear. This could of course be attributed to the lack of time owing to the sheer weight of other work the prime minister was inevitably suffering under during this phase (though the amount of thought and effort that went into courting the press during this period would appear to discount this). On the other hand, we could take Eden's word for it when he claimed that at this juncture 'public opinion in our country held steadier than appeared from press reports', and that therefore there was no need for him to appear before the microphone or cameras.[1] Either way, to infer from Eden's silence that the government left the BBC entirely to its own devices at the start of the crisis, and that the corporation was therefore able to formulate its editorial policy in the autonomous manner decreed by its Charter, would be a mistake. Owing to a combination of pure chance and the closed nature of the British establishment, the BBC found itself inextricably part of the crisis from the very outset.

Amongst the dignitaries at the ill-fated dinner at Number 10 on the night of 26 July 1956, during which news of the nationalization of the Suez Canal Company broke, was the BBC's director-general himself. (Jacob had that day been involved in the entertainment of the young guest of honour, King Faisal of Iraq, who had expressed a desire to see the facilities of the BBC Arabic Service.)[2] It is not known whether Eden said anything specifically to Jacob, an old wartime colleague,[3] at this juncture. However, the director-general's own reaction to Nasser's coup cannot fail to have been influenced, if only in the short term, by hearing at first hand the prime minister's and others' swift condemnation of the Egyptian ruler. He may not, as Eden would later claim of those present, have 'understood at once how much would depend upon the resolution with which the act of defiance was met'.[4] Nevertheless, his being so close to the centre of events can only have served to increase Jacob's determination to direct the BBC as 'responsibly' as possible throughout the crisis ahead.

Also intimately involved in the crisis within hours of its outbreak was Sir Alexander Cadogan, chairman of the BBC's Board of Governors. Cadogan had been Eden's permanent under-secretary at the Foreign Office during the war and was now a government-appointed director of the Suez Canal Company. Telephoned later that night by Guy Millard, the prime minister's private secretary, he volunteered to come to Downing Street immediately (despite 'being in my pajamas').[5] The result was that even before dawn broke on the first morning of what would develop into the most serious crisis to have hit Britain since World War Two and arguably the biggest test yet of the BBC's independence, the institution's two top figures, both of whom could determine editorial policy to a remarkable degree, were deeply caught up in events. Whilst this by no means assured the government of their, and the corporation's, support for war, there was no escaping the fact that the BBC's objectivity and impartiality was already compromised. There was certainly no doubting Cadogan's own reaction to Nasser's act, as his diary entry for 30 July testifies:

> Evening papers carried a statement by Anthony, including a declaration that we could not accept a solution by which the Canal is left in the control of a single power. That is a good formula, and I only hope we are decided to take all measures necessary to ensure it![6]

A few days later, on 31 July, we come across the first evidence of William Clark seeking to cast his spell on the broadcasters via the same sort of confidential briefings he was then affording the press. Clark saw both Sir Ian Jacob and Geoffrey Cox, an old friend and one-time co-TV presenter, now editor of ITN, to give them a preview of the Suez situation 'so as to try and ensure sensible coverage'. He also stressed the need for them to keep an eye on disclosing military information of value to 'the enemy'.[7] Clark made a point of seeing them both again in the early days of August, but on this occasion he was significantly more upbeat and forthcoming. With Eden's 2 August parliamentary announcement of the necessity for 'certain precautionary measures of a military nature' ringing in their ears, according to Cox:

> William came straight to the point. The government meant business. The partial mobilisation was not a bluff. Whatever happened in the weeks ahead, it was important to bear in mind the government was not going to let Nasser get away with seizing the Canal.
>
> Clark made it clear he had taken the decision to tell me this entirely on his own initiative. It was not a statement I could use, or attribute, in any way to him. It was intended only as guidance in a situation which was likely to get confused in the weeks ahead. 'However different things may seem from time to time, as events unfold, I think you will find that this is what the policy turns out to be.'[8]

This was a clear example of the press secretary exploiting his position to use the broadcasting medium to wage his master's war of nerves on Nasser. As Cox goes on to admit, there was certainly no hint of ITN blindly following the government line as the crisis assumed a new and more formidable shape, friendly press secretary and all. However, until this point in the crisis he had thought that Eden was bluffing and that if Nasser failed to back down then ultimately the prime minister would be willing to meet him halfway. Clark's secret guidance radically altered this viewpoint, and with it the situation. It now appeared that unless the Egyptian regime adhered to the Anglo–French demands and agreed to internationalize the Suez Canal Britain would be at war. Cox therefore calculated that the only course to take in these circumstances was to make plain to Cairo the utter seriousness of the British government's protests. Such an approach would, it was hoped, help to break down Nasser's resistance to negotiations and thereby make a peaceful settlement more likely. Accordingly, both ITN and BBC news bulletins in early to mid-August put a sudden and increased emphasis on official statements that stressed the need for a tough line with the Egyptians.[9]

Getting television and radio to help frighten Nasser was one thing. However, as was the case with the press during this period, it was also essential to persuade the broadcasters to play down the extent to which the government was actually arming for war. Nothing could do Eden's firm yet conciliatory image more damage than to have television cameras intruding into the size and purpose of the task force gathering in the Mediterranean.

Unfortunately for Eden, the government started off its attempt to control the BBC's dissemination of military information by effectively shooting itself in the foot. When the subject was first raised in a meeting of the Egypt Committee, including military chiefs, on 2 August there was a clear disagreement between Mountbatten, First Sea Lord, and Boyle, chief of air staff, on the one hand, and Eden and Templer, chief of the imperial general staff, on the other. 'We should say as little as possible', stated the prime minister. The problem was that William Clark, following an earlier informal agreement with Mountbatten and Antony Head, secretary of state for war, had already released some of the more obvious information which, according to the press secretary, 'the public could see with its own eyes'. Whether this information, which included such items as the preparation of a landing strip in the Mediterranean, really was as anodyne as Clark claimed is open to debate. The point is that the prime minister, for one, certainly did not think so. Consequently, when the information appeared that evening on radio's Nine O'Clock News Eden 'blew his top' and got Guy Millard (again) to ring the BBC. This, however, only resulted in what Clark describes as 'a very sharp rebuff from Sir I.J.'. Not surprisingly, the BBC did not take kindly to being chastised by a government which had its own publicity wires crossed.[10]

In its first clash with the government since Suez had erupted, therefore, the BBC had scored a victory, but this would quickly prove to be pyrrhic. The corporation's disclosure of material which Eden interpreted as politically embarrassing galvanized the Egypt Committee into immediate retaliatory action. Thus on 3 August, whilst Eden and Monckton induced Fleet Street's editors to suppress coverage of the military manoeuvres at Number 10, next door Macmillan and Salisbury saw Ian Jacob to 'put him in the picture' also. Unfortunately, exactly what transpired at this meeting remains a mystery, as, again, no record of it exists. Despite this, in the light of Salisbury's verbal assault on Michael Berry only three days earlier and the chancellor's own un-rivalled bellicosity throughout this phase,[11] the director-general must have been put under great pressure to see things from the government's point of view. That Jacob had been military assistant secretary to the cabinet during World War Two, and was therefore close to both Eden and Macmillan, increased the scope for emotional blackmail.[12] It was following this meeting, on 4 August, that the Services, Press and Broadcasting Committee issued its first D-Notice. The BBC (and the ITA) complied with this, as well as with the second, delivered on 15 August.[13] Britain's 'independent' broadcasting medium had thus subjected itself to the same reporting restrictions on Operation MUSKET-EER as had the press.

It is necessary at this juncture to examine in greater detail what impact the government's efforts to influence broadcasting during the first stage of Suez actually had on the BBC's output. The first point in this regard is that, MUSKETEER preparations aside, the BBC's news bulletins had on the whole been admirably straight and impartial from the moment the corporation had broken the news of Nasser's act to an unsuspecting British public at II o'clock on the night of 26 July. Nevertheless, considering how very brief and strictly informational these bulletins were in the 1950s – compared with the 'news' programmes of today, which carry a great deal more comment – one could argue that it would have difficult for them to have played it in any other fashion.[14] The most reliable way therefore of discovering whether the BBC had really been true to its principles is to examine its current affairs programmes. And it was here that we see unmistakable signs of a pro-government bias.

The two programmes which dealt directly with the subject within the first twenty-four hours of Nasser's coup – *Highlight* on television and *At Home and Abroad* on the radio – both added significant weight to the government's assertion that the Egyptian president had indeed acted illegally and that 'sanctions' were therefore justified. Commenting in the latter programme on the wider implications of Nasser's 'expropriation of the Canal' (note, not just the Company), Sir Thomas Rapp, former head of the British Middle East Office in Cairo, went even further:

> It is a melancholy reflection that the Anglo-Egyptian Treaty of 1954, under which we agreed to evacuate our troops from the Canal Zone, was calculated to make possible – in the words of Sir Anthony Eden – 'a new pattern of friendship between ourselves and Egypt.' Britain has loyally carried out her part of the bargain and has held out in many ways the hand of friendship, but in my judgement there is no appeasement possible of revolutionary dictatorship. For its pretensions are unlimited. The latest arbitrary decisions of the Egyptian Government now make far-reaching decisions inevitable.[15]

To some extent Rapp's line of thought, which set the tone for the BBC's commentaries in late July,[16] was to be expected, given the overall shocked state of public and parliamentary opinion during the first heady days of the crisis. It is therefore during the second phase of Suez, after the initial jingoistic knee-jerk reaction had begun to die down, that the corporation's output begins to look even more suspect. By early August, as an analysis of the press shows, a serious split was already beginning to emerge in Britain over the government's right to use force. However, little if anything of this important cleavage was

LIVERPOOL JOHN MOORES UNIVERSITY
LEARNING SERVICES

reflected in the BBC's commentaries during this period. Owing in part to the Fourteen Day Rule, Suez was dealt with in an extremely cautious, not to say insipid, manner. *Radio Link*, *From Our Own Correspondent*, *At Home and Abroad* and *Highlight* all concentrated on the foreign and, to a great extent, peripheral aspects of the crisis. Even *Panorama*, BBC Television's investigative flagship, was reduced to skirting round the fundamental issues involved. Its highly respected 'anchor-man', Richard Dimbleby, relied instead upon 'eliciting a few facts', as he put it.[17] Little wonder that Michael Peacock, who worked on the production side of the programme, would later claim that *Panorama* covered Suez 'with a degree of neutrality which denied the proper function of journalism'.[18] The net effect of the BBC's prudence was to hide from its licence-payers the growing domestic upheaval surrounding Eden's policy and, by its unequivocally anti-Nasser stance, to give the impression that the corporation supported the government. Certainly, whenever the BBC did stray from the non-committal, its tendency to favour the Egypt Committee's interpretation of events and motives was very noticeable.[19]

All this suggests that at least part of the reason why Eden chose not to make a personal broadcast as early in the Suez crisis as one might have expected was indeed because he had no need to. However, this perhaps had rather less to do with the 'steadiness of public opinion', as he implied in his memoirs, and more to do with the fact that public opinion's single most influential informer was, at least during this early period of Suez, doing the government's bidding without his help anyway (give or take the occasional phone call and confidential briefing). This did not mean of course that the prime minister had crossed the Rubicon and actually now trusted the BBC. He was as prone as ever to wild anti-BBC outbursts. On 7 August, for example, he rang up William Clark to complain at the corporation's failure that night to swallow another item of guidance, this time from the Foreign Office News Department concerning the invitations to the London Conference. 'Are they enemies or just socialists?' he demanded to know. The point is, however, that Eden's anger in this instance, as had also been the case when he 'blew his top' on 2 August, could be attributed more to a muddled publicity policy than to a bravely recalcitrant BBC.[20] The mere fact that there was so very little evidence of Eden criticizing the corporation during this period, certainly compared with the press, was perhaps a measure of how impartially the institution hitherto had acted.

The BBC itself might not have given Eden many sleepless nights during early August, but the perceived shift in domestic public opinion, away from support for the use of force, certainly did. Clearly, something had to be done, and quickly, to arrest this slide, which threatened to leave the government in the potentially fatal position of having condemned Nasser as a second Hitler and amassed an invasion fleet itching to have a crack at the 'gyppos', and then being forced ignominiously to stand it down owing to taxpayers' opposition.[21] Whilst William Clark and Sir George Young got to work on the press, therefore, Eden decided that it was time for him to try and cut through the various lines of argument and put his case directly to the nation on his favourite medium, television.

Having given his press secretary 'a royal rocket' for suggesting, over the 4–6 August Bank Holiday weekend, that he should wait until events were more developed and let Selwyn Lloyd do a sound broadcast first,[22] Eden was immediately presented with a prime-time spot by the BBC for the evening of 7 August. This was then rescheduled for the night after – contrary to BBC practice – so that it could also be relayed by ITV. Eden was adamant that what was to be only the second ministerial broadcast on television should make the biggest impact possible. It was also to be broadcast simultaneously by domestic radio and on short wave by the General Overseas Service, as well as being relayed by all four radio networks in the US, in all dominions and in many colonies.[23]

The prime minister prepared assiduously for his appearance before the cameras, assisted by a group of expert advisers including Robert Allan, his parliamentary private secretary, Norman Brook, the cabinet secretary, and George Christ, the former political correspondent of the *Daily Telegraph*, now employed by Conservative Central Office. These sat around Eden's bed, according to William Clark, 'like a TV panel'.[24] The result was a speech, delivered live from a tiny studio at Lime Grove, which perfectly encapsulated the style and technique of the government's anti-Nasser propaganda campaign that summer. All of Eden's favourite themes were included: how the canal, which many of those watching and listening had fought to defend 'in one or other of the Great Wars', was almost a part of Britain; how the government's quarrel was not with the Egyptian people, still less with the Arab world, but with Colonel Nasser alone; how Nasser's pattern of lies and deceit evoked foreboding memories of fascism and could therefore not be appeased – 'With dictators you always have to pay a higher price later on, for the appetite grows with feeding'; how the government's military moves were entirely precautionary; and, last but not least, despite the government not seeking a solution by force, how the dispute amounted to 'a matter of life and death to us all'.[25]

Eden was on the whole pleased with his performance, especially when he learned that the domestic audience alone for the broadcast topped fifteen million and that the opposition, despite invitations from both the BBC and ITV, did not wish to reply. Gaitskell preferred to withhold any statement until after the forthcoming London Conference.[26] Eden's confidence was given a further boost by reports on how well his speech had been received abroad. Gladwyn Jebb wrote from Paris: 'Everybody thought it first class.'[27] Yet, all was not entirely well with the prime minister. After the broadcast, Eden railed against 'those Communists at the BBC' who he felt were shining the studio lights in his eyes. This, he argued, forced him to wear his glasses, thus tarnishing his forceful image. Clarissa Eden, who even before Suez had grown increasingly over-protective towards her husband and tended to feed his suspicions of the media, angrily complained to William Clark that Sir Anthony's eyes 'were made up like an early Charlie Chaplin'. She concluded, 'I consider it a scandal that the Prime Minister, wanting to give an important message to the nation, should be so hampered by a handful of inefficient and conceited amateurs.'[28] This resentment was a foretaste of things to come.

Earlier in August, Sir Robert Menzies, the Australian prime minister and one of Eden's oldest and most trusted political colleagues, had arrived in London to lend his assistance. Eden was immensely grateful to Menzies for this and genuinely seems to have taken much strength from his presence: 'at this sharp testing time for myself, it was good to be able to sit down and assess the situation with Mr Menzies. We had been through this kind of thing before [a reference to their membership of the Churchill war cabinet].'[29] After first reassuring himself that he and Menzies saw eye to eye on how to deal with Nasser, Eden then persuaded the Australian leader that it would be in both their interests if he were to conduct a broadcast on the BBC publicly reaffirming the Commonwealth's wholehearted support for the British government's policy.[30] With large elements of domestic and international opinion still open to persuasion in the run-up to the London Conference, Eden hoped that such a broadcast would help tip the balance in his favour. This led to the most serious clash yet between the government and the BBC during Suez; Eden himself later cryptically referred to it as merely 'a strange interlude'.[31]

The BBC had invited Menzies to make a broadcast in June 1956, during the London Commonwealth Prime Ministers' Conference. Despite being turned down on that occasion, the corporation repeated the invitation when Menzies returned to the country in August. Thus, on 8 August the BBC offered Menzies a slot on the radio on Tuesday, 14 August – two days before the London Conference was due to open. Soon after issuing this, however, the BBC learned, much to its consternation, that Selwyn Lloyd wanted to make a sound ministerial broadcast on the same day. Clearly, if two broadcasts, both pro-government, were allowed to go ahead in such close succession the BBC's political balance would inevitably be called into question. The issue therefore became a test of the corporation's objectivity.[32]

Two days later, on the morning of 10 August, William Clark telephoned the BBC to say that the prime minister, obviously encouraged by his own recent appearance before the cameras, would now like Menzies to appear on television rather than radio, on either the Monday or Tuesday (13 or 14 August). At this, John Green, controller of Talks (Sound), who was deputizing for the hospitalized Harman Grisewood as the BBC's liaison with the political parties, argued that two official or quasi-official broadcasts in two days would 'be out of place'; Clark therefore agreed, quite amicably, to find the Australian a platform elsewhere. Later that day, however, Hugh Dash, Menzies' own press secretary, telephoned to ask how he should request the television appearance on Monday suggested by Eden. Green stood his ground, replying that a Commonwealth premier could not ask the BBC to break programmes for a quasi-ministerial broadcast as could a member of the British cabinet. Such a move would be 'both a precedent and an act of emphasis'. Green and other senior BBC officials were in fact becoming increasingly concerned about the corporation's one-sided coverage of Suez. Any broadcast by Menzies would, they believed, only exacerbate this pro-government bias.[33]

This was by no means the end of the matter, however. That same evening William Clark re-entered the fray, telephoning Green to warn him, 'off the record', that Eden himself would be making a personal request for Menzies to appear on TV on 13 August and that Green ought to inform either the director-general or chairman of this.[34] When this threat failed to do the trick, Clark decided to approach the BBC from a different angle and so contacted Grace Wyndham-Goldie, acting head of Television Talks. For this the press secretary also switched to using his very best scaremongering tactics. Eden, he said, was extremely angry and had found the corporation's refusal to offer a broadcast to Menzies quite intolerable. In fact, according to Wyndham-Goldie's memoirs, 'Clark was afraid that in his anger the Prime Minister might take some drastic action which would be permanently harmful to the BBC.' This was not actually true but it had its desired effect on Wyndham-Goldie, who professed to being 'dumbfounded'. She could not understand her seniors' attitude to Menzies: 'in view of his position in the Commonwealth and the active part he was playing in the Suez negotiations anything he could say would surely be a contribution to public information.'[35]

By now livid with what he regarded as the BBC's arrant disloyalty,

Eden decided to pull rank. Sir Alexander Cadogan's diary entry for 10
August makes it clear what happened next:

> After dinner, an excited Anthony on the telephone, saying that Menzies
> wanted to broadcast on Suez on Monday but he had been refused by
> Norman Bottomley [acting Director-General]. This really nonsense, so I
> rang up Ian in Suffolk and said we really must comply with Menzies'
> request at this time, no matter what our traditions and inhibitions might
> be. He rang me up later to say that all was arranged.[36]

And apparently it was. Green was rung up the next morning and
bluntly told that the Australian premier would after all appear on
television in *Highlight* the following Monday evening.[37] This went
ahead accordingly, with Menzies berating those 'beset with intellectual
doubts' about the government's right to use force and making a com-
pelling case for the illegality and immorality of Nasser's act.[38] 'Many
congratulations. Absolutely first class', was Eden's telegrammed reply.[39]

The fact that a foreign politician had been allowed to do a quasi-
ministerial broadcast on the BBC was not the real issue here; rather, it
was the BBC's independence and the role it was playing during the
Suez crisis. When it came to conduct its own post-mortem on this
little episode five years later, the BBC was adamant that it had committed no wrong. 'The pressure exercised by 10 Downing Street was
not instrumental in forming the Corporation's decision', it concluded.[40]
This clearly was not the case. Had it not been for Cadogan's personal
intervention on Eden's behalf, there is little doubt that Menzies would
not have got on the air at such an opportune time for the government.
On his return from hospital soon afterwards, Harman Grisewood was,
for one, extremely unhappy at what had happened and what the
burgeoning close relationship between Cadogan and Eden during the
crisis signalled. If Eden insisted on communicating directly with anyone
at the BBC it should have been the director-general or his assistant.
'What worried me about this – I heard about it both in Broadcasting
House and at Number Ten – was not so much the contact itself, as the
danger that the Chairman would misunderstand his role and the Prime
Minister would encourage him to assume more of an executive responsibility than was practical or constitutionally proper.' Grisewood
knew how 'devoted' Cadogan was to Eden.[41]

Allowing Downing Street to meddle with the already complicated
rules governing ministerial broadcasts, and in the process favouring
the government's cause, was bad enough. However, this was no isolated
example of the BBC's pusillanimity. In the midst of the Menzies
debacle, the BBC's Television Talks Department conceived the idea of
sending one of its senior commentators to Cairo to interview Nasser.

Such a move, it was judged, would be both a bold journalistic scoop and would help to put the other side of the Suez story, something which many inside the corporation felt the BBC was failing to do. However, instead of going straight ahead with this, as the BBC had the perfect right, if not duty, to do as a provider of public information, Grace Wyndham-Goldie asked John Green first to sound out official circles to find out their reaction to the proposal. As was now the custom, Green immediately got in touch with William Clark, who, after consultation, said that the prime minister thought the project 'unwise' because the BBC would be 'laying itself open to criticism from strong forces in the Commons who would almost certainly argue that the Corporation was thwarting the national interest by giving Nasser a platform'. Considering the lengths to which Eden had already gone in seeking to muzzle the BBC it was more than a touch ironic to hear him now depict himself as a champion of the institution's interests. Nevertheless, the ploy worked. Green reported all this back to Wyndham-Goldie, who, despite having earlier strongly supported the Menzies broadcast on the basis of its 'contribution to public information', thereupon decided to abandon the whole idea. Perhaps the best chance of initiating a genuinely open discussion of the reasons behind the nationalization of the Suez Canal Company thus went by the wayside.[42]

Meanwhile, the BBC was beginning to come under fire for its slanted coverage of Suez. On 10 August, Cadogan received a letter from Reginald Sorenson, MP, chairman of the National Peace Council, who complained that 'in its treatment of the present Suez crisis the Corporation has fallen short of its own high standards'. Sorenson went on to point out in detail where the failures lay:

The points of view of the British, French and US Governments have been adequately developed over the wireless, but – apart from a short mention in last night's programme – nothing has been said in the talks and discussions of how the world East of Suez has responded, of the response of the Arab world itself, or even of the reasons which caused Colonel Nasser to make his recent move. Nor, perhaps we should add, has there been mention of the very varied opinion within this country which has been voiced, for example, in the correspondence columns of *The Times* and the *Manchester Guardian* … we are anxious that the picture of world opinion available to the listening public here should be comprehensive, not selective, and that against the background thus provided, there should be a serious discussion in which the points of view of this country, of Egypt (and perhaps other countries East of Suez) should be put with equal responsibility and feeling.[43]

Cadogan's response, written with the assistance of Norman Bottomley, was disingenuous in the extreme. Rather than answering Sorenson's criticisms directly, the chairman argued instead that the BBC had thought it right in the pre-conference period to confine itself to 'factual expositions and background information, save when it fulfilled its constitutional duty to accede to requests from the Government to give time for Ministerial broadcasts'.[44] However, this had plainly not been the case. The BBC had consistently strayed from the 'factual', and consistently in the government's favour. And yet even if it had not done this, there still remained the question of whether it was right for the BBC not to comment. To keep quiet about the serious rift in opinion that by now existed at home in the run-up to the London Conference, presumably in order to increase the pressure on Nasser and with it the chances of his coming to the negotiating table, merely played into Eden's hands. In circumstances verging on war it was surely the BBC's responsibility to discuss all the issues as fully as possible and not have its agenda dictated by Whitehall.

Neither could the corporation blame its 'selectivity' on the inhibitions of the Fourteen Day Rule. Parliament had gone into recess on 2 August, after which the law's restrictions on the coverage of Suez no longer applied. It was certainly true when Cadogan claimed that throughout this period the opposition had been free to seek a right of reply to any of the government's ministerial broadcasts. However, the fact that Hugh Gaitskell had, for the time being, drawn back from appearing on the BBC was no excuse for the corporation's failure to achieve something akin to a balance in its current affairs coverage of the crisis. Still less was this, as Cadogan's letter implied, evidence of the Labour party's satisfaction with the way the BBC was handling the crisis and therefore a clear vindication of the corporation's editorial policy so far. The opposition's complaints about the one-sided picture of the dispute being presented on the broadcasting media were mounting.[45]

In spite of Cadogan's repudiation of criticism, the growing element within the BBC asking questions was not to be denied. At a Board of Management meeting on 13 August, Lindsay Wellington, the director of Sound Broadcasting (DSB), called attention 'to the need to reflect in Home Sound Broadcasting the conflicting views about British policy which had begun to be voiced'. Coverage had so far been 'mainly informational' and 'a round-up of opinion would now be valuable'. The board therefore agreed that, subject to Selwyn Lloyd's sound broadcast planned for the 14th, Wellington should arrange for a discussion to be mounted the day after.[46] Quite why it was felt necessary to delay still further this round-up programme, which was obviously already long overdue, and make it conditional on another government ministerial, is unclear. Be that as it may, when the foreign secretary had appeared on the radio the next night, taking the opportunity to make yet another call to arms, this time delivered in arguably the most apocalyptic fashion yet,[47] the BBC broke its regular Light Programme service the night after and at long last made a positive contribution to the Suez debate now raging in Britain.

Given Eden's ever-increasing distrust of the BBC – despite the support it had hitherto lent his cause – it is probably fair to say that even if this programme had been slanted almost entirely in the government's favour he would still have found fault with it. After all, if there was one thing that had come out of the crisis so far it was that the prime minister's definition of impartiality and of the national interest differed markedly from that of many of his countrymen. This helps to explain why Eden at one point on the evening of 15 August considered trying to ban the programme outright, only to be dissuaded by William Clark.[48] In the event, the twenty-five-minute programme, *Special Survey of the Suez Crisis*, was well-balanced. However, by including a minute's contribution by Major Salah Salem, Nasser's former minister of national guidance, and a hate figure within the Foreign Office and popular press,[49] it opened up the whole question of the BBC's independence during the crisis.

It was Eden himself who contacted the BBC immediately after the broadcast, again via Sir Alexander Cadogan. The letter he then sent Cadogan on 16 August was typical of the tactics the government used to manipulate not only the BBC but the media as a whole throughout Suez. He started off by accusing the corporation, quite wrongly, of misrepresentation:

My Dear Alec, since we spoke on the telephone last night about Major Salem's broadcast, I have had several reports of the programme in which he spoke. All of these reports have been critical, and I have heard that the programme gave a deplorably misleading picture of British opinion as uncertain and hesitant.

This was accompanied by the customary reference to the institution's burden of 'responsibility':

Of course the Government have no intention of interfering with the freedom of the BBC to try to reflect, as well as educate, public opinion in this country. But I hope that the Governors will bear in mind the very heavy responsibility which rests on the BBC at this crucial time when an international conference is meeting in London. Many people will judge the strength and determination of Britain by what they hear on the BBC.

Then came the obligatory disclaimer and the curious implication that all of this amounted to nothing more than simple 'advice':

> I do not need to tell you how grave the present crisis is for this country and the whole of the western world. This is not a Prime Minister's representation but a personal comment which I thought you should have in view of our talk about this programme last night.[50]

Eden then ordered an inquiry into the broadcast, led by Alan Lennox-Boyd. The colonial secretary was more than happy to act as troubleshooter – along with a number of other ministers, including Harold Macmillan, he was even angrier than the prime minister with the BBC.[51] As a result, these enquiries soon had the makings of a full-scale investigation into how the government might control broadcasting. Having consulted the Tory Party chairman and the chief whip, who had themselves already grilled the BBC, in a letter to Eden Lennox-Boyd expressed anger and frustration at the corporation's behaviour:

> The BBC told the Chief Whip that they put on the broadcast as a matter of policy because they felt that up to now only the Government point of view had been put across. It was time, they claimed, that they should give expression to another point of view which was widely held in the country. Whatever the merits of this argument it seems to me inexcusable that it should be put across in a way which virtually monopolised what they claimed to be a balanced survey. As to Major Salem's recording, I think it an outrage that a body widely believed to be in part at least associated with the British Government should broadcast at such a moment a speech by a notorious enemy. It does not seem to be in any particular person's responsibility to draw our attention in time to proposals of this kind – or any procedure whereby consideration is given as to whether or not an attempt should be made to stop a particular broadcast.[52]

Watching events unfold, William Clark was struck with 'the extent to which the BBC was regarded as completely under government control'.[53]

Cadogan's reply to Eden arrived at Number 10 the next morning, Friday, 17 August. According to his diary editor, Cadogan had not been fazed in the slightest by Eden's outburst. He simply 'viewed the business of Major Salem less seriously than did the Prime Minister'.[54] However, this is only half the story. True, in his letter the chairman did refer to the issue as a mere 'triviality' but he also wholly misinterpreted Eden's warnings. Whereas Cadogan felt 'it is a few people round him who always stir him up about the BBC',[55] implying that Eden was in fact an innocent party in this attempt to lean on the corporation, records show that the prime minister was far from being a mere puppet, controlled by the arch anti-BBC zealots in Whitehall. His distrust of the BBC – and of the media as a whole, for that matter – was in reality both deep and highly irrational. As to the upshot of Cadogan's reply, this was far from the firm rebuff of BBC mythology. On the contrary, it suggests that the chairman had once more overstepped his constitutional position to help out his former chief. Thus, whilst Cadogan made it clear to Eden that he simply could not agree with 'your friends'' criticism of the Salem broadcast, he then added:

> I spoke yesterday to Norman Bottomley, who is in charge until Ian Jacob returns. He has warned all his people to be especially careful while the Conference is sitting, and, apart from straight news, they will not stage any programmes of this sort.[56]

Even this significant measure of compliance, however, did little to quell Eden's mounting fury with an institution he now regarded as little short of treacherous. William Clark was sent for that morning to 'hear more anger against the BBC'. Eden was under the false impression that the Salem broadcast had been deliberately designed to balance the government's three ministerial broadcasts. 'The result at PM's level is passion and determination to teach them a lesson.'[57] Consequently, Sir Ian Jacob was called back from his Suffolk holiday, told by Eden personally of the BBC's duty to 'educate' the nation as to the 'seriousness of the situation', and warned of the possible need for a Foreign Office official to be attached permanently to the BBC as in World War Two – for 'liaison' purposes. Eden even raised with the director-general the idea of appointing a senior minister as general overseer of broadcasting.[58] In the meantime, in order to get the best out of the broadcasters during the immediate period ahead and ensure that no mistakes akin to the Salem broadcast recurred, the prime minister agreed with the line advocated by the postmaster-general. The conclusion Charles Hill had reached was that, rather than complaining about how little formal control they could exert over the BBC and ITA, ministers ought to exploit more fully the potential that already existed for 'informal control', either in the form of an extension of prior consultation or via more high-level contact between government spokesmen and the heads of the two broadcasting organizations. This would serve to 'put the latter "in the picture" and by doing so influence their treatment of current affairs matters of national importance'.[59]

To what extent Sir Ian Jacob was rocked by Eden's thinly veiled threats we cannot be sure.[60] However, given the aggressive campaign simultaneously being mounted on the BBC's External Services by the Foreign Office, few in the higher echelons of the BBC can have had doubts about the precarious position the corporation was in by the

time of the London Conference. Whitehall seemed determined to
secure a larger measure of control over the contents of the BBC's
overseas broadcasts, particularly to the Middle East.[61] Significantly, on
the day of his meeting with Eden, Jacob had acceded to a request from
the Foreign Office that the BBC be represented on a special advisory
committee, chaired by Douglas Dodds-Parker, designed 'to achieve
closer coordination between those departments most directly concerned
with the Suez Canal question'. This helped tie the BBC more firmly
into the government's overseas propaganda machinery.[62] The question
now appeared to be whether the government would go to the same
lengths to control the BBC's Domestic Services. Judging by the tone
of a letter Eden despatched to Churchill during the London Conference this was a distinct possibility:

> The BBC is exasperating me by leaning over backwards to be what they
> call neutral and to present both sides of the case, by which I suppose
> they mean our country's and the Dancing Major's. However, I am seeing
> Jacob this afternoon. He and nearly all the seniors have been away on
> leave. I hope we can improve on past performances.[63]

10

Division and disunity

At this stage, most accounts of the relationship between the government and the BBC during Suez move straight on to deal with the controversial events surrounding the outbreak of hostilities in the Middle East in late October 1956. The implication is that between the London Conference and the issuing of his ultimatums to Egypt and Israel a full two months later, Eden lost interest in trying to use the BBC as a vehicle for his propaganda campaign on the home front. Explanations for this abrupt change of mind on the prime minister's part vary, from the argument that the more the government lost the initiative in the diplomatic field the less point it saw in bothering to compete in the sphere of publicity, to the theory that Eden was simply forced to give up in the face of the BBC's continued intransigence and stubborn attachment to its independence. Neither of these in reality holds much water. There certainly is a case for saying that the government was more concerned with the BBC's Overseas, especially Arabic, Service during this phase of the crisis. However, to suggest that as a consequence Eden left the Domestic Services to their own devices, thereby allowing the BBC to recover its composure and reflect more coolly on where it should stand, would be incorrect. This period of diplomatic and political drift witnessed yet further attacks on British broadcasters' freedom of manoeuvre, and its analysis is therefore vital if we are fully to understand the state of play between the government and the BBC when war eventually did arrive.

Even before the Lancaster House conference ended on 23 August, Eden had confirmed the importance he attached to the continued use of broadcasting during Suez by asking the BBC for permanent broadcasting facilities to be installed in Number 10. This meant that by the time that the prime minister next chose to appear on the air – at the height of the crisis in early November – he was able to do so live from Downing Street (where, presumably, he could control the lights himself).[1]

A week later, on 28 August, Ian Jacob met another wartime colleague, the permanent under-secretary at the Foreign Office, Ivone
Kirkpatrick. Their discussion marked a new low in the already poor
relations between Whitehall and BBC. Although the main thrust of
Kirkpatrick's message was to impress upon the director-general how
'preoccupied' ministers were 'with the state of the Overseas Service',
the generally threatening nature of the interview was clearly designed
to influence BBC output as a whole. 'There were two powerful schools
of thought,' Kirkpatrick told Jacob, 'one of which was disposed to
favour governmental control in the Overseas Service and the other, the
curtailment of the £5 million grant in aid to the BBC and its expenditure on other propaganda enterprises.' According to Kirkpatrick's
own account of this episode, which he related to Jack Rennie of the
Information Research Department whose job it was to compile a list
of complaints against the Overseas Service,[2] Jacob gave as good as he
got. 'He denied that the Home Service was lowering its standards and
claimed that the Overseas Service was doing its job. He defied any
impartial inquiry to come to any other conclusion.' Whether the
director-general's subsequent actions were as brave as his words is,
however, debatable. Kirkpatrick also noted, with cruel relish, how Jacob
'looked stricken like a mother about to be deprived of her child'.[3]

That same day, the 28th, Jacob was also on the receiving end of a
copy of a circular sent from Number 10 and entitled 'Broadcasts by
Ministers', which purported to describe the procedures that Eden now
wished ministers to follow in making ministerial broadcasts. Unfortunately, no trace of either this copy or the original circular can be
found in cabinet or BBC records, and it is impossible to state its
contents exactly. However, judging from a report on the whole subject
of ministerial broadcasts written by Harman Grisewood in the immediate aftermath of Suez, it would appear that Eden was seeking at
this point to rewrite the terms of the 1947 *aide-mémoire* on political
broadcasting. The BBC itself had for years been unhappy with the
system agreed in the *aide-mémoire*, believing that the definition of what
constituted a ministerial broadcast was too vague and consequently
open to exploitation by government.[4] Nevertheless, one look at Eden's
own scheme for the system's revision told the corporation that this
was far from being the solution to the problem. The prime minister
appeared to be both questioning the very need for a formal agreement
between the BBC and the parties on the matter, and threatening the
opposition's right to reply.[5] What was interpreted as a clumsy attempt
to turn the BBC into the government's lap-dog during Suez was too
much for Jacob. His letter to Norman Brook at the Cabinet Office on
30 August, referring to the circular, makes this abundantly clear:

I am not sure what is intended by the words 'general broadcasting policy'. There was never any guidance in the past, nor do I believe that we require any ... I don't imagine there was any idea that the government would take it upon themselves to regulate the output of the BBC at this time more than any other.[6]

The BBC might have successfully fought off this attempt to alter radically the system of ministerial broadcasts in favour of the government, but the dispute over this most intractable of issues had only just begun.

On 4 September, Alfred Robens, Labour's senior spokesman on foreign affairs, was interviewed by Richard Goold-Adams in *At Home and Abroad*. According to the BBC's own account, this took place as a result of direct intervention from the corporation itself, 'since no Opposition view had yet been expressed in broadcasting except in news bulletins'.[7] Was the BBC, six weeks into the crisis, at last beginning to do something positive about the deficiencies in its Suez coverage? Possibly, but the Labour party had its own ideas. By mid-September Gaitskell had decided that the time for him to appear on the air had arrived. On the morning of 13 September, therefore, Labour's chief whip, Herbert Bowden, informed Harman Grisewood that Gaitskell now wished to take up the BBC's offer of a month ago, and preferred his broadcast to be in the Television Service, possibly in the form of a *Press Conference*.[8] This request served to strain still further the terms of the *aide-mémoire* and consequently heaped even greater pressure on the BBC.

It is a mark of how nervous the BBC had become since the start of the Suez crisis – of how frightened it was to tread on the government's toes – that the Labour leader's decision caused the corporation any distress whatsoever. Gaitskell was not asking for permission to make a formal, direct appeal to the nation in the manner in which Eden, Lloyd and Menzies had in August. He was instead willing to take part in a regular BBC television programme in which questions would be put to, and, most importantly, criticisms made of, him by leading journalists. As already noted, there was clear and incontrovertible provision for such a request within the *aide-mémoire*.[9]

Paralysed by indecision, Ian Jacob sought the advice of the BBC's Board of Governors, which was holding its regular fortnightly meeting on 13 September. At this meeting the director-general, setting off immediately on the wrong foot, said that in his view the Labour party's request could not be regarded in any sense as a response to the BBC's August invitation. 'The situation had changed considerably since then: there had been the London Conference, the Menzies Committee, and the recall of the House. Moreover, the Parties were now more than ever sharply divided on this issue.' The matter was further complicated by the knowledge that Downing Street was expected at any moment to make its own request for another television ministerial broadcast, which 'could hardly fail to be controversial'. As far as Jacob was concerned, the BBC was therefore faced with three choices: either to accept the government's request for a ministerial broadcast and grant the opposition the right to reply; to proclaim that all broadcasts on this subject must be of a party political nature (thereby allowing for any amount of controversy); or, to take the initiative in inviting both a leading member of the government and opposition to appear in a *Press Conference* type of programme. 'This was an unusual situation for the BBC,' he concluded, 'because for the first time for many years there was a foreign policy issue of great gravity on which there was a sharp division on party lines.'[10]

If the director-general showed signs of painful hesitation, so too did the Board of Governors. Instead of divorcing itself from outside pressures, as was its responsibility, and interpreting Gaitskell's request as coming entirely within the bounds of ordinary, informal political broadcasts, the board wavered and decided that the best course would be for Jacob and Cadogan to meet both the government and the opposition to discuss the problem. This took place the next day, with the Lord Privy Seal, R. A. Butler, and Gaitskell attending.[11] The upshot was that the Labour leader did after all appear in *Press Conference*, on 21 September, but was followed three days later by Selwyn Lloyd's interview on *Panorama*. Sandwiched between (on 22 September) was a sound broadcast on Suez given by Alan Lennox-Boyd, defined by the BBC as strictly party political.[12] This meant that since the start of the crisis the opposition had made a total of two broadcasts – ministerial or otherwise – compared with the government's five.

In his account of this episode, the BBC's official historian, Asa Briggs, argues the case that the corporation had no alternative to seeking advice from the politicians. The fault lay not in the BBC's weak editorial policy but in the inadequacy of the *aide-mémoire*. 'The Board was thus being steadily driven into a difficult political position in which existing machinery would not work.' As proof of this Briggs goes on to cite Jacob, who, in his own post-mortem on Suez, wrote that 'the procedures which govern political broadcasting were designed for domestic controversy of the kind that normally accompanies political life; a national emergency when Government action was not nationally supported presented a new problem.'[13]

There is, it must be said, some truth in this. Having evolved in a piecemeal fashion over the years, the rules governing political broadcasting were complex and could be interpreted in many different ways.

The BBC's misjudgement of Gaitskell's entreaty was therefore to some extent understandable. However, what both Briggs and Jacob fail to mention is that the board's guiding principle throughout this episode was not, as it should have been, to make its coverage of Suez as objective and as full as possible. It was instead, as the board's minutes state, 'that the BBC should do nothing to underline the existence of party division and disunity at a time of crisis'.[14] This was a complete misreading of the BBC's constitutional role. The corporation was not supposed to be in the business in hiding anything. Surely, with, as Jacob himself admitted, British politics now more than ever divided on Suez, it was all the more important to tell the British people the full truth. To make Britain appear more united behind Eden than it actually was both increased the psychological pressure on Nasser and strengthened the government's mandate for force.

There is one final, and important, point to be made about this matter. In managing to forge an agreement between itself, the government and the opposition on the awkward question of Gaitskell's request, the Board of Governors naturally felt that it had gone some way towards both solving the seemingly intractable problem of ministerial broadcasts and setting relations between the BBC and the politicians during the present crisis on a new and less volatile footing.[15] In reality, the opposite turned out to be the case. In the panic to extricate itself from this 'unusual situation', the BBC had, without realizing it, made an agreement which further confused rather than clarified the rules of political broadcasting. According to the BBC's director of Spoken Word in his investigation into this affair in the immediate aftermath of Suez, the corporation had for the first time explicitly accepted that both the government and the opposition could 'in times of crisis' make ministerial broadcasts of a 'politically controversial nature'. 'As I see it,' Grisewood lamented, 'this really breaks the *aide-mémoire* definition wide open.'[16]

The result was that instead of affirming its attachment to longstanding principles, as it should have done during a time of crisis, the BBC had made even more trouble for itself. There was, after all, still the problem of defining what constituted 'controversial' material, and even, for that matter, what amounted to a 'crisis'. Moreover, there now appeared to be no distinction between a ministerial and a party political type of broadcast whatsoever. The heated argument over political broadcasts that ensued when Suez reached its climax in early November was, therefore, entirely predictable.

As October arrived and the Suez crisis slipped into its third month, it became ever more apparent that events on the diplomatic front had reached a deadlock. The Menzies mission to Cairo in early September had failed to budge Nasser, whilst Secretary of State Dulles' idea of a Suez Canal Users' Association, designed to deprive Egypt of the canal tolls, quickly proved to be a non-starter. It was after the second international gathering in London, in late September, which Downing Street interpreted as another failure to create the necessary *casus belli*, that Eden decided to take the government's case to the United Nations. These unmistakable signs of drift and indecision had an inevitable effect on British public opinion. Most British people now saw the crisis as less of a personal contest between Eden and Nasser, and more of a complicated, international dispute which should be settled by negotiation rather than by brinkmanship. As early as 6 September, polls showed that the shift in opinion away from the use of force, apparent long before the first London Conference, had continued apace.[17] In these circumstances it is not surprising to find William Clark showing signs of increased disillusionment with the government's publicity policy in general and its use of broadcasting in particular. The latter was, after all, considered to be the prime minister's forte. In Clark's opinion, Eden's over-emphasis on ministerial broadcasts to present the government's case was proving counter-productive. 'I feel sure that this is not the way to go about it; it is too direct, too propagandistic.' In his view, a sort of persuasion-by-osmosis would be more effective. 'The ministerial speech which may – or may not – be reported is the thing that is needed and neglected.'[18]

Given this increase in public and party political opposition to the government's continued hardline stance, one would have expected the BBC to have realized the errors of its ways during the first phase of the crisis and recover its impartiality. However, there is little evidence to support this in terms of output. For all Ian Jacob's words of defiance, the BBC's External Services practised little of its much-vaunted even-handedness in the summer and autumn of 1956. This was particularly the case with the Arabic Service, which became an integral part of the Foreign Office's psychological campaign against Nasser. A report by the director of External Broadcasting in September outlined how the talks output of the Arabic Service had consistently stressed the solidarity of the views expressed in Parliament, the 'futility of Nasser's economic plans', the danger of running the canal without experienced pilots, and the threat posed by the seizure to Asian as well as Western interests.[19] Analysis of the service's surviving scripts for the period confirms this.[20] The service also broadcast jokes produced by its Features Unit alluding to the oppressiveness of Nasser's regime and the dangers of living under communism.[21] Douglas Dodds-Parker, with whom the Arabic Service had been in close touch throughout the crisis, was particularly pleased with the 'vigorous line' which had been taken.[22] 'The BBC's Arabic Service has represented our case pretty well,' the head of the Information Research Department revealingly told Ivone Kirkpatrick in late September.[23] Despite this, ministers continued to search for ways of legally exerting greater influence over the External Services.[24]

As the crisis developed, the BBC was also involved in overseas operations of a more covert nature. These were directed by Dodds-Parker's powerful Advisory Committee set up in August and run jointly by the Foreign Office and MI6. The Committee's task was to co-ordinate propaganda – black, grey and white – to the Middle East, thereby acting as a bridge between the Egypt Committee and another body established by Selwyn Lloyd in mid-August, the Information Coordination Executive. Amongst the items it produced for Arab consumption included threats of interference with the flow of the Nile waters (the lifeblood of Egypt's society and economy), the existence of 'concentration camps' in Egypt, and Egyptian pamphlets amended to make it appear that Cairo planned to control the whole Middle Eastern oil trade.[25] One of the main organs of dissemination used was SCANT radio station, supposedly run by an Egyptian 'national freedom group', which had been broadcasting disinformation almost from the outset of the crisis.[26] Precisely what role was played on this committee by the BBC, represented by Hugh Carleton-Greene, controller of the External Services (and a future director-general), is unclear owing to the paucity of records. From existing files, however, it is apparent that the BBC helped to transmit much of the propaganda material to the Arab world, and that Carleton-Greene was, crucially, fully aware of the committee's aim – 'to get rid of Colonel Nasser'.[27]

As for the BBC's Domestic Services, in general its current affairs output continued to show a pro-government bias during this period, perhaps owing partly to the anti-Nasser material with which it too was supplied by the Foreign Office's Information Research Department.[28] Whilst Menzies was in Cairo between 3 and 9 September, for instance, the BBC appeared to act under the same constraints imposed on it by Sir Alexander Cadogan during the Lancaster House conference, deliberately refraining from broadcasting any programmes of an investigative nature. One particular radio programme, *Next Steps on Suez*, due to go out on 6 September, therefore had to be replaced at the last moment by one which merely provided background to the crisis. 'In the circumstances we cannot kick the ball,' wrote a frustrated J. C. Thornton, assistant controller of Talks (Sound), 'but this may be useful dribbling.'[29] In later commentaries Nasser was consistently portrayed either as desperate, with his fellow Arabs slowly turning against him, or as a megalomaniac whose irrational hatred of Britain was being exploited by the Russians.[30] American policy was condemned from all sides for its ambiguity, if not duplicity, whereas the United Nations came under fire for having yet again illustrated its customary pusillanimity.[31] At the same time, despite Parliament having been in recess since early August – except for the Suez debate on 12 and 13 September – the BBC persisted in imposing restrictions on how it reported the domestic political upheaval surrounding the potential use of force. In *Radio Link* on 19 September, for example, chairman and distinguished historian, Alan Bullock, announced a ban on the participants making any comments on British views of Eden's policy.[32]

There were some notable exceptions to this line of policy on the BBC's part. On 14 September, for example, *At Home and Abroad* included a debate between MPs Walter Elliot and Kenneth Younger on the parliamentary differences over Suez. This was followed on 27 September by Bickham Sweet-Escott's passionate defence of the UN as an international peace-keeping organization in *The World and Ourselves*.[33] Nevertheless, on the whole, the BBC's commentaries during this period painted a false picture of a country if not fully behind, then at least tolerant of, a belligerent stance on the Suez dispute. In this sense, the BBC continued to do the government's bidding, even though, according to the polls, a majority of British people was now against any resort to force. At the same time, the longer the crisis had progressed and the more pacific Eden had sought to present himself, the more taboo any mention of the government's 'military precautions' had become. Throughout this whole period there was not one single BBC current affairs programme that dealt at length with the size and ramifications of the huge military build-up taking place in the Mediterranean. It is unclear whether this oversight was due simply to the BBC's adherence to the D-Notices, or whether the Egypt Committee or Ministry of Defence imposed other more stringent restrictions on the filming of these 'secret' manoeuvres.[34] Either way, the fact that the BBC agreed so readily to censor its coverage of such newsworthy material said little for its independence. Nor did it augur well for the corporation's ability to report objectively should the crisis turn into war.

The crucible

Up to this point in the crisis, the government had, for all the BBC's later complaints about bullying, largely relied on a mixture of persistent lobbying and the discreet use of censorship powers to persuade British broadcasters to play its tune. As has been shown, this had worked to a remarkable degree. However, once Eden had decided in mid-October to activate Operation MUSKETEER REVISE, there was, as he saw it, no alternative but to turn the broadcasting medium into an arm of war. This would, after all, be no ordinary 'war' in Egypt. Parliament was likely to be split down the middle on the issue, and there was little that the government could do to stop at least some sections of the press from accusing it of an illegal resort to arms. The broadcasters' role was therefore pivotal. If the government could go at least some way towards controlling the BBC and ITV coverage of the military operation, the propaganda conflict at home would be half won. Conversely, if the broadcasters were allowed to report on issues and events when and how they pleased, given the dubious nature of the enterprise the government could find itself seriously, if not fatally, discredited. William Clark offers us this insight into Eden's thinking at this stage: 'He really believed that anything that was said pro the enemy and any questioning of the motives, legality and rightness of our cause were acts of sabotage and treason.'[1]

The real test had therefore now arrived for broadcasting, especially television, considering the powerful visual images that war would be expected to produce and the effect that these could have on public opinion. Would it report events in accordance with Parliament's ruling to commercial broadcasting two years earlier, that is, 'with due accuracy and impartiality',[2] or instead succumb to increased government manipulation? Geoffrey Cox, ITN's editor throughout this period and beyond, for one had no doubts about the answer to this question. Putting the crisis in the wider context of the development of television as the prime source of information in Britain, Cox praised the new medium's performance highly:

> The constant pressure of major news throughout the five months since Nasser had nationalised the Suez Canal had hardened and sharpened our bulletins into a form which was not only to endure for some years ahead within ITN, but which was to influence the format of BBC bulletins and to have repercussions on television news presentation in many other countries. Suez and Hungary were the crucible in which television news was to be shaped for a decade.[3]

It is impossible to appreciate how much pressure the BBC's Domestic Services were put under during this phase without also taking into account the degree to which Eden simultaneously sought to muzzle the External Services. The cabinet had signalled its intent in this regard, long before its decision to collude with the French and Israelis, by the establishment in late September of a new committee under R. A. Butler designed 'to review the whole basis of the existing arrangements for overseas broadcasting'. This coincided with Butler's appointment as the government's emergency public relations chief, charged with injecting much-needed adrenalin into Eden's propaganda operation.[4] As the earlier meeting between Ivone Kirkpatrick and Ian Jacob intimated, by October 1956, despite Foreign Office praise for the Arabic Services' 'vigorous' output, ministers were fast running out of patience with what they saw as the External Services' failure to present the nation's policy in a sufficiently aggressive and loyal fashion. It therefore now fell to Butler's powerful committee to decide how the BBC could best be brought to book at this critical juncture.

On 25 October, less than a week before the start of hostilities in the Middle East, the minister of state for foreign affairs, Anthony Nutting, accordingly acquainted Ian Jacob with Butler's recommendations. Designed 'partly as a means of administering a shock to the BBC, and inducing them to reconcile their independence with the need for greater care in conducting those services in the national interest',[5] these proposals threatened fundamental change in the External Services. First of all, the services' grant was to be cut by £1 million (one fifth of the total). This saving would be devoted, in part, to an intensification of the BBC's services to the Middle East and Asia, and to enable the government to invest in those information services over which it had more direct control. Secondly, the government required the appointment of the much-discussed Foreign Office liaison officer 'to advise the BBC on the content and direction of their overseas programmes'. The director-general, who was about to leave for a Commonwealth Broadcasters' Conference in Australia, an assignment which would enforce his absence during the impending crisis, protested strongly. Such measures, he argued, would have the effect of destroying a large and integral part of the corporation's organization built up to carry out work on behalf of the government. Nutting was adamant, however, and closed the interview by emphasizing

> the Government's concern, now that a 'bipartisan' foreign policy had broken down, for the Government's case to be put over in a clear and unambiguous way; they must reserve the right to have material made to their order, without having contrary views also carried to the confusion of peoples in certain parts of the world who do not understand our political system.[6]

The next day, following urgent talks between Jacob, Cadogan and Butler, the latter somewhat surprisingly agreed to reduce the proposed cut in funding to £500,000.[7] This was interpreted as something of a victory for the BBC, especially when the subsequent letter outlining the financial arrangements was sent via Douglas Dodds-Parker on 26 October only in draft form, allowing the director-general to use delaying tactics. As Peter Partner, historian of the BBC's Arabic Service, writes: 'If the intention had been to administer a short, sharp shock to the BBC, this was an odd way of doing it.'[8] Despite this, contrary to conventional wisdom, the government had not come away from this episode empty-handed. The BBC may not have acted as ministers would have wished and completely buckled under the weight of these threats, thereby guaranteeing the government its support in the weeks ahead; nevertheless, Bush House had, at last, agreed to the installation of a Foreign Office liaison officer in its midst in the near future (to be of some use to the government in November).[9] Moreover, the above sequence of events cannot fail to have had a knock-on effect in terms of how the BBC's other half, the Domestic Services, would handle the forthcoming national crisis. Pressure from the government on one service inevitably impacted on the other; recognizing this interaction is the key to assessing the BBC's overall coverage during the military phase of Suez in particular.

We come next to the single most notorious incident in the relationship between the government and the BBC during Suez. Writing his personal account of the crisis a decade later, Harman Grisewood, the BBC's director of Spoken Word, claimed that, 'one day towards the end of October,' William Clark told him 'that the prime minister had instructed the Lord Chancellor [Kilmuir] to prepare an instrument which would take over the BBC altogether and subject it wholly to the will of the government'.[10] This has since entered into BBC folklore,[11] but is now largely dismissed as a typical example of William Clark letting his imagination get the better of him; Clark himself later admitted that 'he might have exaggerated in talking to Grisewood about the specific plans afoot'.[12] This appears to be confirmed by the absence of any trace of the Lord Chancellor's 'instrument' either in the records that have been released or in Clark's diary.

It seems likely that the origin of Clark's message lay in fact in the 25 October meeting between Nutting and Jacob, during which the minister stated that the government had considered taking over and operating the External Services itself.[13] On returning to work on 29 October, Clark possibly heard of this via garbled office gossip, misleading himself and Grisewood.[14] Nevertheless, even if we accept that Eden was not planning to take over the BBC, the matter is still of the highest importance. What Clark told Grisewood might not have been true, but there is every indication that the BBC man thought it genuine. Grisewood had come increasingly to rely on the 'hardworking' press secretary to keep him in touch with Eden's real mood. 'I was never kept in the dark,' he claims.[15] Given that Grisewood was, together with Norman Bottomley, deputy director-general, effectively running the BBC's day-to-day affairs after Jacob's departure, this is highly significant. Grisewood was already aware of the mounting tension between Eden and the External Services at this juncture;[16] Clark's latest secret can only have added to the pressure on the BBC to act 'in the national interest', especially when hostilities broke out a few days later. Moreover, the fact that Grisewood decided not to pass on this 'burdensome information' to Sir Alexander Cadogan, whom he considered to be none too firm in his support of the BBC's editorial policy at that time of the crisis and overly close to Eden, said little for the degree of trust and solidarity that existed between the BBC's most senior officials on the verge of a crisis which would test the corporation's independence to the limit.[17]

If we are to understand the full significance of this 'takeover' episode, it should not be viewed in isolation but rather placed within the wider context of the government's almost continual harassment of broadcasters immediately prior to the launching of MUSKETEER REVISE. This reached its peak when Grisewood and Bottomley were asked to call at the Ministry of Defence in the last week of October, shown the war room and told that military operations, 'which were soon to start', would necessitate the introduction of the full apparatus of wartime censorship.[18] The similarities between this and Eden's earlier confession to *The Times*'s Iverach McDonald about the collusion plan are strikingly apparent. For the BBC's acting director-general and his chief assistant to be given advance knowledge of the plot to invade Egypt speaks volumes for the role the government assigned to broadcasting in the weeks ahead. By confiding in the BBC and brandishing the threat of strict censorship, we can reasonably presume that it was Eden's intention to persuade the corporation to present the military operations as a national war; it is difficult to think of another motive for the prime minister taking such a risk. That the two men left Whitehall, according to Grisewood, 'with heavy hearts' suggests that Eden's ploy did not work. On the other hand, as had been the case with Iverach McDonald, it apparently did not occur to either Grisewood or Bottomley to disclose what they knew to be the truth, war or no war. Consequently, no one else was given this information, either within the BBC or outside.[19] This accords little with Grisewood's later assertion that throughout Suez Eden's aim was secrecy whereas the BBC's was enlightenment.[20]

As if to prove that Eden was not conducting a private little war against the BBC during this period and was not concerned with just its coverage of the events ahead, at some point in late October (it is impossible to say exactly when) the prime minister also made an approach to Independent Television. He chose as his conduit Sir Kenneth Clark, chairman of the Independent Television Authority and an old personal friend. 'I was on my way to give a lecture on Raphael', Clark recalls, 'when Eden asked me to see him at Number 10. He asked me, in the national interest, to slant the news about Suez.' Clark appears, however, to have taken the prime minister's request entirely within his stride: 'Even had we inclined to do so – which I was not – I told him it could not be done. We were working under an Act of Parliament which called for impartiality. I left, and went on my way to give my lecture, and never heard another word about it.'[21]

The undeclared Israeli war on Egypt started on 29 October, followed on the afternoon of the 30th by Eden's announcement of the Anglo-French ultimatums to Tel Aviv and Cairo. Throughout the rest of that day the prime minister faced a barrage of criticism. The Labour opposition reacted with incredulity and hostility, dividing the House and leaving the government with a majority of only 52. President Eisenhower, angered by having first learned of the ultimatums from press reports, sent a stunningly cold and formal message to Eden, making it clear that the US administration completely dissociated itself from his action. To make matters worse, this was then released to the media. Finally, that evening, the Anglo-French declaration was brought before the Security Council, where the American ambassador, Cabot Lodge, introduced a resolution demanding Israel's withdrawal from Egypt and calling on all UN members to refrain from the use or threat of force. This was blocked by Britain's first ever use of her veto.[22]

In telling his cabinet on 24 October that the attack against Egypt had to be 'quick and successful',[23] Eden had clearly expected some opposition to his policy, but not on this scale and with such ferocity. We can reasonably presume that the resulting sense of shock played at least some part in William Clark's inviting Harman Grisewood to Number 10 the next morning to request another ministerial broadcast, this time for Eden personally. With the RAF bombings due to start that afternoon Eden must have realized the importance of putting his case directly to the nation as soon as possible. Consequently, after consulting Bottomley and Cadogan, Grisewood informed the Number 10 office that the BBC would accede to Eden's request, but also made the point that if the opposition then sought a right of reply this would likewise be granted. According to the BBC's records, Clark said that this was understood and expected by the prime minister.[24]

Simultaneously, the government meddled yet further with the BBC's overseas operations. On 30 October, following an emergency ministerial meeting presided over by Eden, the government announced that it had instructed the governor of Cyprus to 'requisition' the Near East Arab Broadcasting Station, or Sharq al-Adna.[25] This was a station which had been secretly run by British Intelligence since World War Two under the guise of a commercial company – a fact long known by certain senior BBC staff, despite claims to the contrary before, during and after Suez.[26] Henceforth, the station was to be known as the Voice of Britain and would be used to 'carry official announcements of HMG in the UK' as well as 'the Arabic Services of the BBC as soon as circumstances permit'.[27] This constituted a radical change from a plan previously drawn up between the BBC and the Foreign Office, whereby the Arabic Services would have used Sharq al-Adna's powerful transmitters as a relay station solely for its own output.[28] Following this, on 31 October, the assistant under-secretary with responsibility for information matters, Paul Grey, telephoned Norman Bottomley stating that the 'sudden crisis in the Middle East' required the immediate appointment of the liaison officer, under the terms of Dodds-Parker's draft letter of 26 October. This the BBC agreed to on the understanding that it should not 'derogate in any way from the existing independence of the BBC',[29] only for the official to arrive at Bush House with the obvious intention of shaping the Arabic Services' output in the government's image.[30] Taken together, these two measures made clear to the BBC the government's determination to control broadcasting, either directly or indirectly, throughout whatever lay ahead.

On Thursday, 1 November, the BBC's Board of Governors assembled for what Harman Grisewood later called its most critical meeting of the whole crisis. According to the director of Spoken Word, the BBC was at this point on the verge of a damaging split over its coverage of the emerging hostilities. Eden, it appears, had lost no time in raising with Alexander Cadogan the sensitive question of broadcasting opinions contrary to the military operation which the British troops would be able to listen to on the eve of battle. The chairman subsequently told the acting director-general that in his opinion this would be both demoralizing and dangerous. Bottomley and Grisewood disagreed, however, arguing with Cadogan before the board meeting that it would be neither proper nor practical to suppress news in one service and allow it in another. The sense of real tension in the BBC at this point is graphically described by Grisewood:

> The whole staff, we knew, backed the traditional policy of the BBC. If the Board had decided to side with Eden the BBC would have broken into revolt. If Eden had his way, it would, in my view, have been the end of the Corporation as it had been known up till then. I believe most of the senior people would have resigned rather than try to carry out orders of suppression.[31]

Unfortunately, because the records of this particular meeting have been partially withheld, it is impossible to gauge exactly how close the BBC came to splitting on 1 November. According to Grisewood, whose account is verified by several other sources, the Board of Governors in fact stood firm under pressure from Eden and decided that the BBC should 'continue to apply the policy ... it had followed hitherto both at home and in the External services.'[32] Thus, despite having declared in September how anxious it was to 'do nothing to underline the existence of party division and disunity at a time of crisis', the governors appeared to have revised their attitude somewhat. The issuing of explicit instructions to the effect that the External Services' press reviews, which had already contained material denouncing Eden's ultimatums, should continue as normal seemed to confirm this.[33]

By the time of this board meeting, Operation MUSKETEER REVISE had begun in earnest. At intervals throughout the night of 31 October– 1 November, RAF Canberras and Valiants bombed targets in and around Cairo; a total of eleven sorties were flown that night alone. Over the next few days, with weather conditions perfect and enemy resistance virtually non-existent, allied aircraft dropped a total of almost 2000 bombs, destroying upwards of 300 aircraft on the ground and paralysing the Egyptian air arm.[34]

What part the BBC was to play in the reporting of this bombing offensive appears to have been given little prior thought by the government. There is evidence of field operators like Ralph Murray, General Keightley's political adviser in charge of propaganda operations in

Cyprus, stressing the value of providing adequate media coverage of the military attack. His message on 24 October to the MoD's standing Committee on Public Relations Policy in Services, responsible for the accreditation of journalists in the event of war, is an example: 'The contribution of correspondents, cameramen, etc. may well be important to the operations themselves, as well as to our general political position during and after them.'[35] Such appeals for sufficient groundwork on the whole, however, seem to have fallen on deaf ears in Whitehall. Consequently, the government's broadcasting policy which accompanied the launching of military action against Egypt in the first days of November showed tell-tale signs of confusion and improvisation.

Notwithstanding this, the government managed to control the broadcasters' coverage of the bombing campaign very well. This can be attributed to a combination of positive, selective guidance and censorship, much as was used to manage the press. On 31 October, the MoD Committee on Public Relations Policy in Services met, having been informed by the Defence Transition Committee earlier that morning that arrangements for accreditation and censorship should be put in hand at once. During this meeting, it was suggested that it would be useful to have a BBC liaison officer in close touch with the MoD and Service Departments. In this way, guidance about the RAF's actions could be given to the BBC along the same lines as that to Fleet Street.[36] This matter was then passed on to Monckton's newly established, more senior Public Relations Committee, which floated the idea of combining the Foreign Office liaison officer (about to be installed at Bush House) with something even more direct, namely to have a BBC representative actually attend meetings of the Public Relations Committee.

The next day, however, this far-reaching proposal was dropped, 'to avoid giving the BBC the impression that this was an attempt to influence their presentation of news and to avoid the press learning that the BBC was receiving special treatment'. Instead, the Committee delegated Richard Chilver, the MoD's deputy secretary, whom Norman Bottomley had, interestingly, already contacted on his own initiative with a view to some form of 'consultation' between the BBC and the Service Ministries, to discuss the whole issue of liaison with Harman Grisewood that afternoon. This resulted in the establishment of liaison arrangements between the BBC and the government during MUSKET-EER REVISE on two levels: the Number 10 Press Office with Harman Grisewood, and the MoD's deputy secretary with the BBC's senior news editor (Tahu Hole). By providing the BBC with such high-level, supposedly reliable sources, Monckton hoped that its bulletins would be 'accurate and up to date'; or, to put it another way, that the BBC's output would faithfully reflect the allegedly limited nature of the government's military action.[37]

However, even before this mutually 'helpful machinery' of liaison could begin to operate smoothly,[38] it was already apparent that the BBC's coverage of the hostilities in the Middle East was going to be far from comprehensive. The government had immediately issued a further D-Notice to the media on 1 November. This the BBC automatically complied with, thereby placing serious restrictions from the outset on how it could report MUSKETEER REVISE, particularly concerning casualties.[39] Added to this, owing to the delayed accreditation of its correspondents, the BBC failed to produce a single genuinely objective, first-hand report of the RAF bombings. News bulletins were instead based either on 'guided' interviews with the pilots themselves (who were given explicit orders not to act in a 'gung-ho' fashion)[40] or on the official communiqués being released regularly from Allied Headquarters in Cyprus. In some cases it seems the BBC simply rehashed press reports which were themselves already tainted with having come from the same reputedly authoritative sources.[41]

Given that the majority of the bombing raids on and around Cairo had been carried out under cover of darkness, realistically one could not have expected a series of detailed and precise eye-witness reports of how accurate (or otherwise) these sorties had been. On the other hand, by relying almost entirely, and apparently without question, on second-hand reports served up courtesy of the government or MoD, the BBC contrived to paint a distorted picture of the opening salvos of MUSKETEER REVISE. Thus, rather than insisting on seeing for themselves what had been the cost in people and property of these raids, and why, if they had been as accurate as the authorities claimed, all airfields bar Cairo West were still serviceable for operations afterwards,[42] reporters instead repeatedly stressed the 'unprecedented precautionary measures' which the RAF, under government orders, had taken to save lives. Not one news bulletin gave an estimate of the Egyptian casualties, military or otherwise, that would be expected to accrue from an attack on such a scale.

Having no film of the actual bombings, the BBC's Television Service could only show comparatively innocuous scenes of aircraft either taking off from or landing in Cyprus.[43] As for the BBC's commentaries, to which many people instinctively turned for informed opinion, these either considered the subject off limits owing to the Fourteen Day Rule or tended to lend further support to the 'police action' thesis by employing former RAF chiefs whose instant judgements were themselves based mainly on official guidance and re-emphasized the avoidance of casualties.[44] Had viewers and listeners been made sufficiently aware of the censored nature of the 'news' they were receiving, the BBC might have been more justified in using what little information it could get its hands on; however, it conspicuously failed to reveal such facts, presumably because it would detract from the corporation's reputation as the purveyor of the truth, even, or especially, in wartime. All of this boded ill for the assault phase, by which time the work of Monckton's news coordination committee would be more finely tuned.

Controlling the media's presentation of the war was one thing; however, getting the public to actively support the government's policy was another. On 2 November, Oliver Poole, the Conservative Party chairman, sent Eden the latest in a long line of memoranda outlining Central Office's assessment of public, and particularly Tory, opinion. This amounted to a stiff warning that unless he started to explain his policy – and quickly – the prime minister would lose the propaganda war by default:

> Nearly all reports indicate that whilst there is a steady majority of the Party behind the Government, people are bewildered by the speed of events and are confused by the lack of knowledge about what is really happening. The Socialist Party are organising a major campaign against the Government under the slogan 'Law Not War' and in view of the concern which is being felt all over the country this campaign is bound to have some impact.

Both as a means of countering what he perceived as the left-wing bias in the media and settling national opinion, Poole made one major suggestion:

> By far the most important point arising from a quick survey of feeling in the country is that you should go on the air both on TV and radio as quick as possible. I understand that you are planning to do this tomorrow and I much hope that nothing will arise which will prevent you from doing this.[45]

Judging from William Clark's diary, ministers were in complete agreement with Poole. Preparations for Eden's broadcast, scheduled for Saturday, 3 November, closely resembled those for his appearance in August: intense, with an acute attention to detail.[46] This is hardly surprising. It is difficult to exaggerate the pressure the government was under at this particular point in the crisis. With the first stage of MUSKETEER REVISE – the bombings – complete, the government could now do nothing but wait whilst the invasion fleet advanced from Malta slowly towards Port Said. The delay – of three whole days – merely gave further strength to domestic and international criticism.

Eden had to contend with a ruptured Commonwealth, combined with an American-led United Nations demanding that he call an abrupt halt to the operation. At home, he faced aggressive street demonstrations coupled with near fights in Parliament itself.[47] In the strained circumstances of this phoney-war period, many on the government's side therefore thought it was essential that the prime minister should address the nation in a cool, detached manner on television, as much for their own morale as for wider public opinion.[48]

Eden's broadcast on the evening of 3 November went out on the BBC's Television, Home, Light and General Overseas Services, as well as being relayed by ITV. Given the pressure he was under, the prime minister arguably made one of the best speeches of his political life, showing no signs of nervousness or indecision, which could have proved highly damaging in the circumstances. The emphasis on his record as 'a peacemonger', which William Clark had stressed whilst helping to prepare the script the day before,[49] was the overriding theme. 'All my life,' Eden declared, 'I have been a man of peace ... a League of Nations man and a United Nations man ... but I am utterly convinced that the action we have taken is right.' Once again, as in his own and Selwyn Lloyd's broadcasts earlier in the crisis, the spectre of the 1930s was evoked. 'Between the wars we saw things which were happening which we felt were adding to the danger of a great world war. Should we have acted swiftly to deal with them, even though it meant the use of force, or should we have hoped for the best and gone on hoping and talking as in fact we did? There are times for courage, times for action and this is one of them.' The government had no alternative, Eden argued, but to intervene militarily in order 'to put out the forest fire' of war in the Middle East. Finally, the British and French were not working against the UN, but for it. It was for this reason that the military operation, now started, must be completed. 'Once British and French forces have occupied key points on the Canal, HMG will ensure that the Israelis withdraw from Egyptian territory ... If the UN will take over this police force we shall welcome it.'[50]

Having made what was to him a wholly justified patriotic call for unity as British troops were about to go into action, the prime minister's attitude towards the Labour party's being allowed to use the same facilities to argue its own case was entirely predictable. 'Eden wanted to put the national point of view,' said William Clark later. 'He would appear as a summation of our national interests without the right of reply by the Opposition, which he felt ought not to be in opposition at all.'[51] Consequently, when Labour's chief whip, Herbert Bowden, rang his counterpart, Edward Heath, immediately after Eden's appearance his request for a right of reply was met with stiff resistance.

Bowden was told that the prime minister's broadcast had 'been as uncontroversial as possible', that it had complied with the requirements of a ministerial broadcast as defined in the *aide-mémoire*, and therefore Gaitskell's request had to be rejected. (There is some evidence that at this point Number 10 toyed with the idea of using the designated three days to make up its mind on this issue, only to dismiss it, presumably for fear of the damage the government would incur from the inevitable allegations of flagrant censorship.)[52]

Heath's message ran directly counter to William Clark's statement to Grisewood on 31 October, and put the ball awkwardly in the BBC's court. The corporation now found itself in the onerous position of having to fulfil its role as official adjudicator and 'exercise its own judgement' whether to grant the opposition the right to reply in the midst of acute political turmoil. It was in this situation that the BBC discovered how it had to some extent made a rod for its own back. By appearing to agree, in mid-September, that ministerial broadcasts could, after all, be controversial 'in times of crisis', and that this was provided for in the 'right of reply' system, the BBC seemed to have clarified the rules governing political broadcasting. All it had done in reality, however, was to give the impression to the opposition that it had the automatic right to reply to a ministerial broadcast. Consequently, if, as happened in this instance, the government then claimed that its ministerial broadcast had in fact been impartial, prohibiting any reply, the corporation found itself under even greater pressure. Harman Grisewood alluded to the dangerously arbitrary fashion in which the BBC was negotiating with the politicians when he wrote to his chief in early November: 'I do think in these matters we must try to keep some body of principle effectively in being. At the moment, I do not think we are very far from dealing with these matters as a sequence of merely *ad hoc* arrangements.'[53] In fact, had the BBC simply ordered both Eden and Gaitskell to make party political broadcasts, the more correct procedure in view of the national row over the government's policy, it might have saved itself a great deal of trouble.

In the event, the BBC passed this particular test of its impartiality, though only by making enemies on both sides of the Suez divide in the process. Thinking that the BBC was being deliberately obstructive in not acceding to Bowden's request, at midnight on 3 November Gaitskell himself rang up Grisewood in a furious rage and insisted that he be allowed to broadcast the following evening. When this was not forthcoming – Grisewood telling him that the chairman's ruling on the subject would have to wait until 'a Christian hour' in the morning – the Labour leader threatened the BBC with public exposure for suppressing the opposition. When even this failed to work, Gaitskell

then put through a call direct to Sir Alexander Cadogan, who failed –
or more likely refused – to answer, thereby angering Gaitskell still
further.[54] Eventually, the next morning, Cadogan authorized the reply
for that evening. Even he could not ignore the flaw in the government's
argument against allowing Gaitskell's broadcast to go ahead. Eden's
confession that his own broadcast had been 'as uncontroversial as
possible' was, as Cadogan himself put it, 'tantamount to admitting that
it *was* controversial'.[55] Edward Heath sought, even then, to cajole the
BBC into restricting Gaitskell's freedom of speech, but to no avail.[56]

Gaitskell was clearly as aware as Eden of how much public and
parliamentary opinion was in the balance at this juncture. Hence his
devotion of the whole of Sunday, 4 November, to preparing his own
broadcast, assisted by the party's two media experts, Tony Benn and
Woodrow Wyatt.[57] For all this, the Labour leader seems to have made
a serious error of judgement and, as a result, done the opposition's
cause more harm than good. What he had to say was, for the most
part, extremely effective, scrutinizing, as it did, Eden's own words
from the previous evening. Thus, Gaitskell argued that, contrary to
the prime minister's claims, Britain had used its veto not to assist the
UN but to obstruct it; that the government's real intention was not to
secure peace in the Middle East but to solve the Suez Canal problem
by force; and that, as a consequence, it had split the country and the
Commonwealth, betraying in the process all that Britain had long stood
for in world affairs.

However, by his appeal to those Conservatives 'who like us are
shocked and troubled by what is happening' to vote against the government, coupled with an explicit call for the prime minister to resign,
Gaitskell played into Eden's hands. Instead of encouraging potentially
dissident Tory MPs, his appeal seems to have provided them with a
pretext with which to give Eden a second chance. As Philip Williams,
Gaitskell's biographer, says, 'The appeal was counter-productive, and
rallied waverers to Eden.' [58] Neither was this effect confined to Westminster. Coming when it did, as British ground troops were known to
be only hours away from launching their assault, Gaitskell's broadcast
seemed to many people at the very least insensitive, if not downright
treasonable. Would not the troops themselves be able to hear this as
they nervously waited to fight for Queen and Country?[59] Even Gaitskell
himself had admitted that Britain was effectively at war.[60] Alexander
Cadogan, for one, was in no doubt as to who had actually gained most
from Gaitskell's performance. The speech was, in the chairman's view,
'disgraceful ... But I don't mind, we have given him enough rope!'[61]

There is little doubt that given the need to depict the long-awaited
landings in Egypt as a 'police action', Eden would have wished to

control broadcasting's coverage of them better than he did. Geoffrey Cox gives a vivid account of the scoop which ITN itself managed to pull off, enabling its viewers to see a long and explicit film of Port Said only the day after the invasion, showing, amongst other things, the charred remains of Egyptian civilians. For a viewing public raised on the relatively corpse-less footage of D-Day, and used to watching any such scenes at the cinema rather than in their own front rooms, this was certainly emotive material.[62] Two further sound broadcasts made by Hardiman Scott on the BBC's *From Our Own Correspondent* on 11 and 18 November, in which he compared the shell-shocked Port Said with London during the Blitz, only serve to underline how unsuccessful the prime minister's attempts at turning broadcasting into an arm of war had been.[63] Nonetheless, overall, the medium's coverage of the final and most critical stage of MUSKETEER REVISE was by no means as full or as critical as the above reports imply.

By severely limiting radio and television correspondents' access to Port Said in the first twenty-four hours of the invasion – despite its being the obvious landing target and there having been ample time after the bombings to transfer journalists to the ships – the MoD ensured that there would be no graphic eye-witness accounts of the fighting in the town. By insisting on pooling arrangements, only one television cameraman, Cyril Page of ITN, was allowed to accompany the invasion fleet.[64] Although Page can take the credit for the searing pictures which ITN showed on 6 November, even his filming contained no scenes of the lengthy street battles and certainly no shots of either wounded or dead British soldiers. Moreover, Page's film was shown when it was only because of a serious mishap in the censorship process.[65] As with the press, all other reports of the landings bound for radio and television in Britain had first to be passed by the military authorities in Cyprus, who decided what scenes should or should not be shown. To assist them further in their work, the MoD also assigned the correspondents a public relations officer, or minder, whose job it was to point the media in the right direction.[66]

As a consequence, the vast majority of broadcasting reports concentrated on the aftermath of the troops' actions, thus missing most of the dirtiest material which might have proved politically damaging. News bulletins also tended to echo newspaper reports in terms of the scale of casualties inflicted on Port Said. The mysterious figure of one hundred dead and wounded Egyptians, again so prevalent, smacked of official guidance, either from the authoritative sources in Cyprus or Monckton's committee. Indeed, the fact that the BBC's bulletins on the whole bore such a close resemblance to so much of the officially released information on the invasion suggests that the government's machinery of liaison paid dividends.[67] Overall, the image of the war broadcasting presented to the British public mirrored that which was provided by the press: one in which the allied strategy worked perfectly and the body count was negligible. This was a central factor in legitimizing the government's interventionist policy.

As to the coverage of the wider political debate surrounding the Anglo-French landings, it must be stated that the BBC's news bulletins remained as straight as they had been from the very start of the crisis. Given the considerable pressure the BBC's senior officials were under, either implicitly or explicitly, to slant the news in favour of the government this was no small achievement. Once again, however, the BBC's current affairs output showed serious flaws. Reviewing the corporation's performance since the outbreak of hostilities, on 5 November the Board of Management itself recognized that the BBC was failing in its duty to reflect opinion because of the Fourteen Day Rule, but decided it could do nothing about it.[68] Television commentaries during the period reflected this cautiousness. *Press Conference* on 2 November, for example, focused on Suez, but the interviewee, Harold Watkinson, minister of transport, was not asked a single question related to the rights and wrongs of the government's policy.[69] On the very day of the landings, *Panorama* carried only one small item relating to the crisis, of a strictly apolitical nature, whereas *Highlight* ignored the subject altogether, choosing instead to discuss the topic of mental health.[70] When Michael Peacock, *Panorama*'s producer, sought to improve matters by proposing that the BBC should interview Selwyn Lloyd, the Board of Management refused point-blank. Years later, Jonathan Dimbleby underlined how discreetly circumscribed had been his father's broadcasting during Suez: 'in the aftermath no one outside the BBC noticed that the whole fiasco had still been reported without a single critical voice being heard; not once was the massive authority of Richard Dimbleby's *Panorama* challenged.'[71]

It was a similar story with radio. One of the first programmes in a position to comment on the dramatic turn of events at the end of October, *At Home and Abroad* on 30 October, conspicuously steered clear of the furore surrounding Eden's ultimatums to Egypt and Israel that afternoon. In his so-called survey of British reaction to the Israeli invasion of Egypt, Richard Scott of the *Manchester Guardian* instead simply outlined the facts of, and justification behind, the prime minister's Commons statement.[72] This set the pattern for a great many of the BBC's sound commentaries during the first two weeks of November, with programmes either explicitly announcing that owing to the Fourteen Day Rule no comment could be made on Suez whatsoever, or getting around this by sticking to the foreign (and politically safer) aspects of the crisis.[73] There are even examples of controllers having to black out live programmes in which it was felt the rule was being dangerously transgressed. The speakers on one such programme, *Any Questions?*, broadcast on 3 November, resorted to referring to Egypt as Ruritania as a device to circumvent the restrictions.[74]

Episodes like this could be passed off as faintly amusing were it not for the fact that during this period Britain was, for all Eden's claims to the contrary, at war, both in Egypt and with itself. The degree to which the BBC (and ITV) was willing to censor itself at a time when people naturally turned to broadcasting to provide them with the information they required to make sound judgements was one thing. (The audiences for the BBC's main news bulletins doubled in early November 1956.)[75] Added to this, however, was that many of these same people instinctively conflated censorship in wartime and such vague but powerful concepts as deference and national duty. In short, the conspicuous air of silence surrounding many of the most contentious issues, most notably about the political storm on the home front, contrived to lend the government's actions a respectability they ill deserved.

On the occasions when BBC commentaries did brave the waters of controversy, they invariably came down on the government's side. *At Home and Abroad* on 2 November, whilst by no means an isolated example, is perhaps the best illustration of this bias. The programme contained three items on Suez. Firstly, Sir Alec Kirkbride, former ambassador to Jordan and a respected Arabist, strongly defended Eden's action in terms both of the Arab world and Britain's wider policy in the Middle East. Geoffrey Goodwin from the London School of Economics then added his support to the government by alluding to the UN's impotence in times of crisis. In his view, the use of force had provided the organization with the 'teeth' it so urgently required and could be likened to the UN's role in Korea. Finally, Christopher Serpell, the BBC's chief American correspondent, rounded off the programme with an analysis of why the United States' policy diverged so widely from that of its NATO allies in the present crisis. However, instead of referring to such factors as the adverse international implications of the war, the UN's position and the strong feeling within the US of Anglo-French dishonesty, Serpell attributed the American opposition to a mixture of Eisenhower's need to win the peace vote and the country's obsession with colonialism:

> It is impossible to exaggerate the emotional effect that this word 'colonialism' has on Americans. In the same breath that they criticise Colonel Nasser as a dictator, they will compare his attitude towards Great Britain

with that of the Founding Fathers towards George III. Mr Dulles has revealed in his own press conferences how much his thinking is coloured by ancestral reaction.[76]

Aside from Hardiman Scott's two reports from Port Said, which questioned the veracity of the official figures of Egyptian dead and alleged a political war,[77] militarily the operation was represented as having been a great success. News of the ceasefire was treated as a vindication of the government's daring action rather than what it actually was, an enforced and humiliating halt to MUSKETEER REVISE. The Anglo-French action tended to be presented as having achieved its objectives: of separating the combatants and preventing Armageddon in the Middle East. Moreover, thanks to the allies, the UN now had a police force in the region which could help to produce a lasting solution to the Arab–Israeli question. The consensus was that all this had been done with astonishingly little loss of life. In this regard, many commentaries were at pains to stress the very great differences – morally, politically, as well as militarily – between what had taken place in Egypt and the Russians' 'atrocities' in Hungary. There was only a tiny hint that the two crises could in fact be linked by implying that the use of force was infectious.[78] Again, the part played by Monckton's committee in providing news-hungry broadcasters with a ready supply of easily digestible stories designed to counter Nasser's own 'atrocity' stories and switch the focus of the media's attention towards the Russians' misbehaviour (both in Eastern Europe and the Middle East) was perhaps important here.[79]

Despite the Fourteen Day Rule, therefore, the BBC was willing to enter into the debate concerning some of the contentious aspects of the crisis, albeit in a decidedly unbalanced way. However, the one issue that the corporation fought shy of almost completely was the most important: collusion. Of the commentaries from this period which survive in the BBC's archives, none dared to tackle this subject head-on. This can only be described as a lamentable oversight, given how widespread the allegations of a tripartite conspiracy were in early to mid-November, including in Parliament,[80] and the pride which the BBC traditionally had in its investigative capacities. Moreover, when any programme did touch on the issue it was either played down or dismissed as unsubstantiated rumour.[81]

Whilst it is difficult to say for certain, there is a strong possibility that the almost unprecedented criticism which Conservative backbenchers heaped on the BBC in the aftermath of the ceasefire at least played some part in the corporation's treatment of this most sensitive of issues. On 7 November, Peter Rawlinson, Conservative MP for

Epsom, sent Norman Bottomley a telegram demanding an inquiry into what he saw as the BBC's systematic bias against the government during the recent crisis. So bitter was Rawlinson that the next day he gave notice in the Commons that he would raise the subject of the 'BBC Charter – Political Balance', on the adjournment on Wednesday, 14 November.[82] In the resulting debate, a whole bevy of MPs launched a vociferous attack on the BBC, accusing it essentially of having worked for the opposition. The assistant postmaster-general, Cuthbert Alport, who was expected to defend the BBC, then increased the pressure on the corporation still further by making ominous allusions to certain 'plans and proposals' which the government had in mind to improve its voice abroad.[83]

Despite numerous allegations, there is no evidence that Rawlinson was actually put up to this by a devious Tory Central Office trying to frighten the BBC into compliance with the government's wishes at a still sensitive point in the crisis. Nevertheless, there is little doubt that the corporation was severely shaken, so much so that Bottomley ordered a comprehensive review of output.[84] Consequently, when, in the third week of November, Fleet Street began publishing fresh evidence of collusion via American sources, it is perhaps not altogether surprising to find Harman Grisewood advising the BBC's director of Television Broadcasting to take 'great care in handling the story'.[85] Only the same day, the director of Spoken Word had made clear his apprehension in a letter to his chief: 'All this is heavy foreboding for political broadcasting, for our relations with the Government and for the continuance of the role of the BBC.'[86] The last thing the BBC wanted to do in these circumstances was to aggravate the government even more by exploring the one issue which could arguably have brought it down. Judging from the BBC's current affairs programmes during this later phase of the crisis, it seems Grisewood's advice was taken to heart: the subject was almost wholly suppressed and allowed to die a quiet death.

In the weeks after the 7 November ceasefire, both the government and the opposition continued to invest energy in presenting their cases on radio and television. Selwyn Lloyd made another national broadcast on 7 November, for instance, to be answered by James Griffiths, Labour's deputy leader, the following evening.[87] Walter Monckton, Douglas Dodds-Parker and Edward Heath all made important representations to the BBC during this period, intent on getting the government as good a hearing as possible.[88] However, with broadcasting's unwillingness to explore fully the potentially explosive issue of collusion, any chance of it playing a truly decisive role in what was left of the crisis, say in terms of the government's survival, had in reality gone. By the time the BBC governors met to examine the Commons' charges of bias on 22 November, therefore, Suez was to all intents and purposes over. All that was left was for the government to agree to relinquish its 'gage' on the canal unconditionally, for the Conservative party to ditch Eden, and the Board of Governors to conclude triumphantly that, for all the mud which had been thrown at the BBC during the crisis, the corporation had 'fulfilled [its] obligation for impartiality, objectivity and for telling the truth'.[89]

12

The BBC: conclusion

It is indisputable that during the Suez crisis the BBC's editorial independence was subjected to a most severe test. Bar invoking the reserve powers written into the BBC's Licence and Agreement which enabled the government to 'take over' the corporation in certain circumstances,[1] Eden did everything possible to turn it into his official mouthpiece. This was not the first occasion on which the BBC had been forced to examine its constitutional role – the 1926 General Strike and World War Two itself stand out in this respect.[2] However, Suez contained within it a unique element. As Sir Ian Jacob wrote in the BBC's in-house magazine in January 1957:

> Not for many years has our country dispatched a considerable expedition on warlike operations without there being a high degree of unanimity among the parties and among the people in support of the Government's decision, and without the accord of the other members of the Commonwealth. Thus the situation which recently confronted the BBC was in some respects unprecedented.[3]

Given that the BBC was therefore treading new ground during the summer and autumn of 1956, it must take some credit for refusing to truckle to Eden. For one thing, the corporation's news output was on the whole admirably straight and objective, if not as comprehensive as it might have been. Consequently, the BBC played a vital role in helping to challenge the prime minister's assertion that he was acting in the national interest. That the corporation also granted the leader of the Opposition the right of reply at the very peak of the crisis makes nonsense of one Labour MP's allegation that Sir Alexander Cadogan was 'a Foreign Office deadbeat' and Sir Ian Jacob 'a Tory stooge'.[4]

Whether all this amounted to, as one historian put it, 'the obvious hostility of the BBC to the whole Suez operation'[5] is, however, highly doubtful. If anything, the opposite was the case. As this study has shown, throughout the crisis the BBC's current affairs programmes – in both the Domestic and Overseas Services – evinced a discreet, yet distinct, pro-government bias. From the very start of the dispute BBC commentaries were in no doubt as to the illegality of Nasser's action and the government's subsequent right to take military 'precautions'. When the initial domestic consensus on policy disappeared the BBC then took to using the Fourteen Day Rule as a device to withhold the full truth of the opposition to the government from the public. (In December 1956, Parliament suspended the rule, initially for a six months' trial then indefinitely.)[6] During the first London Conference and the Menzies mission to Cairo no broadcasts were allowed which might harm the government's position, despite the fact that by this time half of the British people were at odds with Eden's stance. Finally, when it came to the government's eventual use of force, the BBC was not, admittedly, manoeuvred into treating the military conflict as though it was a national war; nevertheless, by agreeing to various forms of self-censorship, the corporation contrived to sanitize Operation MUSKETEER REVISE and keep from licence-payers much of the evidence of collusion. The extent to which all of this assisted Eden in his war of words against both Nasser and the opposition at home cannot be quantified but should certainly not be underestimated. Such partiality, of course, ran directly counter to the rules laid down in the BBC's charter.

As was the case with the press, Suez highlighted a number of inherent weaknesses in the British broadcasting system in general and the BBC in particular which the Eden government was able to exploit. Firstly, the fact that the opposition only had the right to make a reply to a ministerial broadcast – and only then if that broadcast had been deemed to be controversial – gave the government an unfair advantage in terms of setting the agenda during the crisis. Secondly, William Clark's ability to persuade broadcasters via confidential briefings that the government meant business, thereby increasing the psychological pressure on Nasser unattributably, showed that all journalists, from whatever medium, were open to exploitation by so-called authoritative sources. The official information disseminated by the MoD during the military operation itself told the same story. Thirdly, even before the 'war' started, both the BBC and ITV displayed an unhealthy over-willingness to suppress their coverage of the government's military preparations. This deference to authority, symptomatic of the in-stitutionalized nature of broadcasting in Britain,[7] helped to foster Eden's conciliatory image significantly. Finally, the extent to which the chairman of the BBC's Board of Governors, prompted by the prime minister, was able to overstep his constitutional position and interfere in executive decisions revealed flaws at the very heart of the corpora-tion's organizational and policy-making structure.[8]

PART THREE

The Campaign in the United States

13

The 'special relationship' and the role of public opinion

Our real concern is to persuade the USA that no one can trust Nasser to live up to his promises or to maintain freedom of navigation of the Canal by himself. We must keep US public opinion continuously aware of this, and of the manifold dangers of being hoodwinked by him ... I am sure you realise the extreme importance of having US opinion behind us, and we are confident that you will be as successful in influencing current opinion over Suez as you have been over other issues. [Foreign Office to A. B. Horn, Deputy Director-General of British Information Services, New York, 1 August 1956][1]

From the outset of the Suez crisis, the British government considered the stance taken by the United States administration as crucial to its freedom of manoeuvre. This accounts for Eden's summoning Andrew Foster, the American chargé d'affaires, to Number 10 immediately after hearing the news of nationalization on 26 July. Having been allowed to attend the hastily arranged meeting between senior ministers and service chiefs that night, Foster was left in no doubts as to the cabinet's 'extremely grave view of the situation ... and very strong feelings ... to the effect that Nasser must not be allowed to get away with it'.[2] The next afternoon Eden cabled Eisenhower warning him of the threat which Nasser's action posed to Western interests in the Middle East and asking for the president's help in bringing 'the maximum pressure to bear on the Egyptian government'.[3]

On the face of it, the prospects of Eden getting the administration's support in his campaign against the Egyptian regime looked very bright. The Americans could, after all, hardly be described as Nasser's friends. Throughout 1955 the State Department had, together with the Foreign Office, sought in secret to broker an Arab–Israeli peace settlement, centred on Tel Aviv and Cairo. Project ALPHA, as it became known, would, it was hoped, produce a permanent solution to the Palestine problem, thereby eliminating the major source of instability in the Middle East, off which communism threatened to feed.[4] By March 1956, however, ALPHA had clearly failed, owing primarily, in Eisenhower's opinion, to Nasser's need to play the anti-Zionist card as part of his quest to assume the leadership of the Arab world.[5] The frustration felt, combined with Cairo's recent overtures to Moscow, heralded a significant shift in Washington's Middle Eastern policy, set out in a State Department memorandum labelled OMEGA at the end of March 1956. Egypt's most-favoured-nation status with the US was revoked. Emphasis was instead placed on building up King Saud of Saudi Arabia as an opposite pole to Nasser in the Arab world. Simultaneously, the US punished Nasser for having sought to play West off against East by, amongst other things, allowing the negotiations on the Aswan high dam to languish.[6] Nasser then managed to alienate the White House yet further in May 1956 when he opened diplomatic relations with Communist China, which the United States itself stubbornly refused to recognize.[7] The net result was that it was the State Department, and not the Foreign Office, which took the lead in completely withdrawing the West's loans for the high dam scheme in mid-July 1956. From Eden's point of view, surely the Americans therefore shouldered at least part of the blame for Nasser's shock announcement only a week later.[8]

On the other hand, if the 'special relationship' had conspicuously floundered anywhere since World War Two it was in the Middle East. Here, Anglo-American cooperation had tended to be based upon what one historian describes as 'a tenuous convergence of aims',[9] often marked by conflicting methods. To Washington the British appeared to be out of touch with local issues and political forces, with a dangerous tendency to over-react; to London the Americans all too often wanted the influence but without the necessary commitment (their refusal to join the Baghdad Pact being a case in point). Some in the Foreign Office suspected that behind this prevarication lay an ambition to 'take our place in the Middle East'.[10] This conflict of interests was illustrated most graphically less than a year before Suez by the deep split between the State Department and the Foreign Office over the little-known oasis of Buraimi. Ownership of this tiny area amounting to only eight villages, lying between Saudi Arabia and the Trucial Sheikhdoms of Abu Dhabi, Muscat and Oman on the eastern coast of the Arabian Peninsula, had been disputed since the 1930s. British and American oil companies, as well as local rulers, expressed interest for strategic and economic reasons. However, matters came to a head in October 1955 when London, fearing the negative results of international arbitration, ordered troops into the oasis to evict what it saw as an occupying, and potentially expansionist, Saudi force.[11] Washington regarded this sudden, violent action as confirmation of the weaknesses of British policy in the region: it was gratuitous, counter-productive and smacked of outright colonialism.[12] Although the Americans did not press their objections in the face of the British *fait accompli*, the issue continued to sour relations. Dulles described Buraimi as the most difficult difference between the two countries at the Washington summit conference in January 1956.[13]

When Nasser expropriated the Suez Canal Company, therefore, Eden was acutely aware of the need to coordinate action as fully as possible with the Americans. This did not mean that he would allow the United States to dictate the crisis agenda or Britain's actions. Indeed, on the morning of 27 July the cabinet agreed that should the United States and France default it would be willing to act alone.[14] However, the ministers' decision to concert common action with Washington and Paris, strongly supported by the service chiefs, signalled more than mere diplomatic etiquette. For instance, the efficacy of economic sanctions against Egypt would to a great extent depend on Western solidarity. More importantly, should it come to war, the role to be played by the United States in deterring Moscow from coming to Nasser's rescue was vital. As early as 30 July, at a lunch with the deputy under-secretary of state, Robert Murphy, Eden requested that, in the event of Anglo-French action, the US 'keep an eye on the Soviet Union'.[15]

Hitherto, accounts of Anglo-American affairs during the Suez crisis have for the most part concentrated on the relationship at its highest level, that is between the two governments, even the two leaders themselves. Personalities have been uppermost, peoples almost forgotten.[16] Part Three of this book seeks to add another dimension to the 'alliance' by examining how the Eden government sought to recruit US support for its policy by appealing over the heads of the Eisenhower administration to the American public itself. In doing so, attention is drawn, firstly, to the considerable scope which the government believed existed for influencing the White House via a discreet propaganda campaign, and the impressive machinery at its disposal; secondly, Eden's need, and ability, to fashion a case for international opinion – one which would differ subtly from, yet not contradict, that presented to the British people; and, thirdly, the competition that the Foreign Office faced not only from Cairo but also from the State Department's own propaganda offensive.

Propaganda – or 'information' as ministers called it publicly – had emerged as an essential ingredient of British diplomacy after World War Two. This was especially the case in relation to the United States. Conscious of their growing financial dependence on the Americans, and alert to the United States' isolationist tradition, post-war British governments sought to broaden their relationship with the US as fully as possible. The need to explain British policies to the American people *in American terms* was all the more important because of the continuing suspicions which many Americans harboured of British 'imperialism' and London's apparent refusal to face up to modern-day realities.[17] (Attlee's 'socialist' policies until 1951, seen by many Americans as pseudo-communist in the context of a developing Cold War, gave a further impetus to the establishment of an official, easily accessible and active British voice in the US.)[18] Added encouragement was given to these propaganda efforts by the common belief that public opinion played a special, arguably unique, role in the foreign policy-making process in the US. Owing to the separation of powers and divided authority enshrined in the Constitution, the US administration was considered to be far more sensitive to short-term movements of public opinion and the pressure of regional and sectional interests than was the British government. According to this school of thought, it was therefore possible to draw a direct link between American public opinion and the fulfilment of British interests.[19]

The machinery for influencing American opinion (constructed mainly by the Foreign Office) was impressive and complex. In London, the Foreign Office News Department, the US Regional Adviser's Office in the Information Policy Department, and the Number 10 Press Office liaised closely with the large corps of American newspapermen and radio commentators resident in Britain, supplying background material and current news guidance.[20] The North American Service of the BBC (which in 1956 broadcast 36 programme hours per week, more than any other single overseas service) was used to disseminate British views, with extensive rebroadcasting of BBC material being promoted by a Foreign Office eager to exploit 'non-official' communication channels.[21]

In the United States, the propaganda effort was conducted under the authority of the ambassador in Washington and the information counsellor. However, the operational focus was British Information Services (BIS) in New York, the headquarters of the mass distribution media in the US. Housed in the Rockefeller Center with a staff of around 140, and headed by a director-general, this operated as a production, adaptation and distribution centre serving a branch office in Chicago and key information offices in Atlanta, Boston, Cleveland, Houston, Kansas City and Los Angeles. The organization was divided into five sections (Press and Radio, Public Relations, Films and Publications, Reference and Library, and Economic), each of whose heads had a wide circle of friends and contacts in their respective spheres.[22] In 1953 the Drogheda Committee's investigation into Britain's Overseas

Information Services showed that more money was spent on information work in the US than in any other single country, with the exception of Germany; the Foreign Office's budget for information staff involved in American operations was greater than that for the Middle East and Asia put together.[23] The 1954 Drogheda Report believed this was a sound investment, praising BIS as 'a model ... of what can be done in the information field in a highly developed country'. [24]

Behind these multifarious Foreign Office activities lay a dual approach towards courting American opinion. Whilst British Information Services was forced to work in the open lest it contravene the terms of the 1938 Foreign Agents Registration Act, the embassy and the consulates, together with information personnel back in London, were able to operate in a more subtle, unaccountable fashion.[25] This was important given the traditional suspicion of British propaganda in particular in the United States (dating from World War One).[26] The art of discretion dovetailed with the doctrine that influence in the United States should be sought through access to the influential few. Little attempt was made to persuade directly the American man in the street. Not only would this require a larger and more costly organization, it would also appear too propagandistic and therefore prove counter-productive. The strategy was instead to concentrate on getting to know, talking to and influencing key personalities, especially those who had a voice in the native organs of public opinion. By cultivating this leadership opinion – Congressmen, journalists, financiers, foreign affairs organizations, religious and racial groups – a greater understanding of British interests would then percolate down to the masses whilst also reaching those holding the reins of power.[27]

It will be shown that during Suez the British government employed a combination of four main methods to persuade the American people to endorse its case against Nasser. In the US itself, British Information Services operated in the public arena, disseminating material direct to leading American opinion, by means of pamphlets, articles and speakers. At the same time, BIS worked in unison with the embassy and consulates, devising the most appropriate publicity themes and disseminating these more discreetly through contacts with friendly journalists. In Britain, the Foreign Office News Department and the Number 10 Press Office liaised closely with American correspondents, offering them the same sort of unattributable guidance dealt out to the Fleet Street lobbies. Finally, ministers themselves went on the propaganda offensive by making a number of broadcasts or major speeches at key points in the crisis, either at home or in the US, designed for American consumption. These were then further publicized by the

Foreign Office's readily equipped and extensive communications net-work in the United States.

It is the intention of this study to analyse how integral a part publicity played in British diplomacy towards the United States during the crisis and how American public opinion, as opposed to the US administration, reacted to these efforts. Attention throughout therefore focuses on the formulation of propaganda and on the decision-making behind its thematic selection, together with the Foreign Office's own systematic reviews of American opinion as manifested in the mass media.

14

Mobilizing American opinion

An identity of interests?

On 28 July 1956, Sir Roger Makins, British ambassador in Washington, sent the Foreign Office his assessment of the American mass media's immediate reaction to Nasser's nationalization of the Suez Canal Company. Such reports, which analysed leading press and radio comment in detail, would come to form the basis of the Foreign Office's estimate of US opinion throughout Suez. Clearly, Nasser's action had surprised the American public as much as the British, and by and large was similarly deplored. Makins noted that a strong editorial in the *Philadelphia Inquirer*, which referred to the coup as 'an act of banditry' and 'one of the biggest attempts at thievery in history', was representative of the vast majority of press and radio opinion. Nevertheless, views were divided on the extent to which the United States itself should intervene. There were some good signs for Eden. Several highly influential 'internationalist' newspapers had taken a similar line to that of the *New York Herald Tribune*: 'In the consultations which Great Britain, France and the United States are holding ... the central theme should be that the Free World, the world of law, is not powerless in the face of a plain act of economic aggression.' At the same time, some of these papers had seemingly ruled out the use of force already, the authoritative *New York Times* amongst them: 'Nasser's bluff will have to be called – not by force, but by reason, economics and law.' Meanwhile, the *Chicago Daily Tribune*, taking a line which, according to Makins, 'may well prove representative of the isolationist press', argued that the United States should simply turn a blind eye to the whole situation because it did not directly threaten its interests.[1]

Given this mixed reaction of US leading opinion, Makins urged the Foreign Office to waste no time in setting out its case to the American public. The ambassador pointed out that the US administration itself had not yet given a clear lead, having merely issued a statement on 27 July cautiously alluding to the 'far-reaching implications' of Nasser's act.[2] However, officials back in London had themselves been caught off guard by the Egyptian's announcement, owing to a combination of poor intelligence and clever concealment.[3] Consequently, it was a matter of days rather than hours before the Information Policy Department, which took overall responsibility for handling propaganda policy, managed to despatch a set of clearly defined guidelines to its missions abroad. (It was not until 3 August, for instance, that a full-scale meeting took place to discuss how to present the government's policy in the Middle East.)[4] Nevertheless, from the outset of the crisis it was apparent that when ministers and information officials spoke of the need to 'mobilise international opinion' their priority was the United States.[5] Given his diplomatic experience, Eden himself was probably more aware than most of the need to cultivate the American public. Whilst foreign secretary he had made a point of lunching regularly with the Association of American Correspondents in London. As for his press secretary, it is unlikely that a person more attuned to the idiosyncrasies of American opinion and mass media could have been found. Clark had worked for British Information Services in Chicago during the war, then was press attaché in the Washington embassy immediately afterwards.[6]

The first evidence of the Foreign Office issuing guidance to its Washington embassy on how it should present the government's case against Nasser came on 30 July. In two separate telegrams, the foreign secretary, Selwyn Lloyd, emphasized the need to marginalize the legality of Nasser's action and instead portray the issue as a political crisis with potentially grave consequences for the United States itself. As part of this plan, the Egyptian president had to be depicted as both misguided and untrustworthy. His past record, most notably his discrimination against Israeli shipping, was to be cited as graphic proof of the dangers of allowing the Suez Canal to come 'under the unfettered control of a single power'. The Egyptian regime, it was to be argued, had neither the desire nor the ability to operate the canal in accordance with international law; it would soon find itself without the 'indispensable' foreign pilots, for a start. Ultimately, if allowed to get away with it, Nasser would be in a position to threaten oil supplies vital not only to Western Europe but also the NATO alliance. All this was to be used in conversation with 'the [US] government, friendly colleagues and suitable journalists'.[7] Makins' US media review of 1 August, again showing an anti-Nasser consensus, suggested there was ample fertile ground for these publicity themes.[8]

Meanwhile, in London, the Foreign Office News Department needed no prompting to capitalize on its links with the all-important British-based American correspondents. These 'walking propagandists for Britain', as Ivone Kirkpatrick had called them in 1947 when in charge of the Foreign Office's Information Departments,[9] represented the source of nearly all news about Britain and its policies which reached the United States, and were therefore vital to Eden's cause. On the very night of the nationalization at least one of these journalists, Kennett Love of the *New York Times*, was given confidential information by Whitehall sources concerning retaliatory action.[10] Anthony Moore, deputy head of the News Department, met regularly with American correspondents in late July, impressing on his audience the extent of American financial oil interests in the Middle East and the parallels between Nasser and Hitler. Selwyn Lloyd himself then held a special hour-long 'off-the-record and non-attributable' briefing session with a group of American correspondents in early August.[11] By confiding in these journalists the intention was to stiffen their resolve, thereby strengthening support in the United States for force and increasing the pressure on Nasser.

By the end of the first week of the crisis, however, with the initial American outrage at Nasser's action diminishing, it was apparent to Cosmo Stewart, head of the Information Policy Department, that such guidance was by itself insufficient. Sympathetic American correspondents warned the Foreign Office of the difficulties of mobilizing an American public which was ignorant of Middle East affairs, vocally anti-colonialist and distracted by the forthcoming presidential elections.[12] As a result, Stewart despatched a memorandum to Alan Horn, deputy director-general of British Information Services in New York, detailing how he should intensify the campaign on that side of the Atlantic. This memorandum represented the first substantial attempt to devise a propaganda strategy for the United States during the Suez crisis and thus deserves scrutiny.

Stewart opened on an optimistic note, arguing that the reaction of the American press to the Suez situation had so far generally been quite good. The newspapers had certainly been more aggressive towards Nasser than the administration, a trend which the Information Policy Department was anxious should continue. However, what was causing information officials real concern was the stand taken by the key American correspondents in London, whose reaction was 'far from what we would desire them to be'. In order to arrest a further slide in American comment, therefore, it was important that both ends of the Foreign Office's propaganda operation acted in unison and that American opinion be made fully aware of the economic, military, political and ideological ramifications of the dispute. Stewart elaborated:

> Our real concern is to persuade the USA that no one can trust Nasser to live up to his promises or to maintain freedom of navigation in the Canal

by himself. We must keep US public opinion continuously aware of this; and of the manifold dangers in being hoodwinked by him.

Arguments which occur to us are:

(i) Western Europe is entirely dependent on the free navigation of the Canal for oil.

(ii) Consequently, the ability of the NATO powers to defend themselves in war or to develop their economies in time so that they are strong enough to make NATO a significant alliance cannot be left to the whim of one man: more particularly when his whims have proved to be so mercurial.

(iii) Nasser claims to be neutral. But he has flirted dangerously with Communism in the course of his arms deal. Nobody knows what he agreed with Shepilov [the Soviet Foreign Minister] and the Soviet Ambassador [during a high-profile meeting in Cairo in late June 1956], but it can be taken for granted that whatever was agreed was not to the advantage of the US or the UK. Nasser's unnecessary recognition of China, where, in contrast to the UK, he has no interests to defend, was provocative.

It was British Information Services' responsibility to convince the American public, via 'editors who are known to be friendly and whom you can really trust', that the United States was deeply involved in the crisis, whether it liked it or not. Any sign of weakening on its part, it should be stressed, would precipitate major difficulties in the supply of oil to Western Europe to a critical extent. The United States could then not fail to become embroiled in some form of rescue operation. Moreover, Nasser's action directly threatened the Americans' own Middle Eastern interests. If nationalization caught on in the Arab world, the Arabian–American Oil Company (ARAMCO) in Saudi Arabia, Gulf Oil and the Iraq Petroleum Company would inevitably all be on the hit list. Stewart then ended with a call to arms: 'I am sure you realise the extreme importance of having US opinion behind us, and we are confident that you will be as successful in influencing current opinion over Suez, as you have been over other issues.'[13]

British Information Services had in fact been conducting a low-key campaign specifically designed to support British policy in the Middle East since 1945. The intention was to give British imperialism a kinder, gentler face and to emphasize the essential identity, rather than rivalry, of British and American interests in the region. BIS had therefore in many ways prepared the ground for the Suez crisis. Over the years it had assiduously explained to American opinion the importance of the Middle East: its strategic significance as the right flank of NATO, as a major source of oil, the bridge between Asia and Africa, and the site of an international waterway as important strategically as the Panama Canal.[14] Only two months before Suez erupted, in May 1956, BIS had been given explicit instructions by the information office of the Washington embassy to highlight the rising importance of Middle Eastern oil to the United States' own economy – the US had recently moved from being a major exporter of oil to a net importer. According to Foreign Office calculations, American commercial interests in the region were, in absolute terms, greater than those of all other countries, constituting roughly 60 per cent of the whole Middle East oil investment. Prophetically, the directive also referred to the potentially disastrous repercussions of the closure of the Suez Canal.[15] Having established a sophisticated network through which to channel this type of information to the American people – economic and financial columnists, influential broadcasters, foreign affairs organizations such as the Council of Foreign Relations, even sympathetic politicians[16] – BIS was therefore poised to go on the offensive as soon as it heard the news of Nasser's coup.

Before it had had the opportunity to act on Stewart's advice from London, however, came proof that British Information Services would not be allowed to operate in a propaganda vacuum. During the first week of the crisis, the Eisenhower administration had declined to commit itself publicly on the question of force against Nasser, for fear of causing a rift with the British and sending Cairo the wrong signals.[17] Given that Eden already had serious misgivings about the White House's attitude towards military action (for good reason),[18] this silence had worked to his advantage. Affairs changed on 3 August, however, when Secretary of State Dulles, having only just returned from consultations with the British and French in London, made a nationwide broadcast strongly espousing the virtues of a negotiated settlement and implicitly distancing the US from its allies in the process.[19] Such statements, often issued by Dulles at hurried press conferences, came to cause the British government regular headaches throughout Suez. Their effect was to undermine severely the image of Anglo-American solidarity which Eden tried to convey and invariably increase the American public's desire for a diplomatic solution.

It was perhaps partly to counter the damage done by Dulles' speech, but also in response to Makins' latest media review showing increased moderation,[20] that the next day the Foreign Office devised its most novel publicity scheme yet. This comprised a series of tape recordings made by 'suitable British personalities' specifically designed for American consumption. It was envisaged that, for example, Sir Stephen Gibson, managing director of the Iraq Petroleum Company, or the *Daily Telegraph*'s deputy editor, Donald McLachlan, could speak of the implications of the dispute for US oil interests.[21] BIS in New York thoroughly approved, replying with information both on how the tapes might be disseminated via the BBC and contacts in the American broadcasting networks, and on what points they should focus. The recommended themes were a synthesis of those which the Information Policy Department had recently suggested and others that BIS felt would most make an impact on leading American opinion, namely: the effect on the Western and US economies of the closure of the canal; the effect of raising tolls; the dangers to Western interests in the Middle East; the danger that Egyptian control might lead to Soviet control; and the identity of interests of the Western powers and the need for a single policy.[22]

One organization that was particularly anxious to help disseminate these and other publicity lines in the United States was the English-Speaking Union (ESU). Founded in 1918 to promote greater understanding between Britain and the United States via inter-country cultural, literary and educational activities, the ESU had by the mid-1950s sixty-one branches and 22,000 members throughout the US.[23] As a privately funded, non-sectarian, apolitical organization it functioned independently of government, but this did not preclude liaison altogether. In early August 1956, Lord Baillieu, chairman of the ESU in Britain, contacted the Foreign Office Information Policy Department to volunteer his organization's assistance in guiding American opinion during the developing crisis. Mindful of the ESU's considerable influence in American establishment circles, and its experience in explaining British foreign policy to the chosen few, Cosmo Stewart accepted gratefully. Consultations ensued between the Foreign Office and Lewis Douglas, the visiting chairman of the ESU in the United States, over publicity tactics.[24] These came to form the basis of the ESU's discreet efforts to generate support for British interests over the following months, whether via lectures, letters to the mass media, pamphlets or its magazine (*English-Speaking World*). The work was shared with the Commonwealth–American Current Affairs Unit, an offshoot of the ESU formed in 1953, which specialized in publications. Its chairman was Sir Alexander Cadogan.[25]

There is little doubt that Eden's own keynote television broadcast on 8 August was designed primarily for domestic rather than foreign consumption. But, as with Selwyn Lloyd's highly charged radio appearance a week later,[26] there are clear signs that the prime minister sought to use this valuable air time also as a means of stiffening international opinion, American especially. Throughout his speech, which was relayed on four radio networks in the United States, Eden made every effort to appeal to American sentiment by painting the Suez dispute in Cold War colours. Nasser's 'act of plunder', he argued, had to be seen as a threat to the West as a whole, not just Britain;

hence he had consulted his two closest allies immediately. To accuse Britain of harbouring colonialist motives – BIS's chief bugbear throughout Suez – was entirely bogus; over the past few years he personally had gone out of his way to foster Anglo-Egyptian friendship. As for Nasser's claim to the moral high ground, namely that Egypt had the right to use the resources of the Suez Canal Company to help pay for the much-needed Aswan dam, this was entirely flawed. If Egypt was so short of money why was she spending millions on new arms shipments? It was the failure of the Egyptian 'dictator' to provide answers to such questions which had, Eden claimed, caused the United States government itself to pull out of the Aswan dam loan scheme. By implication, the White House therefore distrusted Nasser as much as did Britain.[27]

Whilst Eden was particularly aware of the need publicly to allay any suspicions Americans might have of the ulterior motives of his policy,[28] this did not necessarily prevent him at the same time suggesting otherwise privately. Consequently, the morning after the broadcast William Clark put a further gloss on the prime minister's words by disclosing unattributably to a group of American correspondents that Whitehall's experts had calculated the effects of the speech in advance, including the possibility that Egypt would break relations and stiffen her resistance to international control of the Suez Canal. The speech was intended at least to isolate and weaken Nasser and at best to provoke an act or a chain of actions that would turn world opinion against him and justify an attack. In fact, divulged the press secretary, the cabinet believed that a settlement was virtually impossible so long as Nasser remained in power, and it was therefore exerting military, economic and diplomatic pressures towards his overthrow.[29] This was another example of Eden exploiting the rules of press confidentiality, the aim on this occasion being to whip up American opinion in favour of force and increase further the pressure on the Egyptian regime.

Eden's address appears on the whole to have gained a good reception in the United States. Sir Roger Makins believed it had 'clarified the issues very well and ... hit just about the right note'.[30] Nevertheless, despite all these early efforts to influence the Americans, in the run-up to the London Conference in mid-August it was the Eden government, rather than Cairo, that found itself increasingly out of step with the prevailing mood of international opinion. In a frank and plainly depressing conversation on 9 August, William Clark and the cabinet secretary, Sir Norman Brook, agreed that 'Britain now found herself isolated, the Arab world against us, Asia against us, America wobbly, the old Commonwealth wobbly, only France as an ally and she is a definite liability with world opinion.'[31] As Eisenhower and Dulles had progressively moved further away from a policy of force, both in private and in public,[32] so, it seemed, had leadership opinion in the US. Many commentators who had previously been willing to contemplate military action fairly readily now took a far more cautious line. Others, such as Walter Lippmann, the doyen of American columnists who hitherto had been marking time on the issue of force, had by now come out firmly against it.[33]

Reflecting this shift in opinion, Makins' media reviews grew increasingly pessimistic. There was, he intimated on 10 August, very little chance of the American president committing troops during an election campaign in which peace was a fundamental issue. Indeed, in this respect, 'Nasser could not have chosen a better time for his action in terms of US politics.'[34] Prompted by Eden, William Clark tried his best to arrest this slide by again courting the American correspondents in London,[35] but to no avail. A few days later, on the eve of the London Conference, Makins was at his lowest point yet, lamenting that 'the whole trend of press and radio opinion is away from the use of force, at any rate so long as there is no interference with shipping in the Canal'.

By this stage, the American media had also started to pick up on the deep split over Suez emerging within Britain itself. Such front-page headlines as 'Labourites break with Eden on use of force' only served to provide yet more ammunition for those sections of US opinion urging restraint.[36] Dulles himself made the most of this cleavage during the London Conference.[37] The British government's cause was further hampered by the Egyptians running their own propaganda campaign in the United States. This might not have been as professional or as discreet as that operated by the Foreign Office, but it was not without a certain degree of sophistication. The Washington embassy was particularly impressed with one widely distributed pamphlet issued by their Egyptian counterparts which set out a strong case both for Cairo's right to nationalize the Suez Canal Company and its ability to run the canal efficiently.[38]

Communism versus colonialism

Eden came away from the London Conference, which concluded its proceedings on 23 August, with mixed feelings concerning the strength of the 'special relationship'. On the one hand, the United States had played a full and active part both in condemning Nasser's action and in forcing through the strong resolution insisting upon international control of the Suez Canal. Publicly, at least, the United States, Britain and France appeared united. On the other hand, serious doubts now existed about the US administration's willingness to support any resort to force. Following a dinner with Dulles on 18 August, Eden had to inform the Egypt Committee that the secretary of state 'was not in favour of provoking Colonel Nasser into taking further action which would justify the use of military force', nor would American troops join in an operation because 'the US government could not justify going to war over oil in the Middle East'.[39] The day after the conference ended, the inner cabinet showed major signs of division for the first time since the start of the crisis. Walter Monckton, minister of defence, expressed deep anxiety about the continued determination to use force at the earliest opportunity, in large part because of the predictable international reaction to it.[40] Despite such problems, Eden and most other ministers were not at this stage prepared to compromise their objectives. Having staked his reputation on Nasser's humiliation, to retreat now in the face of what he perceived as American weakness would probably render Eden's position as prime minister untenable. The only viable course of action in these circumstances was to exert even greater pressure on the US administration, including via public opinion, in the hope that the president was at least willing to acquiesce in any Anglo-French operation. Should Nasser actually accept the Eighteen Power proposals, or do the opposite and create a genuine *casus belli*, all the better.[41]

Over the next fortnight, with the Menzies mission to Cairo in early September acting as the focal point, the Foreign Office increased its propaganda activity in the United States significantly. On 29 August, Sir Roger Makins could be found once again lamenting the state of leading American opinion. The arrival of French troops in Cyprus – designed as part of the psychological campaign against Nasser – had struck the American mass media as a 'needless piece of muscle-flexing' and fuelled suspicions of colonialist gunboat diplomacy.[42] It was in response to this recent 'souring' on the part of the US press that Selwyn Lloyd took the initiative in asking Makins how he personally might help to counter such allegations of warmongering. The result was a widely reported speech emphasizing the threat to Western prosperity from dictators allowed to flout their engagements, and underlining the strength of international support (the United States' included) for Robert Menzies' crucial visit.[43] This was followed, on 6 September, by the UK delegation at the United Nations in New York, another of the Foreign Office's propaganda outlets in the US, whose information secretary liaised closely with British Information Services at all times, asking the Information Policy Department on behalf of Lloyd for publicity in relation to the Egyptian army's mobilization at the time of the seizure of the canal. Such a theme, together with extracts of the more poisonous Cairo wireless broadcasts, especially those hostile to the United States, was thought 'likely to impress American public opinion'. This was put in the hands of the Information Research Department.[44]

In the meantime, as if to confirm that he too saw a direct link between US policy and American public opinion, Eden sent Lloyd an article taken from the *News Chronicle* of 3 September focusing on the fears which many of the Arab states had of extremist threats to destroy the Middle East's oil wells and pipelines should Britain invade Egypt. Opposition to this 'scorched earth policy' would, thought the prime minister, 'be useful in persuading the Americans that the whole of the Arab world is not behind Nasser'. The article was passed on to British Information Services in New York. A few weeks later, Eden and Lloyd gave enthusiastic approval to the publicizing of a letter sent to the Arab League by one of Nasser's ministers, Salah Salem, in which the latter had proposed the Arabs' cancellation of contracts with Western oil companies and the establishment of treaties with the Soviet bloc. Such information was thought likely 'to strike American opinion especially well'.[45]

It is difficult to gauge the impact of these efforts to provide leading American opinion with material useful to the government's cause, in part because of the brevity of BIS's records. Some of the above themes were certainly covered in the mass media, and by authoritative journalists. In early September, for example, Joseph Alsop, a syndicated columnist on the *New York Herald Tribune* with whom BIS had strong links, warned against any compromise solutions which allowed Nasser to claim a success in defying the West. This would, he argued, merely serve to whet his appetite.[46] On the whole, however, this propaganda appears to have had little influence on an American public seemingly growing increasingly weary of the Suez dispute. Attempts to somehow shock American opinion into supporting force by informing correspondents that if Nasser rejected internationalization armed intervention would follow immediately merely backfired.[47] In the wake of the Menzies mission, Makins had to report that the American media had 'no enthusiasm whatsoever for the use of force' and now felt that 'the psychological moment for vigorous retaliation had passed'.[48] To make matters worse, Eisenhower now started to use the cautionary nature of American public opinion as extra leverage against what he saw as a dangerously aggressive prime minister. As he warned Eden in no uncertain terms on 8 September:

> The use of military force against Egypt under present circumstances might have consequences even more serious than causing the Arabs to

support Nasser. It might cause a serious misunderstanding between our two countries because I must say frankly that there is as yet no public opinion in this country which is prepared to support such a move, and the most significant public opinion that there is seems to think that the UN was formed to prevent this very thing.[49]

This did nothing to stop William Clark, on 10 September, discussing with Max Ways, head of the *Time-Life* bureau in London, how the government's case could get a better hearing in the United States. (Ways suggested an article on Eden for *Life.*) Nor did it prevent the permanent secretary, Ivone Kirkpatrick, showing the same publicist, a few days later, a confidential Foreign Office document which quoted the Jordanian newspaper *Addifa'a* calling for a unanimous Arab decision to stop oil supplies and the abrogation of all treaties with Western powers. The obvious intention was to prove to the American people the dangers of allowing Nasser to get away with tearing up an international agreement.[50]

Initially at least, Eden had high hopes for the 'ingenious' Suez Canal Users' Association scheme which Dulles had introduced to him in the middle of Menzies' Cairo talks. Together with the planned withdrawal of the Suez Canal Company pilots on 15 September, the prime minister believed that this offered the best chance yet of producing a *casus belli*. It was this inability to establish a diplomatic pretext for force which recently had caused Eden, much to his distress, to revise completely his military options.[51]

Hopes quickly turned to disappointment and bitterness, however. British Information Services did its utmost in this period to explain to American opinion why the foreign pilots felt forced by Nasser's truculence to walk out. It managed, for example, to have a *Daily Telegraph* article reproduced in the US press highlighting Egypt's manipulation of the pilots and the growing threats against their liberty.[52] Contrary to all expectations, however, the new Egyptian Canal Authority maintained the normal flow of traffic perfectly well without the former company's employees. By 18 September, Harold Watkinson, minister of transport, had to tell the Egypt Committee that PILEUP, the operation to over-congest the canal, had failed.[53] When Dulles then effectively broke the back of the SCUA project in the eyes of the Egypt Committee by telling American journalists during the second London Conference that it was 'not a device for denying Egypt any income at all with respect to the Canal', depression set in amongst ministers. For someone who had told Selwyn Lloyd during the conference how 'deeply disturbed [he was] by the manner in which Nasser was winning the propaganda battle', Dulles' behaviour seemed to many hypocritical if not duplicitous.[54] The disillusionment felt by those who had to explain such statements to the public was typified by William Clark, writing on 21 September:

> It was a ghastly day with all the worst expectations turning up. Dulles pulled rug after rug from under us, and watered down the Canal Users' Association ... till it was meaningless. Tony Moore came in half way through the afternoon almost in tears about the whole thing – how could we prevent it all seeming a total disaster.[55]

Harold Macmillan's trip to the United States between 20 September and 1 October 1956 has been the focus of intense historical debate, centred largely around his false assurance to Eden on returning that if it came to war Eisenhower would 'lie doggo'.[56] What has attracted less attention is the use the Chancellor of the Exchequer made of his visit to carry the Egypt Committee message direct to the American people. Both before and after his talks in Washington, Macmillan made a number of exceptionally strong speeches about Suez, candidly admitting that stopping Nasser was the main issue. Whilst on a visit to his mother's home state of Indiana, for example, he warned an audience of the parallels between the Rhineland and Suez crises and that, if the Egyptian's action went unchallenged,

> The determination to seize other property – whether it be British-owned, American-owned, Dutch-owned or what you will – will be too great; and before we know where we are it may well be that the control of vital oil supplies, on which Western Europe at any rate must live, will be in the hands of powers which have in effect become satellites of Russia.

The deliberate parading of the communist bogey, accompanied by emotive images of appeasement, was designed partly in this instance to counter local papers such as the *Indianapolis Star* which Macmillan noted had run 'some really bad isolationist leaders about "Colonialism" and the rest'.[57] The chancellor's public statements, often reported coast to coast, reflected both his fervently 'hawkish' stance and his own acute awareness of Britain's dependence on American financial assistance.[58] Macmillan might also have observed the relatively ambiguous results of Gallup's first opinion poll on the Suez crisis, conducted in the United States between 20 and 25 September. On the one hand, Gallup's findings appeared to bear out Eisenhower's warning to Eden of 8 September: that a majority of Americans was against military support for the British and French if they decided to use force against Egypt. Whether the American public was opposed to the use of force *per se*, however, or merely against any US military involvement was left unanswered. Indeed, the fact that a sizable section of opinion (23 per cent) at this stage actually wanted to send in troops and ships suggested that if it came to war the American people might favour a policy of watch and wait.[59]

Macmillan's visit was immediately followed by that of Selwyn Lloyd, who arrived in New York on 2 October to present Britain's case at the UN. Seen by many as perhaps Britain's last chance to corner Nasser before the Suez issue disappeared altogether from the front pages, this visit galvanized information officials in the United States into their most intense activity yet. The detailed groundwork for this was laid by Sir Pierson Dixon, Britain's permanent representative at the UN. On 29 September, Dixon cabled Lloyd's private secretary arguing that the forthcoming trip would provide 'a valuable opportunity for putting over our case on Suez to the US press, TV and Wireless'. A detailed publicity itinerary was duly prepared for the foreign secretary by Dixon, Makins and British Information Services in New York. This included a statement to the press and television on arrival at Idlewild Airport, a luncheon with prominent publishers and television commentators, an appearance on one of the major TV networks (two of which BIS professed to be 'in contact' with), and a further press conference towards the end of the visit.[60]

The highlight of all this in terms of publicity value was Lloyd's interview by the veteran broadcaster and Anglophile, Ed Murrow, on CBS's *See it Now* on 7 October. Drawing on the latest advice from Alan Horn and others as to the points most likely to sway American opinion, the foreign secretary gave a most persuasive performance, much belying his reputation as a dour debater. What was especially noteworthy was the skill with which Lloyd impressed upon Murrow the 'imperialist' nature of Nasserism and the scope which existed within the UN Charter for the unilateral use of force. In accordance with the Foreign Office's propaganda strategy, he also managed to emphasize the need for Anglo-American unity without actually admitting that the United States' help was essential. This would have smacked of weakness and contravened one of the guiding principles of diplomatic persuasion: to appeal to a nation's self-interest rather than its capacity for charity.[61]

If Lloyd's activities were aimed at any section of American opinion in particular it was probably the business community. American industrialists and bankers with international investments were naturally concerned with the implications of the nationalization of the Suez Canal Company, and it was in the Foreign Office's interest to play on their fears. A prominent adviser in this field was Harry Kern, senior editor of *Newsweek* and the president of *Foreign Report* in New York. The latter was a 'confidential' weekly news-sheet published by *The Economist* but sold separately to a select but influential circle of subscribers. Kern was in regular contact with Selwyn Lloyd throughout the crisis offering his views on the state of mind of American business-men and how the British government could tailor its propaganda appropriately. Whilst Lloyd was in New York, Kern recommended that the foreign secretary should publicly emphasize the damage Nasser's action had caused in terms of 'international equity' and the threat posed to the 'sanctity of contracts'. 'I know that stressing this theme will produce the maximum support for the British case in quarters where this counts,' wrote Kern on 4 October. Both of these themes were indeed significant features of Lloyd's messages to the American public in early October.[62]

Running in tandem with these high-profile ministerial visits in late September–early October was information work of a less noticeable, though arguably equally valuable, nature. As the crisis progressed, the embassy and consulates in the United States devoted an increasingly large percentage of their time to cultivating American opinion. One embassy official, David Muirhead, conducted an exhaustive tour of the southern United States in October. In twenty-three days he had driven 4000 miles, made fourteen set speeches, given twelve press interviews and appeared twice on television. He had spoken to local branches of the English-Speaking Union, a church group, a rotary club, a chamber of commerce, several universities, and the Air War College on the issues of Eastern Europe, the Middle East and Anglo-American unity.[63] For the most part these forays into public relations by British diplomats attracted little controversy; discretion was, after all, considered essen-tial. Perhaps the one exception was when the British consul general, Sir Robert Hadow, nearly came to blows with Senator George Malone of Nevada, a well-known anti-British isolationist, during a meeting held at the Commonwealth Club in San Francisco. What was reported as a comical affair in the *New York Times* illustrated well the potential divisiveness of the Suez issue.[64]

Had this concerted, if belated, attempt to bolster American opinion been allowed to operate without interference, the Foreign Office might have recovered some lost ground. The perceived increase in American support for Britain's policy could then have acted as a useful bargaining tool in the Security Council negotiations. Once again, however, Eden's campaign in the United States ran headlong into Foster Dulles' own propaganda strategy and his determination to distance the State Department's stance from that adopted by the British government. On 2 October, the very day that Lloyd arrived in New York, at a press conference the secretary of state first declared that 'there were no "teeth" in [SCUA], if that means the use of force', and then openly attacked Britain and France:

The US cannot be expected to identify itself 100 per cent either with the colonial powers or with the powers uniquely concerned with the problem of getting independence as rapidly and as fully as possible ... I hope that we shall always stand together in treaty relations covering the North Atlantic, [but] any areas encroaching in some form or manner on the problem of so-called colonialism will find the US playing a somewhat independent role.[65]

It is hard to think of a form of words likely to cause the British government greater embarrassment on the eve of the crucial Security Council debate. This was grist to the mill not only for Nasser, who all along had asserted that he was fighting against imperialism, but also for the many Americans who by nature were still extremely suspicious of 'perfidious Albion'. The consensus amongst the American media was that, despite being tactless, Dulles' remarks contained a great deal of truth.[66] Thus, although Dulles privately apologized almost immediately for his 'blunder', there was little Eden could do publicly except retaliate unattributably via *The Times*.[67] The Foreign Office News Department itself decided to play Dulles' remarks down as much as possible, although the BBC American Service did offer a sharp riposte in the form of a commentary by H. V. Hodson, editor of the *Sunday Times*.[68] The general feeling amongst information officials in London and Washington was that to have entered into a slanging match would only have given Nasser even greater succour and deepened Anglo-American wounds still further.

Dulles' failure of judgement, or 'betrayal' as many in the Egypt Committee saw it,[69] seems to have acted as the final straw for Eden, and convinced him that Britain and France must do as appeared best to themselves. 'And now what have you to say for your American friends?' he angrily asked Anthony Nutting, the Foreign Office minister who throughout the crisis had urged the prime minister not to get too far out of step with the United States. 'How on earth can you work with people like that?' Eden asked Iverach McDonald on 3 October. 'It leaves us in a quite impossible position. We can't go on like this.'[70] With Lloyd's subsequent failure to reach a wholly satisfactory agreement with the Egyptians at the United Nations, combined with the Israelis' offer to attack Egypt in mid-October, Eden made the decision to do the previously unthinkable and go ahead without the Americans.

It was at this point that relations between the Egypt Committee and the Foreign Office entered something approaching a twilight zone. Eden's thinking seems to have been that the fewer people who knew of the collusion plans the better. The result was that no one in the Foreign Office involved with Anglo-American relations or with information work in the United States had prior knowledge of the project, let alone any guidance on how it might be presented to international opinion. When Sir Roger Makins arrived in London on 15 October to take up his new duties as permanent secretary to the Treasury – thereby leaving a vacuum in Washington until his successor, Harold Caccia, turned up on 8 November – nobody wanted to see him.[71] John Coulson, chargé d'affaires in Washington and acting ambassador, was not sent instructions from London until 6pm on 29 October, more than two hours after the Israeli invasion of the Sinai. John Peck, director-general of British Information Services and perhaps the most important official in terms of the Americans' perception of the intervention, was kept entirely in the dark.[72] Whether knowing of the plans afoot would have enabled information officials in the US to prepare the ground somehow is of course highly debatable. As was the case in Britain, to have primed the American public would probably have given the game away. Either way, judging from a most instructive report on Midwest opinion drafted by the British consulate in Detroit on 12 October, the battle for American public opinion by this juncture seemed well and truly lost:

> If Mr Dulles and the President had given a more positive and consistent lead from the beginning it seems to me that the US public could have accepted a considerably more couragious [sic] policy over the Suez issue. Perhaps, in an election year, that was more than could be hoped for. In any case it is too late now.[73]

Going it alone

Having, in their view, been continually frustrated by an indecisive, at times mendacious, US administration, and opted instead to work with the Israelis, one might have expected ministers to care little for the Americans' reaction to what lay ahead. The manner in which relations with the White House were virtually severed during the latter half of October whilst collusion plans were completed seemed to confirm this.[74] Despite its resentment, however, the cabinet realized that the American attitude towards military intervention could not simply be ignored. On the very eve of Eden's ultimatums to Egypt and Israel on 30 October, Selwyn Lloyd asked the cabinet to consider whether Britain 'should attempt to persuade [the US] to support the action which we and the French are proposing'. Although ministers were not prepared to postpone military action for this, they did approve an immediate, last-ditch, approach to the Americans:

> Even though it was unlikely that the US government would respond to

such an appeal, we should do our utmost to reduce the offence to American public opinion which was liable to be caused by our notes to Egypt and Israel. Our reserves of gold and dollars were still in need of assistance, and we could not afford to alienate the US government more than was absolutely necessary.[75]

This indicated that, as far as the cabinet was concerned, the battle to capture the hearts and minds of the American people was far from over; if anything, the need to court US opinion and use it against Eisenhower and Dulles was now more important than ever.

Unfortunately for British information officials in London and those on the ground in the United States, the apparent concern shown for American opinion at the highest levels of government failed to manifest itself in the form of appropriate action, that is essential policy guidance. Over the next week, as the 'special relationship' threatened to be torn asunder, ministers on the whole made very little effort to cultivate American opinion themselves. Having swiftly reopened the channels of communication with the White House, Eden himself seemed content to rely on heartfelt, though ultimately forlorn, appeals to Eisenhower.[76] Moreover, owing to the atmosphere of secrecy surrounding events in the Middle East and the fact that so few officials were told of the plans afoot, much of the Foreign Office's elaborate and efficient machinery of publicity was of little use. This was especially the case in relation to the United States where the Foreign Office had always favoured a sober, unobtrusive approach based on a continuous stream of reliable, positive information rather than bursts of high-pressure propaganda aimed at third countries.

Despite this, it would be wrong to think that the British government's case in the US went entirely by default. The explosion of anger in Washington, caused in large part by the cabinet's having acted blatantly behind the administration's back,[77] certainly left the British embassy there in moral and diplomatic quarantine. But the situation in New York was very different. This was a scenario with which the elastic, personal-contact system of British Information Services was well-equipped to deal. Starved of any clear political instructions on how to present the war in the Middle East to the American people, BIS therefore simply devised explanations of its own, ably assisted by the British delegation at the UN.[78]

The most graphic evidence of British Information Services' ability to act independently during this critical period came in the form of a memorandum written by John Peck, its director-general (and a former head of the Information Research Department). This set out a coherent and persuasive case for Britain's right to use force and seems to have acted as the cornerstone of the government's propaganda campaign in the United States following the launching of MUSKETEER REVISE. Clearly of the opinion that the best form of defence was attack, Peck urged his officials to make no apologies for the military intervention, nor for the lack of prior consultation with the US administration. Americans had to realize that Britain had in fact had no alternative but the immediate use of force: first, because only she had the capability of acting promptly and effectively in the Middle East in a military sense; secondly, because a halt had to be called to the Egyptian–Israeli fighting before it inflamed the region; and, thirdly, because Soviet support for Nasser's destabilizing of the region ruled out any possibility of the United Nations acting in time. Leading on from this last point, Peck argued that it was the responsibility of all the Western powers to support each other against the threat posed to their interests in the Middle East by the Soviet-backed Egyptian regime, if not actively then at least passively. Indeed, if the NATO allies acted in concert, the Anglo-French intervention could be used as a platform from which to build 'a more positive Western policy in the Middle East'. Reading between the lines, the first prerequisite of this was the neutering of Nasserism.[79]

By emphasizing Nasser's ambitions to destroy Israel, Peck also recognized the value of co-opting the support of the Jewish lobby in the US. Zionists had for years constituted a powerful pressure group in American politics, as the Foreign Office had discovered to its own cost in the latter period of the Palestine mandate.[80] Following the Soviet–Egyptian arms deal of September 1955, the United Jewish Appeal, along with other organizations, had conducted an intense campaign of lobbying to persuade the State Department to allow the sale of American arms to Israel to counter the growing Arab threat.[81] Whilst this had not succeeded, it meant that by the summer of 1956 the Israeli lobby could boast of an increasingly influential network of sympathizers, and one which any administration, particularly in an election year, ignored at its peril.[82] As Eisenhower's campaign to remain in the White House reached its climax in early November, Peck's strategy appeared shrewd and opportune. Discretion was essential, however, lest any impression were given that Britain and Israel had concocted a pact against Egypt.

Publication of this 'think piece' in any open, attributable sense would naturally have caused immediate controversy in the United States. The British government's official motive for intervention had after all merely been to 'separate the combatants', not to turn the Israeli attack on Egypt into an overdue Western assault on Cairo. In order for Peck's trenchant memorandum to get an airing, therefore, it had to be disseminated confidentially amongst British Information Services' most trusted contacts. Chief amongst these appears to have been George

Sokolsky, influential columnist and broadcaster, whose material through-out November and into December was a model of consistent support for Eden. On 4 November, for example, Sokolsky made a prime-time broadcast on the ABC network quoting parts of Peck's thesis virtually word for word. On 5 November, the day of the Anglo-French landings in Egypt, he followed suit, this time in an article which appeared in the *New York Journal America*. This was then ensured even greater pub-licity by being syndicated to the entire Hearst Press and over three hundred newspapers throughout the United States.[83]

As the crisis progressed and Foreign Office personnel managed to get a firmer grip on the Egypt Committee's policy, so the Information Policy Department felt sufficiently confident to issue specific guidance to its overseas missions. On 6 November, Cosmo Stewart suggested to Peck that a potentially profitable line of argument to use with American opinion was to draw a parallel between the present Anglo-French intervention in the Middle East and that by the British in Greece at the end of 1945. The latter had been heavily censured initially, both in the United States and at home, and yet only two years later it was the Americans themselves who were bearing the main burden of supporting the Greek government against communist guerrillas. By exploiting this theme, Stewart argued that the American people would hopefully wake up to the dangerous instability of the Middle East and recognize just who the real enemy was.[84]

As well as devising suitable publicity themes to justify the resort to force, the Foreign Office also made strenuous efforts to ensure that the fighting itself got the best possible coverage in the US. American correspondents seeking accreditation for the battle zone were con-sistently afforded preferential treatment, although, like their counter-parts from Fleet Street, they too were prevented from witnessing either the bombing sorties or the amphibious landings. Following the ceasefire and the lifting of censorship on 7 November, the Information Policy Department and the psychological warfare experts in Cyprus gave the Ministry of Defence explicit orders to allocate US journalists the same status as British correspondents. 'You had better keep this dark,' Newling at the MoD warned the Foreign Office, 'as I am already in very hot water with the British and Commonwealth Press for what they allege to be gross over-representation of the American Press.'[85] American correspondents with troublesome reputations were treated with kid gloves, especially if their papers showed signs of sympathy for Britain's case. For example, when the governor of Cyprus refused to issue a visa to Alexander Sedgwick of the *New York Times* on the grounds of his commitment to Enosis (union with Greece), this was swiftly overturned after an urgent appeal by British Information Services in New York: 'In the present difficult phase of Anglo-American relations the *New York Times* is one of the few journals only moderately critical of ourselves. The action proposed would antagonise not only the *New York Times* but the entire American press.'[86]

By allowing American journalists such privileged, yet controlled, access to Port Said, the Foreign Office also helped to refute what it called the 'atrocity stories' being widely disseminated by the Egyptians' own propaganda machine in the United States. These took the form of articles, films, photographs and specially commissioned magazines depicting the Anglo-French 'police action' as an indiscriminate massacre which had claimed the lives of up to twelve thousand civilians.[87] Ministers, including Eden, attached great importance to the countering of these allegations and worked on discrediting their sources personally.[88] The Ministry of Defence, Foreign Office News Department and Information Policy Department acted in unison to produce their own printed guidance material, feature articles, photographs, films and radio broadcasts on Port Said for circulation in the United States and elsewhere. The Washington embassy assisted by 'taking all possible steps, both overt and covert, to counteract' the Egyptian material.[89] Eventually, whilst at the UN in mid-November and mindful of the damage that could be done to Britain's reputation in the United States if Egypt's charges were given a greater airing, Selwyn Lloyd ordered a full-scale assault on Cairo's campaign. 'The stink will last for years unless we mount a major operation in reply.' The resulting publicized reports by Walter Monckton and Sir Edwin Herbert, based on enquiries in Port Said, had the overall desired effect.[90]

If, by dint of censorship and guidance, the Foreign Office managed to control the American media's coverage of MUSKETEER REVISE, the same most certainly could not be said of the collusion controversy. It was on this issue that Eden's propaganda campaign met the State Department's head-on. Furious at the way in which the British had connived with the French and Israelis, and with ample intelligence material to prove it, throughout November the State Department leaked the whole story to the American people via its own press contacts.[91] The Information Policy Department wrote to British Information Services suggesting a number of ways of 'killing the collusion bogey'. It was to be argued, for example, that if there really had been collusion, then surely the timing of the Anglo-French military action would have been better (this referred to the delay between the initial bombings and the actual landings).[92] The BBC's North American Service added weight to this thesis by claiming that the British government had prevented the Israelis from achieving their purpose of getting at the heart of Egypt.[93]

Such weak reasoning had very little impact, however. Even BIS's well-cultivated links with normally pro-British opinion-formers could not help in this matter. For example, when Bill Ormerod of the New York office sought to persuade his friend Tom Griffith, foreign editor of *Time* magazine, of Britain's innocence, he got very short shrift. Griffith believed that HMG had had wind of Israel's plan to attack Egypt for weeks and had deliberately refrained from warning her against undertaking such an act in the conspicuously firm manner the Foreign Office had over Jordan.[94] The damage which the copious evidence of a conspiracy did to Britain's case in the United States was very real. Allegations of deceit added genuine anger to what was already deep shock. This caused grave pessimism in the Foreign Office's American Department:

> The Americans appear to have little intention of accepting our denial that such collusion took place and this suspicion is going to make it difficult to re-establish really good relations with the US administration.[95]

As for BIS's hopes that careful exploitation of the power of the American Israeli lobby might encourage White House moderation, this too proved a chimera. Eisenhower was determined not to act as he believed Harry Truman had in the late 1940s and allow electoral expediency – and the Zionist lobby especially – to cloud his political judgement.[96] When the president heard of Israel's Sinai invasion, he showed no hesitation in initiating a condemnatory resolution in the UN Security Council, even though his own fate was about to be decided in national elections. The accompanying economic sanctions against Tel Aviv were relatively mild, in part for fear of causing what secretary of the Treasury George Humphrey called 'terrible political activity'.[97] Nevertheless, once the fighting had ceased, and his fight for the White House had succeeded, Eisenhower then used the threat of powerful sanctions via the UN to force the reluctant Israelis to return to their pre-war boundaries. When American Jewish spokesmen complained about these demands, the State Department retaliated by threatening to lift the tax exemptions of the United Jewish Appeal.[98] The overall result was a subdued Zionist lobby, 'powerless to affect [US] foreign policy',[99] and a further weakening of Britain's case in the United States.

What helped more than anything else in this period to offset the damage done to the Anglo-American alliance by collusion was a growing realization on the part of the US media and public that the real enemy in the Middle East was the Soviet Union, not Britain. It is difficult to say exactly when and why this shift in opinion took place. There can be little doubt that Bulganin's notes to Eisenhower, Eden and Mollet on 5 November, in which he threatened the use of 'rocket weapons' against Britain and France unless they immediately withdrew from Egypt, following this by offering Nasser Soviet 'volunteers', were a propaganda godsend for the cabinet. The American media regarded these moves as very menacing. Together with the Red Army's simultaneous crushing of the Hungarian uprising, it was these actions, arguably, more than anything else that made many Americans think twice about their heavy criticism, and alienation, of their allies.[100] That the Foreign Office's scare tactics also heightened anti-Soviet sentiment in the United States, is, however, undeniable. If the propaganda surrounding the allies' discovery of Soviet military equipment in Egypt had a positive impact on British opinion, this was perhaps even more the case in the United States, where many leading commentators had for years been critical of the State Department's apparent lack of a Middle Eastern policy, which, they warned, would eventually play into the communists' hands.[101]

Throughout November and into December, British information officials on both sides of the Atlantic conducted a systematic campaign designed to persuade Americans to view the recent events in the Middle East through a Cold War prism. In London, the Foreign Office News Department and Monckton's Public Relations Committee presented American journalists with proof that Nasser was a Soviet pawn; in the United States, the Washington embassy and British Information Services did 'everything to encourage those American commentators who had recently been emphasising the extent of Soviet manoeuvres in the Middle East'. The Information Research Department, whose remit was anti-communist propaganda, provided much of the necessary background material.[102]

These efforts appear to have paid dividends. On 17 November, the newly appointed ambassador in Washington, Sir Harold Caccia, wrote that there was a growing burden of comment in the American media on reports that 'Soviet military penetration of Egypt and Syria had progressed far beyond Western intelligence estimates'. Furthermore, speeches about HMG's policy in the face of Soviet intervention made by, amongst others, the colonial secretary, Lennox-Boyd, in the Commons on 13 November, were reported as having been given 'a good reception in most quarters'.[103] This was particularly the case amongst such distinguished commentators as Joseph and Stewart Alsop, Joe Harsch, Walter Lippmann and Ed Murrow, with whom British Information Services was later credited with having had conspicuous influence. Joseph Alsop's line might be attributed in part to Caccia's having told him of his and Selwyn Lloyd's now legendary conversation with Dulles in Walter Reed Hospital on 17 November, during which the secretary of state asked Lloyd why the British forces had halted before they were in complete control of the Suez Canal.[104] So sympathetic to Eden's cause was Ogden Reid, president of the *New York Herald Tribune*, that he went as far as sending the prime minister a personal telegram, dated 16 November:

> Have just had a talk with Selwyn Lloyd and told him that I stand ready to help in current MidEast situation if I can be of any service to you or him.

Reid's offer of assistance, which was readily accepted,[105] came at a critical point in the crisis for the British government. In order to save face, Eden was fighting for a phased withdrawal from Suez to match the arrival of the UNEF contingents, thus ensuring an orderly takeover; and for the allies' own salvage fleet to be allowed to clear the debris from the canal. Jeopardizing this more than anything else was the tremendous pressure now being felt in Britain from the economic effects of the intervention. Ministers had agreed to call a premature halt to military operations on 6 November on the implicit understanding that American sanctions would be replaced by financial aid.[106] In the event, Washington continued to use its monopoly on the world's dominant currency as a crude weapon in order to ensure the swift Anglo-French evacuation of Egypt.[107] On 9 November, C. F. Cobbold, the governor of the Bank of England, told the Treasury that sterling had been a major casualty of the crisis and only radical treatment could save it. Three days later, the Treasury's senior officials concluded that if Britain went on losing reserves at the existing rate a second devaluation would be unavoidable. Coming so soon after the 1949 devaluation, many believed that this would destroy the sterling area.[108]

The government's predicament then worsened when, on 18 November, after the latest in a series of relapses which had dogged him throughout the crisis, Eden was told by his doctors that he needed a complete rest, preferably in warmer climes; he would leave for Jamaica on 23 November. It was in the midst of this, on 20 November, that a distinctly chastened Harold Macmillan gave the cabinet the grim details of the state of the British economy. The only way to stop the potentially fatal run on the pound was, he argued, to appeal to the 'goodwill of the US' in the hope that she might call a halt to her policy of financial retaliation. In this the cabinet saw a significant role for the American people. Ministers noted with great interest the 'increasing evidence that unofficial opinion in the US was showing a greater understanding of our policy in the Middle East. We should do all we could to ensure that our actions and motives were presented to public opinion in the US as fully and convincingly as possible.' Lord Reading, minister for foreign affairs, was entrusted with this task.[109]

Whilst he was at the United Nations between 12 and 27 November, the foreign secretary again went out of his way to cultivate American opinion. This included another nationwide television broadcast, designed to appeal to the American public in general, followed by two keynote after-dinner speeches intended to influence leading opinion in a more subtle, indirect fashion. The first was delivered at a meeting of the Pilgrims of the United States, an elite dining club promoting Anglo-American relations; the second, which made a strong attack on American anti-colonialism, to the English-Speaking Union.[110] The latter body did its best to soothe Anglo-American relations in November, including the cultivation of newspaper editors.[111] During this period both Lloyd and Harold Caccia also briefed the American press. The best example of this was the detailed interview Lloyd accorded Roy Howard, editor of the *New York World-Telegram and Sun*, on the eve of his return to London. The result was an extremely sympathetic and widely publicized article emphasizing the inherent strength and essential elasticity of the 'special relationship'. When sent the text of this, together with Howard's 'excellent editorial', the Information Policy Department was very impressed, citing it as 'evidence that we have our friends in the USA'.[112]

It is of course impossible to measure the effectiveness of this campaign to influence American opinion with any acceptable degree of accuracy. To isolate one particular influence from the total sum exerted – through the family, politicians and the media – presents an insurmountable task. What we can say for certain is that the Foreign Office's efforts made no difference to the US administration's demand that Britain and France withdraw their troops from Egypt unconditionally. This the cabinet – minus Eden – acceded to in the first week of December.[113] Nor is there any evidence that the United States gave the Treasury any financial support during this period; sanctions were eased only after the military withdrawal started.[114] Looked at from this angle, therefore, Britain's propaganda campaign in the US during the most critical phase of Suez failed to achieve any of its short-term objectives. Eisenhower's determination to punish London's insolence was stiffened by his own political assuredness. On 6 November he had been re-elected by an overwhelming majority of ten million votes (almost double the margin of 1952). This result was seen by the president as a vindication of his Middle Eastern policy and for the time being rendered the White House almost impervious to domestic and overseas criticism.[115]

The question, nevertheless, remains whether these efforts paid off in the long term by helping Britain to mend its fences with the Americans, and thereby helping to ease the pressures on the Conservative government. There seems little doubt that even when American public opinion was at its angriest, in early November, it was by no means as critical of the Anglo-French action as was the administration. One poll published on 10 November claimed that only 45 per cent disapproved of the intervention; 31 per cent approved and 24 per cent did not know.[116] This itself might arguably be interpreted as a victory for British propaganda. As November passed into December, however, and the pace and intensity of the Foreign Office's campaign increased, it is striking that even those elements of leading opinion initially most offended by Eden's decision to 'go it alone' showed clear signs of having come round to the prime minister's point of view. Any anger seems on the whole to have subsided remarkably quickly. It was now generally accepted that the intervention was more of 'a stupid blunder' than anything immoral; that the British, French and Israelis had suffered from considerable provocation; and that the US administration itself had to bear at least some responsibility for what had happened in the Middle East. Moreover, except for the professional isolationists, all of the major newspapers and comment throughout the United States now insisted that the time had come for a major effort to repair the structure of the Western alliance, regardless of who was right or wrong over the Suez issue.[117]

Given the dramatic events that also took place in Eastern Europe in November 1956, inevitably drawing the NATO allies closer together, one would certainly have expected some sort of improvement in Anglo-American relations once the fighting in Egypt had stopped. For American opinion on Eden's 'police action' to have shifted so markedly, and in such a relatively short space of time was, however, curious. It is difficult to believe that Britain's multifarious propaganda activities in the US, both at the height of the Suez crisis, and in its immediate wake, did not play at least some part in this. Certainly, the Foreign Office itself had no doubts on this score.[118]

15

The campaign in the United States: conclusion

Foreign Office propaganda policy in the United States post-1945 had been characterized in the main by a low-key, passive approach, geared to deflecting criticism rather than re-educating opinion. Suez constituted a marked departure from this. From the moment that the crisis broke and it chose to embark on a policy of force, the Egypt Committee attached the utmost importance to winning over American opinion to its cause. Ministers saw a direct link between the American people's stance on the issue and the position that the Eisenhower administration itself would take. This, it was assumed, would in turn have important implications for the attitude of other states, including ultimately Egypt itself. The result was an unprecedented emergency propaganda campaign designed to persuade the American public of the legitimacy of the use of force against the Egyptian regime. Within this, four specific tactics emerged: an attempt to depict Gamal Abdel Nasser as both a second Hitler and a crypto-communist; an attempt to emphasize the identity of interests of the Western powers in the Middle East, chiefly oil; an attempt to counter allegations of British imperialism with references to Britain's past contributions to Arab unity and the present decolonization process; and an attempt to drive a wedge between the 'isolationists' and the 'internationalists' by underlining the wider strategic and political implications of the issue as a whole.

This campaign ran into difficulties almost from the outset. For all its well-established contacts, the Foreign Office found it impossible to exert anything like the degree of control over the American mass media that it could over the British. The failure to enlist the support of the American correspondents in London, many of whom were pro-British by inclination and were subjected to the most thorough guidance, was particularly illuminating. The result was that within a fortnight of Nasser's coup, the vast majority of the United States' leading opinion-formers had come out firmly against the use of force as a means of solving the dispute. Most Americans had little time for the British government's rhetoric. Nasser clearly was no innocent champion of anti-colonialism; yet neither was Egypt another Nazi Germany. The United States did indeed have a number of valuable economic interests in the Middle East, but their loss would not prove life-threatening. Only 25 per cent of her oil imports came from the region, for example.[1] As for Nasser being a Soviet pawn, there may have been some truth in this, but the consensus was that to use his latest act as a pretext for invasion would only serve to inflame anti-Western sentiment in the Arab world still further, and thereby increase Russia's influence in the Middle East. After all, to most Arabs the Suez Canal Company was one of the most powerful symbols of imperialism (and with ample justification, in many Americans' eyes).

Information officials might have been able to direct or refine some of this American thinking; however, they could not hope to over-turn it, not at least without some help from the US administration itself. As it was, the State Department's desire to fashion the press to its own liking rendered the Foreign Office's task even more problematic. It was one thing for the US government to be non-committal, leaving the American people to make up their own mind on the Suez issue; it was quite another for it to publicly label its 'allies' as colonialists whilst privately urging them 'to make Nasser disgorge what he was attempting to swallow'.[2] This gave the impression to many in the cabinet that the Americans wanted to have their cake and eat it. One cannot help feeling that the presidential election campaign, in which the Republican party's principal plank was its peace-keeping record, played at least a part in this.

In this regard, the cabinet's unanimous decision to manufacture a *casus belli* the very week before the Americans went to the polls was impolitic in the extreme. For Eden then not to have the decency to give Eisenhower prior notice of his ultimatums to Egypt and Israel added insult to injury. The prime minister was ostracized, and the State Department took the lead in exposing the transparency of his plan to the American press, rather than acquiescing as Eden envisaged. At the height of the crisis, therefore, British Information Services in the United States found itself bereft of Whitehall guidance and having to compete on two fronts: disproving Egyptian 'atrocity' and American collusion propaganda. Added to this was Eden's failure to gain acceptance of his policy at home, surely a *sine qua non* of any foreign propaganda operation.[3] Finally, for the military operation itself to be so ill-timed that there was a five-day delay between the bombings and the actual landings was arguably the biggest publicity blunder of all. Besides allowing criticism to build up, because it meant that the Anglo-

French invasion occurred on the very eve of the presidential elections, this appeared to many Americans as though London and Paris were trying to deliver their finishing stroke to Nasser whilst America's back was turned.

Sensibly, in these circumstances, British Information Services chose in the main to concentrate its efforts on patching up Britain's relations with the US as quickly as possible rather than wasting time on negative counter-propaganda. The key to this was to switch the Americans' focus of attention from the Middle East to Eastern Europe and from the Suez Canal dispute to the Cold War. This it appears to have done very successfully by giving maximum publicity to the Budapest 'massacres', the Kremlin's threats of a third world war and the 'discovery' of Soviet arms in Egypt. Whilst this improvisation was not enough to save Eden, it does seem to have helped to pave the way towards the relatively swift reconciliation between London and Washington, confirmed at the Bermuda Conference in March 1957.[4] By this stage, however, it was clear that the 'special relationship' had taken on a new meaning. The Eisenhower Doctrine, announced in January 1957, had also signalled the United States' replacement of Britain as the dominant power in the Middle East.[5]

16

Conclusion and epilogue

The received impression of Sir Anthony Eden during the Suez crisis is one of a man wracked by indecision, living up to his reputation as an habitual Downing Street 'ditherer'. This might serve as an accurate description of his behaviour a month or so into the crisis but certainly not at its outset. Within hours of hearing the news of the nationalization of the Suez Canal Company on 26 July 1956, the prime minister and his closest advisers had made two firm decisions. The first was that, regardless of the legal complications, Gamal Abdel Nasser could not be permitted to have unfettered control of the Suez Canal, with 'his hand on our windpipe', as Eden put it.[1] The second was that the Egyptian dictator's act should be used as a pretext for his removal from power.

This resolution was in sharp contrast to two previous British setbacks in the Middle East in particular: Musaddiq's nationalization of the Anglo-Iranian Oil Company in 1951 (under the previous Labour administration) and, more recently, the dismissal of Sir John Glubb as the head of the Jordanian army in March 1956. On both of these occasions the government in London had backed away from a confrontation only to see its domestic popularity sink and regional nationalism soar.[2] Eden was determined not to make the same mistake this time around. To him and many others in the cabinet, this was the test case on which Britain, her prestige and world status already severely in decline, would stand or fall.

The result of these decisions was one of the most intensive propaganda campaigns conducted by a British government since World War Two. From the very start of the crisis, Downing Street and the Foreign Office, supported by the Quai d'Orsay, sought to blur the legal and financial verities of the dispute and keep the issue as political and emotional as possible. This was intended both to increase the public's hostility towards Nasser, thus providing the climate for aggression, and to rasp Egyptian nationalist sensibilities in the hope of provoking a *casus belli*. Nasser was to be isolated internally and internationally; the use of force was to be presented as justifiable, necessary even. Unlike the Egyptian president, Eden was not able to direct the British media entirely how he would have wished. He was, therefore, at a propaganda disadvantage throughout. On the other hand, any success he did manage with the press and broadcasting services would, owing to their perceived independence, count double. The extent to which the prime minister did control these opinion-formers during Suez should therefore be viewed in this context.

The signs are that this campaign succeeded, particularly in the first weeks. By and large, the question of Egypt's legal right to nationalize the Anglo-French company was overlooked by the British media. Attention immediately focused instead on the manner and implications of Nasser's act. Whilst this angle of approach was to some degree to be expected of the market-orientated press, the same excuse could not be made for the BBC. After all, its function was, as William Clark himself pointed out during the course of the crisis, to 'inform and educate', not just 'entertain'. It is difficult not to conclude that the government's immediate efforts to dictate the agenda of the dispute played at least some part in the media's conspicuous failure to address this most vital of issues. Had they done so, the basis of Eden's whole case against Nasser would have been severely weakened from the outset (as the cabinet itself recognized).

With the legalities of the dispute marginalized, this left the government free to concentrate on building up a picture of 'the enemy' as a serious military and ideological threat to Britain and the Free World. Here, ministers sought and obtained the active support of a number of highly placed media acquaintances. A large contingent of the national press volunteered not only to lead the campaign of hate against the Egyptian 'dictator', but also to do the government's bidding for military action. Whitehall spokesmen then increased the war mentality simply by tapping into the lobby system, where they could brief print and broadcasting journalists 'anonymously'. Bearing in mind Eden's need to disguise his objectives, this helped the inner cabinet's propaganda immeasurably.

The overall result was a tirade of abuse and threats against a foreign leader the like of which arguably had not been seen since Hitler had torn up the Munich agreement in March 1939. It would of course be absurd to see the hand of the government behind all the vitriol. However, looking back after thirty-five years, it is possible to spot the fruits of official guidance in numerous places: from the uncharacteristic aggression of papers like *The Times*, through to the loyalty of others like the *Daily Telegraph*; and from the BBC's emphasis on national unity, through to the media's wholly inadequate coverage of the so-called 'precautionary measures'. One can only speculate but had Eden in fact been able to mount a military assault on Egypt early in the summer 1956, the odds on him having had the support of the vast majority of British people seem very strong. The manner in which his propaganda had helped prepare the ground for war would have taken much of the credit for this.

In the event, as the crisis entered into its third week without any sign of an imminent Anglo-French riposte, serious cracks began to appear in the government's public relations strategy. Central to this was the prime minister himself. Eden had already shown, even before Suez, that he lacked the personal characteristics to cope under the critical scrutiny of modern media coverage. During the crisis his over-sensitivity to criticism increased. This proved to be a major handicap, not only precluding rational response, but also alienating journalists. Thus, when the BBC gave a few minutes' air time to a minor Egyptian official in August, Eden's reaction was to try and ban the broadcast. This took no account of the fact that hitherto the BBC had been on the whole extremely supportive of the government. Similarly, a few months later, when actual hostilities started, his answer to press critic-ism was to bully newspaper editors personally. These manoeuvres might have been effective occasionally. However, in a democracy where, as outlined in the Introduction, successful propaganda requires subtlety and sophistication, such tactics were far too clumsy and ultimately counter-productive. In Eden's case, his panicky, direct dealing was interpreted by many in the media as a sign of a weak policy.

Closely related to this problem was another – that of the breakdown in communications between the prime minister and his press secretary. The relationship between Eden and William Clark was already tense prior to Suez. In the heat of the crisis it disintegrated. In Eden's eyes, Clark became a subversive, working for his opponents. To Clark, Eden's attempts to suppress dissent were misguided and futile. It was not long, therefore, before he found himself banished from the small circle of intimates who had full knowledge of policy. This left the govern-ment's propaganda policy rudderless. Instead of appointing a more trustworthy replacement, the prime minister fudged the issue by asking Robert Allan, his parliamentary private secretary, to brief journalists and appointing R. A. Butler to the role of publicity coordinator. Neither had the experience or the nose for effective media management; Butler's remit was too loosely defined. The result was that, during the crucial later stages of the crisis, the government lacked someone with the important advantage of distance, who could identify which policies were unacceptable to the public and media because the policies were

LIVERPOOL JOHN MOORES UNIVERSITY
LEARNING SERVICES

not his own. Such a person would have alerted Eden to the fact that no amount of manipulation or intimidation could guarantee wholly favourable coverage of a British military operation at such a late stage in the crisis, and on such an implausible pretext.[3]

The government managed to build up a climate for war very successfully in the early stages of the crisis. Maintaining this over a period of three whole months, however, proved to be an impossible task. Had Eden acted in a similar fashion to Margaret Thatcher at the outset of the Falklands crisis in 1982 things may have been different. On that occasion, too, no immediate military response was physically possible – and could not be so for many weeks. Nevertheless, it was made apparent to the world that force would be used if the Argentinians failed to withdraw their troops. This clarity of commitment not only enabled information officials to work more in the open, thus allowing them greater scope for persuasion; it also gave the media and the public a fixed point of reference.[4] Because the cabinet lacked the confidence to issue a similar ultimatum to Nasser in 1956, so its propaganda lacked the clearly identifiable aims central to sustaining public support over a long period. Crucially in this regard, the MoD was prevented from using the task force sent to the Mediterranean as a means of engendering a national war psychology lest it scared Nasser into going to the United Nations or served to reveal the government's hidden agenda.

This comparison between Suez and the Falklands brings us to another problem faced by information officials in 1956. During the Falklands crisis the Reagan administration, whilst acting as honest broker between Britain and Argentina, morally sided with the former. Ultimately, it would countenance force to recover the islands should negotiations fail. This gave the Thatcher government a distinct propaganda advantage over Buenos Aires and domestic opponents who saw the dispute in old-style colonial terms.[5] During Suez, however, the White House clearly saw Nasser as the guilty party but argued that the use of troops would drive a wedge between the Arabs and the West. This damaged Eden's campaign in three ways. Firstly, it directly undermined a number of the government's key propaganda themes. For example, the fact that the US herself was so opposed to the use of force said little for Eden's argument that Nasserism represented a threat to the Free World. Secondly, it exposed the government to the State Department's own powerful publicity machinery. Finally, it rendered the Foreign Office's task of enlisting the strong support of American opinion almost impossible.

By the later stages of the crisis, therefore, it was evident that Eden was less in control of his propaganda and more a captive of it. During the negotiations at the United Nations in early October 1956 a number of cabinet ministers – the influential Lloyd and Monckton amongst them – were in favour of a compromise settlement. The prime minister and others, however, feared any sort of agreement which Nasser could claim as a victory. Doubtless part of the reason for this was the effect such a triumph would have on the Arab world and Britain's standing within it. What was also on Eden's mind, however, was the government's loss of face at home. How could he explain to those newspapers who knew his real motives that the UN plan was a success for British interests? On a wider, more open, level, how could he justify signing any sort of agreement with someone he himself had compared with Hitler and Mussolini? Eden, in fact, was now in a desperate situation, trapped by his own rhetoric. His propaganda had helped to create expectations which he felt had to be fulfilled.

Viewed from this perspective, Eden's acceptance of the Franco-Israeli collusion plan in mid-October was entirely predictable. So, for that matter, was the public relations fiasco that followed. Having effectively dismissed William Clark, the prime minister was now dangerously out of touch with the media and public opinion. Incredible though it may seem, the cabinet appears not to have fully thought through what the public's reaction would be to a military operation three months after the start of a crisis which most people now thought and hoped would end peacefully. The only proviso was that the operation should be 'quick and successful' (which, of course, it could not be, owing to the distance of 1100 miles between Port Said and Malta, where part of the task force was based). Keeping the tripartite plot a secret was acknowledged as essential if the government was to carry with it the majority of domestic and international opinion. Yet this very secrecy also had the effect of causing confusion and contradiction. What the public needed were clear, comprehensible and demonstrably achievable aims. What it got was a government apparently making things up as it went along, one which did not even know whether Britain was officially at war.

The sheer ferocity and universality of criticism which greeted the government's Egyptian intervention in early November 1956 testified to the cabinet's miscalculations. Eden's policy was excoriated by the UN, stringently opposed by the majority of Commonwealth states,[6] and condemned as crooked by sections of the American administration and mass media. At home, unruly scenes in Parliament were matched by angry protest meetings and petitions against the so-called 'police action'. Opposition to the government embraced academics, senior religious figures and many ordinary British citizens who were affected by what Leon Epstein has described as a 'Suez fever', which compelled people to publicize their opinions.[7] Fittingly, the cabinet's crucial decision on Sunday, 4 November, to push ahead with the Anglo-French landings was itself punctuated by the sounds of mounted police charging anti-war demonstrators who were converging on Downing Street from a mass rally in Trafalgar Square.[8]

To dismiss the government's propaganda as completely ineffective during this period would, nevertheless, be erroneous. Many historians point out the strong support that the military action received in Britain, but imply that this occurred despite, rather than because of, any presentational efforts on the part of the government.[9] There is some truth in this. Many of those who backed the government did so for relatively straightforward reasons: either they were loyal Conservatives, die-hard imperialists, Israeli sympathizers, or they believed that Britain ought to assert her independence (especially from the Americans), or they thought that to criticize an on-going operation amounted to stabbing the troops in the back. Given the flaws in the government's case, however, together with the open discontent within its own ranks, these factors are, by themselves, unpersuasive.

What must also be taken into account are the government's powers of recovery in propaganda terms. By drawing upon the earlier support for force it had established in Fleet Street, issuing threats to the BBC's independence, and censoring coverage of MUSKETEER REVISE, the government was to some extent able to determine what the public saw, heard and read about its policy. The machinery of coordination it urgently set up, although by no means perfect, ensured greater consistency of stated objectives. Monckton's Public Relations Committee also played an invaluable role, partially filling the hole left by William Clark's departure, acting as a reliable source of information for the media and thereby reconstructing the crisis agenda in the government's favour.

One of the most curious phenomena of the Suez campaign was its greater popularity (judging by opinion polls) after the ceasefire on 6 November. This occurred despite the gross failure marked by the ignominious forced withdrawal and the economic repercussions, which included the introduction of petrol rationing.[10] The common explanation for this is one of relief based on the fear that the military operation might have spiralled out of control, leading to a serious war with even greater human and economic consequences.[11] An alternative thesis, however, is that the shrewd and systematic exploitation of Moscow's real or alleged actions in early to mid-November by the government's propagandists persuaded many waverers that Eden's policy ought to be given the benefit of the doubt. This theme certainly appears to have had success in the United States, where, as in Britain, many people were naturally confused by the various allegations and counter-allegations surrounding the intervention. By playing the Cold War card effectively, and switching from a defensive to offensive approach, the government targeted the one theme on which there was a considerable consensus on both sides of the Atlantic. This, in turn, arguably played a major part in limiting the diplomatic and political fall-out from the Suez crisis.

Despite this partial recovery, Suez remained a watershed for Britain's influence in the Middle East and for her very status as an independent world power. The imbroglio provided, in Anthony Nutting's famous phrase, 'no end of a lesson' for British policy-makers,[12] not least in the realm of public persuasion. Suez had demonstrated the dangers of allowing propaganda to outpace policy and the flaws within the propaganda machinery. Consequently, in the immediate aftermath of the crisis, Charles Hill, the postmaster-general, was appointed by Eden to undertake a comprehensive review of the government's information services.[13] Together with Fife Clark, head of the Central Office of Information, Hill built on the recommendations of the 1953 Drogheda Report on the overseas information services to improve coordination between departments and increase expenditure. When Macmillan became prime minister in January 1957, Hill was made Chancellor of the Duchy of Lancaster with a seat in the cabinet and no departmental responsibilities. Although Hill was no 'minister of information' with control functions – thus leaving the propagandists' role in the policy process unaltered – he could bring propaganda factors to bear on the consideration of policies at the highest levels. The outcome of these changes was to upgrade the role of propaganda at home and overseas whilst ensuring that ministers and officials spoke with one voice.[14]

How this new regime might have handled the Suez crisis had it been in place was illustrated in the summer of 1958. On 14 July 1958, the last large bastion of British authority in the Middle East collapsed when nationalist officers under Brigadier Karim Qassem overthrew the Hashemite monarchy in Iraq. This caused panic in London and Washington, where the coup was seen as pro-Russian and a potential catalyst for other revolutions throughout the region. The Anglo-American reaction was swift and decisive. Within a week, British forces had entered Jordan, at the solicited invitation of King Hussein, whilst American troops went into Lebanon at the behest of President Camille Chamoun.[15]

Being a largely American initiative, and conducted with the overwhelming approval of Parliament and the two Arab leaders directly concerned, this operation had quite different propaganda requirements to that which the Eden government had ordered in 1956. What was striking, however, was how closely propaganda and policy were interwoven. Charles Hill coordinated matters via a special news executive consisting of representatives of the Foreign and Commonwealth Relations Offices, the four defence departments, and a number of other public relations experts, including Harold Evans, Macmillan's press secretary. Hill also liaised regularly with the Chairman and senior officers of the Conservative party, coordinated ministerial guidance, monitored the BBC's output, and advised the prime minister on whether to broadcast. The overall result was a text-book propaganda exercise: problems were pre-empted; the government's objectives were clearly projected; relations with the media were cordial; and ministers avoided potentially compromising rhetoric, especially in relation to Nasser, whom the Foreign Office again suspected of acting in unison with Moscow.[16]

Within a few years this coordinating machinery had itself undergone changes, to the point in 1964 when no single minister was responsible for the government's information services.[17] Nevertheless, the Suez debacle continued to set the tone for Britain's propaganda activities in the years ahead, particularly in relation to foreign policy issues. Above all, it acted as a salutary warning to successive governments of the perils of taking actions abroad without sufficient internal and external public support. This was spelled out in strong and unequivocal terms by the commander-in-chief of the Anglo-French forces in 1956, General Sir Charles Keightley, in his own post-mortem on the crisis in 1957:

> The one overriding lesson of the Suez operations is that world opinion is now an absolute principle of war and must be treated as such. However successful the pure military operations may be they will fail in their object unless national, Commonwealth and Western world opinion is sufficiently on our side.[18]

Appendix A

Circulation of the principal British newspapers in 1956

The papers are grouped together by proprietor.* (E) evening; (S) Sunday.

Lord Beaverbrook	*Daily Express*	4,042,334
	Sunday Express	3,331,127
	Evening Standard	662,608
Mirror Group	*Daily Mirror*	4,649,696
	Sunday Pictorial	5,624,010
Lord Rothermere	*Daily Mail*	2,071,708
	Daily Sketch	1,123,855
	Evening News	1,221,195
	Sunday Dispatch	2,420,159
Cadbury Brothers	*News Chronicle*	1,442,438
	The Star (E)	926,884
Michael Berry	*Daily Telegraph*	1,075,460
Odhams (Lord Southwood)	*People* (S)	4,948,215
Odhams/TUC	*Daily Herald*	1,653,997
National Cooperative Trust	*Reynolds News* (S)	516,445
Eyre Trust	*Financial Times*	80,518
The Times Trust	*The Times*	220,716
News of the World Limited	*News of the World* (S)	7,493,463
Manchester Guardian Trust	*Manchester Guardian*	163,585
Observer Trust (Chairman Hon. David Astor)	*Observer* (S)	601,402
Lord Kemsley	*Sunday Times*	618,540
	Empire News (S)	2,550,308
	Sunday Graphic	2,420,159

* Based on the *Newspaper Press Directory* (107th annual issue, London, 1957). This listing of national newspapers includes all London papers. The *Manchester Guardian* was a provincial paper but it ranked alongside *The Times* as part of the elite press and its influence was nationwide.

Appendix B

**Readership of the main British newspapers
in 1956**

Figures for July 1956–June 1957*

Daily Mirror	14,223,000
Daily Express	12,203,000
Daily Mail	6,275,000
Daily Herald	5,789,000
News Chronicle	4,793,000
Daily Sketch	4,313,000
Daily Telegraph	2,797,000
The Times	977,000
Manchester Guardian	739,000
Sunday Times	1,920,000
Observer	1,976,000

* Based on the 'National Readership Survey', published by the Institute of Practitioners in Advertising (London, 1957). No estimate available for the *Financial Times*.

Appendix C

A classified index of Suez publicity and guidance material

This index was constructed by the Foreign Office in February 1957 and provides a guide to the propaganda themes focused upon, and sources used, by the FO during the Suez crisis (*source*: PRO FO 953/ PG 11639/69).

Key to index

Bk	=	Booklet
Cmd	=	Command Paper
F	=	Feature Article
FDO	=	Further details omitted
GUID	=	Guidance
HANS	=	Hansard
INTEL	=	Intels
LPS	=	London Press Service
R	=	Reference Paper
SR	=	Second Rights Feature Material

British policy

Sir Anthony Eden's speech in the Commons on 2 August (HANS Columns 1610 to 1616)	R 3377	3.8.56
Sir Anthony Eden's broadcast	R 3382	10.8.56
Supplement to R 3382	R 3396	17.8.56
Foreign Secretary's broadcast	GUID 35–6	14.8.56
The Pot and the Kettle (William Bluett)	F LPS 7	26.8.56
Suez – Records compared (Lord Birdwood)	F LPS 2	13.8.56
Mutual Respect (John Lawrence)	LPS MECO	25.8.56
Britain's Evolving Overseas Policy (James Morris)	LPS FEASTCO	8.9.56
Anglo-French action in the Middle East: Statements by members of the UK Government	R 3444	21.10.56

The campaign in Egypt

Clearance of Canal

Importance of Anglo-French Salvage	F 4359	
(Admiral Nicholl)	LPS 7	22.12.56

Conferences

(Selected Documents London, 2–24 August
   1956)   Cmd 9853

1. Invitation extended by Her Majesty's Government to certain foreign Governments, 2 August 1956

2. Tripartite Proposal for the establishment of an International Authority for the Suez Canal communicated to the Governments attending the Conference, 5 August 1956

3. Proposal tabled by the Hon. J. Foster Dulles on behalf of the United States Delegation, 20 August 1956

4. Draft Declaration tabled by Mr Krishna Menon, leader of the Indian Delegation, 20 August 1956

5. Proposal tabled by the Delegates of Ethiopia, Iran, Pakistan and Turkey

6. (i) Spanish Proposal, 21 August 1956

    (ii) Statement by Spanish Delegation, 22 August 1956

7. Proposal tabled by the Ceylonese Delegation, 21 August 1956

8. Statement by the Hon. T. L. MacDonald, leader of the New Zealand Delegation, 24 August 1956

9. The '18-Nations Proposals'

10. Speech by the Secretary of State for Foreign Affairs at the Fourth Plenary Session of the Suez Canal Conference on 18 August 1956

11. Speech made by the Secretary of State for Foreign Affairs at the opening of the Seventh Plenary Session, 22 August 1956

Statement issued after Tripartite Talks	GUID 22	2.8.56
The Suez Conference (W. N. Ewer)	F LPS 5	10. 9.56
Suez summing up (Maurice Latey)	F LPS 5	24. 8.56
Report of the Suez Committee on the mission entrusted to it by 18 of the nations which attended the Conference on the Suez Canal	Bk	9.9.56
Proceedings of the Second London Conference (including Declaration on establishment of a Suez Canal Users' Association)	GUID 69–85	20–21.9.56
Summing up the Suez Conference (Michael Andrews)	F 3946 (for *Englische Rundschau*)	FDO

Documents on the Suez Crises, 26 July to 6 November – Chatham
House publication

Dues

Guidance issued 31 July by General		
Council of British Shipping	GUID 23	
Suez Canal Dues	GUID 65	7.9.56
Payment of Transit Dues	GUID 86	29.9.56
Suez Canal Dues	GUID 28	FDO

*Exchange of correspondence between the Suez [Menzies] Committee
and the President of the Republic of Egypt regarding the future
operation of the Suez Canal*

(a) Composition of the Suez Committee
(b) *Aide-Mémoire* to President Nasser from the Suez
     Committee, 3 September 1956
(c) Letter from the Chairman of the Suez Committee
     to President Nasser, 7 September 1956
(d) Letter from President Nasser to the Chairman of
     the Suez Committee, 9 September 1956

Financial and trade aspects

(a) General

Economic implications of the Suez issue		
(Patrick Seale)	F LPS 2	6.8.56
Effects on UK payments and trade with		
Egypt	INTEL 148	13.8.56
Canal Balance Sheet (Patrick Seale)	F LPS 7	9.9.56
The Picture in Full (W. Bluett)	F 3808	26.8.56
What is at stake (W. Bluett)	F 3790	29.8.56
Effects of the Suez crisis on the financial		
markets (W. T. C. King)	F 3274	5.9.56
Cape Route Costs (Patrick Seale)	F LPS 7	19.9.56
The Economic Consequences of the Present		
Events in the Middle East	INTEL 217	12.12.56

(b) Egypt

Nasser mortgages the future (William		
Bluett)	F LPS MECO	4.8.56

Where is Colonel Nasser going to find
the money? (Patrick Seale)   F LPS 5   9.8.56
Egypt's economy and the Canal (Patrick Seale)   F LPS 7   16.8.56
The Risks involved (William Bluett)   F 3789   29.8.56
The New Situation (William Bluett)   F 3788   29.8.56
Egyptian Monetary Area   INTEL 149   15.8.56

History

The Suez Canal   R 2451   22.2.52
The Suez Canal (Supplement)   R 3375   31.7.56
The Suez Canal Traffic Figures   'GUID 60   25.8.56
                                                    GUID 61   26.8.56
The Suez Dilemma - Engineering a
predominant factor   SR 280 (7/112) 17.8.56
The Security of the Middle East   Bk R F P 3379 Aug 56
The West and Middle East Development   R 3420   Sept.56.
Suez and Panama Canals   INTEL 155   30.8.56
Suez Canal Legal Position   GUID 24–27   3–4.8.56
Analysis of Canal Traffic   GUID 87   29.9.56

International aspects

An International Problem (Lord Birdwood)   F LPS 5   3.8.56
Nations and nationalisation (Guy Wint)   LPS FEASTCO   11.8.56
Suez Canal – Nationalisation or
Internationalisation (Elizabeth Barker)   F LPS 5   18.8.56
Suez and the United Nations   GUID 30–31   10.8.56
The folly of Pure Sovereignty (James
Thomson)   F LPS 5   7.9.56
Suez Canal and the Middle East (James
Thomson)   LPS MECO   18.8.56
Russians and Asia and Africa (W. N. Ewer)   F LPS 5   24.8.56
Suez and Asia (Guy Wint)   LPS FEASTCO   27.8.56
India, Russia and the West (W. N. Ewer)   F LPS 5   31.8.56
Iraq stands firm (William Bluett)   F 3792   29.8.56.
Majority verdict (William Bluett)   F LPS 5   1. 9.56.
The Security of the Middle East   Bk R F P 3379 Aug. 56
The Suez and Panama Canals   INTEL 155   30.8.56
Proverbial Wisdom (William Bluett)   F LPS MECO   17.9.56
Current Events – Questions of
Confidence   F LPS MECO   22.9.56
Humble victims (Guy Wint–John
Lawrence)   LPS FEASTCO   249.56

Iraq Government Statement on the Suez Canal	GUID 29	6.8.56
Suez Canal Soviet Statement	GUID 32–33	10.8.56
The Suez Canal and Asia	GUID 37	15.8.56
The UN and Arab–Israel relations	R 3407	15.10.56
Egyptian subversive activities in Middle East	INTEL 208	28.11.56
Russian activities in the Middle East	INTEL 209	30.11.56
Security Council and Suez (Maurice Latey)	F 3821 (for *Gazet van Antwerpen*)	FDO
The Suez Nationalisation	GUID 66	10.9.56
Question of Confidence (John Lawrence)	F 3888 MECO	22.9.56
M.E. Commentary: Long Term Lines (William Bluett)	F 3824 MECO	29.9.56
World Affairs Commentary: Egypt and Russia (Maurice Latey)	F 3886 LP 82	1.10.56
Pause for Reflection (John Lawrence)	F 3889 MECO	6.10.56
Suez and Cyprus (Maurice Latey)	F 3898 (for *Englische Rundschau*)	FDO
A Lesson in the Weakness of Nationalism (Maurice Latey)	F 4010 LPS 7	14.10.56
Suez and Nationalism (Maurice Latey)	F 1014 (for *Gazet van Antwerpen*)	FDO
Hungary, Suez and the UN (Maurice Latey)	F 4019 (for *Gazet van Antwerpen*)	FDO
Suez Situation Today (D. Mitchell)	F 4071 LP 55	24.10.56
Middle East Crisis (James Thomson)	F 4120 LPS 7	2.11.56
Middle East Commentary: A Chaotic Campaign (William Bluett)	F 4158 MECO	10.11.56
Soviet Policy and Suez (Jules Menken)	F 4168 LPS 5	12.11.56
Soviet Objectives in the Middle East (Admiral Nicholl)	F 4170 MECO	15.11.56
Suez provides opportunity as well as danger (U. Tristram)	F 4016	FDO
Suez and NATO (Admiral Nicholl)	F 4254	FDO
Egypt: The Task Ahead (James Thomson)	F 4194 (for *Gazet van Antwerpen*)	FDO
Russia, Egypt and Syria (Sir Alec Kirkbride)	F 4296 LPS 2	3.12.56

The Bottomless Well (Hugh Cavendish)	F 4304 MECO	15.12.56
Middle East Highlights (James Thomson)	F 4361 LPS 5	28.12.56

Nasser's policy and action

Colonel Nasser and the Suez Canal (James Thomson)	F LPS 5	8.8.56
Nasser's Refusal (Maurice Latey)	F LPS 5	13.8.56
The Expropriation of the Suez Canal (Sir Thomas Rapp)	SR 3740	14.8.56
Colonel Nasser's Word (Guy Wint)	LPS PAKINCO	21.8.56
A Choice of Pure Policies (John Lawrence)	LPS MECO	4.9.56
Nasser's Philosophy (William Bluett)	LPS 2	24.9.56
Suez Canal Control or Chaos (William Bluett) (4)	F 3874	2.10.56
Suez Canal: Nasser's Statement of August 12	GUID 34	12.8.56
Nasser and the Canal (James Thomson)	F LPS 7 (3993)	5.10.56
Colonel Nasser's Second Thoughts (James Thomson)	F LPS (3826)	27.10.56
Why Nasser is a bad Landlord (Patrick Seale)	F 4088	FDO
The Fruits of Dictatorship (William Bluett)	F 4129 MECO	9.11.56
Cairo's Military Claims to Reality (Admiral Nicholl)	F 4136 LPS 7	8.11.56
Nightfall for Nasser:		
The Myth Destroyed (William Bluett)	F 4221	16.11.56
A World Betrayed (Bluett)	F 4222	19.11.56
Bluster Discounted (Bluett)	F 4223	22.11.56
Danger of Dictatorships (John Lawrence)	F 4202 MECO	1.12.56
Nasser's Egypt (Walter Laqueur)	FDO	FDO

Oil

Britain and Middle East Development	Bk R F P 3291	April 56
World Petroleum Production and Refining Capacities	R 3077	2.8.56
Middle East Oil	R 3398	2.8.56
Middle East Oil (*Financial Times*)	SR 279	13.9.56
Super-tankers and Oil Supplies	FDO	FDO
Middle East Outlook (David Mitchell)	FDO	FDO

Saving Middle East Oil (Neville Wray)   F 4207 MECO   11.11.56
I.P.C. Payments to the Syrian Government   INTEL 8   30.1.57

Pilots

Suez Canal Pilots   INTEL 156   30.8.56
Suez Canal Pilots play a vital part
  (James Thomson)   F LPS 5   1.9.56
Suez as a Pilot sees it (G. W. Wood)   F LPS MECO   5. 9.56
Pilots are People (J. M. Spey)   F LPS FEASTCO   11.9.56
Suez Canal Pilots   GUID 67   11.9.56
Dropping the Company: The Pilots'
  Fears (Patrick Seale)   F 3876 WESCO   20.9.56

Suez Canal Users' Association

Inaugural Meeting of SCUA   GUID 88–100   Oct. 56

Parliament – Debates and Statements

House of Commons, 2 August   HANS   3.8.56
The Suez Canal   F LPS 5   4.8.56
House of Commons, House of Lords,
  12 September   HANS
Suez Debate Summing Up   F LPS 5   14.9.56
  (Maurice Latey)   GUID 68   14.9.56
Suez Canal Statement by Selwyn   Commons HANS
  Lloyd   Col.493   23.10.56
Statement: The Suez Canal   Lords HANS
    Col.936   23.10.56
Egypt and Israel – Debate and   Commons HANS
  Situation   Cols.1256, 1277, 1435   30.10.56
    Commons HANS
    Col.1450   31.10.56
The Israel–Egyptian Conflict Statement   Lords HANS
    Cols.1225–62   30.10.56
Egypt   Lords HANS
    Col.1243   31.10.56
Military Situation Statement by   Commons HANS
  Mr Head   Col.1623   1.11.56
UN Resolution   Commons HANS
Egypt British Civilians   Cols.1751, 1768   2.11.56
UN Resolution - UK Reply (Prime
  Minister)   Cols.1861

Military Situation (Mr Head)	1877	3.11.56
UN Resolution Statement by Selwyn	Commons HANS	
Lloyd and Military Situation	Cols.1960, 1974	5.11.56
(Mr Head)		
Middle East Situation Settlement	Lords HANS	
	Col.1373	5.11.56
Statements by the Prime Minister and		
Mr Butler on the Middle East	Commons HANS	
Situation	Cols. 106, 138	7.11.56
The Military Situation Statement by	Commons HANS	
Mr Head	Col.257	8.11.56
Prime Minister's Statement and		
Debate on the Middle East	Commons HANS	
Broadcast	Cols.421, 518	9.11.56
Statement by Mr Butler on the	Commons HANS	
Middle East Situation	Col.1555	20.11.56
Statement by Mr Butler on the	Commons HANS	
Middle East Situation	Col.1949	22.11.56
Statement on Egypt	Lords HANS	
	Col.541	22.11.56
Expulsion of British Subjects by		
Commander Noble	Col.30	26.11.56
Statement by Selwyn Lloyd	Commons HANS	
	Col.581	29.11.56
Statement on Egypt	Lords HANS	
	Col.690	29.11.56
Statement by Selwyn Lloyd on the	Commons HANS	
Middle East Situation	Col.581	28.11.56
Statement by Selwyn Lloyd on the	Commons HANS	
Middle East Situation	Col.879	3.12.56
Statement on Egypt	Lords HANS	
	Col.718	4.12.56
Port Said (Sir Walter Monckton) and	Commons HANS	
Debate	Cols.1247, 1258	5.12.56
Debate	Col.1457	6.12.56
Debate on Egypt	Lords HANS 11–12.12.56	
Suez Canal Clearance Statement by	Commons HANS	
Selwyn Lloyd	Col.392	17.12.56
Port Said Casualties (Mr Head)	Commons HANS	
	Col.1467	20.12.56
Statement on Compensation for Expelled	Lords HANS	
Britons	Col.453	5. 2.57

Notes

Preface

1. David Carlton, *Anthony Eden* (London, 1981); Robert Rhodes James, *Anthony Eden* (London, 1986); Keith Kyle, *Suez* (London, 1991); W. Scott Lucas, *Divided We Stand: Britain, the United States and the Suez Crisis* (London, 1991); Steven Z. Freiberger, *Dawn Over Suez: The Rise of American Power in the Middle East, 1953–7* (Chicago, 1992).

2. Valerie Adams, *The Media and the Falklands Campaign* (London, 1986); Derrik Mercer, Geoff Mungham and Kevin Williams, *The Fog of War* (London, 1987); Tom Hopkinson, *Relations between Governments, Armed Services and the Media: A Case Study of the 1956 Suez Conflict* (Unpublished, 1987).

3. See, for example, R. A. Butler, *The Art of the Possible* (London, 1971); Anthony Eden, *Full Circle* (London, 1960); Lord Kilmuir, *Political Adventure* (London, 1964); Ivone Kirkpatrick, *The Inner Circle* (London, 1959); Selwyn Lloyd, *Suez 1956* (London, 1978); Harold Macmillan, *Riding the Storm, 1956–59* (London, 1971).

4. Kennett Love, *Suez: The Twice Fought War* (London, 1970).

5. References to the Eden government's cultivation of Arab, including Egyptian, opinion during the Suez crisis are to be found in Peter Partner, *Arab Voices: The BBC Arabic Service, 1938–88* (London, 1988); M. Abdel-Kader Hatem, *Information and the Arab Cause* (London, 1974); Roy Fullick and Geoffrey Powell, *Suez: The Double War* (London, 1979); Kyle, *Suez*; Lucas, *Divided We Stand*; Mohamed H. Heikal, *Cutting the Lion's Tail* (London, 1986).

1. Introduction: the propaganda strategy

1. Cited in Michael Cockerell, Peter Hennessy and David Walker, *Sources Close to the Prime Minister* (London, 1984), p. 149. For the record, later that day Admiral Lewin was able to tell the prime minister that the SAS and SBS men aboard the helicopters were in fact safe. The point is, however, the public were not told about the crashed helicopters – even after the operation to retake South Georgia was successfully completed. Mrs Thatcher was fully aware of the need to massage the war news.

2. PRO AIR 8/40 Annex to JP(57)142 (Final), Sir Charles Keightley, 'Lessons of Suez', 11 December 1957.

3. Derrik Mercer, Geoff Mungham and Kevin Williams, *The Fog of War* (London, 1987), p. 17. This book is one of the most comprehensive on the relationship between the government, military and the media during the Falklands crisis. Others of interest are David Morrison and H. Tumber, *Journalists at War: the Dynamics of*

News Reporting during the Falklands Conflict (London, 1988), and Valerie Adams, *The Media and the Falklands Campaign* (London, 1986).

4. How the government sought to control the cinema newsreels, the fourth main source of news for British people in 1956, is outside the scope of this book. For an interesting analysis of how British newsreels did cover Suez, see *Film As Evidence; 'We Were Right'*, written and produced by Howard Smith, distributed by BBC Film Sales, 1976. The film shows how the newsreels were overwhelmingly hostile to Nasser and supportive of government policy.

5. See, for example, Eden's first nationwide broadcast on 8 August 1956, transcript in BBC Written Archives Centre (hereafter referred to as BBC WAC), R34/1580/1, and statements by Antony Head, minister of defence, in the Commons on 21 November 1956, *Hansard*, Fifth Series, Vol. 560, c.1742–6.

6. Quoted in J. A. C. Brown, *Techniques of Persuasion: from Propaganda to Brainwashing* (Harmondsworth, 1963), p. 19.

7. For one of the best accounts of the collapse of the Aswan dam negotiations see Keith Kyle, *Suez* (London, 1991), pp. 123–30.

8. Ibid.

9. Mohamed H. Heikal, *Cutting the Lion's Tail* (London, 1986), pp. 128–31.

10. Ali E. Hillal Dessouki, 'Nasser and the Struggle for Independence' in W. R. Louis and Roger Owen (eds), *Suez 1956: The Crisis and its Consequences* (Oxford, 1989), pp. 36–7.

11. Ibid., pp. 37–9; Heikal, *Cutting the Lion's Tail*, p. 134.

12. See Sydney W. Head (ed.), *Broadcasting in Africa* (New York, 1976), pp. 15–23; Adeed Dawisha, *Egypt in the Arab World: the Elements of Foreign Policy* (London, 1976), pp. 162–73.

13. Miles Copeland, *The Game of Nations* (New York, 1969), p. 209; Douglas A. Boyd, 'The Development of Egypt's Radio: "Voice of the Arabs" under Nasser' in *Journalism Quarterly*, Vol. 52, No. 4 (Winter 1975), pp. 645–53.

14. M. Abdel-Kader Hatem, *Information and the Arab Cause* (London, 1974), p. 166ff; Mahmoud Shalabieh, 'A Comparison of Political Persuasion on Radio Cairo in the Eras of Nasser and Sadat' (unpublished Ph.D. thesis, Ohio State University, 1975); Rais Ahmad Khan, 'Radio Cairo and Egyptian Foreign Policy, 1956–59' (unpublished Ph.D. thesis, University of Michigan, 1967).

15. Speech by Nasser on 22 July 1955 filed in BBC WAC E1/1, 848/1.

16. Munir K. Nasser, *Press, Politics and Power* (Iowa, 1979), pp. 53, 66, 124.

17. The French ambassador in Washington, Couve de Murville, predicted that the West's refusal to finance the Aswan Dam would cause Nasser to seize the revenues from the Suez Canal. Despite this, and the fact that the Canal Company was an obvious target, London, Washington and Paris were taken by surprise. See Kyle, *Suez*, pp. 135–41.

18. Heikal, *Cutting the Lion's Tail*, pp. 138–9.

19. For the full text of Nasser's 26 July speech see Noble Frankland (ed.), *Documents on International Affairs, 1956* (London, 1958), pp. 77–113. For a useful though somewhat melodramatic account of how this speech was received see Heikal, *Cutting the Lion's Tail*, pp. 140–1.

20. Cited in W. Scott Lucas, *Divided We Stand: Britain, the United States and the Suez Crisis* (London, 1991), p. 142.

21. W. R. Louis, 'The Tragedy of the Anglo-Egyptian Settlement of 1954' in Louis and Owen (eds), *Suez 1956*, p. 47.

22. Ibid., pp. 66–71.

23. See David R. Devereux, *The Formulation of British Defence Policy Towards the Middle East, 1948–56* (London, 1990), pp. 161–77; Kyle, *Suez*, pp. 56–60.

24. For British and American motives involved in Project ALPHA, together with its misconceptions and eventual failure, see Shimon Shamir, 'The Collapse of Project Alpha' in Louis and Owen (eds), *Suez 1956*, pp. 78–100.

25. David R. Devereux, 'Britain and the Failure of Collective Defence in the Middle East, 1948–53' in Ann Deighton (ed.), *Britain and the First Cold War* (London, 1990), pp. 247–51.

26. Gamal Abdel Nasser, *The Philosophy of the Revolution* (New York, 1959).

27. Foreign Office–BBC paper, sent by R. H. Ellingworth to Gordon Waterfield, Head of BBC's Eastern Service, on 'The activities of Cairo Radio and their impact on territories towards which they are directed', dated 30 August 1956, BBC WAC E1/1, 848/1; Humphrey Trevelyan, *The Middle East in Revolution* (London, 1970), p. 59; Copeland, *Game of Nations*, p. 181.

28. Peter Partner, *Arab Voices: The BBC's Arabic Service, 1938–1988* (London, 1988), pp. 90–9; Report by John Rae, the BBC's representative in the Middle East, on 'Broadcasting in the Middle East', January 1956, BBC WAC E1/1, 850/1; PRO FO 953/1641/PB1011/18, Grey to Dodds-Parker, draft Cabinet paper on BBC External Services, 6 June 1956; Avon Papers, AP 20/21/93, Eden to Lloyd on need to establish an Iraqi broadcasting station, 4 May 1956.

29. Heikal, *Cutting the Lion's Tail*, pp. 79–81.

30. David Reynolds, *Britannia Overruled* (London, 1991), p. 203.

31. Quoted in Richard Lamb, *The Failure of the Eden Government* (London, 1987), p. 174.

32. PRO CAB 128/29, CM(55)36, Minute 1, 20 October 1956. Talks between Egypt, Britain and the US on the financing of the Aswan High Dam opened in Washington on 21 November 1955.

33. PRO CAB 128/29, CM(55)36, Minute 1, 20 October 1956.

34. Kyle, *Suez*, pp. 92–3.

35. The Templer mission to Amman lasted from 7 to 14 December 1955. PRO FO 371/115650, 'Report of General Sir Gerald Templer on Mission to Jordan'; Trevelyan, *Middle East in Revolution*, p. 57.

36. See, for example, *Daily Mail*, 3 March 1956, front-page leader, 'We Get the Boot'; *Daily Telegraph*, 3 March 1956, first leader, p. 6, 'Exit Glubb Pasha – and Good Sense'.

37. Anthony Eden, *Full Circle* (London, 1960), p. 432; Robert Rhodes James, *Anthony Eden* (London, 1986), pp. 431–3; Evelyn Shuckburgh, *Descent to Suez* (London, 1986), pp. 344–5.

38. Ibid., pp. 327, 346.

39. William Clark, *From Three Worlds* (London, 1986), p. 166.

40. Shuckburgh, *Descent to Suez*, p. 345.

41. PRO PREM 11/1098, EC(56) 3rd Meeting, 30 July 1956.

42. Nasser did make an estimation of Britain's military strength immediately prior to nationalizing the Canal Company, but this was confined to its forces in the Mediterranean. See Heikal, *Cutting the Lion's Tail*, p. 136.

43. Lucas, *Divided We Stand*, p. 143.

44. PRO CAB 128/30, CM(56)54, 27 July 1956. For a brief explanation of the Suez Canal Company's legal status see Peter Calvocoressi, *World Politics since 1945* (London, 1982), p. 212.

45. For an analysis of the Suez Group and its pressure upon Eden see Leon Epstein, *British Politics in the Suez Crisis* (London, 1964), pp. 41–60, and Julian Amery, 'The Suez Group: A Retrospective on Suez' in Selwyn Ilan Troen and Moshe Shemesh (eds), *The Suez–Sinai Crisis of 1956: Retrospective and Reappraisal* (London, 1990), pp. 110–11. For evidence of the wider criticism of Eden prior to the Suez crisis, particularly from Fleet Street, see Private Papers of William Clark, MSS William Clark, 7, p. 97, 16 July 1956.

46. PRO CAB 128/30, CM(56)54, 27 July 1956.

47. Figures taken from a Conservative Party Archives, Research Department paper, CRD 2/34/7, 11 September 1956.

48. For details of how the British military presence in the Middle East had been run down during the early and mid-1950s but was still considerable in 1956 see Devereux, *Formulation of British Defence Policy Towards the Middle East*, pp. 185–95.

49. See James A. Bill and W. R. Louis (eds), *Musaddiq, Iranian Nationalism and Oil* (London, 1988), pp. 261–95.

50. Lucas, *Divided We Stand*, pp. 325–6.

51. PRO DEFE 4/89, COS(56) 75th Meeting, 31 July 1956.

52. For an indication of the sort of propaganda the Foreign Office disseminated throughout the Arab world, for instance, during the crisis see PRO FO 953/1688/ PG11639/7, Minutes of Meeting attended by members of the Africa, Levant, Eastern, Information Research, Information Policy and News Departments, 3 August 1956.

53. Heikal, *Cutting the Lion's Tail*, p. 78; Trevelyan, *Middle East in Revolution*, pp. 64–5.

54. PRO FO 371/119228/JE1451/1, F. R. Murray (Cairo) to J. H. A. Watson (African Department) on the working of the Egyptian propaganda machine, 30 January 1956.

55. For early evidence of the use of many of these propaganda themes see Eden's TV broadcast, 8 August 1956, and Selwyn Lloyd's radio broadcast, 14 August 1956, BBC WAC, R34/1580/1.

2. Eden and the press

1. Francis Williams, 'Fleet Street Notebook', in *New Statesman*, 6 October 1956, p. 403.

2. Kyle, *Suez*, p. 191.

3. See, for example, Ralph Negrine, 'The Press and the Suez Crisis: A Myth Re-examined' in *Historical Journal*, Vol. 25, No. 4, 1982, pp. 975–83; Kyle, *Suez*, pp. 404–7.

4. See Appendix B.

5. Heikal, *Cutting the Lion's Tail*, p. 163.

6. Rhodes James, *Anthony Eden*, p. 411; James Margach, *The Abuse of Power* (London, 1978), p. 106.

7. Margach, *Abuse of Power*, p. 107; Rhodes James, *Anthony Eden*, p. 196.

8. In pursuit of more about government–press relations during the 1930s see Richard Cockett, *Twilight of Truth: Chamberlain, Appeasement and the Manipulation of the Media* (London, 1989).

9. Rhodes James, *Anthony Eden*, p. 142.

10. MSS William Clark, 7, p. 2, 20 September 1955; Clark to Wadsworth, 17

September 1955, *Manchester Guardian* Archive (hereafter 'MGA'), B/C134/1–2.

11. MSS William Clark, 7, p. 25, 25 October 1955.

12. MSS William Clark, 7, p. 70, 6–9 April 1956.

13. For a detailed examination of how the lobby system operates see Jeremy Tunstall, *The Westminster Lobby Correspondents: A Sociological Study of National Political Journalism* (London, 1970). For a useful insider's view see James Margach, *The Anatomy of Power* (London, 1979), p. 125ff.

14. MSS William Clark, 7, p. 7, 3 October 1955.

15. Ibid.

16. Margach, *Abuse of Power*, p. 106.

17. Lamb, *Failure of the Eden Government*, pp. 12–14.

18. MSS William Clark, 7, p. 24, 24 October 1955.

19. MSS William Clark, 7, p. 47, 5 January 1956.

20. *Daily Telegraph* 3 January 1956, p. 6. Butler was present as Eden read McLachlan's article and recalled how it 'drew a pained and pungent oath'. R. A. Butler, *The Art of the Possible* (London, 1971), p. 183.

21. There is no archival evidence, in *The Times*, for instance, of any conspiracy between the papers involved. The Beaverbrook papers took no part in the campaign. Michael Berry, the *Daily Telegraph*'s proprietor, intended to deliver a shock to Eden following the large number of letters his paper had received indicating the despair in Tory constituency parties about the government's performance. McLachlan himself wrote to Eden apologizing for the reaction his article had provoked. See Duff Hart-Davies, *The House the Berrys Built* (London, 1990), pp. 170–1.

22. *New Statesman*, 14 January 1956, p. 38.

23. Butler, *Art of the Possible*, p. 183.

24. Margach, *Abuse of Power*, p. 106.

25. MSS William Clark, 7, p. 67, 27 March 1956.

26. MSS William Clark, 7, p. 85, 5 June 1956.

27. MSS William Clark, 7, p. 97, 16 July 1956.

28. PRO CAB 128/30, CM(56)47, Minute 2, 5 July 1956; PREM 11/1886, 'Government Publicity', draft by Frederick Bishop, Eden's private secretary, undated but returned from Treasury on 11 July 1956.

29. MSS William Clark, 7, p. 97, 16 July 1956.

3. Nationalization

1. *News Chronicle*, 28 July 1956, leader, p. 4; *Daily Herald*, 28 July, front-page leader. The *Daily Herald* was owned by Odhams and the TUC; until 1960, when a revised agreement between the two conceded a greater measure of editorial discretion, the paper solidly supported Labour party policy. See Stephen Koss, *The Rise and Fall of the Political Press in Britain* (London, 1990), pp. 1090–3. The ownership and the political affiliation of the *News Chronicle* are outlined later in this chapter.

2. *Daily Mail*, 27 July, front-page leader. The last British troops had left the Suez Canal Zone on 13 June 1956.

3. For a typical, conventional analysis of how the press reacted to Nasser's nationalization coup see Kyle, *Suez*, p. 137. For a more detailed survey of the press's performance during Suez, complete with the same oversight, see Guillaume Parmentier, 'The British Press in the Suez Crisis' in *Historical Journal*, Vol. 23, No. 2 (1980), pp. 435–48.

4. It is impossible to know exactly how Eden reacted to press comment on the morning of 27 July 1956 because William Clark's habit of keeping a daily record of his duties as press secretary temporarily deserted him at the very outset of Suez, owing, he later wrote, to his heavy workload. Given Eden's obsession with the press, however, we can reasonably presume that he read the papers on this of all days with even greater interest.

5. *Daily Telegraph*, 27 July, third leader, p. 6, 'Seizing Suez'; *Daily Mail*, 27 July, front-page leader, 'Hitler of the Nile'; *Daily Express*, 27 July, first leader, p. 4, 'A Time To Resist'.

6. *Daily Express*, 27 July, first leader, p. 4; *Daily Mail*, 27 July, front-page leader: 'We have always said that Britain should have brought him [Nasser] to heel when he first opened the gates of Egypt to Communist Russia and started preparing for war. It shows how misguided the Foreign Office were ever to think of playing ball with him'; the *Daily Telegraph*, 27 July, first leader, p. 6, was severely critical of Eden's record since becoming prime minister. It is significant that despite Nasser's coup this remained the paper's main leader. As far as the *Telegraph* was concerned, Eden was still very much on trial; Suez would be his big test.

7. PRO CAB 128/30, CM(56)54, 27 July 1956, p. 3.

8. Margach, *Abuse of Power*, p. 107.

9. Iverach McDonald, *A Man of The Times* (London, 1976), p. xiii and Chapter 17.

10. Ibid., pp. 29–40.

11. Ibid., pp. 75–80.

12. *Hansard*, Fifth Series, Vol. 557, c.777–80, 27 July 1956.

13. Memorandum by McDonald to William Haley, editor, 27 July 1956, in *The Times* Archive (hereafter 'TTA').

14. *The Times*, Friday, 27 July, first leader, p. 11: 'It is a clear affront and threat to western interests, besides being a breach of undertakings which Egypt has freely given and received in recent years ... It is much too soon to work out all the implications of the act or to say what the counter-action of the British and other directly affected Governments should be.'

15. Haley was abroad and out of touch with Printing House Square when Suez erupted. When he returned a few days later, however, he gave McDonald's line his firm backing.

16. See for example *The Times*, Saturday, 28 July, first leader, p. 11, 'Time for Decision': 'The truth is that Colonel Nasser's Government has such a bad record in such international dealings that it can be relied upon to use its control of the Canal as an instrument of blackmail even if it does not violate the international convention forthwith ... The act is political and nationalistic. The all too probable consequences would affect the free world as a whole.' Eden had been 'justifiably reticent' in saying what the government's response should be, though the paper dismissed any reference to the UN (because of the Soviet veto), and claimed that economic sanctions were apt to be two-edged weapons.

17. Compare *The Times*'s first leader, 1 August, p. 9, with Eden's telegram to Eisenhower on 27 July in Rhodes James, *Anthony Eden*, pp. 462–3. Paragraphs 1 and 4 of the telegram bear an uncanny resemblance to the phrasing in key passages of the 1 August editorial.

18. Eden, *Full Circle*, p. 441.

19. Iverach McDonald, *The History of The Times: Volume V, Struggles in War and Peace, 1939–1966* (London, 1984), pp. 263–4.

20. Memorandum by McDonald to Haley, 27 July 1956, TTA.
21. McDonald, *History of The Times*, pp. 263–4.
22. Examples to be found in *Hansard* are by John Harvey, MP, and Julian Amery, MP, both during the Suez Commons debate on 2 August (Vol. 557, c.1687 and c.1700), and J. E. S. Simon, MP, during the emergency Suez debate on 12 September (Vol. 558, c.119–20).
23. Kyle, *Suez*, p. 136.
24. *Daily Express*, 28 July 1954, first leader, p. 4.
25. Arthur Christiansen, *Headlines All My Life* (London, 1961), p. 282. Research has shown that Christiansen's birthday was indeed on 27 July.
26. Ibid., p. 283.
27. See A. J. P. Taylor, *Beaverbrook* (London, 1972), pp. 635–6; Anne Chisholm and Michael Davie, *Beaverbrook: A Life* (London, 1992), pp. 494–5.
28. According to Taylor, Beaverbrook and Eden were not the best of friends. The former had often criticized the latter in his early days and since the war had had no time for Eden's attachment to the UN. Taylor, *Beaverbrook*, pp. 354, 620.
29. Christiansen, *Headlines*, p. 282.
30. 'Beaverbrook watched every detail of his papers until the last day of his life. During his four months in England [early summer] he met all the senior members of the staff and many junior ones so that he knew what was going on personally. He telephoned his editors two or three times a day.' Taylor, *Beaverbrook*, p. 579.
31. See p. 6.
32. Eden to Beaverbrook, 17 January 1957, Beaverbrook Papers, BBK C/17.
33. *Daily Mail*, Saturday, 28 July, front-page leader, 'We Want Action'; *Daily Telegraph*, Tuesday, 31 July, first leader, p. 6, 'Fifth Day on the Canal'. Compare these with the two leaders in the *Daily Express*, Monday, 30 July and Tuesday, 31 July, both p. 4.
34. The Egypt Committee had been set up on 27 July, during the first cabinet meeting after the news of nationalization, 'as a kind of inner Cabinet and was also responsible for supervising the military operations and plans'. Its membership fluctuated during the crisis but at its core were Eden, Macmillan (chancellor), Salisbury (leader of the House of Lords), Selwyn Lloyd (foreign secretary), Monckton (minister of defence until October, thereafter paymaster-general) and the Earl of Home (Commonwealth secretary). Its secretary was Norman Brook.
35. PRO CAB 134/1216, EC(56) 4th Meeting, 30 July 1956.
36. Christian Pineau, *1956 Suez* (Paris, 1976), p. 41; Maurice Vaisse, 'France and the Suez crisis' in Louis and Owen (eds), *Suez 1956*, pp. 134–8.
37. PRO CAB 134/1216, EC(56) 4th Meeting, 30 July 1956.
38. PRO CAB 134/1216, EC(56) 2nd Meeting, 28 July 1956. For more details see Part Three above.
39. MSS William Clark, 7, p. 102, 29 July 1956.
40. PRO CAB 134/1216, EC(56) 4th Meeting, Minute 4, 30 July 1956.
41. MSS William Clark, 7, p. 103, 31 July 1956.
42. *Daily Express,* Wednesday, 1 August, first leader, p. 4.
43. *Daily Mail*, Saturday, 28 July, front-page headline. As already stated, so aware were the chiefs of staff of Britain's military unpreparedness they had threatened to resign on 26–27 July if Eden insisted on an immediate use of force.
44. *Daily Mail*, 1 August, front-page headline; MSS William Clark, 7, p. 103, 31 July–1 August 1956.

45. *Daily Mail*, 3 August, front-page leader, 'This is an Ultimatum'.

46. Margach, *Abuse of Power*, pp. 110–11.

47. Ibid., pp. 104–5.

48. This is explained later; see p. 76–7.

49. MSS William Clark, 7, p. 70, 6–9 April 1956; p. 97, 16 July 1956.

50. MSS William Clark, 7, p. 100, 24 July 1956; Shuckburgh, *Descent to Suez*, pp. 42–3.

51. See for example *Daily Telegraph*, 31 July, first leader, p. 6, 'Fifth Day on the Canal'.

52. I am grateful to Michael Berry (Lord Hartwell) for providing me with his contemporaneous notes of the meeting between Butler, Salisbury and himself on 31 July 1956.

53. Ibid. Berry wrote that he got the impression that if it did indeed come to 'war' then the government was probably not quite as certain of itself as Butler and Salisbury had said.

54. See for example *Daily Telegraph*, 4 August, first leader, p. 6 'Entente Beyond Europe'.

55. See Appendix B.

56. *Hansard*, Vol. 557, c.1602–721, 2 August 1956. Eden announced these 'precautionary measures' himself.

57. *Daily Herald*, 30 July, leader, p. 4, 'Answer To Nasser'; *News Chronicle*, 30 July, leader, p. 4, 'Uphold the Law of Nations'; *Manchester Guardian*, 31 July, first leader, p. 6, 'Pause for Thought'; *Observer*, 29 July, comment, p. 6.

58. Koss, *Rise and Fall of the Political Press*, pp. 1088–9.

59. Ibid.

60. MSS Clark, 7, p. 103. Butler and Salisbury had also told Michael Berry on 31 July that they particularly knew that 'the editor of the *News Chronicle* would be against war in any circumstances'. This presumably came from Eden's meeting with Michael Curtis earlier.

61. *News Chronicle*, 28 July, leader, p. 4, 'Suicide of the Sphinx'.

62. *News Chronicle*, 30 July, leader, p. 4, 'Uphold the Law of Nations.'

63. *News Chronicle*, 2 August, leader, p. 4, 'Firmness but not Folly': 'Whatever the hotheads may say and however responsible the quarter from which the cry comes, immediate and unilateral military intervention, simply to prevent the nationalisation of the Suez Canal, is the worst possible solution ... There remains the UN: and it is here that we part company with the Prime Minister, with his plan for a meeting of the Maritime Powers only. What are the UN for if not to deal with an international emergency of this kind?'

64. See Margach, *Abuse of Power*, Chapters 7 and 8.

4. 'Rattling the sabre'

1. Had Dulles had his way during the tripartite discussions in London in early August 1956, the canal conference would have taken place at the end of August and not in the capital of any interested power. Selwyn Lloyd insisted on only a fortnight's interval and that London be the venue, thus ensuring Britain's primacy during the crisis. For these discussions see PRO PREM 11/1098 ff 77–84, 7th Meeting, Council Chamber, FO, 2 August 1956.

2. 'I said that I thought they ought to act quickly whatever they did and that,

as far as Great Britain was concerned, public opinion would almost certainly be behind them.' Gaitskell to Eden and Selwyn Lloyd at Number 10 on the night of 26 July 1956. Philip Williams (ed.), *The Diary of Hugh Gaitskell, 1945–56* (London, 1983), pp. 552–3.

3. *Hansard*, Vol. 557, c.1609–17, 2 August 1956.

4. Eden, *Full Circle*, p. 438.

5. Kyle, *Suez*, p. 175.

6. PRO CAB 134/1216, EC(56) 10th Meeting, Minute 2, 3 August 1956.

7. 'Please let us keep quiet about the UN', minute by Eden, 7 August 1956, cited in Kyle, *Suez*, p. 166.

8. PRO FO 800/725 file, 'Memorandum on diplomatic exchanges and negotiations from Egyptian nationalisation to outbreak of hostilities between Israel and Egypt', undated, written by Donald Logan. In a conversation with Chauvel on 3 August, Lloyd called for coordination of the guidance which the British and French governments would give to the press in the run-up to the London Conference.

9. William Clark, *From Three Worlds* (London, 1986), p. 166.

10. *Observer*, 3 October 1976, p. 9, 'Suez – an inside story' by William Clark. Clark wrote that it was as important to be seen to be prepared to use force as it was to be capable of using force. 'For this reason there was a well-orchestrated campaign of sabre-rattling. I was charged with rattling my sabre in the direction of the Press, and felt that I had had some success when [Labour MP] Dick Crossman started warning his colleagues and the Press that the future was dark with the threat of "Clark's War".'

11. *Daily Mail*, 3 August, p. 1. See also on the same day reports by diplomatic correspondents in the *Daily Telegraph* (p. 1), *Manchester Guardian* (p. 1), *News Chronicle* (p. 1), as well as political correspondents in *The Times* (p. 8). The same thing happened the next day, 4 August: see *Daily Telegraph* (p. 8), *Manchester Guardian* (p. 1) and *News Chronicle* (p. 1).

12. *Hansard*, Vol. 557, c.1602–721, 2 August 1956.

13. In his speech to the House of Commons during the emergency Suez debate on 12 September 1956 Gaitskell raised the question of inspired government leaks, only for the prime minister and other ministers to simply look the other way. For Gaitskell's instructive speech see *Hansard*, Vol. 558, c.19–21, 12 September 1956.

14. *Observer*, 3 October 1976, p. 9.

15. MSS William Clark, 7, p. 112, 13 August 1956.

16. PRO CAB 128/30, CM(56)59, p. 6, 14 August 1956. This is one of the few cabinet meetings at which British public opinion was referred to explicitly.

17. MSS William Clark, 7, p. 113, 15 August 1956. Eden himself used this phrase during his first TV broadcast to the nation on 8 August. Transcript of broadcast: BBC WAC R34/1580/1.

18. *Daily Mail*, 16 August, article, p. 4, 'This is your Crisis'. A number of papers, both pro- and anti-force, showed evidence of having been influenced in some way by Clark's briefings on the eve of the conference. The *News Chronicle*'s leader on 16 August, 'Matter of Life and Death' (p.4), is a case in point.

19. For the News Department's duties and operational procedures see John B. Black, *Organising the Propaganda Instrument: the British Experience* (The Hague, 1975), pp. 21–4. For a closer examination of the Department's origins and development see Philip M. Taylor, *The Projection of Britain: British Overseas Publicity and Propaganda* (Cambridge, 1981).

20. Kirkpatrick, significantly, had been at the Berlin embassy throughout the whole of Hitler's peacetime rule. For the clearest evidence of his fear of repeating the mistakes of the 1930s during the Suez crisis see his memorandum, subsequently amended slightly, sent by Eden to Eisenhower on 6 September 1956, *Foreign Relations of the United States*, Vol. XVI, Doc.681, pp. 400–3.

21. Sir George Young should not be confused with his unknighted namesake who was MI6's deputy director in charge of Middle East operations in 1956.

22. MSS William Clark, 7, p. 108, 7 August 1956; author's interview with Anthony Moore, August 1991.

23. Richard Scott to Alastair Hetherington, editor-elect of the *Manchester Guardian*, 14 October 1956. Hetherington correspondence: C4/B36/91, MGA.

24. For Dodds-Parker's involvement in the Sudan lobby see, for example, PRO FO 371/96913/JE1051/411, Dodds-Parker and Mott-Radcliffe to Foreign Office, 20 November 1952. For Dodds-Parker's chairing of an *ad hoc* committee, established in June 1956, directed to oversee non-military measures to maintain Britain's Middle East position see PRO FO 371/120812/UEE10062/9G, Minute by Dodds-Parker, 19 June 1956. This committee worked alongside a Middle East (Official) Committee which, amongst other things, was looking into the increased use of broadcasting to counter Egyptian radio propaganda. For the establishment in July 1956 of an official Committee on Overseas Broadcasting, chaired by Dodds-Parker, see FO 953/1641/PB1011/18, Paul Grey to Dodds-Parker, 6 June 1956, and FO 953/1641/PB1011/19, Dodds-Parker to Kirkpatrick, 10 July 1956. The work of this latter committee is covered in greater detail in the BBC chapters (Part Two below).

25. PRO FO 371/119113/JE14211/977, Minute by Dodds-Parker, 17 August 1956.

26. PRO PREM 11/1162, Monckton to Eden, 13 August 1956.

27. PRO FO 371/119113/JE14211/977, Minute by Dodds-Parker, 17 August 1956.

28. PRO PREM 11/1162, Monckton to Eden, 13 August 1956.

29. By 14 August, President Eisenhower was warming to the idea of a 'supervisory board of five persons designated by such countries as Egypt, France, India, and Sweden, who would have a voice in the selection of a general manager who would be in charge of Canal operations'. Dulles agreed: 'It might even be necessary to minimise the role of Britain and France, assuming dependable alternatives could be found.' This was a far cry from the sort of internationalization and Anglo-American solidarity which Eden was looking for. Cited in Lucas, *Divided We Stand*, p. 168.

30. Walter Monckton Papers, MSS Dep. Monckton, 7, p. 126, 13 August 1956.

31. PRO PREM 11/1099 f230–1, FO to Paris, 8 August 1956.

32. Macmillan's diary, 3 August 1956, cited in Alastair Horne, *Harold Macmillan: Volume 1, 1894–1956* (London, 1988), p. 400; MSS William Clark, 7, p. 105, 2 August 1956; Churchill to Eden, 6 August 1956, cited in Martin Gilbert, *Never Despair, Winston S. Churchill, 1945–65* (London, 1988), p. 1203. In the first week of August the Egypt Committee spent a great deal of time discussing censorship: see PRO CAB 134/1216, EC(56) 9th Meeting, Minute 1, 2 August; EC(56) 10th Meeting, Minute 2, 3 August; EC(56) 12th Meeting, Minute 1, 9 August 1956.

33. PRO CAB 134/1217, EC(56)13, 8 August Memorandum by Monckton on 'Press Censorship'.

34. For a more detailed analysis of the D-Notice system see Annabelle May and

Kathryn Rowan (eds), *Inside Information, British Government and the Media* (London, 1982), p.79ff. Also Report of the Committee on Security Procedures in the Public Service, Chapter 9, Cmnd. 1681 (April 1962).

35. Curiously, there is no record of the discussions on publicity and censorship in the Cabinet minutes for 3 August, despite references to them elsewhere, especially in William Clark's papers (MSS William Clark, 7, p. 106, 3 August 1956). What do survive, however, are records of the discussions the Egypt Committee had on the morning of 3 August on the same subjects: PRO CAB 134/1216, EC(56) 10th Meeting, Minute 2, 3 August. One of the main conclusions of this meeting was that 'the PM would see editors of the chief UK newspapers to seek their cooperation in restricting speculation about the nature and purpose of military movements in the Mediterranean'.

36. MSS William Clark, 7, p. 106, 3 August 1956. This is corroborated by Arthur Christiansen, editor of the *Daily Express*, who recalls there were so many journalists 'that there was no room for us all at the Cabinet table'. Christiansen, *Headlines*, p. 285.

37. Ibid.

38. William Clark writes of this meeting that Eden offered the editors every sort of help with military information. 'I was a bit horrified at his own extension of my suggestion [of offering the press a *quid pro quo* in return for restraint], but undoubtedly it went well because as a result the press began to backpeddle [*sic*] and say – not too much information for gawd's sake. Finally we all agreed that Admiral Thomson [secretary of the Services, Press and Broadcasting Committee] should send out a D-Notice limiting mention of numbers of troops and their destinations.' MSS William Clark, 7, p. 106, 3 August 1956.

39. PRO FO 953/1617/P10127/3E, D-Notice sent on behalf of Services, Press and Broadcasting Committee, 4 August 1956.

40. See, for example, PRO CAB 134/1217, EC(56)13, 8 August 1956.

41. PRO PREM 11/1162, Monckton to Eden, 10 August 1956. Memorandum on D-Notices and daily press conferences.

42. Ibid.; FO 953/1617/P10127/4(A), D-Notice sent on 15 August 1956.

43. See, for example, Alastair Hetherington, *Guardian Years* (London, 1981), pp. 5–6; George P. Thomson, *Blue Pencil Admiral* (London, 1947).

44. See, for example, *News Chronicle*, 31 August, leader, p. 4, 'A Pointless Exercise'; *Daily Herald*, 31 August, leader, p. 4, 'Going to the Brink'; and *Manchester Guardian*, 30 August, first leader, p. 6, 'A Sabre Rattled'.

45. *Manchester Guardian*, 1 September, second leader, p. 4, 'Suez'.

46. PRO CAB 134/1216, EC(56) 10th Meeting, Minute 2, 3 August 1956.

47. MSS William Clark, 7, p. 108, 7 August 1956.

48. David Ayerst, *Guardian: Biography of a Newspaper* (London, 1971), pp. 588–91; Richard Cockett, 'The *Observer* and the Suez Crisis' in *Contemporary Record*, Vol. 5, No. 1, Summer 1991, p. 10; Koss, *Rise and Fall of the Political Press*, pp. 1059–60.

49. *Manchester Guardian*, 2 August, first leader, p. 6, 'Military Action'; 4 August, first leader, p. 4, 'Ends and Means'.

50. Hetherington, *Guardian Years*, pp. 4–5.

51. *Manchester Guardian*, 10 August, first leader, p. 4 'In Perspective'.

52. *Observer*, 29 July, first leader, p. 6.

53. *Observer*, 5 August, first leader, p. 4, and 11 August, two leaders, p. 6.

54. *Observer*, 29 July, first leader, p. 6; *Manchester Guardian*, 29 July, first leader, p. 4.

55. Hugh Cudlipp, *Walking on Water* (London, 1976), pp. 226–7.

56. *Daily Mirror*, 14 and 15 August; MSS William Clark, 7, p. 113, 14 August 1956.

57. MSS William Clark, 7, p. 112, 13 August 1956.

58. Hetherington, *Guardian Years*, pp. 7–8. This episode was confirmed in private correspondence with Hetherington, July 1991.

59. MSS William Clark, 7, p. 111, 9 August 1956.

60. Memorandum by Iverach McDonald to Haley, 10 August 1956, TTA.

5. Losing the initiative

1. PRO CAB 128/30, CM(56)59 p. 6, 14 August 1956.

2. PRO PREM 11/1152, Lennox-Boyd to Eden, 24 August 1956.

3. Kyle, *Suez*, pp. 192–9.

4. PRO PREM 11/1100 f.277, Conversation between Lloyd and Henderson, 27 August 1956.

5. PRO CAB 134/1216, EC(56) 21st Meeting, 24 August 1956; CAB 134/1216, EC(56) 23rd Meeting, 28 August 1956.

6. *Foreign Relations of the United States*, Vol. XVI, Doc 99: Memorandum of a conversation, Ambassador's residence, London, 19 August 1956, pp. 233–5. Eden countered Dulles' remarks by arguing that, except for the 'Left-Wing Labour element', the British public was strongly behind the government, despite the fact that hitherto he had refrained from building up public sentiment for the use of force.

7. At meetings on 21 and 23 August the cabinet discussed the timing of a meeting of Parliament to review the Suez situation, that is, whether it should be called immediately after the end of the London Conference. The cabinet agreed on 23 August that it would be inexpedient to recall Parliament as early as 28 August. It was feared that the ensuing debate might reveal a division of opinion between government and opposition, thus influencing Egypt's attitude towards the con- clusions of the conference, and that it might also lead other countries to doubt whether public opinion in the UK was solidly in support of the stand the govern- ment had taken on the Suez issue. PRO CAB 128/30, CM(56)60 and 61.

8. *The Times*, 27 August, first leader, p. 9, 'Escapers' Club'.

9. MSS William Clark, 7, p. 121, 27 August 1956. Interestingly, Eden also clipped the editorial for his personal file: Avon Papers, AP 20/34/3.

10. MSS William Clark, 116/1/1, p. 154, 27 August 1956. One such message came from Reginald Maudling, minister of supply: 'May I say how much I have admired *The Times*'s leaders in the last few weeks about Suez. Today is the best of the lot – how I agree with all that's said in it.' TTA, 27 August 1956.

11. PRO FO 371/119175/JE14214/35, Young to I. Pink, 31 August 1956. For the Haley memo, 29 August 1956, see TTA.

12. *Manchester Guardian*, 28 August, first leader, p. 6, 'Escapers'. See also *News Chronicle*, 28 August, leader, p. 4, 'Britain can be Great'; *Observer*, 2 September, first leader, p. 6, 'The Great Debate'.

13. On 31 August 1956, A. P. Wadsworth wrote to Donald Tyerman, editor of

the *Economist* and former deputy editor of *The Times*: 'What has come over W.J.H.?' Wadsworth editorial correspondence: 149/T19/2, MGA.

14. *Daily Herald*, 29 August, front-page article. See also *Manchester Guardian*, 27 August, front-page article by Richard Scott.

15. The only two national dailies which failed to give this news as their lead story were *The Times* and *Daily Sketch*. For a typical reaction to this news see *Manchester Guardian*, 31 August, first leader, p. 6, 'To War?', and *Daily Mirror*, 1 September, front-page leader, 'Suez: A grave Warning'.

16. MSS William Clark, 7, p. 123, 29 August 1956.

17. See, for example, *The Times*, 15 August, first leader, p. 9, 'What is at Stake'.

18. *The Times*, 1 September, first leader, p. 7, 'Widening the Circle'; PRO FO 371/119175/JE14214/35, Young to I. Pink, 31 August 1956.

19. PRO FO 371/119110/JE14211/866, Letter from J. A. N. Graham to Foreign Office, 10 August 1956.

20. PRO PREM 11/1286, Cairncross to Logan, 1 September, and reply, 6 September 1956.

21. Avon Papers, AP 14/4/33, 1 and 7 September 1956. For the correspondence between Eden and Churchill during August and September 1956 concerning Suez see Gilbert, *Never Despair*, pp. 1203–4, 1208–9, 1210.

22. Ibid., p. 1211. For Churchill's published statement on 5 November, and Eden's message of gratitude, see pp. 1220–1.

23. MSS William Clark, 7, pp. 124–5, 5 September 1956.

24. Cecil King, *Strictly Personal* (London, 1969), pp. 130–1. King is vague about when exactly he spent this 'hour' with Macmillan, though his estimate – 'about two months before the landing' – puts it at late August/early September, when the government was preparing the ground for the Menzies mission.

25. PRO FO 371/119130, A. D. M. Ross, 'The Egyptian Proposal of September 10', 11 September 1956.

26. Heikal, *Cutting the Lion's Tail*, p. 133.

27. See Lucas, *Divided We Stand*, pp. 188–91.

28. PRO PREM 11/1104, EC(56)43, 'Operation MUSKETEER: Implications of Postponement', 6 September 1956.

29. PRO CAB 134/1216, EC(56) 25th Meeting, 7 September 1956.

30. PRO CAB 134/1216, EC(56) 21st Meeting, 24 August 1956; PREM 11/1152, Brook to Eden, 25 August 1956.

31. PRO CAB 134/1216, EC(56) 26th Meeting, 10 September 1956.

32. Rhodes James, *Anthony Eden*, p. 512.

33. PRO FO 371/119137/JE14211/1622, Makins to Foreign Office, 14 September 1956.

34. PRO CAB 21/3093, 'Proceedings of SCUA Conference'; MSS William Clark, 7, p. 134, 21 September 1956.

35. George M. Gallup, *The Gallup International Public Opinion Polls, Great Britain, 1937–75* (New York, 1976). For a detailed analysis of public opinion polls during Suez see Leon D. Epstein, *British Politics in the Suez Crisis* (London, 1964), pp. 141–53.

36. The Security Council met to consider the Suez issue on 5 October. Agreement was reached on the 'Six Principles' on 13 October.

37. See Appendix B.

38. For the relationship between the *Mirror* and the Labour party during Suez,

and Gaitskell's reign as party leader in general, see Maurice Edelman, *The Mirror: A Political History* (London, 1966), pp. 155–63; Cudlipp, *Walking on Water*, pp. 226–30; King, *Strictly Personal*, pp. 130–1.

39. *Daily Mirror*, 5 September, p. 4; Janet Morgan (ed.), *The Backbench Diaries of Richard Crossman* (London, 1981), p. 504ff.

40. Philip Williams, *Hugh Gaitskell* (London, 1979), p. 427. Gaitskell's piece appeared in *Reynolds News* on 26 August. The interview in the *Manchester Guardian* appeared on the 31st. The initiative for the latter had in fact come, not from Gaitskell, but from A. P. Wadsworth, the *Guardian* editor, who felt that Labour had so far failed to assert itself publicly. Wadsworth editorial correspondence: 149/G1/1; 149/V2/1, MGA.

41. Williams, *Hugh Gaitskell*, p. 425; *Daily Mirror*, 18 September, front-page interview with Gaitskell. The letter to *The Economist* appeared on 22 September.

42. *Daily Mirror*, 1 and 5 September, front-page leaders.

43. See, for example, *News Chronicle*, 4 September, p. 4, article by James Cameron, and *Daily Mirror*, 14 August, front-page leader.

44. *Daily Mirror*, 5 September, front page.

45. Cudlipp, *Walking On Water*, pp. 229–30.

46. See, for example, *Daily Telegraph*, 2 October, first leader, p. 6, 'Socialists, Suez and SCUA'.

47. For ministerial efforts to persuade the press to minimize this embarrassment see Monckton Papers, MSS Dep. Monckton, 8, pp. 217–22, letter from Hugh Cudlipp to Antony Head, 23 November 1956.

48. PRO CAB 128/30, CM(56)67, p. 3, 26 September 1956.

49. For the preparation of this paper see PRO FO 371/119153 file. For the paper itself, 'The importance of the Suez Canal', see MSS Dep. Monckton, 7, pp. 273–7, 330–1.

50. PRO PREM 11/1102, Eden to Lloyd, T 440/56, 7 October 1956.

51. Carlton, *Britain and the Suez Crisis*, pp. 52–3; Kyle, *Suez*, pp. 281–90. The 'Six Principles' were: free and open transit through the Suez Canal without discrimination, overt or covert; respect for the sovereignty of Egypt; insulation from the politics of any one country; dues to be decided between Egypt and the users; a fair proportion of the revenue to be allocated to development; and unresolved points between Egypt and the old Suez Canal Company to be settled by arbitration.

52. Lucas, *Divided We Stand*, pp. 224–6. Lucas argues that Eden had dismissed force as an option by 14 October, citing the chiefs of staff's imminent replacement of MUSKETEER REVISE by a 'Winter Plan' as crucial. According to this plan, the combination of approaching adverse weather conditions and the necessary release of reservists and ships from duty meant that no landing of troops on open beaches could be attempted until Spring 1957.

53. Carlton, *Britain and the Suez Crisis*, p. 53.

6. Collusion and war

1. The threat of an Israeli–Jordanian war was explored in detail by the cabinet on 18 October 1956, PRO CAB 128/30, CM(56)71, p. 7; Anthony Nutting, *No End of a Lesson* (London, 1967), p. 89ff.

2. PRO CAB 128/30, CM(56)74, 25 October 1956.

3. Carlton, *Britain and the Suez Crisis*, pp. 65–8; Selwyn Lloyd, *Suez 1956*, pp.

239–50; W. S. Lucas, 'Redefining the Suez "Collusion": A Regional Approach' in *Middle Eastern Studies*, Vol. 26, No. 1, January 1990, pp. 88–112; Mordechai Bar-On, 'David Ben-Gurion and the Sevres Collusion' in Louis and Owen (eds), *Suez 1956*, pp. 145–60 .

4. PRO CAB 128/30, CM(56)71, p. 6, 18 October 1956; David Thorpe, *Selwyn Lloyd* (London, 1989), pp. 235–6.

5. McDonald is a little vague about when exactly he learned of the tripartite plan, and from whom. He says that he wrote the memo to Haley outlining the whole plan a few days after Eden and Lloyd had returned from Paris on 16 October but shortly before the first Sèvres meeting (22 October). This would put it on or around 18 October. Given that those in the cabinet who heard of the deal were naturally sworn to secrecy, and McDonald had been briefed by Eden personally so often before, evidence suggests it was the prime minister himself who told McDonald. See McDonald, *History of The Times*, p. 268.

6. MSS William Clark, 7, p. 139, 29 October 1956; see the conversation between Clark and Tony Benn after the hostilities in Egypt had ceased in Benn Archives, 18 November 1956. According to this, Clark had been sent on leave against his wishes after he had explained to the prime minister what the likely public reaction would be to the use of force against Egypt.

7. MSS William Clark, 7, p. 147, 1 November 1956.

8. Harold Macmillan, *Riding the Storm* (London, 1971), pp. 112–3; Hugh Thomas, *The Suez Affair* (London, 1967), pp. 63–4.

9. Lamb, *Failure of the Eden Government*, pp. 301–2.

10. Via CIA reports, the US administration knew that the French and Israelis – probably with the British – were planning something in late October, but nothing had been said publicly. Eisenhower initially refused to believe that London would get dragged into any collusion. See Kyle, *Suez*, p. 345.

11. *Hansard*, Vol. 558, c.1274–5, 30 October 1956.

12. Hetherington, *Guardian Years*, pp. 11–12; Donald Edgar, *Express '56* (London, 1981), p. 152; Kyle, *Suez*, pp. 310–11, 323.

13. On 24 October, the cabinet did discuss the question of international opinion's reaction to the forthcoming intervention and concluded: 'If ... a military operation were undertaken against Egypt, its effect on other Arab countries would be serious unless it led to the early collapse of Colonel Nasser's regime. Both for this reason, and also because of the international pressures that would develop against our continuance of the military operation, it must be quick and successful.' PRO CAB 128/30, CM(56)73, p. 7, 24 October 1956.

14. William Rees-Mogg, then chief leader-writer for the *Financial Times* as well as speech writer for Anthony Eden, vividly recalls being given this information by Allan at Number 10 'as it was proven so spectacularly untrue'. Interview with Rees-Mogg, 15 January 1992. That Rees-Mogg was not the only journalist given this story is borne out by what the vast majority of newspapers wrote the next day. Evidence suggests that Allan therefore also briefed the lobby.

15. *The Times*, 31 October, p. 8 headline, 'British move into Egypt reported: Taking over key positions'; *Manchester Guardian*, 31 October, p. 1 headline, 'Proposal to send in troops today'; *News Chronicle*, 31 October, p. 1 headline '3.30 am – Suez Zero Hour. Allied force ready to go in'; *Daily Express*, 31 October, leader, p. 6, began with the news that by the time the reader got his paper there was a strong possibility that British forces would have received their orders to take up positions

alongside the canal; *Daily Mail*, 31 October, p. 1, reported that British and French paratroops had already dropped at 4.30am; *Daily Mirror*, 31 October, p. 1 headline, 'Our troops in today'.

16. *News Chronicle*, 31 October, leader, p. 4, 'A gigantic gamble'; *Daily Mirror*, 31 October, no editorial whatsoever.

17. For the pressures on Curtis and the split in the *News Chronicle* office during this period see David Hubback, *No Ordinary Press Baron: A Life of Walter Layton* (London, 1985), p. 235, and George Glenton and William Pattison, *The Last Chronicle of Bouverie Street* (London, 1963), pp. 105–6.

18. Neither Cecil King (*Strictly Personal*, p. 131) nor Hugh Cudlipp (*Walking on Water*, pp. 226–30) accounts for the Mirror's conspicuous silence on 31 October. Indeed, both put the paper alongside the *Manchester Guardian* as being against the intervention from the very outset, when this was clearly not the case. The only conclusion one can reach is that the *Mirror* was beset with the same problem as in late July: King and Cudlipp split over whether to criticize the government whilst troops were about to go into action.

19. *Manchester Guardian*, 31 October, first leader, p. 6, 'To War?': 'The Anglo-French ultimatum to Egypt is an act of folly, without justification in any terms but brief expediency.' *Daily Herald*, 31 October, leader, p. 4, 'This is folly': 'Eden's decision will rouse the entire Arab world against Great Britain and France and, whatever the immediate outcome, will destroy the last vestige of British influence in the Middle East.'

20. *The Times*, 31 October, first leader, p. 9, 'Intervention'. This did, as Iverach McDonald claims in the paper's official history (p.270), list three reasons for deep concern – the lack of consultation with the US, the one-sidedness of the ultimatum, and the fact that the Arabs were bound to say that HMG's policy helped Israel. But the leader also praised the government for taking immediate action: 'Boldness often pays.'

21. *Daily Mail*, with its leader 'Stopping a war?' (31 October, p. 6), clearly had doubts about the wisdom of Eden's ultimatum, but was certainly not hostile to the government, as Hugh Thomas states (*The Suez Affair*, p. 133).

22. *Manchester Guardian*, 31 October, first leader, p. 6, 'To War?': 'Israel will be wrong if it supposes that there could be any collusion between itself and the Western forces which may be sent to occupy the Canal, so that they would in practice (though in disguise) act together in holding down the Arabs.'

23. Geoffrey Moorhouse, *The Diplomats* (London, 1977), p. 172.

24. *New Statesman*, 8 December 1956, p. 733. Derick Heathcoat Amory was minister of agriculture, David Eccles minister of education.

25. MSS William Clark, 7, p. 146, 1 November 1956.

26. *Hansard*, Vol. 558, c.1619–744, 1 November 1956.

27. *Daily Mail*, 2 November, front-page leader, 'A Police Action'; *Daily Express*, 7 November, leader, p. 6, 'Now for the Settlement'.

28. *News Chronicle*, 1 November, leader, p. 4 'Only a miracle can save Eden now', and 2 November, leader, p. 4, 'Reverse this Folly'; *Daily Mirror*, 2 November, front-page leader, 'Disastrous Folly'. The *Chronicle*'s editor, Curtis, was stiffened by support from Sir Walter Layton, who, though no longer chairman of the board, was still a major influence on the paper's editorial policy. See Hubback, *No Ordinary Press Baron*, p. 235; Glenton and Pattison, *Last Chronicle of Bouverie Street*, pp. 105–6.

29. See Hetherington, *Guardian Years*, p. 15, and *Hansard*, Vol. 558, c.1441–572, 31 October 1956. For examples of these papers' strong opposition to Eden's intervention see *Manchester Guardian*, 5 November, first leader, p. 8, 'To Quell the Flames'; *Daily Herald*, 3 November, front-page leader, 'He Must Go'; *Observer*, 4 November, first leader, p. 10, 'Eden'.

30. A. P. Wadsworth had retired owing to ill health in mid-October. He died on 4 November. For the background to the *Manchester Guardian*'s close relationship with Zionism see David Ayerst, *Guardian: Biography of a Newspaper* (London, 1971), pp. 381–6, 620.

31. See, for example, *Manchester Guardian*, 2 November, third leader, p. 8, 'Trade Unions and War' and 5 November, first leader, p. 8, 'To Quell the Flames'; *Daily Herald*, 3 November, front-page leader, 'He Must Go'; *Observer*, 4 November, first leader, p. 10, 'Eden'.

32. See Richard Cockett, 'The *Observer* and the Suez Crisis' in *Contemporary Record*, Vol. 5, No. 1, Summer 1991, pp. 9–31. As this article shows, contrary to popular mythology, the *Observer* did not lose circulation because of its anti-Eden stance on Suez. It did, however, lose a number of its regular advertisers, angered by what they regarded as the paper's anti-patriotic or anti-Jewish attitude. This weakened the *Observer*'s financial position significantly in the years ahead as competition for advertising in the Sunday press stiffened. For an analysis of the complex relationship between newspapers' policies during Suez and their subsequent changes in circulation see Ralph Negrine, 'The Press and the Suez Crisis: A Myth Re-examined' in *Historical Journal*, Vol. 25, No.4, 1982, pp. 975–83.

33. For evidence of the *Observer*'s continued opposition to Eden despite internal wranglings caused by the ferocity of its attack on 4 November see the three leaders on 11 November, p. 9, 18 November, first leader, p. 8, and 25 November, first leader, p. 8.

34. Kyle, *Suez*, pp. 353–4, 359–61, 363–5 (29–31 October 1956). For the UN General Assembly's resolution demanding an immediate ceasefire on 4 November, following Britain and France's use of the veto in the Security Council, see Kyle, pp. 436–8.

35. *Daily Telegraph*, 3 November, first leader, p. 6, 'International Police'; *Daily Express*, 1 November, leader, p. 6, 'The Safety of Us All'; *Financial Times*, 2 November, first leader, p. 6, 'Economic Consequences'. By 2 November the line-up amongst the national daily papers was the *Express*, *Mail*, *Sketch* and *Telegraph* pro-force; the *Mirror*, *News Chronicle*, *Herald* and *Manchester Guardian* (which, although a provincial paper, carried national and international weight) anti-force; *The Times* neutral. For a more detailed breakdown of the editorial position on Suez of the principal newspapers, including Sundays and provincials, see Epstein, *British Politics in the Suez Crisis*, pp. 154–5.

36. Ibid., pp. 144–5.

37. Margach, *Abuse of Power*, pp. 109–10.

38. Ibid., p. 110.

39. MSS William Clark, 7, p. 151, 2 November 1956. Clark writes that the request for this came from the Conservative party's chief whip (Edward Heath) via Philip de Zulueta of Eden's private office.

40. Avon Papers, AP 14/4/208, 2 November 1956. Thomson had bought *The Scotsman* in 1953.

41. Avon Papers, AP 14/4/111–114, 6 and 14 November.

42. Although this telegram is undated, its nature and Eden's reply (on 12 November) more than suggest it was sent in reaction to the government's use of force in Egypt: 'My dear Gomer, Thank you so much for the telegram which you and Edith sent. I have been infinitely grateful for your kindness and help throughout all this tough business.' Avon Papers, AP 14/4/126.

43. For the split in the *Sunday Times* office in early November see Harold Hobson, Philip Knightley and Leonard Russell, *The Pearl of Days – An Intimate Memoir of the Sunday Times, 1822–1972* (London, 1972), pp. 292–3.

44. *Hansard*, Vol. 558, c.1956–78, 5 November 1956.

45. MSS William Clark, 7, p. 154, 5 November 1956.

46. See Carlton, *Britain and the Suez Crisis*, pp. 74–5.

47. *The Times*, 6 November, p. 10, 'Support for PM stiffening'. Sir Edward Boyle, economic secretary to the Treasury, announced his resignation from the government on 9 November.

48. For an account of the Hungarian crisis of 1956 and how it proceeded quite independently of Suez events see John C. Campbell, 'The Soviet Union, the United States and the twin crises of Hungary and Suez' in Louis and Owen (eds), *Suez 1956*, pp. 233–56.

49. See, for example, *Daily Mirror*, 5 November, leader, p. 2; *Daily Herald*, 4 November, front-page leader; *News Chronicle*, 4 November, leader, p. 4.

50. See, for example, *Manchester Guardian*, front-page main headline, 'Soviet Tanks Crush Resistance'; *Daily Telegraph*, 5 November, front-page main headline, 'Soviet Tanks Crush Hungarian Uprising'. Television and radio also made the most of these reports from Hungary during the period of relative quiet on the Suez front. See Geoffrey Cox, *See it Happen: The Making of ITN* (London, 1983), pp. 81–5.

51. See, for example, *Hansard*, Vol. 558, c.1946–55, 5 November, statement by Selwyn Lloyd, and Vol. 559, c.114–18, 7 November, statement by joint under-secretary of state at the Foreign Office, Lord John Hope.

52. *Daily Telegraph*, 10 November, front-page headline; *Manchester Guardian*, 10 November, front-page headline.

53. Major General P. Shortt, director public relations, War Office, to Brigadier G. Hobbs, director of public relations, AFHQ, during Operation MUSKETEER REVISE, 19 November 1956. Liddell Hart Archive: Private papers, G. P. Hobbs, 20. For a more detailed analysis of military-media relations during Suez see the private papers of General Sir Hugh Stockwell, also lodged in the Liddell-Hart Archive. Stockwell papers 8/2/3 Operation MUSKETEER: Annex 'A': Arms and Services Reports. Number 4 on 'Public Relations', submitted by assistant director of PR, Lt Colonel T. W. Stubbs. Number 11 on 'Signals' by the chief signals officer, Brigadier W. G. Tucker.

54. Author's interview with Anthony Moore, deputy head of the Foreign Office News Department during the Suez crisis, August 1991. General Keightley himself thought the Egyptians would fight well, and, like Mountbatten, the First Sea Lord, saw the 1952 Ismailia resistance as proof. See Kyle, *Suez*, pp. 41, 236–7. For details of the events of 1952 see Michael Mason, '"The Decisive Volley": the Battle of Ismailia and the Decline of British Influence in Egypt, January–July 1952' in *Journal of Imperial and Commonwealth History*, Vol. 19, No. 1, January 1991, pp. 45–64.

55. Woods apparently managed to convince the military that he had parachute experience. His account of the paras' drop on Port Said airfield made it into the

press on 7 November 1956. See Donald Edgar, *Express '56*, p. 164, in relation to Woods' injuries.

56. Ibid., p. 157. Edgar strongly suspected that the Army Public Relations Unit had rigged the ballot held to decide which two journalists would be allowed to travel with the assault ships. It was widely known that his paper, the *Daily Express*, was solidly in favour of the government's policy and would therefore presumably report the landings in the appropriate manner. Baldwin was chosen because of the *New York Times'* influence in the US and further afield.

57. Private correspondence with Alastair Hetherington, February 1992. The correspondent in question was the *Manchester Guardian's* Michael Butler.

58. According to Lt.-Col. Stubbs in his summary report on the work of his unit, Number 4 PR Service, these officers should have been captains. This lack of status of PR officers was noticed by the journalists, who, as a result, valued their assistance even less. See Stockwell Papers 8/2/3 Report Number 4, p. 12.

59. Ibid., p. 8.

60. See, for example, *The Times*, 2 and 3 November; *Manchester Guardian*, 2 and 3 November.

61. See, for example, *The Times*, 6, 7, 8 November; *Manchester Guardian*, 6, 7, 10 November.

62. *News Chronicle*, 9 November, p. 4.

63. A detailed discussion of the technical problems of communications at Suez can be found in reports 4 and 11 in Stockwell Papers 8/2/3.

64. PRO FO 953/1617/P10127/3(H), D-Notice, 1 November 1956.

65. Butler's report was very much an isolated case. Most papers did not start to question the official figures for another week, particularly those supporting the government's case. See Edgar, *Express '56*, p. 170 for the *Daily Express's* unwillingness to print most of the despatches sent by its on-site correspondent. Where this official figure of 100 dead and wounded Egyptians originated is unclear. Given that Lt.-Gen. Stockwell himself put the number of Egyptians killed and wounded at 500 almost straight away, the most rational explanation is that it came from within government circles itself, most probably the Monckton publicity coordinating committee. Whatever the source, this extremely low figure was the one most British papers believed and published for a long time.

66. The first poll was conducted by the *Daily Express*, the second by Gallup. Figures in Epstein, *British Politics in the Suez Crisis*, pp. 143–5.

67. MSS William Clark, 7, p. 162, 2–6 November 1956.

68. For the background to the creation of this committee see PRO CAB 134/1216, EC(56) 37th Meeting, Minutes 1 and 2, 1 November; CAB 130/121/GEN 558 1st Meeting, 1 November; CAB 134/815, DTC(56) 18th Meeting, item 1, 1 November. For the daily work of the committee see DEFE 7/1127 file. The committee met daily in Monckton's room until 16 November, and on alternate weekdays thereafter. On 26 November, it was superseded by Charles Hill's Committee appointed to review and coordinate the government's publicity policy as a whole.

69. PRO DEFE 7/1127, MISC/M(56)149, Minutes of MoD PR Committee, 4 November 1956.

70. In the early hours of 6 November, Eden received a telegram from the Soviet premier, Marshal Bulganin, condemning the tripartite assault on Egypt and threatening, in a veiled manner, rocket attacks. This appears in fact to have had little impact on the government's subsequent actions in the Middle East (see Kyle,

Suez, pp. 456–60), though it certainly was useful for Eden's propaganda purposes, in the US especially. This is examined in Part Three.

71. PRO DEFE 7/1127, MISC/M(56)152, 6 November; MISC/M(56)154, 9 November 1956.

72. See, for example, *Sunday Times*, 11 November, leader, p. 8, 'The Greater Issue'; *Manchester Guardian*, 12 November, p. 1, 'Soviet Arms in Egypt'; *News Chronicle*, 10 November, p. 1, 'The Great Russian Riddle'; *Daily Telegraph*, 8 November, p. 1, and 10 November, p. 1.

73. Stockwell Papers 8/2/4 Annex 'B': Lessons and Recommendations, Public Relations.

74. Sir Edwin Herbert, president of the Law Society, was persuaded by the government to undertake an official investigation into the casualties resulting from MUSKETEER REVISE in December 1956 (foreign dignitaries having declined British requests to undertake the enquiry). He concluded that 'a reasonable estimate' was 650 killed in Port Said and another 100 in Port Fuad. Another 900 were sufficiently wounded to be detained in hospital. The US Naval Attaché estimated 1000 deaths. For details of this report and how its findings were presented to the public see Dep. Monckton, 8, pp. 209–10, 261–76, 370–7, 436–51.

75. Ibid.

76. For an analysis of the part US pressure on the British economy played in bringing about the ceasefire see Diane B. Kunz, *The Economic Diplomacy of the Suez Crisis* (Chapel Hill, 1991), pp. 128–52.

77. During the post-ceasefire period, great emphasis was placed by ministers on Britain being allowed to form a key component of the international force to be sent to Egypt under the UN's auspices. Its role would be to maintain order and supervise a return to the previous armistice lines. See PRO PREM 11/1105 ff 58–62. C.M.(56) 41st Meeting, 7 November 1956.

78. McDonald, *History of The Times*, p. 272.

79. McDonald was perhaps trying to cover his tracks at this stage, obscuring how much he knew by encouraging, via *The Times*, a spirit of rapid reconciliation in Britain. The sooner the country got back to normality, the fewer questions would be asked about who knew what and when.

80. *The Times*, leading editorials on 7, 8, 9 and 12 November.

81. For an account of how vulnerable Eden was during this period, and the pressure on him from within Conservative ranks especially, see Rhodes James, *Anthony Eden*, pp. 573–81.

82. Lord Beaverbrook to Brendan Bracken, 13 November 1956. Beaverbrook Papers BBCK C/58; Chisholm and Davie, *Beaverbrook*, p. 495.

83. According to the same letter sent to Bracken on 13 November 1956, Beaverbrook's son, Max, did not entirely agree with his father's assessment of Eden's decision to cease fire, and by this stage it was he who was in charge of the papers' policy.

84. Richard Bourne, *Lords of Fleet Street – The Harmsworth Dynasty* (London, 1990), p. 173.

85. *Daily Mail*, 7 November, front-page leader, 'Objective Achieved', and 9 November, 'Ceasefire'; *Daily Telegraph*, 7 November, first leader, p. 6, 'Ceasefire and After'.

86. Stockwell, commander of the allied land forces, later claimed that the whole length of the canal would have been captured within 48 hours of the main seaborne landings. Cited in Carlton, *Britain and the Suez Crisis*, p. 76.

87. PRO DEFE 7/1127, MISC/M(56)154, 9 November; MISC/M(56)158, 16 November 1956.

88. PRO DEFE 7/1127, MISC/M(56), 9 November; MISC/M(56)155, 12 November 1956.

89. PRO FO 953/1614/P10118/191(A), Major David Colbeck, Directorate of Forward Plans, MoD, to Pirie-Gordon, Foreign Office News Department, 20 November 1956. FO 953/1615/P10118/192(A), C. C. B. Stewart to Trend at Cabinet Office, 16 November 1956. The cabinet had suggested a few publicity points itself on 16 November, one of which was the publication of the full details of the Soviet arms discoveries.

90. For an estimate see PRO FO 953/1612/P10118/151(A), Guidance Paper 'Egypt-Israel and Suez: Notes on Policy', Annex A, sent by Foreign Office to overseas missions, November–December 1956. For a more detailed, retrospective analysis of the strength of the Egyptian armed forces during Suez and the extent of Soviet equipment and training see Yonah Bandmann, 'The Egyptian Armed Forces during the KADESH Campaign' in Troen and Shemesh (eds), *The Suez–Sinai Crisis 1956*, pp. 74–99.

91. *Daily Express*, 9 November, first leader, p. 6, 'Eden Sees Through It'; *Daily Express*, 12 November, first leader, p. 6, 'Nasser's Big Brother'; *Daily Telegraph*, 12 November, first leader, p. 6, 'New Plots for Old'; *Sunday Times*, 11 November, leader, p. 8, 'The Great Issue'.

92. PRO FO 953/1614/P10118/92(A), Guidance Telegram No.133 sent to Middle East posts, UK Delegation in New York, Paris and Washington, 13 November 1956.

93. Maurice Vaisse, 'France and Suez Crisis' in Louis and Owen (eds), *Suez 1956*, pp. 134.

94. The need to coordinate propaganda was firmly established at one of the first meetings between Selwyn Lloyd and Christian Pineau in London, on 31 July 1956. PRO FO 371/119083/JE14211/22/G, 31 July 1956.

95. PRO FO 800/727, Murray to Kirkpatrick, 1 November 1956.

96. PRO FO 800/727, Eden to Mollet (Telegram 2363), 1 November 1956.

97. PRO FO 371/118909/JE1094/144/6, Lloyd to Jebb, 8 November 1956.

98. For the *Guardian*'s investigation into collusion, and the problems caused by Israeli censorship, see Hetherington, *Guardian Years*, pp. 21–27.

99. For an account of David Astor's private efforts to bring down Eden see Cockett, 'The *Observer* and the Suez Crisis', pp. 24–5.

100. Laurence Cadbury to Michael Curtis, 30 November 1956, in Walter Layton Papers, Box 92, 62.

101. Ibid., Egbert Cadbury to Layton, 16 November 1956.

102. See, for example, *Daily Telegraph*, 21 November, first leader, p. 6, 'A Plot without a Plan', and *Daily Express*, 23 November, article, p. 2.

103. *The Times*, 21 November, p. 8, article by military correspondent.

104. Rendel sent Haley three handwritten letters in mid-November informing his editor of the truth behind the allegations of collusion. Rendel's firm opinion was based on evidence he had amassed from contacts in the Foreign Office. None of this made it into the paper. Letters found in TTA (Suez file).

105. PRO CAB 128/30, CM(56)85, 20 November 1956.

106. *News Chronicle*, 4 December, leader, p. 4, 'A Chance to Advance'; *Manchester Guardian*, 4 December, first leader, p. 2, 'The Recovery of Britain'.

107. Rhodes James, *Anthony Eden*, p. 583.
108. Lucas, *Divided We Stand*, pp. 312–23.
109. Rhodes James, *Anthony Eden*, pp. 591–8.
110. See, for example, *Daily Telegraph*, 10 January 1957, first leader, p. 6; *The Times*, 10 January 1957, leader, p. 9; *News Chronicle*, 10 January 1957, leader, p. 4.

7. The Press: conclusion

1. See, for example, Parmentier, 'British Press in the Suez Crisis', pp. 435–48; Epstein, *British Politics in the Suez Crisis*, pp. 153–65.
2. It was T. B. Macaulay who, in 1828, popularized the designation of the press as the fourth estate. See Tom Baistow, *Fourth Rate Estate* (London, 1985), p. 1; Francis Williams, *Dangerous Estate* (Cambridge, 1984), p. 6. For an interesting analysis of the contemporary relevance of this concept see George Boyce, 'The Fourth Estate: the reappraisal of a concept' in G. Boyce, J. Curran, and P. Wingate (eds), *Newspaper History* (London, 1978), pp. 19–40.
3. See, for example, Parmentier, *British Press in the Suez Crisis*, p. 435.
4. Cited in Cockerell, Hennessy and Walker, *Sources Close to the Prime Minister*, p. 144.
5. Eden, *Full Circle*, p. 446. How the Eden government sought to control the BBC's output during Suez is examined in Part Two.

8. Collision course

1. Quotation from Hugh Carleton-Greene, then BBC director-general, in 1961, cited in Asa Briggs, *The BBC: A Short History of the First Fifty Years* (Oxford, 1985), p. 320.
2. Cited in Burton Paulu, *Television and Radio in the UK* (London, 1981), p. 39.
3. F. R. MacKenzie, 'Eden, Suez and the BBC – A Reassessment', *The Listener*, 18 December 1969, pp. 841–3; John King, 'The BBC and Suez', *The Round Table*, Vol. 304, October 1987, pp. 510–17; Asa Briggs, *Governing the BBC* (London, 1979), pp. 209–17. The 1960 Pilkington Committee on Broadcasting praised the BBC for showing no signs of deference to the government, instancing the 1956 Suez crisis. See Anthony Adamthwaite, '"Nation Shall Speak Unto Nation": The BBC's Response to Peace and Defence Issues, 1945–58', *Contemporary Record*, Vol. 7, No. 3, Winter 1993, p. 560; This article seeks to counter the traditional view of the BBC as an independent body promoting public debate, and provides a useful context for the Suez crisis.
4. See note 1 above.
5. For brief details of the finances of the BBC's Home and External Services see *BBC Handbook 1957* (London, 1957), pp. 27–8.
6. See Cox, *See it Happen*, p. 72.
7. Briggs, *Fifty Years*, p. 386.
8. Jonathan Dimbleby, *Richard Dimbleby* (London, 1975), pp. 253–71; Briggs, *Fifty Years*, pp. 292–3, 302–3.
9. For an account of how ITN changed the face of television political reporting see Michael Cockerell, *Live from Number Ten* (London, 1988), pp. 41–4, and Cox, *See it Happen*, p. 71ff.
10. For details of the origins of the Fourteen Day Rule see Paulu, *Television and*

Radio, pp. 168–70. For a more critical analysis see Anthony Smith, *The Shadow in the Cave* (London, 1976), p. 198. See also Adamthwaite, '"Nation Shall Speak Unto Nation"', pp. 558–9.

11. For the details of the formulation of the *aide-mémoire* see Asa Briggs, *The History of Broadcasting in the UK, Volume 4, Sound and Vision* (Oxford, 1979), pp. 632–3, 636–7, 672, Appendix.

12. Briggs, *Sound and Vision*, p. 636.

13. Grace Wyndham-Goldie, *Facing the Nation: Television and Politics* (London, 1977), p. 165.

14. Briggs, *Fifty Years*, p. 292.

15. Sir Alexander Cadogan's Papers, 1955 Diary, ACAD 1/26, 27 June.

16. Briggs, *Fifty Years*, p. 292.

17. For details of the failed attempts, particularly in 1953, to seek a new definition of the term 'ministerial' see BBC WAC R34/1508/1, Report on Ministerial Broadcasts by Harman Grisewood sent to Norman Bottomley, 22 November 1956, p. 2.

18. Minutes of meeting between representatives of the government, opposition, BBC and ITA, 6 March 1956, in Conservative Party Archives, Central Office Records, CCO 4/7/348. For the detailed discussion between the political parties and the broadcasters on the issue of television ministerial broadcasts in the 1950s see PRO PREM 11/596 file, PREM 11/2604 file.

19. CCO 4/7/348; CCO 4/17/362, Heath to Donald Kaberry, Central Office Publicity Department, 12 April 1956.

20. Cockerell, *Live from Number Ten*, p. xiii.

21. Ibid., pp. 11–13.

22. Ibid., p. 36.

23. Avon Papers, AP 14/4/214, 22 May 1955. This is filed mistakenly under 1956.

24. Cited in Cockerell, *Live from Number Ten*, p. 38.

25. Paulu, *Television and Radio*, p. 213.

26. PRO PREM 11/1210 file, Eden to Conservative Central Office, 23 December 1955; CCO 4/7/346, Publicity Department report on broadcasting requested by Eden, dated 16 February 1956.

27. PRO PREM FO 953/1640/PB1011/12/G, Dodds-Parker to Paul Grey, 24 May 1956. Dodds-Parker wrote that the permanent under-secretary, Ivone Kirkpatrick, had also written to Sir Ian Jacob, the BBC's director-general, about the TV film.

28. PRO FO 953/1640/PB1011/6, J. B. Clark memorandum on the External Services, December 1955; FO 953/1640/PB1011/13, Sir Ian Jacob memorandum on the External Services, May 1956.

29. PRO FO 953/1641/PB1011/17, Paul Grey to Kirkpatrick, 20 April 1956; Avon Papers, AP 20/21/93, Eden to Lloyd, 4 May 1956; Conservative Research Department records, CRD 2/34/2, Minutes of joint meeting between Conservative Foreign Affairs and Defence Committees, 10 May 1956.

30. PRO FO 953/1641/PB1011/17, Nutting to Grey, 20 February 1956; same file, Grey to Kirkpatrick, 10 April 1956; FO 953/1641/P1011/18, Grey's draft Cabinet paper, 6 June 1956.

31. PRO CAB 128/30, CM(56)47, Minute 1, 5 July 1956; CAB 130/119/GEN 542.

32. PRO FO 800/738/19 Record of conversation, between Lloyd and Jacob, noted by Dodds-Parker, 11 July 1956.

33. PRO PREM 11/1212 file, Bishop to Hill, 15 June 1956; Hill's reply to Eden, 21 June 1956.

34. Ibid., Hill to Eden, 29 June 1956.

35. PRO CAB 128/30, CM(56)47, Minute 2, 5 July 1956.

36. MSS William Clark, 7, p. 96, 11 July 1956.

37. MSS William Clark, 7, p. 5, 27 September 1955. For details of this first period of competition between the BBC and ITV, and the impact it had on the BBC's news policy in particular, see Briggs, *Fifty Years*, pp. 299–308.

9. 'Are they enemies or just socialists?'

1. Eden, *Full Circle*, pp. 444–5.

2. BBC WAC R34/1580/1, director-general's desk diary for 26 July 1956.

3. Jacob was director-general of the BBC from 1952 until 1960. From 1939 to 1946 he had been military assistant secretary to the war cabinet, and in 1952 chief staff officer to the minister of defence and deputy secretary (military) to the cabinet.

4. Eden, *Full Circle*, p. 424.

5. Cadogan's Papers, 1956 Diary, ACAD 1/27, 26 July.

6. Ibid., 30 July 1956. The editor of Cadogan's diaries, who writes a somewhat sympathetic account of his role during Suez, declares: 'It is perhaps best to say at this point that Cadogan shared Eden's view of Nasser as an unscrupulous demagogue of paranoic tendencies.' *The Diaries of Sir Alexander Cadogan, 1938–1945*, edited by David Dilks (London, 1971), p. 796.

7. MSS William Clark, 7, p. 103, 31 July 1956.

8. Cox, *See it Happen*, p. 73; BBC WAC R34/1580/1, director-general's desk diary records a meeting with Clark at Broadcasting House at 6pm on 2 August.

9. Cox, *See it Happen*, p. 73.

10. MSS William Clark, 7, p. 105, 2 August 1956.

11. See Kyle, *Suez*, p. 257.

12. Ibid. Jacob's desk diary records an appointment with Macmillan and Salisbury at 11 Downing Street at 4.45pm on 3 August 1956. BBC WAC R34/1580/1.

13. PRO FO 953/1617/P10127/3E, 4 August; FO 953/1617/P10127/4(A), 15 August 1956.

14. BBC home news bulletins in the 1950s were, on average, little over five minutes long.

15. *At Home and Abroad*, Radio Home Service, 9.15–9.45 pm, 27 July 1956. Transcripts of all programmes cited can be found in BBC WAC, filed under programme title. Unfortunately these holdings are not complete, but a significant cross-section is available. Rapp had been head of the British Middle East Office in Cairo from 1950 to 1953.

16. See, for example, *From Our Own Correspondent* (radio), 29 July, *Panorama* (TV) 30 July, and *At Home and Abroad* (radio), 31 July.

17. *Panorama*, 8.30–9.15 pm, 30 July 1956. Dimbleby stated that because of the Fourteen Day Rule they could not discuss the rights and wrongs of the Suez situation that evening, but could 'elicit a few facts'. Even these, however, were couched in a discreetly anti-Nasser tone. *Panorama* had an average weekly audience of eight million in 1956 (*BBC Annual Report and Accounts 1956–7*, Cmd. 267, p. 39).

18. Dimbleby, *Richard Dimbleby*, p. 282.

19. See, for example, *At Home and Abroad*, 3, 17 and 21 August.

20. MSS William Clark, 7, p. 108, 7 August 1956.

21. Ibid.; Clark, *From Three Worlds*, p. 172, warnings by Sir Norman Brook, cabinet secretary, to Eden, 9 August 1956.

22. MSS William Clark, 7, p. 107, 4–6 August 1956.

23. See 'The Suez Crisis and the BBC: A Study of Successful Resistance to Government Pressure', compiled by Gordon Mosley and dated July 1961, BBC WAC R34/1508/3, p. 2.

24. MSS William Clark, 7, p. 108, 8 August 1956.

25. Transcript of Eden's broadcast, 10pm, 8 August 1956, BBC WAC R34/1508/1.

26. BBC WAC R34/1508/1, note of a telephone conversation between Gaitskell and unknown BBC official, 13 August 1956; R34/1508/3, 'Study of Successful Resistance', p. 4; for audience figures see R34/1508/1.

27. PRO PREM 11/1126, Jebb to Eden, 10 August 1956. The reaction to Eden's broadcast in the United States was also favourable. This is explained in greater detail in Part Three.

28. Cited in Cockerell, *Live from Number Ten*, p. 445; Avon Papers, AP 3/2/1, Clarissa Eden to Clark, 9 August 1956. Clark often got the impression that Clarissa came between Eden and himself, and even began to take over as the prime minister's public relations adviser. See, for example, MSS Clark, 7, p. 97, 16 July 1956.

29. Eden, *Full Circle*, p. 448.

30. Robert Menzies, *Afternoon Light* (London, 1967), p. 151.

31. Eden, *Full Circle*, p. 448.

32. BBC WAC R34/1508/1. See also 'Study of Successful Resistance', pp. 2–3, R34/1580/3.

33. BBC WAC R34/1580/1, Conversation between Green, Lindsay Wellington, director of Sound Broadcasting, and Norman Bottomley, director of Administration and acting director-general, 10 August 1956.

34. BBC WAC R34/1580/1. At this, Green telephoned Bottomley to reiterate his and Wellington's views and suggested that Bottomley should consult Cadogan. Bottomley said he would do so.

35. Wyndham-Goldie, *Facing the Nation*, pp. 178–9.

36. Cadogan's Papers, ACAD 1/27, 10 August 1956.

37. BBC WAC R34/1508/1, 11 August 1956.

38. Transcript of broadcast in PRO FO 371/119110 file, 13 August 1956.

39. Avon Papers, AP 14/4/61, Eden to Menzies, 13 August 1956.

40. BBC WAC R34/1508/3, 'Study of Successful Resistance', pp. 2–3.

41. Harman Grisewood, *One Thing at a Time* (London, 1968), p. 196.

42. BBC WAC T16/204/1, Green, controller, Talks (Sound), to Wellington, director Sound Broadcasting, 13 August 1956.

43. BBC WAC R34/1508/1, Sorenson to Cadogan, 10 August 1956.

44. Ibid., Cadogan to Sorenson, 14 August 1956.

45. Ibid., King, 'The BBC and Suez', p. 513.

46. BBC WAC R34/1508/1, Board of Management Minutes, BMM 391, 13 August 1956.

47. Transcript of Lloyd's broadcast, 9.30pm, 14 August 1956, in BBC WAC R34/1508/1. Lloyd's speech ended: 'I believe that there have been three essential times for us in the past ten years. First there was the threat to Berlin in 1948, which

was defeated by the Berlin air lift. Secondly, there was the communist aggression in Korea in 1950. That was repelled by force of arms. The third threat, and in my view the most serious of all for us in Britain, is this act of aggression against this great international waterway. The strength and prosperity of much of the world depends upon it. For us it is a question of our national livelihood, jobs, standard of living, and position in the world.'

48. MSS William Clark, 7, p. 114, 15 August 1956.

49. Salem had aroused the anger of the Foreign Office and parts of the British popular press in the mid-1950s for organizing an intensive anti-British propaganda radio campaign in Sudan. (See, for example, Shuckburgh, *Descent to Suez*, p. 233.) When he was then photographed jigging in his underwear at a Sudanese village ceremony, his nickname in the press became that of 'the dancing major'. For the transcript of Salem's short, and moderately toned, contribution to the programme, broadcast at 10.15–10.40 pm, 15 August 1956, see BBC WAC R34/1580/1.

50. PRO PREM 11/1089A file, Letter from Eden to Cadogan, 16 August 1956.

51. MSS William Clark, 7, pp. 114–15, 16 August 1956.

52. PRO PREM 11/1089A, PM(56)66, Lennox-Boyd to Eden, 16 August 1956.

53. MSS William Clark, 7, pp. 114–15, 16 August 1956.

54. Dilks (ed.), *Diaries of Sir Alexander Cadogan*, p. 797.

55. Cadogan's Papers, ACAD 1/27, 17 August 1956.

56. PREM 11/1089A file, Letter from Cadogan to Eden, 17 August 1956. Contrast this with Dilks (ed.), *Diaries of Sir Alexander Cadogan*, p. 797.

57. MSS William Clark, 7, p. 115, 17 August 1956.

58. PRO PREM 11/1089A file, Clark to Eden, 17 August 1956.

59. PRO PREM 11/1089A file, Hill to Eden, 20 August; Bishop to Hill, 21 August 1956.

60. There is no record of Jacob's reaction to the prime minister's message other than that of Eden himself, who afterwards felt that the director-general 'now more fully understands the strength of the Government's feeling that the BBC should take account of the national interest'. PRO PREM 11/1089A file, Bishop to Hill, 21 August 1956.

61. For the government's attempts to increase control over the BBC's External Services in the weeks immediately after the start of the Suez crisis see Peter Partner, *Arab Voices: The BBC Arabic Service, 1938–88* (London, 1988), pp. 99–101. George Young, head of the Foreign Office News Department, expressed the frustration which many in the FO felt towards the BBC during this phase when he referred to the corporation's resentment of interference as 'a permanent virginity complex'. PRO FO953/1652/PB1041/79, Young to A. D. M. Ross, 10 August 1956.

62. BBC WAC R34/1508/1, Kirkpatrick to Jacob, 16 August, and Jacob's reply, 17 August 1956. The BBC's representative on this Advisory Committee was to be the BBC's overseas services controller, Hugh Carleton-Greene.

63. Cited in Gilbert, *Never Despair*, pp. 1208–9.

10. Division and disunity

1. BBC WAC BMM 406 Board of Management minutes, 20 August 1956. The BBC installed a special coaxial cable in Downing Street.

2. PRO FO 953/1643/PB1011/43/G, Kirkpatrick to Rennie, 28 August 1956. Such a list was indeed compiled and sent to Kirkpatrick on 20 September, having

first passed through the hands of Paul Grey, assistant under-secretary at the Foreign Office with a special responsibility for information. Grey thought that this would give R. A. Butler's newly established Committee on Overseas Broadcasting plenty of ammunition with which to browbeat the BBC. FO 953/1643/PB1011/54, Grey to Kirkpatrick, 20 September 1956.

3. PRO FO 953/1643/PB1011/43/G, Kirkpatrick to Rennie, 28 August 1956.

4. BBC WAC R34/1508/1, Report on Ministerial Broadcasts by Harman Grisewood, sent to Norman Bottomley, 22 November 1956, pp. 1–2. The BBC in 1952 and again in 1953 tried to put forward suggested revisions of the definition of the *aide-mémoire* but neither party would agree to the changes. The politicians turned a blind eye to the abuse of the restrictions, probably in the hope that they would one day find the vagueness of the procedures useful.

5. Ibid., pp. 2–3.

6. BBC WAC R34/1508/1, Jacob to Brook, 30 August 1956.

7. BBC WAC R34/1508/3, 'Study of Successful Resistance', p. 4.

8. BBC WAC R1/1/24, Board of Governors minutes, 13 September 1956.

9. See Briggs, *Sound and Vision*, Appendix: *aide-mémoire* paragraph 6, (iii).

10. BBC WAC R34/1508/1, Account of meeting between Jacob, Cadogan, Butler and Gaitskell, 14 September 1956, in which Jacob describes why the latter two came to be consulted.

11. Ibid.

12. See BBC WAC R34/1508/3, 'Study of Successful Resistance', p. 6. Transcripts of all three broadcasts can be found in WAC. Gaitskell was interviewed by a group of four well-known journalists, H. V. Hodson of the *Sunday Times*, Ed Newman of the American National Broadcasting Company, Kenneth Harris of the *Observer* and Francis Williams of the *New Statesman*. Selwyn Lloyd was interviewed on 24 September by Hugh Cudlipp, editorial director of the *Daily Mirror*. So keen was Eden that his foreign secretary should say the right thing he sent Lloyd a list of points to put in the broadcast. Eden thought it very important, for example, that the government's imminent reference of the dispute to the UN should not be seen as a change of plan. Nor should the Security Council procedure be viewed as a panacea. It was imperative, in other words, that the government should not limit its freedom of manoeuvre. Lloyd followed his chief's advice very closely. PRO FO 371/119144/JE14211/1890, Eden to Lloyd, 24 September 1956.

13. Briggs, *Governing the BBC*, p. 211; Sir Ian Jacob, 'The Suez Crisis and the BBC', *Ariel*, Vol. 2, No. 1, January 1957, p. 3.

14. BBC WAC R1/1/24, Board of Governors, 13 September 1956.

15. BBC WAC R1/1/24, Board of Governors, 27 September 1956.

16. BBC WAC R34/1508/1, Grisewood's report on Ministerial Broadcasts, p. 1.

17. See Epstein, *British Politics in the Suez Crisis*, p. 142. On 5–6 September, a British Institute of Public Opinion (BIPO) poll asked, 'If Egypt will not agree to international control of the canal, what should we do? Would you approve or disapprove if we were to give Egypt an ultimatum that unless she agrees to our proposals we will send troops to occupy the canal?' Thirty-four per cent approved, 49 per cent disapproved, whilst 17 per cent did not know.

18. MSS William Clark, 7, p. 135, 1 October 1956.

19. BBC WAC R34/1508/1, Report by director of External Broadcasting, June to August 1956, dated 18 September 1956, p. 4.

20. See, for example, *Mirror of the East*, 'The Suez Canal as an engineering

problem', 28 August 1956; *As I See It*, 'Strains and Stresses', 1 October 1956; *Topic of Today*, 'Difficulties of maintaining the Suez Canal', 13 September 1956, and 'Economic effects of the Suez Canal crisis on the Middle East countries', 27 September 1956.

21. 'Political asides', in Arabic Service output file for 1956, one dated 29 August.

22. BBC WAC R34/1508/1, Report by director of External Broadcasting, dated 18 September 1956, p. 4.

23. Cited in Partner, *Arab Voices*, p. 102.

24. For details of the Foreign Office's deliberations over the appointment of a liaison officer at Bush House see PRO FO 953/1643/PB1011/53/G, Grey to Kirkpatrick, 24 September 1956, and letter sent to, and reply from, Eden, 1 and 3 October. For Eden's establishment on 26 September of a Ministerial Committee to review Overseas Broadcasting, chaired by R. A. Butler, see FO 953/1643/PB1011/50/G.

25. BBC WAC R34/1508/1, Information Coordination Committee (ICE) Progress Report, undated but probably late September/early October 1956. See also notes of Carleton-Greene's 'reminiscences' on Suez, dated 17 September 1969, R34/1508/3.

26. Ibid.; For evidence of SCANT material in September see text sent to Eden on October 3 1956, PRO PREM 11/1149 ff. 183/190, Langardge (Foreign Office) to Bishop (Number 10). According to the above ICE report, SCANT material, of which scripts had been available to members of the Advisory Committee, occupied about one hour of broadcasting daily at peak times in the Middle East. The transmissions were directed to Egypt, Syria, S. Jordan, Saudi Arabia, Lebanon, Iraq and the head of the Gulf.

27. BBC WAC R34/1508/1, Dodds-Parker's agenda for the next day's ICE/Advisory Committee meeting, 11 October 1956. One of the Advisory Committee's memoranda, dated 19 October and given to the Egypt Committee, had Carleton-Greene's name on the covering letter. See also the article by Richard Norton-Taylor, 'BBC Connived with MI6 to Oust Nasser', *Guardian*, 16 September 1994, p. 8.

28. BBC WAC R34/1508/1, Memorandum on 'Weaknesses in Egypt's Economic Position', sent to BBC by Jack Rennie, head of IRD, 24 October 1956. See minute on economic propaganda, dated 16 October, in same file also.

29. BBC WAC R34/1508/1, J. C. Thornton to Leslie Smith, 4 September 1956.

30. See, for example, reports by Douglas Stuart, the BBC's Middle East correspondent, in *At Home and Abroad* on 28 August and Thomas Barman, the BBC's diplomatic correspondent, in *From Our Own Correspondent* on 15 September. See also the same programme on 7 and 14 October.

31. See, for example, *At Home and Abroad*, 18 September 1956, and *The World This Week*, 15 September 1956. This latter item by Maurice Latey bears a striking resemblance to the government's own publicity memoranda at this point. Extremely well-argued, the item highlighted several popular themes: the weakness of the UN; how Nasser's action jeopardized the whole future of the newly independent states, in contrast with the help they were receiving from the peaceful, progressive British; that behind the Egyptian dictator's moves could be seen the controlling hand of the Soviet Union; and, finally, why the Americans ought to look to their wider international interests rather than accusing the British of colonialism. It is impossible to tell whether Latey was actually being advised by the government. What can be said for certain, however, is that the text of this broadcast (or something very similar to

it) was issued by the Foreign Office as official publicity material during Suez. Latey also produced one of the most useful publicity items for the government during the war period. For an index of the Foreign Office's Suez publicity material, compiled in March 1957, see Appendix C.

32. BBC WAC, *Radio Link*, 19 September 1956. This programme had to be content with looking at opinions on Suez abroad and the policies pursued by the foreign powers.

33. Transcripts of both programmes are available in BBC WAC filed under programme title.

34. There is no evidence of the BBC being given any specific instructions relating to the reporting of the movements in the Mediterranean during September and early October, over and above the D-Notices issued in August. However, Harman Grisewood does mention in his memoirs how he met William Clark almost on a daily basis during this period. Given what Clark had said earlier to Jacob and Cox about the need for broadcasters to cover the military preparations 'sensibly', and that he was periodically urging the press to play down the extent of the military build-up for reasons of security, it is extremely unlikely that Grisewood would not also have been reminded of his responsibility to protect soldiers' lives. For what it is worth, ITN's coverage of the MUSKETEER preparations was also extremely muted. See Grisewood, *One Thing at a Time*, p. 199.

11. The crucible

1. Cited in Cockerell, *Live from Number Ten*, p. 47.

2. Clause Three of the 1954 Television Act insisted on news being presented 'with due accuracy and impartiality'. This rule stemmed from the fears expressed during the debates on the Bill that a broadcasting system financed by advertising might either produce a yellow press of the air, filled with sensationalism, or be biased in favour of the advertisers and of the business interests behind the system. It was also intended to act as a safeguard against pressures from government and other powers. See Cox, *See it Happen*, p. 4.

3. Ibid., p. 93.

4. PRO CAB 128/30, CM(56)67, 26 September 1956; FO 953/1643/PB1011/50/G, Eden orders review of Overseas Broadcasting.

5. PRO FO 953/1645/PB1011/79, Minutes of Butler's Committee on Overseas Broadcasting, 18 October 1956.

6. PRO FO 953/1644/PB1011/60/G, Nutting to Sir Ian Jacob, 25 October 1956. See also conclusions of cabinet meeting of previous day: CAB 128/30, CM (56)73, 24 October 1956.

7. Cadogan's Private Papers, 1956 Diary, ACAD 1/27, 26 October; BBC WAC R34/1508/3, 'Study of Successful Resistance', pp. 11–12.

8. Partner, *Arab Voices*, p. 105. Jacob stalled on the financial question by having his secretary telephone the Foreign Office on 26 October to say that he had 'no comment' on the draft letter sent him that day. For the draft letter see BBC R34/1508/1, Dodds-Parker to Jacob, 26 October 1956.

9. BBC WAC R34/1508/3, 'Study of Successful Resistance', p. 11.

10. Grisewood, *One Thing at a Time*, p. 199.

11. See, for example, MacKenzie, 'Eden, Suez and the BBC', pp. 841–3; Kyle,

Suez, pp. 336–7. The existence of this 'instrument' was even debated in the House of Commons: see *Hansard*, Vol. 764, c.173–82, 6 May 1968.

12. Leonard Miall (BBC History of Broadcasting Unit), Record of Conversation with William Clark, 10 April 1976; MSS William Clark, 127, p. 103, 19 September 1969, Clark to research student; Gerard Mansell, *Let Truth Be Told: 50 Years of BBC External Broadcasting* (London, 1982), p. 232.

13. PRO FO 953/1644/PB1011/60/G, Nutting to Sir Ian Jacob, 25 October 1956.

14. BBC WAC R34/1508/3, Grisewood 'Reminiscences', dated 9 April 1969. When interviewed in 1969 Grisewood was at least prepared to accept this possibility. Grisewood saw Clark at Number 10 on 29, 30 and 31 October. It is not known on which particular date Clark passed on the 'takeover' information.

15. Grisewood, *One Thing at a Time*, p. 199.

16. BBC WAC R34/1508/3, Grisewood 'Reminiscences', dated 9 April 1969.

17. Ibid., p. 2; Grisewood, *One Thing at a Time*, pp. 199–200.

18. Ibid., p. 197. Unfortunately, Grisewood fails to give an exact date for this visit to Whitehall. MoD files are of no assistance either; there is no record of the meeting at all.

19. At none of the many meetings with senior BBC staff throughout the forthcoming crisis did Grisewood or Bottomley divulge this information. See BBC WAC R34/1508/3, 'Study of Successful Resistance' especially.

20. Grisewood, *One Thing at a Time*, p. 198.

21. Cox, *See it Happen*, p. 92.

22. For details see, for example, Carlton, *Anthony Eden*, pp. 443–6; Epstein, *British Politics in the Suez Crisis*, pp. 68–74; Rhodes James, *Anthony Eden*, pp. 544–6; Kyle, *Suez*, pp. 359–67.

23. PRO CAB 128/30, CM(56)73, 24 October 1956.

24. BBC WAC R34/1508/3, 'Study of Successful Resistance', p. 4.

25. PRO PREM 11/1149, GEN 554/2, FO guidance sent to Middle East posts via Ministerial Committee on Overseas Broadcasting, at 1500 hours, 30 October 1956.

26. PRO PREM 11/1149, GEN 554/6, Note by Dodds-Parker to Eden based on meeting of Ministerial Committee on Overseas Broadcasting, 20 November 1956; Richard Norton-Taylor, 'BBC connived with MI6 to oust Nasser', *Guardian*, 16 September 1994, p. 8.

27. BBC WAC R34/1508/3, 'Study of Successful Resistance', p. 16. The Government's formal requisitioning of Sharq al-Adna turned out to be an unmitigated disaster. Many of the Arab employees walked out when given instructions what they were to broadcast. See Partner, *Arab Voices*, pp. 108–9. For an analysis of the government's psychological warfare campaign in Egypt as a whole during Suez, again largely a failure, see PRO AIR 20/10369 file; AIR 20/9570, Papers by Brigadier Bernard Fergusson; PREM 11/1149 file.

28. BBC WAC R34/1508/3, 'Study of Successful Resistance', p. 16.

29. BBC WAC R34/1508/1, Record of telephone conversation with Paul Grey, 31 October, and J. B. Clark's reply, 1 November 1956.

30. WAC R34/1508/3, 'Study of Successful Resistance', pp. 14–16. A. D. Wilson acted as interim liaison officer from 1 November until John Titchener, an ex-SOE and psychological warfare expert, arrived from Teheran to take up duty in Bush House on 12 November 1956.

31. Grisewood, *One Thing at a Time*, p. 200.

32. Ibid., pp. 200–1; BBC WAC R34/1508/3, 'Study of Successful Resistance', pp. 16–18.

33. BBC WAC R34/1508/3, 'Study of Successful Resistance', pp. 17–18. On 31 October the BBC External Services broadcast a review of the British press which included mention of the *Daily Herald* headline, 'This is Folly', and a brief quotation from the *Manchester Guardian* leader of the same day. The Foreign Office complained vociferously about the BBC's continuation of its normal policy. See, for example, PRO FO 953/1654/PB1041/124, Grey in conversation with Bottomley, 2 November 1956. For a detailed analysis of the press reviews broadcast by the External Services during this stage of the Suez crisis, see FO 953/1755/PB1011/32, J. B. Clark to Ian Harvey, 3 April 1957. This confirms the impartiality of the reviews.

34. PRO AIR 20/10746, Air Marshal Barnett, 'Summary of Operations During Operation MUSKETEER'.

35. PRO FO 953/1606/P10118/25/G, Murray to Powell, 24 October 1956.

36. PRO FO 953/1606/P10119/29/G, MoD Committee on Public Relations Policy in Services, Minutes of Meeting, 31 October 1956.

37. PRO DEFE 7/1127, MoD Public Relations Committee, Minutes of 1st and 3rd Meetings, 1–3 November 1956.

38. BBC WAC R34/1508/2, Grisewood's account of meeting with R. C. Chilver on 2 November, sent to Bottomley 5 November 1956.

39. PRO FO 953/1617/P10127/3(H), D-Notice, 1 November 1956.

40. PRO AIR 20/2098, Powell to Hobbs, 4 November 1956. Powell stressed that the 'undue relish' shown by air-crews returning from Suez operations was damaging. Ministers were concerned about the political repercussions of such enthusiasm. Consequently, pilots were warned against being so 'gung-ho', and correspondents were given extra guidance on how to adjust the tone of such reports to give the 'right' emphasis.

41. See, for example, Home Service News Bulletin, 6pm, 3 and 4 November. The latter included a report by Hardiman Scott from Cyprus based on the best authoritative sources. BBC WAC HNB microfilm 469.

42. The bombing sorties were by no means a complete success. See Kyle, *Suez*, pp. 382–4.

43. This was also the case with ITV bulletins: see composite video material of ITN's coverage of the Suez crisis (courtesy of ITN), in St John's College Library, Oxford.

44. See, for example, *Panorama*, 5 November; *At Home and Abroad*, 2 November. Transcripts in BBC WAC.

45. PRO PREM 11/1123 file, Poole to Eden, 2 November 1956.

46. MSS William Clark, 7, p. 148, 2 November 1956.

47. See especially Rhodes James, *Anthony Eden*, pp. 558–9, 563–5. Rhodes James is particularly informative on how worried Tory backbenchers and ministers were during this period.

48. MSS William Clark, 7, p. 148, 2 November 1956.

49. Ibid.

50. For the full text of Eden's speech on 3 November see *The Listener*, 8 November 1956, pp. 735–6.

51. Cited in Cockerell, *Live from Number Ten*, p. 49.

52. BBC WAC R34/1508/3, 'Study of Successful Resistance', p. 7.

53. BBC WAC R34/1508/1, Grisewood to Bottomley, 1 November 1956.

54. BBC WAC R34/1508/3, p. 7. See also Grisewood's record of events on 3–4 November in R34/1508/1. Compare and contrast with Tony Benn's account of the weekend's events, taken from the political diaries and papers of Tony Benn (3 November 1956, pp. 22–4) in the Benn Archives.

55. Cadogan's Private Papers, 1956 Diary, ACAD 1/27, 3–4 November.

56. Heath talked to Grisewood by phone on the morning of 4 November and asked him to ensure that Gaitskell was as 'unprovocative' as Eden's broadcast had been the night before. BBC WAC R34/1508/1.

57. Taken from the political diaries and papers of Tony Benn (4 November 1956, pp. 25–6) in the Benn Archives.

58. Williams, *Hugh Gaitskell*, p. 435. For the full text of Gaitskell's broadcast see copy in Benn Archives, 4 November 1956.

59. As it happens, some at least would not. Anthony Howard, a young subaltern during Suez, later to become editor of the *New Statesman*, recalled how the troops on board his ship were allowed to listen to Eden's broadcast but not Gaitskell's. The officers who did tune in to the Labour leader considered him a traitor. Kyle, *Suez*, pp. 433–4, and author's personal correspondence with Howard, April 1991.

60. For an assessment of how Gaitskell's speech was received in the living rooms of the nation see Williams, *Hugh Gaitskell*, pp. 434–6, and Rhodes James, *Anthony Eden*, pp. 569–70.

61. Cadogan's Private Papers, 1956 Diary, ACAD 1/27, 4 November.

62. See Cox, *See it Happen*, pp. 88–90; composite video tapes of ITN's coverage of Suez.

63. *From Our Own Correspondent*, 11 and 18 November. Transcripts in BBC WAC. These two commentaries rank as possibly the most critical of the government's action in Egypt which the BBC transmitted. The first described the 'depressing' conditions in Port Said; the second gave the lie to those who argued that MUSKETEER REVISE had uncovered a huge Soviet arsenal in Egypt.

64. Cox, *See it Happen*, p. 88.

65. Page's film should have gone through Army Headquarters in Cyprus. However, the film was given straight to a pilot at Larnaca who was bound for London. He then delivered it to the war office in Whitehall, who handed it on the next day to ITN, apparently without any alterations. See Cox, *See it Happen*, pp. 88–9, for how this gave the company its 'biggest scoop of the year'.

66. Ibid., p. 88. In the account of his own trip to Port Said in the wake of the ceasefire, a young ITN newscaster, Robin Day, also tells of how he was 'shadowed' by a military public relations officer. In both his and Cyril Page's case this happened to be a young National Service officer who would later make a name for himself in broadcasting, Michael Parkinson. Robin Day, *Grand Inquisitor* (London, 1989), p. 105ff. The success which Parkinson, together with Robin Fisher (later of the *Daily Express*), had in winning the confidence of the journalists to whom they were assigned is noted in Colonel T. W. Stubbs' report on Public Relations during MUSKETEER (Number 4) in Stockwell Papers 8/2/3 Operation MUSKETEER: Annex 'A': Arms and Services Reports.

67. See, for example, Home Service News bulletin, 6pm, 5 November. A report by Hardiman Scott, who clearly had not been out to Port Said himself yet, included a statement by the commander-in-chief, Keightley: 'In these operations, the air

forces have done their job with such selectivity and accuracy that not even the pilots of the Egyptian aircraft were killed.' See also Home Service News, 6pm, 6, 7 and 8 November. BBC WAC HNB microfilms 469–70.

68. BBC WAC R2/1/13, Minutes of Board of Management Meeting, 5 November 1956.

69. Watkinson was interviewed by a potentially very hostile group of journalists, including Francis Williams of the *New Statesman* and Richard Scott of the *Manchester Guardian*. However, questions concentrated on the implications of the government's action in terms of transport, such as the closing of the canal and the shortage of oil supplies. Politics was a taboo subject.

70. Transcripts of *Panorama* and *Highlight*, 5 November 1956, in BBC WAC.

71. Dimbleby, *Richard Dimbleby*, p. 270.

72. Transcript of *At Home and Abroad*, 30 October 1956, in BBC WAC.

73. See, for example, *The World and Ourselves*, 1 November; *From Our Own Correspondent*, 4 November 1956.

74. See report on this in *Daily Express*, 3 November 1956, p. 3.

75. BBC research figures showed that, in the four days immediately after the Anglo-French ultimatums to Egypt and Israel on 30 October 1956, the audiences for BBC Radio's Six O'Clock News jumped from the normal five million to nine million a night. Those for the Nine O'Clock News doubled. See *BBC Annual Report and Accounts, 1956–7*, Cmd. 267, pp. 9, 57.

76. Transcript of *At Home and Abroad*, 2 November 1956, in BBC WAC.

77. *From Our Own Correspondent*, 11 November: 'All this devastation, however, was far more than I'd expected from the communiqués I'd read in Nicosia.'

78. *The World and Ourselves*, 8 November. Richard Scott made veiled criticisms of the government, accusing it of being at least partially responsible for the Russians' action in Hungary by having flouted the UN's wishes. His major point was that force was infectious.

79. PRO DEFE 7/1127, MoD Public Relations Committee, Minutes of Meeting on 9 November 1956; *The World This Week*, 17 November; *Panorama*, 12 November 1956, in BBC WAC.

80. Hugh Gaitskell raised the charge of collusion in the Commons, drawing on American press reports, as early as 31 October 1956. For his speech and Selwyn Lloyd's denial, see *Hansard*, Vol. 558, c.1459–63, 1569–71, 31 October 1956. The issue was consistently brought up in debates thereafter. On 22 November it was R. A. Butler's turn to issue a denial (*Hansard*, Vol. 560, c.1932–7). For the debate during which Eden himself directly refuted the conspiracy allegations, see *Hansard*, Vol. 562, c.1456–1518, 20 December 1956.

81. See, for example, *At Home and Abroad*, 2 November 1956, item by Sir Alec Kirkbride: 'Britain's action against Egypt is being widely represented as nothing more than a pretext to seize control of the Suez Canal, or alternatively the whole affair is a conspiracy between Britain, France and Israel. To this I can only say that it seems that our action is clearly designed simply to put a limit to the resumption of hostilities between Egypt and Israel and to safeguard the Canal area from disruption.' BBC WAC.

82. BBC WAC R34/1508/3, 'Study of Successful Resistance', pp. 22–9. 14 November 1956 – Adjournment Debate on BBC (News Broadcasts) in *Hansard*, Vol. 560, c.1023–1102.

83. BBC WAC R34/1508/3, 'Study of Successful Resistance', pp. 24–5.

84. Ibid., p. 25.

85. BBC WAC R34/1508/2, Grisewood to Gerald Beadle, 20 November 1956.

86. BBC WAC R34/1508/2 ,Grisewood to Bottomley, 20 November 1956.

87. BBC WAC R34/1508/3, 'Study of Successful Resistance', p. 8. Both of these broadcasts were party political and made on sound.

88. BBC WAC R34/1508/3, 'Study of Successful Resistance', p. 20, 15 November; R34/1508/2, 20 November.

89. BBC WAC R1/1/24, Board of Governors, discussion and conclusion on Adjournment Debate, 22 November 1956; R34/1508/3, 'Study of Successful Resistance', p. 26.

12. The BBC: conclusion

1. See Briggs, *First Fifty Years*, p. 317.

2. For an account of how the BBC fell in line with the government's policy during the General Strike see Paddy Scannell and David Cardiff, *A Social History of British Broadcasting* (Oxford, 1991), pp. 32–6. For the BBC's role during World War Two, see Asa Briggs, *The History of Broadcasting in the UK, Volume 3, The War of Words* (Oxford, 1970); James Curran and Jean Seaton, *Power Without Responsibility* (London, 1981), pp. 159–91.

3. *Ariel*, Vol. 2, No.1, January 1957, p. 3.

4. The House of Commons adjournment debate on 14 November 1956 was largely used by those who accused the BBC of having worked against the government during Suez. However, George Wigg, Labour MP for Dudley, alleged the very opposite, claiming that the BBC had indulged in 'Tory propaganda' and that it had gone out of its way from the beginning of the crisis to 'withhold the truth from the British people.' Wigg offered very little hard evidence for this and his comments were swamped by those on the benches opposite. *Hansard*, Vol. 560, c.1051ff, 14 November 1956.

5. Hugh Thomas in the *Sunday Times*, 11 September 1966, p. 19 and cited by Grisewood in his autobiography as evidence of the BBC's steadfast opposition to government pressure: *One Thing at a Time*, p. 199.

6. *BBC Annual Reports and Accounts 1956–7*, Cmnd.267, p. 19.

7. For more on the institutionalized nature of British broadcasting see Smith, *Shadow in the Cave*, p. 54ff.

8. The relationship between the BBC Chairman of Governors, the Executive and government is explained in Smith, *Shadow in the Cave*, pp. 209ff; Jeremy Tunstall, *The Media in Britain* (London, 1985), pp. 194–9.

13. The 'special relationship' and the role of public opinion

1. PRO FO 953/1689/PG11639/3, C. C. B. Stewart to A. B. Horn, New York, 1 August 1956.

2. Foster's cable to State Department, 27 July 1956, cited in Lucas, *Divided We Stand*, p. 142. The only other foreign representative at the meeting at Number 10 on the night of 26 July was the French ambassador, Jean Chauvel.

3. Anthony Eden, *Full Circle*, pp. 427–8.

4. See Freiberger, *Dawn Over Suez*, pp. 107–32. For the essential ingredients of ALPHA, which centred on Israel ceding land to Egypt and Jordan in exchange for a Western-guaranteed peace treaty, see Shimon Shamir, 'The Collapse of Project Alpha' in Louis and Owen (eds), *Suez 1956*, pp. 81–2.

5. Kyle, *Suez*, p. 99.

6. Lucas, *Divided We Stand*, pp. 104–25; Kyle, *Suez*, pp. 99–101.

7. Peter L. Hahn, *The United States, Great Britain and Egypt, 1945–1956* (Chapel Hill, 1991), pp. 202–3.

8. Ibid., pp. 203–6; Kyle, *Suez*, pp. 123–6.

9. Lucas, *Divided We Stand*, p. 3.

10. Quotation from Sir Roger Makins, British ambassador in Washington, January 1954, cited in Richie Ovendale, 'Egypt and the Suez Base Agreement' in John W. Young (ed.), *The Foreign Policy of Churchill's Peacetime Administration, 1951–55* (Leicester, 1988), p. 152.

11. PRO FO 371/114618, Caccia (deputy under-secretary, FO) to Makins (Washington), 21 October 1955.

12. Lucas, *Divided We Stand*, p. 72.

13. *Foreign Relations of the United States*, 1955–57, Vol. XIII, Doc.213, Memorandum of a Conversation, White House, 30 January 1956, pp. 329–34.

14. PRO CAB 128/30, C.M.(56), 27 July 1956; PREM 11/1098 ff 410–15, C.M.(56) 45th Conclusions, Confidential Annex, 27 July 1956.

15. Lucas, *Divided We Stand*, p. 150.

16. See, for example, Herman Finer, *Dulles over Suez* (Chapel Hill, 1964); Hahn, *United States, Great Britain and Egypt*; Kyle, *Suez*; Lucas, *Divided We Stand*; Neff, *Warriors at Suez* (New York, 1981); Freiberger, *Dawn Over Suez*; Richard Neustadt, *Alliance Politics* (New York, 1970); Robert Bowie, *Suez 1956: International Crisis and the Rule of Law* (Oxford, 1974); Love, *Suez: The Twice Fought War*; D. Cameron Watt, *Succeeding John Bull: America in Britain's Place, 1900–1975* (Cambridge, 1984).

17. For a detailed analysis of 'British Information Work in the United States' in the mid-1950s, including the anti-British prejudice faced by the Foreign Office, see PRO FO 371/1471/P10112/17 and 18 – the former on policy, the latter on machinery – draft paper produced by J. G. Boyd, US regional adviser in Information Policy Department, March 1954.

18. See Caroline Anstey, 'Projection of British Socialism: Foreign Office Publicity and American Opinion, 1945–50' in *Journal of Contemporary History*, Vol. 19, No. 3, July 1984, pp. 417–51.

19. PRO FO 371/1471/P10112/17, Paper by J. G. Boyd, US regional adviser in Information Policy Department, March 1954.

20. Ibid.

21. Anstey, 'Projection of British Socialism', p. 422; *BBC Annual Report and Accounts, 1956–7*, Cmd.267, Appendix IX, pp. 142–3. This figure discounts the General Overseas Service, which broadcast 147 hours per week.

22. PRO FO 371/1471/P10112/18, Paper by J. G. Boyd, US regional adviser in Information Policy Department, March 1954.

23. PRO FO 953/1400/P10113/39, Budgets for Foreign Office information services, submitted to Drogheda Committee, 11 May 1953. £300,000 was the budget for US information staff, plus £88,500 for operations.

24. Cited in Paul Gore-Booth, *With Great Truth and Respect* (London, 1974), p. 199.

25. Anstey, 'Projection of British Socialism', p. 419. The 1938 Foreign Agents Registration Act required that all foreign information activities should be registered with the US Department of Justice, and that all material emanating from a foreign source should carry a label describing its origins.

26. PRO FO 371/1471/P10112/17, Paper by J. G. Boyd, US regional adviser in Information Policy Department, March 1954; CAB 130/121, GEN 561, Memorandum on 'The work of the BIS, New York' by J. Peck, director-general of British Information Services, New York, 8 March 1957; Author's personal correspondence with Peck, 13 July 1991. For details of British propaganda efforts in the US during World War One see Michael Sanders and Philip M. Taylor, *British Propaganda during the First World War* (London, 1982), pp. 167–207.

27. PRO FO 371/1471/P10112/17 and 18, Papers by J. G. Boyd, US regional adviser in Information Policy Department, March 1954; FO 953/1163/PG14537/7, K. G. Younger, minister of state, FO, to Sir John Slessor, Air Ministry, May 1951.

14. Mobilizing American opinion

1. PRO FO 371/119080/JE14211/76, Makins to Foreign Office, 28 July 1956.

2. Ibid.

3. Heikal, *Cutting the Lion's Tail*, pp. 135–43; Lucas, *Divided We Stand*, p. 140.

4. PRO FO 953/1688/PG11639/7, Montgomery-Cunningham memorandum, 3 August 1956.

5. See, for example, PRO CAB 128/30, CM(56)54, 27 July 1956; CAB 128/30, CM(56)59, 14 August 1956; Lloyd, *Suez 1956*, p. 95.

6. PRO PREM 11/974 file; Clark, *From Three Worlds*, pp. 1–74.

7. PRO FO 115/4557/1424/126–7/56, London to Washington, 30 July 1956.

8. PRO FO 371/119082/JE14211/186, Makins to Foreign Office, 1 August 1956.

9. Anstey, 'Projection of British Socialism', p. 423. See also PRO FO 953/1471/P10112/17, Gaydon to Foreign Office, 10 March 1954.

10. Love, *Suez: The Twice Fought War*, p. 363.

11. PRO FO 371/119093/JE14211/441, Minute by Anthony Moore of the News Department, 1 August 1956.

12. Ibid.

13. PRO FO 953/1688/PG11639/3, C. C. B. Stewart to Alan Horn, New York, 1 August 1956. Stewart's pin-pointing of the threat which Nasser's action posed to NATO was very astute. On 30 July Dulles himself held a meeting on the subject of oil which concluded that the interruption of supplies would indeed be catastrophic for NATO security. For details of how seriously the US administration viewed this threat see Diane Kunz, 'The Importance of Having Money' in Owen and Louis (eds), *Suez 1956*, pp. 215–32.

14. PRO FO 371/1471/P10112/17–18, Boyd Memorandum to Information Policy Department, March 1954, Part I – Policy, Paragraph 18.

15. PRO FO 953/1689/PG11639/2, Washington embassy to British Information Services, New York, 15 May 1956.

16. PRO FO 371/1471/P10112/17–18, Boyd Memorandum to Information Policy Department, March 1954, Part II – Machinery.

17. See Lucas, *Divided We Stand*, pp. 142–53.

18. See, for example, Eisenhower's letter to Eden, written on 31 July and delivered by Dulles on 1 August, in Rhodes James, *Anthony Eden*, pp. 471–3. Eden might indeed have been right to assert that 'The President did not rule out the use of force' at this stage (Eden, *Full Circle*, p. 436). Nevertheless, it was apparent to Eden and other ministers by the end of the first week of the crisis that the US administration preferred a negotiated solution to the dispute and the toppling of Nasser by covert rather than overt means (as OMEGA had envisaged). See Carlton, *Anthony Eden*, pp. 411–14; Lucas, *Divided We Stand*, pp. 154–6.

19. PRO FO 115/4560/1424/216/56, Transcript of Dulles' broadcast as printed in *New York Times*, 4 August 1956.

20. PRO FO 371/119088/JE14211/311, Makins to Foreign Office, 4 August 1956. The *Philadelphia Inquirer*, for example, very aggressive at the start of the crisis, made much of Dulles' 'moderating influence' in London, which, it said, had 'calmed down hot-heads clamouring for immediate show of force'.

21. PRO FO 115/4560/1424/223/56, Foreign Office to BIS, New York, 4 August 1956.

22. PRO FO 115/1424/252/565, BIS to Washington embassy, 6 August 1956. Wheeler of NBC and Smith of CBS appeared to be BIS's network contacts.

23. *English-Speaking Union: A Decade of Progress, 1945–1955* (London, 1955).

24. PRO FO 953/1688/PG11639/15, C. C. B. Stewart to Beeley, 7 August 1956.

25. Ibid.; *English-Speaking World*, September 1956, Vol. XXXVIII, No. 5, especially the reference to a revised background brief on the Middle East problem produced in August 1956 by the Commonwealth-American Current Affairs Unit. For Eden and the Foreign Office's support for the Unit in May 1956 see FO 800/731 file, Lloyd to Eden, 11 May 1956.

26. BBC WAC R34/1580/1, Transcript of Selwyn Lloyd's radio broadcast, 14 August 1956. Lloyd made every effort to associate the US administration with the Anglo-French stand on Suez, consistently emphasizing the measure of agreement between the three of them in London in early August. Like Eden's broadcast on 8 August, Lloyd's was also relayed in the US.

27. BBC WAC R34/1580/1, Transcript of Eden's broadcast, 8 August 1956.

28. See instructions given to Gladwyn Jebb, ambassador in Paris, PRO PREM 11/1099 f.264, Lloyd: 'France and the Middle East', 7 August 1956; Rhodes James, *Anthony Eden*, p. 485.

29. Love, *Suez: The Twice Fought War*, p. 396.

30. PRO FO 371/119099/JE14211/617, Makins to Foreign Office, 10 August 1956.

31. MSS William Clark, 7, p. 111, 9 August 1956.

32. PRO FO 115/4563/1424/288/56, Makins to Foreign Office, 8 August 1956. On 7 and 8 August, the secretary of state for defence, Wilson, and Eisenhower both made statements which came very near to ruling out the use of force against Nasser completely.

33. PRO FO 371/120313/AU1013/38, Makins to Foreign Office, 11 August 1956. In the light of this latest report, on 14 August A. M. MacCleary of the American Department concluded that the consensus of opinion in the US press was now that: (i) an international solution for the running of the canal must be found; (ii) this solution must have a chance of being acceptable to Colonel Nasser; (iii) the solution must not be imposed upon Egypt by force.

34. PRO FO 371/119099/JE14211/617, Makins to Foreign Office, 10 August 1956.

35. Love, *Suez: The Twice Fought War*, p. 411.

36. PRO FO 371/119109/JE14211/840, Makins to Foreign Office, 15 August 1956.

37. See, for example, PRO FO 800/739 file, Makins to Lloyd, 14 August 1956; CAB 134/1216, EC(56) 18th Meeting, Minute 2, 20 August 1956, and EC(56) 21st Meeting, Minute 1, 24 August 1956.

38. PRO FO 371/119132/JE14211/1484, Washington embassy to African Department, 14 August 1956.

39. PRO CAB 134/1216, EC(56) 18th Meeting, 20 August 1956.

40. PRO CAB 134/1216, EC(56) 21st Meeting, 24 August 1956.

41. Ibid.; PREM 11/1152 ff 26–41, Lennox-Boyd to Eden, 24 August 1956; CAB 134/1216, EC(56) 23rd Meeting, 28 August 1956.

42. PRO FO 371/119124/JE14211/1269, Makins to Foreign Office, 31 August 1956; FO 371/120313/AU1013/41, Makins to Foreign Office, 1 September 1956.

43. PRO FO 371/119122/JE14211/1226, Foreign Office to Washington, 2 September 1956; FO 371/119124/JE14211/1289, Makins to Foreign Office, 3 September 1956. For how the British press reported this, see, for example, *Manchester Guardian*, 6 September 1956, p. 1, and *Daily Telegraph*, 6 September, leader, p. 6.

44. PRO FO 953/1690/PG11639/45, UK Delegation at UN, New York, to Foreign Office, 6 September 1956; personal correspondence with Sir John Peck, director-general of British Information Services during the Suez crisis, July 1991.

45. PRO FO 371/119132/JE14211/1472, D. A. Logan to Lloyd, 4 September 1956; FO 953/1690/PG11639/36, Logan to Information Policy Department, 4 September 1956. This article, entitled 'Arab warnings go to Nasser', was written by Norman Clark. FO 371/119141/JE14211/1795, Eden and Lloyd approval for guidance to BIS, 22 September 1956.

46. PRO FO 371/119128/JE14211/1149, Makins to Foreign Office, 7 September 1956; Dep. Monckton, 8, p. 258, letter written by Dodds-Parker to Rex Benson *vis-à-vis* Suez publicity in North America, 28 November 1956.

47. PRO FO 371/119127/JE14211/1269, Makins to Foreign Office, 5 September; FO 371/119128/JE14211/1149, Makins to Foreign Office, 7 September 1956.

48. PRO FO 371/119133/JE14211/1500, Makins to Foreign Office, 11 September 1956; FO 800/740/33, Makins to Lloyd, 9 September 1956.

49. *Foreign Relations of the United States*, 1955–57, Vol. XVI, Document 192, p. 436, Eisenhower to Eden, 8 September 1956; ibid., Document 163, p. 356, Eisenhower to Eden, 2 September 1956.

50. MSS William Clark, 7, p. 126, 10 September 1956; PRO FO 371/119136/JE14211/1575, Minute by Kirkpatrick, 12 September 1956. The document in question was a telegram sent to the Foreign Office by Charles Duke, ambassador in Amman, dated 11 September.

51. Kyle, *Suez*, pp. 217–41; Lucas, *Divided We Stand*, pp. 188–98.

52. PRO FO 953/1691/PG11639/61, BIS, Los Angeles, to Information Policy Department, undated. For more guidance on the pilots issue, see FO 115/4600/1424/3/124/56, Foreign Office to Washington, 30 August 1956.

53. PRO FO 371/119140/JE14211/1757, Giles to Logan, 18 September 1956. Organized by the Ministry of Transport, PILEUP aimed to test Nasser's ability to operate the Suez Canal without the foreign pilots beyond breaking point. Shipping was bundled together at both ends of the canal to create chaos, whereupon Cairo

would be charged with incompetence. Operation CONVOY would then clear up the mess. This envisaged organizing a convoy of ships piloted by experienced pilots which would demand free and unobstructed passage through the canal. If Nasser objected to this, British and French warships would lead the convoy. See PRO CAB 128/30 Part Two: Memorandum by Watkinson, 10 September 1956. So successfully did the Egyptians run the canal after 15 September, this latter operation was not put into practice.

54. Lucas, *Divided We Stand*, p. 207; Dulles to Lloyd, 19 September 1956, cited in D. R. Thorpe, *Selwyn Lloyd* (London, 1989), p. 225.

55. MSS William Clark, 7, p. 134, 21 September 1956.

56. For an analysis of Macmillan's conversations with Eisenhower and Dulles in the US, and the motives behind his advice to Eden on his return, see Horne, *Macmillan, Volume 1*, pp. 418–26.

57. Ibid., p. 419, Macmillan diary, 22 September 1956.

58. Only a few weeks prior to the chancellor's US visit, for example, Sir Edward Bridges, the permanent secretary at the Treasury, had told Macmillan of 'the vital necessity from the point of view of our currency and our economy of ensuring that we do not go it alone and that we have the maximum US support'. PRO T236/4188, Bridges to Macmillan, 7 September 1956. For Macmillan's failure to convey this and other economic information to the cabinet during Suez see Lewis Johnman, 'Defending the Pound: The Economics of the Suez Crisis, 1956' in A. Gorst, L. Johnman, W. S. Lucas (eds), *Post-War Britain: Themes and Perspectives, 1945–64* (Leicester, 1989), pp. 170–1, 179.

59. George Gallup, *The Gallup Poll, Public Opinion, 1935–1971* (New York, 1972), p. 1455. The poll, dated 20–25 September 1956, asked 'If England and France decide to use armed force against Egypt, should we send troops and ships, or not?' Twenty-three per cent answered yes, 55 per cent no, with 22 per cent having no opinion.

60. PRO FO 371/119181/JE14214/193, Dixon to Lloyd's private secretary, 29 September 1956.

61. PRO FO 371/119155/JE14211/2168, J. H. A. Watson to African Department following conversation with Alan Horn, deputy director-general of British Information Services, 3 October 1956: 'Points most likely to weigh with US opinion'. This list of points was then sent to the Central Office of Information and the BBC by Sydney Hebblethwaite of the Information Research Department. For the transcript of Lloyd's broadcast see FO 953/1691/PG11639/75 file.

62. PRO FO 371/1190888/JE14211/318, Minute by C. R. A. Rae following conversation with Kern, 30 July 1956; FO 953/1991/PG11639/63 and 66, Dodds-Parker to Information Policy Department following conversation between Lloyd and Kern, 26 September 1956; FO 371/119156/JE14211/2175, Kern to Lloyd, 4 October 1956. Kern also gave an overview of American opinion on the Suez crisis on *At Home and Abroad* on 7 August 1956.

63. PRO FO 371/120315/AU1014/5, Muirhead's report on his tour to Hankey in American Department, dated 28 November 1956.

64. PRO FO 371/120333/AU1051/36, Hadow to Foreign Office, 27 October 1956.

65. PRO PREM 11/1174, Washington to Foreign Office, 2 October 1956.

66. PRO FO 115/4584/1424/907/56, Washington to Foreign Office, 4 October 1956; FO 371/120314/AU1015/41, Makins to Foreign Office, 6 October 1956; FO 371/119154/JE14211/2125, Makins to Foreign Office, 11 October 1956.

67. PRO FO 800/741/6, Makins to Eden, 3 October 1956, and Lloyd's reply, 4 October 1956. William Clark spoke to Iverach McDonald, who wrote 'a sharp leader' heavily criticizing Dulles the next day, 3 October. MSS William Clark, 7, p. 137.

68. PRO FO 115/4584/1424/904/56, Foreign Office to Washington, 3 October; transcript of Hodson's broadcast on *This Day and Age*, transmitted on BBC North American Service on 5 October 1956, in BBC WAC.

69. PRO CAB 128/30, CM(56)68, 3 October 1956.

70. Anthony Nutting, *No End of a Lesson* (London, 1967), p. 70; McDonald, *History of The Times*, p. 268.

71. Lucas, *Divided We Stand*, p. 250. Caccia travelled to the US by ship, setting sail on 1 November and arriving on 8 November. He presented his credentials to Eisenhower on 9 November. Why the ambassador chose this slow form of transport during such a critical period in Anglo-American relations is unclear. According to Rhodes James, it was at Caccia's request, to which Eden had agreed, to his subsequent regret (*Anthony Eden*, p. 544). Kyle asserts (though without any evidence) that Caccia's absence from Washington was not accidental, implying either that London preferred to deal with the White House directly in early November or that Caccia should avoid any possibly compromising questions (*Suez*, p. 345).

72. Ibid., p. 257; private correspondence with Sir John Peck, July 1991.

73. PRO FO 371/119163/JE14211/2329, Washington to Foreign Office, 12 October 1956. Report written by Doris Hammond.

74. Lucas, *Divided We Stand*, pp. 253–4

75. PRO CAB 128/30, CM(56)75, 30 October 1956.

76. Much of the personal correspondence between Eden and Eisenhower during the 'war' phase is in Rhodes James, *Anthony Eden*, p. 563ff.

77. Freiberger, *Dawn Over Suez*, pp. 190–4; Finer, *Dulles over Suez*, pp. 371–2.

78. Correspondence with Sir John Peck, July 1991; Gore-Booth, *With Great Truth and Respect*, p. 229.

79. PRO FO 953/1610/P10118/109, Peck's memorandum (undated), copy sent by C. B. Ormerod, British Information Services, to Information Policy Department, 20 November 1956.

80. See W. R. Louis, *The British Empire in the Middle East, 1945–51* (Oxford, 1984), Part 4; Michael J. Cohen, 'The Zionist Perspective' in Louis and Stookey (eds), *The End of the Palestine Mandate* (London, 1986), pp. 79–101; Eliahu Elath, *The Struggle for Statehood, 1945–48, Volume 2* (Tel Aviv, 1982).

81. Nadrav Safran, *The Embattled Ally* (Cambridge, MA, 1978), p. 577; Kyle, *Suez*, p. 98.

82. Ibid., p. 124; Donald Neff, *Warriors at Suez*, pp. 195, 220; Freiberger, *Dawn Over Suez*, pp. 115, 131; Stephen Ambrose, *Eisenhower: The President, Volume Two: 1952–69* (London, 1984), pp. 352–3.

83. PRO FO 953/1610/P10118/109, Peck's memorandum (undated), copy sent by C. B. Ormerod, British Information Services, to Information Policy Department, 20 November 1956; FO 953/1746/P10422/11, Peck to Information Policy Department, January 1957. For BIS's other contacts used during this period see this file.

84. PRO FO 953/1607/P10118/48, Stewart to Peck, New York, 6 November 1956.

85. PRO FO 953/1607/P10118/60(A), Newling to Mennell, Information Policy Department, 9 November 1956; FO 953/1608/P10118/71, Mennell to D'Arcy Edmundson, Washington, 12 November 1956.

86. PRO FO 953/1608/P10118/66, British Information Services to Foreign Office, 11 November 1956.

87. PRO PREM 11/1149, Head to Butler, 13 November 1956; Dixon (New York) to Foreign Office, 22 November 1956; FO 371/118551/JE1027/57, Hadow (San Francisco) to Caccia, 21 December 1956.

88. PRO PREM 11/1149, Eden to Noble, 18 November 1956; Murray to Foreign Office, 21 November 1956; Details of House of Commons statement by Butler concerning Swedish journalist, Perelow Anderson, 10 December 1956. A set of photographs of a devastated Port Said taken by Anderson and put together by the Egyptians in a magazine called *The Scribe*, was distributed internationally in November 1956 and caused the British government great consternation. The Foreign Office, assisted by ministers, consequently conducted a systematic campaign to discredit both the pictures and the journalist. In the Commons on 10 December Butler condemned Anderson as a former member of the Swedish Brownshirt Party with a record of 'fictional' reporting.

89. PRO FO 953/1610/P10118/79, Memorandum by Stewart to Beeley, 23 November 1956; FO 371/118908/JE1094/125, Chiefs of Staff to Allied commander-in-chief, 12 November 1956; FO 371/118908/JE1094/129, Lloyd's comments on Allied commander-in-chief's memorandum, 15 November 1956; FO 371/118909/JE1094/169, Murray to Foreign Office, 20 November 1956; FO 371/118922/JE1094/425, Washington to American Department, 14 December 1956.

90. PRO FO371/118910/JE1094/178, Lloyd to MoD, 21 November 1956; FO 371/118911/JE1094/193, Lloyd to MoD, 22 November 1956; Dep. Monckton, 8, pp. 209–10, 261–76, 370–7, 436–51.

91. PRO FO 371/120314/AU1013/54 Caccia to Foreign Office, 17 November 1956; Love, *Suez: The Twice Fought War*, pp. 573–4.

92. PRO FO 953/1608/P10118/70, Mennell to Peck, 9 November 1956.

93. BBC WAC, *This Day and Age*, broadcast by Ernest Atkinson, 23 November 1956.

94. PRO FO 953/1608/P10118/70, Mennell to Peck, 9 November 1956; C. P. Scott, New York, to Information Policy Department, 20 November 1956; *Time*, pp. 24–5, 12 November 1956.

95. PRO FO 371/120314/AU1013/54, Minute by A. N. MacCleary, 21 November 1956.

96. Ambrose, *Eisenhower, Volume Two*, pp. 352–3.

97. Ibid., pp. 386–7; Safran, *Embattled Ally*, p. 577. Humphrey's comment referred specifically to the potential repercussions of the US administration prohibiting private remittances as part of its sanctions package against Israel.

98. Safran, *Embattled Ally*, p. 577; Stephen Isaacs, *Jews and American Politics* (New York, 1974), pp. 250–1; Paul Findley, *They Dare To Speak Out: People and Institutions Confront Israel's Lobby* (Westport, 1985), pp. 118–19.

99. Isaacs, *Jews And American Politics*, pp. 250–1.

100. PRO FO 371/120314/AU1013/55, Minute by MacCleary, 17 November 1956.

101. CAB 130/121, GEN 561, Memorandum on 'The Work of the BIS' by J. Peck, director-general of British Information Services, New York, 8 March 1957. Peck was alluding to this critical section of American opinion when he stated that Americans themselves had been deeply divided over Middle Eastern policy for many years. This was, he argued, part of the reason why Britain had been given a

reasonably satisfactory press in the US over the Suez campaign. For the Democratic party's opposition to Dulles' Middle Eastern policy prior to the Suez crisis, led by Adlai Stevenson, Eisenhower's challenger for the White House in 1956, see Neff, *Warriors at Suez*, pp. 166, 225.

102. PRO FO 371/118917/JE1094/348/G, Caccia to Kirkpatrick, 20 November 1956. 'The details of Russian penetration in Egypt and Syria consequently raise the doubt whether the Americans really did have the situation in hand and whether after all there was something to be said for us and the French trying to grasp the nettle.' Evidence also here of Caccia's useful liaison with James (Scottie) Reston of the *New York Times*; FO 371/120342/AU1057/3, Memorandum by H. Hankey, 15 November 1956; DEFE 7/1127/Misc/M(56)154, 9 November 1956; DEFE 7/1127/Misc/M(56)155, 12 November 1956; author's interviews with Norman Reddaway and Leonard Figg, both Information Research Department officials during Suez, conducted summer 1991.

103. PRO FO 371/120314/AU1013/54, Caccia to Foreign Office, 17 November 1956.

104. PRO FO 371/120314/AU1013/56, Caccia to Foreign Office, 1 December 1956; Lucas, *Divided We Stand*, p. 307; Dep. Monckton, 8, p. 258, Dodds-Parker to Rex Benson, 28 November 1956.

105. Avon Papers, AP14/4/184, 16 November 1956. Eden replied two days later, thanking Reid and giving him guidance: 'You may have seen what I said yesterday in London. It represents my strongest conviction.' This referred to an unrepentant speech Eden made at a Young Conservatives' rally in London on Saturday, 17 November, in which he argued that had the government not intervened in Egypt, Britain would have been slowly strangled by mounting tension and Soviet infiltration in the Middle East. See, for example, *Sunday Times*, p. 1, 18 November 1956.

106. Kunz, *Economic Diplomacy*, pp. 132–3; Johnman in Gorst, Johnman and Lucas (eds), *Post-War Britain*, pp. 173–4.

107. Kunz, *Economic Diplomacy*, pp. 143–52.

108. PRO T 236/4189, Makins to Macmillan, RM/56/3; T 236/4189, 'Note of a Meeting held in Sir Leslie Rowan's Room', 12 November 1956; Kunz, 'The Importance of Having Money' in Louis and Owen (eds), *Suez 1956*, p. 227. The 'radical treatment' outlined by C. F. Cobbold amounted to three simultaneous steps: the borrowing of three tranches from the International Monetary Fund, the mobilization of Treasury securities and the raising of money on them from New York banks and arrangements about the waiver. None of these objectives could be achieved, however, until relations with the US improved and sanctions ceased.

109. PRO CAB 128/30, CM(56)85, 20 November 1956.

110. Dep. Monckton, 8, p. 258, Dodds-Parker to Benson, 28 November 1956; Lloyd, *Suez 1956*, pp. 230–1.

111. *English-Speaking World*, January 1957, Vol. XXXIX, No. 1.

112. PRO FO 371/1611/P10118/130, British Information Services to Foreign Office, undated. Text of article, as well as Howard's editorial, here. Harold Caccia addressed the National Press Club in Washington during this period. MSS Monckton, 8, p. 258, Dodds-Parker to Benson, 28 November 1956.

113. *Hansard*, Vol. 561, c.877–96, 3 December 1956. Statement by Selwyn Lloyd.

114. See Kunz, *Economic Diplomacy*, pp. 153–60, for details of the American economic aid given to Britain after 3 December 1956.

115. Ambrose, *Eisenhower, Volume Two*, p. 370; Townsend Hoopes, *The Devil and*

John Foster Dulles (London, 1974), p. 386. Eisenhower's euphoria was tempered by the fact that the opposition Democrats had won control of both Houses of Congress. However, this seems to have had little effect on his Suez policy.
  116. PRO FO 371/120342/AU1057/3, Hankey Memorandum, 15 November 1956.
  117. PRO FO 371/120314/AU1013/56, Caccia to Foreign Office, 1 December 1956; FO 371/120314/AU1013/57, Caccia to Foreign Office, 8 December 1956; FO 371/118851/JE1027/48, Caccia to Foreign Office, 13 December 1956.
  118. PRO FO 953/1714/P1011/3, Minute by Dodds-Parker, 31 December 1956; FO 953/1715/P1011/32(A) Paul Grey to Ian Harvey, 28 March 1957.

15. The campaign in the United States: conclusion

  1. PRO FO 953/1689/PG11639/2, Background Note on 'The United States and Middle East Oil', issued as guidance by Information Office, Washington embassy, to British Information Services, 15 May 1956.
  2. PRO PREM 11/1098 f 184, 6th Meeting, Dulles to Eden, Council Chamber, FO, 1 August 1956.
  3. PRO FO 953/1163/PG14573/9, Memorandum on work of British Information Services by Paul Gore-Booth, director-general, BIS, 1949–53, sent to American Department, 16 June 1951; Gore-Booth, *With Great Truth and Respect*, p. 229. During the Suez crisis, Gore-Booth was deputy under-secretary of state (economic) at the Foreign Office.
  4. PRO PREM 11/1838, 'Bermuda Conference Proceedings'; *Foreign Relations of the United States*, 1955–57, Vol. XVII, Docs.239, 241–7 relating to the Bermuda Conference, pp. 450–66, 20–23 March 1957.
  5. Freiberger, *Dawn Over Suez*, pp. 204–9.

16. Conclusion and epilogue

  1. William Clark, *From Three Worlds*, p. 166.
  2. Louis, *British Empire in the Middle East*, pp. 651–89; Kenneth O. Morgan, *Labour in Power, 1945–1951* (Oxford, 1985), pp. 464–71; Eden, *Full Circle*, pp. 347–53; Carlton, *Anthony Eden*, pp. 397–9.
  3. Rhodes James (*Anthony Eden*, p. 533) writes: 'It was plainly, as he [Eden] knew, a pretext for achieving the destruction of Nasser; but it was so obvious a pretext that one still wonders why he believed it would not be seen as such.'
  4. For this and other aspects of government-media relations during the 1982 Falklands crisis, see Mercer, Mungham and Williams, *Fog of War*, pp. 1–212; Cockerell, Hennessy and Walker, *Sources Close to the Prime Minister*, pp. 143–88; Adams, *The Media and the Falklands Campaign*; Robert Harris, *Gotcha! The Media, the Government and the Falklands Crisis* (London, 1983).
  5. Lawrence Freedman, *Britain and the Falklands War* (Oxford, 1988), pp. 42–4; Christoph Bluth, 'Anglo-American Relations and the Falklands Conflict' in Alex Danchev (ed.), *International Perspectives on the Falklands Conflict: A Matter of Life and Death* (London, 1992), pp. 203–23.
  6. Peter Lyon, 'The Commonwealth and the Suez Crisis' in Louis and Owen

(eds), *Suez 1956*, pp. 257–73. Only the prime ministers of Australia and New Zealand offered any support to the Eden government during the military operation in Egypt.

7. Epstein, *British Politics in the Suez Crisis*, pp. 168–9.

8. Lloyd, *Suez 1956*, pp. 206–7.

9. See, for example, Rhodes James, *Anthony Eden*, p. 555; Kyle, *Suez*, pp. 404–7.

10. Epstein, *British Politics in the Suez Crisis*, pp, 141–52. Petrol rationing measures were announced in the Commons by the minister of fuel and power, Aubrey Jones, on 20 November 1956. *Hansard*, Vol. 560, c.1557–62, 20 November 1956.

11. See, for example, Epstein, *British Politics in the Suez Crisis*, pp. 170–1.

12. Nutting, *No End of A Lesson*.

13. For the origins of Hill's Committee on Government Publicity, which met regularly from 26 November 1956, see PRO PREM 11/1186, Eden to Butler, 8 November 1956. For the working of the Committee see CAB 130/121, GEN 561 Series; Fife-Clark Papers, FICA 2/1/10, 20 December 1956.

14. For the Committee on Government Publicity's report on the Overseas Information Services see PRO FO 953/1718/P1011/99/G, July 1957. Details of the coordination machinery in FO 953/1714/P1011/5, Grey to Kirkpatrick, 18 January 1957; FO 953/1716/P1011/49, Harvey to Lloyd, 10 April 1957; FO 953/1723/P1011/183, Harvey to Lloyd, 15 November 1957. For the wider historical significance of these changes and the propaganda lessons learned from Suez see John Black, *Organising the Propaganda Instrument: the British Experience* (The Hague, 1975), pp. 69–72; Marjorie Ogilvie-Webb, *The Government Explains: A Study of the Information Services* (London, 1965), pp. 88–90.

15. Alistair Horne, *Harold Macmillan: Volume 2, 1957–86* (London, 1989), pp. 92–8.

16. PRO PREM 11/2466, Hill to Macmillan, 18 and 23 July 1958. The only propaganda problem concerned the accreditation of journalists, which, as during the Suez crisis, produced a row between the Foreign Office and the Ministry of Defence. See DEFE 7/1385/110/031, Powell to Hoyer Millar, 25 June 1958; DEFE 7/1386/110/031 Hobbs to Drew, 10 July 1958.

17. Black, *Organising the Propaganda Instrument*, p. 72; Ogilvie-Webb, *The Government Explains*, p. 90.

18. PRO AIR 8/1940, Annex to JP(57) 142 (Final). Sir Charles Keightley, 'Lessons of Suez', Part II, p. 4, 12 November 1957.

Bibliography and sources

Unpublished material

Public Record Office, Kew, London. Files have been consulted from the following collections:

ADM 116	Admiralty Secretariat and Cases
AIR 8	Chief of Air Staff Papers
AIR 20	Unregistered Papers
CAB 21	Cabinet Office Registered Papers
CAB 128	Cabinet Meetings
CAB 129	Cabinet Memoranda
CAB 130	Cabinet Committee (Ad Hoc) Files
CAB 134	Defence Committee
DEFE 4	Chiefs of Staff Committee Meetings
DEFE 5	Chiefs of Staff Memoranda
DEFE 7	Registered Files: General Series
DEFE 13	Private Office Papers
FO 115	Records of the British Embassy in Washington
FO 371	Foreign Office, General Political Correspondence
FO 800	Foreign Secretary's Papers
FO 953	Foreign Office, Information Departments
PREM 8	Prime Minister's Correspondence
PREM 11	Prime Minister's Correspondence
T 236	Treasury Overseas Finance Division Files
WO 32	Registered Files, General Series
WO 216	CIGS Papers
WO 288	War Office Intelligence Summaries

Conservative Party Archives, Bodleian Library, University of Oxford: Central Office and Research Department files.

BBC Written Archives Centre (WAC), Caversham, Reading. The following sets of files have been consulted:

BMM	Board of Management Minutes
R1	Board of Governors Minutes
R34	Suez Crisis Files
T16	Director Sound Broadcasting Minutes
Radio and TV Commentaries / News Transcripts	

Manchester Guardian Archive, John Rylands University Library of Manchester, Manchester.

The Times Archive, News International plc, Record Office, London.

Interviews and correspondence

The following journalists, politicians and Foreign Office officials were either interviewed by, or were in correspondence with, the author:

Michael Adams, Sir Philip Adams, Sir Harold Beeley, Tony Benn, MP, Sir Douglas Dodds-Parker, Sir Leonard Figg, Lord Hartwell (Michael Berry), Alastair Hetherington, Teddy Hodgkin, Sir Peter Hope, Sir Donald Maitland, Leonard Miall, Anthony Moore, Sir John Peck, Norman Reddaway, Lord Rees-Mogg, Sir Paul Wright

Private papers

Avon Papers, University of Birmingham
Beaverbrook Papers, House of Lords Record Office, London
Benn Papers, Benn Archives, London
Bracken Papers, Churchill College, University of Cambridge
Butler Papers, Trinity College, University of Cambridge
Cadogan Papers, Churchill College, University of Cambridge
Clark Papers, Bodleian Library, University of Oxford
Fife-Clark Papers, Churchill College, University of Cambridge
Hobbs Papers, Liddell Hart Centre for Military Archives, King's College, University of London
Kilmuir Papers, Churchill College, University of Cambridge
Layton Papers, Trinity College, University of Cambridge
Monckton Papers, Bodleian Library, University of Oxford
Stockwell Papers, Liddell Hart Centre for Military Archives, King's College, University of London

Newspapers and periodicals

Housed either in the Bodleian Library, Oxford, or in the British Newspaper Library, Colindale, London

Daily Express, Daily Herald, Daily Mail, Daily Mirror, Daily Sketch, Daily Telegraph, Economist, Financial Times, Guardian, The Listener, Manchester Guardian, News Chronicle, New Statesman, Observer, Sunday Times, Time, The Times

Film and video material

Film As Evidence; 'We Were Right', written and produced by Howard Smith, distributed by BBC Film Sales, 1976
Independent Television News: Suez coverage (5 VHS video cassettes), in the hands of St John's College, Oxford

Published documents and reports

BBC Annual Report and Accounts, 1956–57, Cmd.267

BBC Handbook, 1957 (BBC, London, 1957)

Documents on International Affairs, 1956, (ed.) Noble Frankland, (RIIA/OUP, London, 1959)

English-Speaking Union: A Decade of Progress, 1945–1955 (London, 1955)

English-Speaking World, 1956–7

Foreign Relations of the United States (Government Printing Office, Washington, DC), 1955–7

Hansard, House of Commons Debates, 1956

Summary of the Report of the Independent Committee of Inquiry into the Overseas Information Services, Cmd.9138 (1954)

Overseas Information Services, Cmd.225 (1957)

Overseas Information Services, Cmd.685 (1959)

Report of the Committee on Security Procedures in the Public Services, Chapter 9, Cmd.1681 (April 1962)

Report of the Study Group on Censorship (the Beach Report), Cmd.9112, (1983)

Diaries and memoirs

Beaufre, Andre, *The Suez Expedition, 1956* (Faber and Faber, London, 1969)

Butler, R. A., *The Art of the Possible* (Hamish Hamilton, London, 1971)

Christiansen, Arthur, *Headlines All My Life* (Heinemann, London, 1961)

Clark, William, *From Three Worlds* (Sidgwick and Jackson, London, 1986)

Cooper, Chester, *The Lion's Last Roar* (Harper and Row, New York, 1978)

Cox, Geoffrey, *See it Happen. The Making of ITN* (Bodley Head, London, 1983)

Cudlipp, Hugh, *Walking on Water* (Bodley Head, London, 1976)

— *At Your Peril* (Weidenfeld and Nicolson, London, 1962)

Day, Sir Robin, *Grand Inquisitor* (Weidenfeld and Nicolson, London, 1989)

Dilks, David (ed.), *The Diaries of Sir Alexander Cadogan, 1938–45* (Cassell, London, 1971)

Dodds-Parker, Douglas, *Political Eunuch* (Springwood, London, 1986)

Eden, Anthony, *Full Circle* (Cassell, London, 1960)

Edgar, Donald, *Express '56* (John Clare, London, 1981)

Eisenhower, Dwight, *The White House Years: Mandate for Change, 1953–6* (Doubleday, London, 1963)

— *The White House Years: Waging Peace, 1956–61* (Doubleday, London, 1966)

Fawzi, Mahmoud, *Suez 1956: An Egyptian Perspective* (Shorouk International, London, 1987)

Fergusson, Bernard, *The Watery Maze* (Collins, London, 1961)

Georges-Picot, Jacques, *The Real Suez Crisis* (Harcourt Brace Jovanovich, New York, 1978)

Gladwyn, Lord, *The Memoirs of Lord Gladwyn* (Heinemann, London, 1983)

Gore-Booth, Paul, *With Great Truth and Respect* (Constable, London, 1974)

Grisewood, Harman, *One Thing at a Time* (Hutchinson, London, 1968)

Heikal, Mohamed, *Cutting the Lion's Tail* (Andre Deutsch, London, 1986)

Hetherington, Alastair, *Guardian Years* (Chatto and Windus, London, 1981)

Hill, Lord, *Both Sides of the Hill* (Heinemann, London, 1964)

Johnston, Sir Charles, *The Brink of Jordan* (Hamish Hamilton, London, 1972)

Keightley, General Sir Charles, 'Operations in Egypt, Nov to Dec, 1956', in *Supplement to London Gazette*, 10 September 1957

Kilmuir, Lord, *Political Adventure* (Weidenfeld and Nicolson, London, 1964)

King, Cecil, *Strictly Personal* (Weidenfeld and Nicolson, London, 1969)

Kirkpatrick, Ivone, *The Inner Circle* (Macmillan, London, 1959)

Lloyd, Selwyn, *Suez 1956* (Jonathan Cape, London, 1978)

McDonald, Iverach, *A Man of The Times* (Hamish Hamilton, London, 1976)

Macmillan, Harold, *Riding The Storm, 1956-9* (Macmillan, London, 1971)

Marett, Sir Robert, *Through the Back Door* (Pergamon Press, London, 1968)

Margach, James, *The Abuse of Power* (W. H. Allen, London, 1976)

Menzies, Robert, *Afternoon Light* (Cassell, London, 1967)

Morgan, Janet (ed.), *The Backbench Diaries of Richard Crossman* (Hamish Hamilton and Jonathan Cape, London, 1981)

Murphy, Robert, *Diplomat Among Warriors* (Collins, London, 1964)

Nasser, Gamal Abdel, *The Philosophy of the Revolution* (Smith, Keynes and Marshall, New York, 1959)

Nutting, Anthony, *No End of a Lesson* (Constable, London, 1967)

Pineau, Christian, *1956 Suez* (Robert Laffont, Paris, 1976)

Shuckburgh, Evelyn, *Descent to Suez* (Weidenfeld and Nicolson, London, 1986)

Thomson, George P., *Blue Pencil Admiral* (Sampson Low, London, 1947)

Trevelyan, Humphrey, *The Middle East in Revolution* (Macmillan, London, 1970)

Williams, Philip (ed.), *The Diary of Hugh Gaitskell, 1945-56* (Jonathan Cape, London, 1983)

Wyndham-Goldie, Grace, *Facing the Nation: Television and Politics, 1936-76* (Bodley Head, London, 1977)

Biographies

Ambrose, Stephen, *Eisenhower: The President, Volume Two: 1952-69* (Allen and Unwin, London, 1984)

Birkenhead, Earl of, *Monckton* (Weidenfeld and Nicolson, London, 1969)

Bourne, Richard, *Lords of Fleet Street - The Harmsworth Dynasty* (Unwin Hyman, London, 1990)

Carlton, David, *Anthony Eden* (Allen Lane, London, 1981)

Chisholm, Anne, and Davie, Michael, *Beaverbrook: A Life* (Hutchinson, London, 1992)

Dimbleby, Jonathan, *Richard Dimbleby, A Biography* (Hodder and Stoughton, London, 1975)

Dixon, Piers, *Double Diploma* (Hutchinson, London, 1968)

Gilbert, Martin, *Winston S. Churchill, Volume VIII: Never Despair, 1945-65* (Heinemann, London, 1988)

Hobson, Harold, Knightley, Philip, and Russell, Leonard, *The Pearl of Days: An Intimate Memoir of The Sunday Times, 1882-1972* (Hamish Hamilton, London, 1972)

Hoopes, Townsend, *The Devil and John Foster Dulles* (Andre Deutsch, London, 1974)

Horne, Alastair, *Harold Macmillan: Volume 1, 1894-1956* (Macmillan, London, 1988)

— *Harold Macmillan: Volume 2, 1957-1986* (Macmillan, London, 1989)

Howard, Anthony, *Rab* (Jonathan Cape, London, 1987)
Hubback, David, *No Ordinary Press Baron: A Life of Walter Layton* (Weidenfeld and Nicolson, London, 1985)
Mosley, Leonard, *Dulles* (Hodder and Stoughton, London, 1978)
Rhodes James, Robert, *Anthony Eden* (Weidenfeld and Nicolson, London, 1986)
Taylor, A. J. P., *Beaverbrook* (Hamish Hamilton, London, 1972)
Thorpe, D. R., *Selwyn Lloyd* (Jonathan Cape, London, 1989)
Williams, Philip, *Hugh Gaitskell* (Jonathan Cape, London, 1979)

Books and monographs

Adams, Valerie, *The Media and the Falklands Campaign* (Macmillan, London, 1986)
Ayerst, David, *The Guardian: Biography of a Newspaper* (Collins, London, 1971)
Baistow, Tom, *Fourth-Rate Estate* (Comedia, London, 1985)
Bartlett, F. C., *Political Propaganda* (Cambridge University Press, Cambridge, 1940)
Belson, William, *The Impact of TV* (Crosby Lockwood, London, 1967)
Bill, James, and Louis, W. R. (eds), *Musaddiq, Iranian Nationalism and Oil* (I.B. Tauris, London, 1988)
Black, John, *Organising the Propaganda Instrument: the British Experience* (Martinus Nijhoff, The Hague, 1975)
Bloch, Jonathan, and Fitzgerald, Patrick, *British Intelligence and Covert Action* (Brandon, Ireland, 1983)
Bowie, Robert, *Suez 1956: International Crisis and the Rule of Law* (OUP, Oxford, 1974)
Boyce, G., Curran, J., and Wingate, P. (eds), *Newspaper History* (Constable, London, 1978)
Braddon, Russell, *Suez: Splitting of a Nation* (Collins, London, 1973)
Briggs, Asa, *Governing the BBC* (BBC, London, 1979)
— *The BBC: A Short History of the First Fifty Years* (OUP, Oxford, 1985)
— *The History of Broadcasting in the UK, Volume 3, The War of Words* (OUP, Oxford, 1970)
— *The History of Broadcasting in the UK, Volume 4, Sound and Vision* (OUP, Oxford, 1979)
Brown, J. A. C., *Techniques of Persuasion: from Propaganda to Brainwashing* (Penguin, Harmondsworth, 1963)
Calvocoressi, Peter, *World Politics since 1945* (Longman, London, 1982)
Camrose, Viscount, *British Newspapers and their Controllers* (Cassell, London, 1947)
Carlton, David, *Britain and the Suez Crisis* (Blackwell, London, 1988)
Cave, Paul, and Waterhouse, Keith, *Britain's Voice Abroad. A Daily Mirror Spotlight on Propaganda* (*Daily Mirror* Newspapers Ltd, London, 1957)
Childers, Erskine, *The Road to Suez* (MacGibbon and Kee, London, 1962)
Cockerell, Michael, *Live from Number Ten* (Faber and Faber, London, 1988)
Cockerell, Michael, Hennessy, Peter, Walker, David, *Sources Close to the Prime Minister* (Macmillan, London, 1984)
Cockett, Richard, *Twilight of Truth: Chamberlain, Appeasement and the Manipulation of the Media* (Weidenfeld and Nicolson, London, 1989)
Copeland, Miles, *The Game of Nations* (Weidenfeld and Nicolson, London, 1969)
Curran, James, and Seaton, Jean, *Power without Responsibility* (Fontana, London, 1981)

Danchev, Alex (ed.), *International Perspectives on the Falklands Conflict: A Matter of Life and Death* (St Martin's Press, London, 1992)

Darby, Philip, *British Defence Policy East of Suez, 1947–68* (RIIA/OUP, London, 1973)

Dawisha, Adeed, *Egypt in the Arab World: The Elements of Foreign Policy* (Macmillan, London, 1976)

Deighton, Ann (ed.), *Britain and the First Cold War* (Macmillan, London, 1990)

Devereux, David R., *The Formulation of British Defence Policy Towards the Middle East, 1948–56* (Macmillan, London, 1990)

Dockrill, Michael, and Young, John W. (eds), *British Foreign Policy, 1945–56* (Macmillan, London, 1989)

Doob, Leonard, *Public Opinion and Propaganda* (Cresset Press, London, 1948)

Edelman, Maurice, *The Mirror: A Political History* (Hamish Hamilton, London, 1966)

Elath, Eliahu, The Struggle for Statehood, Volume 2, (Am Oved, Tel Aviv, 1982)

Epstein, Leon, *British Politics in the Suez Crisis* (Pall Mall Press, London, 1964)

Findley, Paul, *They Dare To Speak Out: People and Institutions Confront Israel's Lobby* (Lawrence Hill, Westport, 1985)

Finer, Herman, *Dulles over Suez* (Heinemann, London, 1964)

Fraser, Lindley, *Propaganda* (OUP, 1957)

Freedman, Lawrence, *Britain and the Falklands War* (Blackwell, Oxford, 1988)

Freiberger, Steven Z., *Dawn Over Suez: The Rise of American Power in the Middle East, 1953–7* (Ivan R. Dee, Chicago, 1992)

Fullick, Roy, and Powell, Geoffrey, *Suez: The Double War* (Hamish Hamilton, London, 1979)

Gallup, George, *The Gallup International Public Opinion Polls, Great Britain, 1937–75* (Random House, New York, 1976)

— *The Gallup Poll, Public Opinion, 1935–1971* (Random House, New York, 1972)

Glenton, George, and Pattison, William, *The Last Chronicle of Bouverie Street* (George Allen and Unwin, London, 1963)

Gorst, A., Johnman, L., Lucas, W. S. (eds), *Post-War Britain: Themes and Perspectives, 1945–64* (Pinter, London, 1989)

Hahn, Peter L., *The United States, Great Britain and Egypt, 1945–1956* (University of North Carolina Press, Chapel Hill, 1991)

Harris, Robert, *Gotcha! The Media, the Government and the Falklands Crisis* (Faber and Faber, London, 1983)

Hart-Davis, Duff, *The House the Berrys Built* (Hodder and Stoughton, London, 1990)

Harvey, Ian, *The Techniques of Persuasion* (Falcon Press, London, 1951)

Hatem, M. Abdel-Kader, *Information and the Arab Cause* (Longman, London, 1974)

Head, Sydney, *Broadcasting in Africa* (Houghton Mifflin, New York, 1976)

Heikal, Mohammed, *Nasser: The Cairo Documents* (New English Library, London, 1972)

Isaacs, Stephen, *Jews and American Politics* (Doubleday, New York, 1974)

Koss, Stephen, *The Rise and Fall of the Political Press in Britain* (Fontana, London, 1990)

Kunz, Diane, *The Economic Diplomacy of the Suez Crisis* (University of North Carolina Press, Chapel Hill, 1991)

Kyle, Keith, *Suez* (Weidenfeld and Nicolson, London, 1991)

Lamb, Richard, *The Failure of the Eden Government* (Sidgwick and Jackson, London, 1987)

Louis, W. R., *The British Empire in the Middle East, 1945–51* (Clarendon Press, Oxford, 1984)

Louis, W. R. and Stookey, Robert (eds), *The End of the Palestine Mandate* (I.B. Tauris, London, 1986)

Louis, W. R., and Owen, Roger (eds), *Suez 1956: The Crisis and its Consequences* (Clarendon Press, Oxford, 1989)

Love, Kennett, *Suez: The Twice Fought War* (Longman, London, 1970)

Lucas, W. Scott, *Divided We Stand* (Hodder and Stoughton, London, 1991)

McDonald, Iverach, *The History of The Times: Volume V, Struggles in War and Peace, 1939–1966* (Times Books, London, 1984)

Mansell, Gerald, *Let Truth Be Told: 50 Years of BBC External Broadcasting* (Weidenfeld and Nicolson, London, 1982)

Margach, James, *The Anatomy of Power* (W. H. Allen, London, 1979)

Martin, L. John, *International Propaganda: its Legal and Diplomatic Control* (University of Minnesota Press, Minneapolis, 1958)

May, Annabelle, and Rowan, Kathryn (eds), *Inside Information, British Government and the Media* (Constable, London, 1982)

Mercer, Derrik, Mungham, Geoff, Williams, Kevin, *The Fog of War* (Heinemann, London, 1987)

Moncrieff, Anthony (ed.), *Suez Ten Years After* (BBC, London, 1967)

Monroe, Elizabeth, *Britain's Moment in the Middle East, 1914–71* (Chatto and Windus, London, 1981)

Moorhouse, Geoffrey, *The Diplomats* (Jonathan Cape, London, 1977)

Morgan, Kenneth O., *Labour in Power, 1945–1951* (OUP, Oxford, 1985)

Morrison, David, and Tumber, H., *Journalists at War: The Dynamics of News Reporting during the Falklands Conflict* (Sage, London, 1988)

Nasser, Munir K., *Press, Politics and Power* (Iowa State University Press, Iowa, 1979)

Neff, Donald, *Warriors at Suez* (Linden Press, New York, 1981)

Negrine, Ralph, *Politics and the Mass Media in Britain* (Routledge, London, 1989)

Neustadt, Richard, *Alliance Politics* (Columbia University Press, New York, 1970)

Nutting, Anthony, *Nasser* (Constable, London, 1972)

Ogilvie-Webb, Marjorie, *The Government Explains: A Study of the Information Services* (A Report of the Royal Institute of Public Administration) (Allen and Unwin, London, 1965)

Partner, Peter, *Arab Voices: The BBC Arabic Service, 1938–88* (BBC, London, 1988)

Paulu, Burton, *Television and Radio in the UK* (Macmillan, London, 1981)

Qualter, T. H., *Propaganda and Psychological Warfare* (Random House, New York, 1962)

Robertson, Terence, *Crisis: The Inside Story of the Suez Conspiracy* (Hutchinson, London, 1965)

Reynolds, David, *Britannia Overruled: British Policy and World Power in the Twentieth Century* (Longman, London, 1991)

Safran, Nadrav, *The Embattled Ally* (Harvard University Press, Cambridge, 1978)

Sanders, Michael, and Taylor, Philip M., *British Propaganda during the First World War* (Macmillan, London, 1982)

Scannell, Paddy, and Cardiff, David, *A Social History of British Broadcasting* (Blackwell, Oxford, 1991)

Seale, Patrick, *The Struggle for Syria* (RIIA/OUP, London, 1965)

Sendall, Bernard, *Independent Television in Britain, Volume 1: Origins and Foundation, 1946–62* (Macmillan, London, 1982)

Seymour-Ure, Colin, *The Political Impact of Mass Media* (Constable, London, 1974)

Smith, Anthony, *The Shadow in the Cave* (Quartet, London, 1976)

Taylor, Geoffrey, *Changing Faces: A History of The Guardian, 1956–88* (Fourth Estate, London, 1993)

Taylor, Philip M., *War and the Media: Propaganda and Persuasion in the Gulf War* (Manchester University Press, Manchester, 1992)

— *The Projection of Britain: British Overseas Propaganda and Publicity, 1919–39* (Cambridge University Press, Cambridge, 1981)

Thomas, Hugh, *The Suez Affair* (Weidenfeld and Nicolson, London, 1966)

Troen, Selwyn Ilan, and Shemesh, Moshe (eds), *The Suez–Sinai Crisis of 1956: Retrospective and Reappraisal* (Frank Cass, London, 1990)

Tunstall, Jeremy, *The Westminster Lobby Correspondents: A Sociological Study of National Political Journalism* (Routledge and Keegan Paul, London, 1970)

— *The Media in Britain* (Constable, London, 1983)

Verrier, Anthony, *Through the Looking Glass: British Foreign Policy in an Age of Illusions* (Jonathan Cape, London, 1983)

Watt, Donald Cameron, *Succeeding John Bull: America in Britain's Place, 1900–1975* (Cambridge University Press, Cambridge, 1984)

Williams, Francis, *Dangerous Estate* (Patrick Stephens, Cambridge, 1984)

— *Nothing So Strange* (Cassell, London, 1970)

Young, John W. (ed.), *The Foreign Policy of Churchill's Peacetime Administration, 1951–55* (Leicester University Press, Leicester, 1988)

Articles

Adamthwaite, Anthony, '"Nation Shall Speak Unto Nation": The BBC's Response to Peace and Defence Issues, 1945–58', *Contemporary Record*, Vol. 7, No. 3, Winter 1993

Anstey, Caroline, 'Projection of British Socialism: Foreign Office Publicity and American Opinion, 1945–50', *Journal of Contemporary History*, Vol. 19, No. 3, July 1984

Boyd, Douglas A., 'The Development of Egypt's Radio: "Voice of the Arabs" under Nasser', *Journalism Quarterly*, Vol. 52, No. 4, Winter 1975

Cockett, Richard, 'The Observer and the Suez Crisis', *Contemporary Record*, Vol. 5, No. 1, Summer 1991

Fletcher, Richard, 'British propaganda since World War Two – A case study', *Media, Culture and Society*, Vol. 4, No. 2, April 1982

Hennessy, Peter, and Laity, Mark, 'Suez – What the Papers Say', *Contemporary Record*, Vol. 1, No. 1, Spring 1987.

Hopkinson, Tom, *Relations between Governments, Armed Services and the Media: A case study of the 1956 Suez Conflict* (Unpublished report, written in 1987, courtesy of Dr Derrik Mercer, Centre for Journalism Studies, University College, Cardiff)

Jacob, Sir Ian, 'The Suez Crisis and the BBC', *Ariel*, Vol. 2, No. 1, January 1957

King, John, 'The BBC and Suez', *The Round Table*, Vol. 304, October 1987

Lucas, W. S., 'Redefining the Suez "Collusion": A Regional Approach', *Middle Eastern Studies*, Vol. 26, No. 1, January 1990.

MacKenzie, F. R., 'Eden, Suez and the BBC – A Reassessment', *The Listener*, 18 December 1969

Mason, Michael, '"The Decisive Volley": The Battle of Ismailia and the Decline of British Influence in Egypt, January–July 1952', *Journal of Imperial and Commonwealth History*, Vol. 19, No. 1, January 1991

Negrine, Ralph, 'The Press and the Suez Crisis: A Myth Re-examined', *Historical Journal*, Vol. 25, No. 4, 1982

Parmentier, Guillaume, 'The British Press in the Suez Crisis', *Historical Journal*, Vol. 23, No. 2, 1980

RAF Historical Society, 'Suez 1956 – Air Aspects', *Proceedings of the RAF Historical Society* (January 1988)

Shaw, Tony, 'Government Manipulation of the Press during the 1956 Suez Crisis', *Contemporary Record*, Vol. 8, No. 2, Autumn 1994

Shaw, Tony, 'Eden and the BBC during the Suez Crisis: A Myth Re-examined', *Twentieth Century British History*, Vol. 6, No. 3, 1995

Smith, Lyn, 'Covert British Propaganda: the IRD, 1947–77', *Journal of International Studies*, Vol. 9, No. 1, Spring 1980

Waterfield, Gordon, 'Suez and the role of Broadcasting', *The Listener*, 29 December 1966

Theses and conference papers

Anstey, Caroline, 'Foreign Office efforts to influence American opinion, 1945–49' (Unpublished Ph.D. thesis, London School of Economics, 1984)

Astor, David, '*The Observer* and Suez' (Institute of Contemporary British History/ London School of Economics Summer School, 1989)

Dajani, Karen Finlon, 'Egypt's role as a major media producer, supplier and distributor to the Arab world: an historical-descriptive study' (Unpublished Ph.D. thesis, Temple University, 1980)

Khan, Rais Ahmad, 'Radio Cairo and Egyptian Foreign Policy, 1956–59' (Unpublished Ph.D. thesis, University of Michigan, 1967)

Shalabieh, Mahmoud, 'A Comparison of Political Persuasion on Radio Cairo in the Eras of Nasser and Sadat' (Unpublished Ph.D. thesis, Ohio State University, 1975)

Index